CARIBBEAN AUTOBIOGRAPHY

Wisconsin Studies in Autobiography

William L. Andrews

General Editor

CARIBBEAN AUTOBIOGRAPHY

Cultural Identity and Self-Representation

SANDRA POUCHET PAQUET

THE UNIVERSITY OF WISCONSIN PRESS

The University of Wisconsin Press
1930 Monroe Street
Madison, Wisconsin 53711

www.wisc.edu/wisconsinpress/

3 Henrietta Street
London WC2E 8LU, England

1   3   5   4   2

Printed in the United States of America

Library of Congress Cataloging-in-Publication Data

Paquet, Sandra Pouchet.
Carribbean autobiography: cultural identity and
self-representation / Sandra Pouchet Paquet.
p. cm.
Includes bibliographical references (p.) and index.
ISBN 0–299–17690–8 (cloth: alk. paper)
ISBN 0–299–17694–0 (paper: alk. paper)
1. Autobiography.   2. Caribbean Area—Biography—History
and criticism.   3. Authors, Caribbean—Biography—History and
criticism.   I. Title
CT25 .P36 2202
920.0729—dc21   2001005425

In loving memory of my parents
Neville Charles Pouchet (1911–1992)
and
Ortensa Teodorini Pouchet (1917–1983)

Contents

Preface

This study began more than a decade ago with an exploratory essay entitled "West Indian Autobiography."[1] Over the years I presented papers on the subject and published several articles as I discovered new texts and my interest in the field steadily grew. Much of that material is incorporated here with changes that reflect my continuing interest in the constitutive forms of Caribbean autobiographical culture and a heightened appreciation of the dynamics of the genre in respect to variables of Caribbean personality and presence.

In this study my focus is on particular people, polities, and institutions represented in selected texts, some dominant and others secondary in the literary canon, with a view to a comparative analysis of specific autobiographical practices. I explore conjunctures between distinct modes of autobiography and the relevance of autobiographical practice to the thematics of diaspora and questions of intercultural identity in the different life worlds of Caribbean islanders and exiles, travelers, and dwellers in various colonial and postcolonial contexts.

Acknowledgments

Several chapters of this book contain portions of or are substantially revised versions of selections that I have previously published. The original publications are duly acknowledged here.

Parts of part 1 text and chapter 1 originally appeared as "Surfacing: Representation, Identification, and Resistance in Nineteenth-Century African Caribbean Women's Texts." *Caribbean Studies* 27, no. 3–4 (July–December, 1994): 278–97.

Parts of chapter 2 originally appeared as "The Heartbeat of a West Indian Slave: *The History of Mary Prince.*" *African American Review* 26, no. 1 (1992): 131–46.

Parts of chapter 3 originally appeared as "The Enigma of Arrival: *Wonderful Adventures of Mrs. Seacole in Many Lands.*" *African American Review* 26, no. 4 (1992): 1–13.

Parts of chapter 5 originally appeared as the foreword to *In the Castle of My Skin* by George Lamming. Ann Arbor: University of Michigan Press, 1991: ix–xxxiii. Reprinted with the permission of the University of Michigan Press.

Part of chapter 6 originally appeared as the foreword to *The Pleasures of Exile* by George Lamming. Ann Arbor: University of Michigan Press, 1992. Reprinted with the permission of the University of Michigan Press.

Parts of chapter 7 originally appeared as "The Poetics of Memory and Authenticity in Derek Walcott's *Another Life.*" In

Memory and Cultural Politics: New Approaches to American Ethnic Literatures, edited by Amritjit Singh, Joseph T. Skerrett, Jr., and Robert E. Hogan, 194–210. Boston: Northeastern University Press, 1996. Reprinted with the permission of Northeastern University Press.

CARIBBEAN AUTOBIOGRAPHY

Introduction

In Caribbean literary discourse the dominant texts of Anglophone autobiography are the works of established creative writers, among them Claude McKay, Edgar Mittelholzer, Derek Walcott, George Lamming, V. S. Naipaul, Jean Rhys, Kamau Brathwaite, and Jamaica Kincaid. Together these works not only provide insight into the creative possibilities of autobiography as a genre but they clarify areas of overlap and discontinuity in the subjective and collective constitution of identity in the heterogeneous Caribbean. They thus enable generalizations about Caribbean cultural formations and the dynamics of genre shifts across different but related levels of meaning in autobiographical discourse.

The autobiographical texts at the center of this study all are different in form, function, and narrative posture. They are written by women and by men, islanders and emigrants, travelers and dwellers; they are dictated and written. Ideologically, they run the spectrum of political debate and social confrontation. They range from slave narrative to travel narrative, narratives of childhood, autobiographical fiction, narrative poem, and more. They include the Hart sisters' "History of Methodism" (1804), *The History of Mary Prince, a West Indian Slave, Related by Herself* (1831), *Wonderful Adventures of Mrs. Seacole* (1857), Claude McKay's *A Long Way from Home* (1937) and *My Green Hills of Jamaica* (1979), Lamming's *In the Castle of My Skin* (1953) and *The Pleasures of Exile* (1960), C. L. R. James's *Beyond a Boundary* (1963), Walcott's *Another Life* (1973), Rhys's *Smile Please* (1979), Yseult Bridges's *Child of the Tropics* (1980), Naipaul's *Finding the Center* (1984) and *A Way in the World: A Novel* (1994), Anna Mahase, Sr.'s *My Mother's Daughter* (1992), Brathwaite's *The Zea Mexican Diary* (1993), and Kincaid's *My Brother* (1997). Each represents a modification of the defining features of autobiography as a social construction and cultural institution (Bruss 5–7).[1] Each autobiographical

3

text articulates, extends, and develops concepts of materially grounded subjectivities peculiar to the Caribbean. Each allows insight into the discursive formations that define the individual autobiographical act. The texts under scrutiny facilitate generic definitions; they also facilitate an understanding of the constitutive relationship of autobiography to the region's cultural formations. In each, issues of self-representation overlap or coincide with issues of gendered racial, ethnic, cultural, and national identities. Each autobiographical act under scrutiny projects an arc of meaning that illuminates the tensions, contradictions, differences, and interpenetrations of heterogeneous community within a variety of opposing modalities.

Each autobiographical act constitutes a different spatial and temporal point in Caribbean literary and cultural history. The selection and chronological arrangement of the texts are not meant to suggest a progressive or causal pattern. Rather, this arrangement is meant to illuminate the centrality and complexity of autobiographical modes in the shifting ground of an ever changing cultural continuum. Ongoing tensions between change and continuity provide different points of reference from which to chart the influence of interculturative processes on racial, ethnic, and gender hierarchies in the multiracial, multiethnic, multinational, and polyglot Caribbean. To claim a neat and mechanical determinism would defeat the quest for overlapping and contradictory subjectivities within an unfolding matrix of cultural associations. The connection between gendered self-figuration and national and regional identities is continually being reinvented. Conflicts between representations of public and private aspects of the self, between representations of community, between self and native space, between lyrical evocation and factual annotation are the elastic substance of an autobiographical culture formed in the intersection of differing interculturative processes.

I seek to assess Anglo-Caribbean autobiography in its many forms as original attempts to encode and re-encode the social machinery that alienates the individual within the community and commingles distinct identities in the shifting dynamics of difference and desire.[2] Autobiography constructs multiple spaces where the private and the personal collapse into projections of a public self, where the individual is represented within the context of mutuality and commonality. When rooted in the specifics of time and place, the study of autobiography and self-representation acquires an archaeological value beyond genealogical fable and personal history.[3] It illuminates the regenerative lineaments of the multilingual, multiethnic, many-ancestored communities of the Caribbean that many of the region's intellectuals have sought to instantiate, among them, Antonio Benítez-Rojo, Michael Dash, Carole Boyce Davies, Edouard Glissant, Wilson Harris, and Evelyn O'Callaghan, as well as C. L. R. James, Lamming, Walcott, and Brathwaite. Brathwaite observes the presence of "differing psychosocial Caribbeans" that interact at times harmoniously and at others antithetically, rather than a single continuous conceptual space ("Caribbean Man" 2).[4]

In *The Repeating Island* Benítez-Rojo comes to the same point from a different angle: "The main obstacles to any global study of the Caribbean's societies, insular or continental, are exactly those things that scholars usually adduce to define the area: its fragmentation; its instability; its reciprocal isolation; its uprootedness; its cultural heterogeneity; its lack of historiography and historical continuity; its contingency and impermanence; its syncretism, etc." (1). The operative concept of Caribbean societies here links island to island; nation-state to associated state and colony; Anglophone to Dutch, Francophone, and Hispanic; African ethnicities to Amerindian, Asian, and European. Broadly or narrowly conceived, such an approach privileges transnational affiliations and hybrid cosmopolitan experiences that tend to blur, if not erase, the boundaries of the nation-state in readings and representations of the literary culture of the region.[5] This study places a similar premium on regional cultural identities for organizing points of view and making comparisons to determine how an individual autobiographical act is approached and evaluated as a culture-building exercise that engages self and collective identities. However, it should be clear that my particular emphasis on the English-speaking Caribbean is not intended as fence building, nor do I seek to minimize the cosmopolitan orientation of Caribbean cultures beyond individual nation-states and regional boundaries.[6] In the face of the multifaceted complexity of the Caribbean experience, any pan-Caribbean paradigm is immediately qualified by the thematics of diaspora, by the tensions between cosmopolitan experiences and rooted ones.[7]

The themes of diaspora in the Caribbean are complicated because Caribbean writers and scholars have been at great pains to represent the region, historically and culturally, as diasporic space—more commonly in terms of the competing claims of African, Asian, and European ethnicities.[8] Diasporic space represents the Caribbean in specific histories of conquest and settlement, population movements, exile and migration. It exists in tension with the concept of community that is inscribed within sites of ancestral dwelling. In *Caribbean Discourse* Glissant observes:

> What makes this difference between a people that survives elsewhere, that maintains its original nature, and a population that is transformed elsewhere into another people (without, however, succumbing to the reductive pressures of the Other) and that thus enters the constantly shifting and variable process of creolization (of relationship, of relativity), is that the latter has not brought with it, not collectively continued, the method of existence and survival, both material and spiritual, which it practiced before being uprooted. (15)

It follows that diasporic cultures are heavily invested in mediating the cultural values of travel and dwelling, and the Caribbean has the added dimension of mediating competing ethnic inscriptions of lineage in any given territory. This self-conscious, often contentious, cultural diversity is important to any discussion of regional cultural identities and further complicates issues of cultural localization. Thus my critical posture is one of interrogation and of dialogue with the contradictions of regional identities that are evident in dominant and in less-well-known autobiographical texts, rather than anticipation of the Caribbean as a single conceptual space based on assumptions of increasing cultural homogeneity.

In his critique of established models of historical analysis in "Caribbean Man in Space and Time," Brathwaite writes, "With regard to the plural model, we shall have to introduce process as well as structure, and open ourselves to inputs of race, creolization and americanization, in ways that we have not attempted before. We shall also have to bear in mind the possibility that the resolution of this process may, but will not necessarily, be socio-cultural homogeneity" (11). By focusing on Caribbean identity formation as an ongoing intercultural process, I hope to differentiate and make specific for further analysis some of the levels and networks of community represented. In *Contradictory Omens* Brathwaite emphasizes personal history as a crucial component in representing the problematics of cultural diversity and integration: "It is my conviction that we cannot begin to understand statements about 'West Indian culture,' since it is so diverse and has so many subtly different orientations and interpretations, unless we know something about the speaker/writer's own socio-cultural background and orientation" (33). More recently, Carole Boyce Davies has used personal history to generate a model of cultural interlap and overlap to challenge the notion that the word *Caribbean* describes only the geographical boundaries of the region (*Black Women* 34). The worlds of Africa, Asia, Europe, and the United States intersect in the Caribbean archipelago in the most unpredictable ways, each a distinct presence continuously refashioning itself, at times contentiously and at others harmoniously.[9]

By using specific autobiographical texts to interrogate some of the conjunctures of these worlds, I am attempting to come to grips with the relevance of autobiographical practice to an understanding of how intermeshing cultural presences are reinvented over time as materially grounded Caribbean subjectivities. I will variously analyze individual texts with respect to environment and history, race and culture, class and caste, gender and sexuality, and language and theory. This will facilitate generalizations about the intersection of multiple contradictory subjectivities of the colonial and postcolonial Caribbean, the role of writing and literacy, concepts of community, and levels of social integration within nation-states that were largely built by and on British colonial practice from the midseventeenth through the midtwentieth century, a practice that generated a persistent pattern of resistance and accommodation.

The radical instability of the Caribbean as a cultural domain coincides with the radical instability of autobiography as a genre.[10] Throughout this study I use autobiography not only as a generic classification but as a mode of representation, which allows for greater flexibility of reference. *Mode* implies use of the conventions of autobiography in combination with other generic forms, for example, travel narrative, fiction, and elegy, and that is my intention as I explore the ways in which autobiographical culture facilitates representation of the multidimensionality and contradictoriness of Caribbean space. Categories of analysis range from the confessional to the historiographical document, the testimonial, written and oral narratives, the relationship between autobiography and the novel, serial autobiography, verse autobiography, autobiography as something else, diaries, journals, parody of autobiography, the autobiographer as a writer, and whatever autobiographical practices are instantiated by the texts under scrutiny here.[11]

This is not a survey of Anglo-Caribbean autobiography. My critical task is to identify and locate strategies of self-representation already in place in Caribbean writing for what they reveal about the fluidity and reciprocity of narrative identity. Though I might easily have chosen other texts, I selected these for the insight that each allows into the literary and cultural systems that it uses, for its singularity and contrasting values in the changing contexts of Caribbean autobiographical practice. The generic values of each text are as important as its contextual conditions; the correlation between the two becomes a measure of the expressive need that autobiography has served in Caribbean literary culture.

Because the unfolding drama of consciousness in autobiography is embedded in the quirkiness of the genre, it follows that each text under scrutiny invites a distinct relationship to a wide range of autobiographical theory. In a study like this one the quest for a Caribbean architecture of consciousness is of necessity engaged with the creative possibilities of the genre that operate within the constraints imposed by the vagaries of print capitalism and the shifting frameworks for expression of a nationally or regionally defined consciousness. What might appear chaotic about the fluidity and multiplicity of the autobiographical forms that I examine may in fact be the measure of an individually and/or collectively drawn self-hood that is straining against the constraints of established models for the representation of gender, race, and ethnicity within the framework of a national or regional consciousness.

I have divided this study into four parts: "Gender, Voice, and Self-Representation," "The Estranging Sea," "Birthrights and Legacies," and "Autobiography, Elegy, and Gender Identification." In each part I pursue a distinct trajectory that explores the correlation between defining features of the genre and other functional aspects, between the conception of the individual identity articulated and the literary and cultural systems within which it is developed. These trajectories are distinct but not necessarily exclusive, because conventions of self-representation are repeated as often as they are reinvented, and conceptions of individual identity are developed with cultural distinctions that are often restated in the changing literary and cultural situations represented.

"Gender, Voice, and Self-Representation," part 1, focuses on issues of gender, voice, and self-representation in the nineteenth-century narratives of four women of color: Anne Hart Gilbert, Elizabeth Hart Thwaites, Mary Prince, and Mary Seacole. These women's narratives are situated within theories of women's autobiography on the one hand and the interweaving of Caribbean life projects with metropolitan institutions and ideologies on the other. Part 2, "The Estranging Sea," explores links between geography and being, exile and otherness, in the narratives of four prominent twentieth-century writers: Claude McKay, C. L. R. James, Lamming, and Walcott. In part 3, "Birthrights and Legacies," I examine the regional dynamic of cultural dislocation and localization in contrastive studies of the works of four writers: Naipaul, Mahase, Bridges, and Rhys. In part 4, "Autobiography, Elegy, and Gender Identification," I focus on cross-gender identifications in recent autobiographical texts by Brathwaite and Kincaid. Through elegy both writers internalize the deceased other and in the process raise different questions about the gender binaries so much in evidence in earlier texts that I discuss in this book.

Part 1

Gender, Voice, and Self-Representation

The nineteenth-century narratives of the Hart sisters, Mary Prince, and Mary Seacole anticipate and disturb many of the gendered assumptions embedded in the colonial and postcolonial paradigms of twentieth-century autobiographical narratives included in this book. Foremost among these, as Carole Boyce-Davies and Elaine Fido observe in their introduction to *Out of the Kumbla,* is "the historical absence of the woman writer's text: the absence of a specifically female position on major issues such as slavery, colonialism, decolonization, women's rights and more direct social and cultural issues" (1). In her afterword to *Out of the Kumbla,* Sylvia Wynter takes this observation a step further. Wynter takes issue with the Prospero-Miranda-Caliban paradigm variously employed by major Caribbean writers and critics in the twentieth century, among them George Lamming, C. L. R. James, Aimé Césaire, Roberto Fernández Retamar, and Kamau Brathwaite; no matter how the discursive paradigm is juggled, the female ancestor is effectively silenced, if not erased. Wynter observes, "not only

her absence, but also the absence of Caliban's endogenous desire
for her, of any longing" (361). She construes this as an ontological absence: "the absence of Caliban's woman as sexual reproductive mate functions to ontologically negate their progeny/
population group" (362). More recently, Belinda Edmondson elaborates on the nature of this historic silencing and erasure:

> In much male-authored anglophone and francophone narrative the
> black woman's body, unlike the white woman's, is often figured as
> maternal, like Sycorax, when it figures at all. In these masculine nar-
> ratives of Caribbean history, the silence of the raped white female
> body is not the same as the silence of the black maternal body, since
> rape is figured as one kind of displaced desire *for* something *through*
> violence, whereas the black female body represents both unrecov-
> erable, nostalgic history associated with Africa (the land, the folk)
> and the tainted history of slavery that requires erasure. (117)

In Caribbean women's writing since the midtwentieth century,
the quest for a female ancestor continues in the imaginary emplotment of a primal mother. Works like Lorna Goodison's "Guinea
Woman" (*Selected Poems*), Grace Nichols's "The Return" (*I Is a
Long Memoried Woman*), Michelle Cliff's *No Telephone to
Heaven,* Maryse Condé's *I, Tituba: Black Witch of Salem,* and
Jamaica Kincaid's *The Autobiography of My Mother* reinscribe the
primal mother as a quasi-historical mythical female ancestor whose
presence is responsive to the twentieth-century Caribbean woman
writer's quest for cultural legitimacy and agency. The absent
mother is reinscribed in ideal terms and immortalized. For Condé
the primal mother as Tituba is a woman of infinite love; for
Michelle Cliff the primal mother as Nanny of the Maroons is the
incarnation of historical awareness and resistant militancy; for
Jamaica Kincaid the primal mother is a vengeful haunting of the
Carib landscape; and for Grace Nichols and Lorna Goodison the
primal mother is a racial and cultural destiny inscribed as reconnection with African origins. These women writers were reconstructing an individual and collective cultural identity in the latter
part of the twentieth century around remote historical figures.[1]
This contemporary reinscription of "the silent presence of a mother

not fully understood" (Zimra 157) is romanticized and heroic in proportion to the individual writer's quest for identity and cultural authenticity.

The historic silencing and erasure of the female ancestor as literary subject takes an interesting turn with the discovery and republication of the nineteenth-century narratives of the Hart sisters, Mary Prince, and Mary Seacole between 1987 and 1993. Though circumscribed by generic function and circumstances of publication, this is hardly a disqualifier in Caribbean literary culture, where writers and critics continue to be dependent on metropolitan publishers and foreign audiences, and transnational capitalist enterprise endures as a facet of the historical disjunctions and economic or cultural dependencies that characterize the post-Columbian Caribbean. Nationalist ideologies in the Caribbean have to contend with transnational networks and cultural attachments that encode practices of accommodation and resistance as a condition of survival.[2] The compromised and often conflictual relationship between textual production and institutional power is the background against which self-identity and group identity are constituted.[3]

The republication of these four nineteenth-century women's narratives effectively restores the woman writer's text to the discourse of decolonization and colonial struggle in the twentieth-century Caribbean. Two were published in Moira Ferguson's *The Hart Sisters* (1993): Anne Hart Gilbert's "History of Methodism" (1804) and Elizabeth Hart Thwaites's "History of Methodism" (1804). The others are Mary Prince's *The History of Mary Prince, a West Indian Slave, Related by Herself* (1831), republished in 1987; and Mary Seacole's *Wonderful Adventures of Mrs. Seacole in Many Lands* (1857), which was republished in 1988.[4] An uneven mixture of intellectual and cultural history, legal deposition, and autobiography, these texts provide detailed, though by no means complete, accounts of strategies available to women who sought to challenge colonial assumptions and practices in their distinct spheres of experience. They throw light on the idiosyncrasies of a female culture of resistance in the Caribbean before and after emancipation and long before women's suffrage became a legal reality in Europe and North America and independence movements coalesced in the British West Indies. Yet these narratives do more than bear witness to strategies of resistance among different groups of Caribbean women in the nineteenth century; they model forms of subject identification that are defining paradigms for modern Caribbean writing, not as a sequence of development but as ongoing literary practice.[5] They illuminate the depth of contemporary paradigms, among them, Brathwaite's "emigrants and the islanders" ("Sir Galahad" 8), and Wilfred Cartey's "I going away, I going home" (in *Whispers from the Caribbean*), that prove to have an analytical value beyond the textual framework for which they were created. By the same token, the narratives of these four women illuminate Caribbean literary culture as a transnational enterprise. Each of these texts is implicated in colonialism and imperialism and each provides a space for the expression of social dissidence and marginality that is directed at a metropolitan audience in an effort to force a change in the status of the colonial subject and slave. The women's narratives under consideration here establish distinct and varied trajectories of Caribbean women's history, resistance, and agency within the contours of specific intellectual and cultural landscapes. In the words of Gramsci, "One does not enter or exit, one continues" (66).

Published in England in the span of more than half a century (1804–1857), across the great divide of the abolition of slavery in England in 1834, the narratives of Elizabeth Hart Thwaites, Anne Hart Gilbert, Mary Prince, and Mary Seacole prefigure styles of being and identity formation in twentieth-century autobiographical narratives.[6] Although they were at the margins of British cultural production, they are at the formative center of an emerging Caribbean literary tradition. In effect, they reconfigure the parameters of Caribbean autobiography, which emerged as a predominantly male enterprise in the twentieth century, around the "submerged" legacy of a few extraordinary women of the nineteenth. These narratives bring into sharp focus the ontological conflicts and contradictions built into the relationship between Europe and the Americas, dependent colony and seat of empire, slave and master, men and women. Within them two issues of paramount importance in the engendering of the modern Caribbean, the emancipation of slaves and the emancipation of women, are fully engaged as vital parts of the way the self and community are conceptualized. In concert with the twentieth-century autobiographical texts that I examine here, they clarify the ongoing process of decolonization, the production of alternative cultural identities in this century, and the ways in which these processes define the parameters of female difference and discrimination in Caribbean writing.

Elizabeth Hart Thwaites (1772–1833) and Anne Hart Gilbert (1773–1834) of Antigua were pioneering educators and missionaries on their native island. Operating under the umbrella of the Antigua Methodist Church, they worked relentlessly to redefine the image and status of free blacks and slaves. Mary Prince was born a slave in Bermuda in 1788, and her quest for freedom took her to England by way of Antigua in 1828. She disappears from historical record shortly after the publication of her life story in 1831. Mary Seacole (1805–1881) was a Jamaican who made a name for herself as an entrepreneur and "doctress" in Jamaica and, by her own testimony, repeated these feats in New Granada, in the Crimea, and in England. Each of their narratives directly and self-consciously challenges the assumptions of a racist, patriarchal, colonial ideology in its distinct sphere of experience.

Nothing is homogeneous about the aesthetic and ideological values of these women's literary production. Differences in class, values, access to circuits of communication, and local and international politics are reflected in their discursive forms and ideological discourses. For example, the Hart sisters were privately educated and accomplished women of letters. They frame their ideological discourse with an autonomy not possible for Mary Prince, who did not write. In "The Changing Moral Discourse of Nineteenth-Century African-American Women's Autobiography," William L. Andrews differentiates the Christian idealism of Harriet Jacobs from the materialist, pragmatic discourse of Elizabeth Keckley as measures of self-evaluation (236). Something similar is apparent in the post-emancipation shift from the Christian idealist discourse of the Harts through Mary Prince to the pragmatic materialist discourse of Mary Seacole, who advertised herself as a self-made professional woman of the world and manipulated the conventions of travel narrative, autobiography, and print capitalism with the explicit intention of making money and reaffirming her good name in the "mother country." The dynamics of slavery and colonialism engender specific patterns of alliance, collusion, and collaboration with metropolitan authorities in the narratives of these women. Read together, they invite complex readings of Caribbean personality and presence in the variables of their discourse of struggle.[7]

Not unexpectedly, the "ideal" woman at the heart of the narratives of Thwaites, Gilbert, Prince, and Seacole, all women of color, both challenges and confirms the assumptions of a patriarchal ideology outlined by Sidonie Smith in *A Poetics of Women's Autobiography*.[8] Their literary production operates within the constraints of an Anglo-American cult of domesticity complicitous in the patriarchal or colonial project, but these narratives remind us that these constraints do not necessarily constitute erasure. The self-inscribed ideal in these narratives emerges as an articulate woman of heroic action, with a highly developed sense of the needs and desires requisite to personal and social fulfillment and of the conflicts and contradictions of life choices. This is not to gainsay or even minimize the strategies of self-erasure imposed and internalized by cultural practice in the narratives of these women.[9] But the texts that these women produced blur the lines of gender difference outlined by Sidonie Smith insofar as they communicate a heartening self-consciousness and sophistication about how "the two universes of discourse" may be manipulated to specific ends (*Poetics of Women's Autobiography* 50). May Chamberlain refocuses the issue when she observes that women are in effect culturally bilingual: "They inhabit simultaneously, not sequentially, a domestic and a public world, and it is this which shapes their experience, the language which expresses it and the priorities allocated within it" (96).

Writing about the legacy of slavery from a nationalist-feminist position in "Shadow of the Whip" (1974), Merle Hodge resists traditional gender distinctions: "In the Caribbean the 'war of the sexes' takes on a very special character. It is not a straight fight between handicapped Woman on the one hand and omnipotent Man on the other. From the very beginning of West Indian history the black woman has had a de facto 'equality' thrust upon her—the equality of cattle in a herd" (114). Hodge misstates the case for "de facto equality," as recent scholarship has documented significant differences in the conditions of women and men, and of slavery, from island to island, even from owner to owner.[10] Marietta Morrissey observes that, although in plantation agriculture much of male and female work was the same, women were consistently subordinate to both whites and male slaves: "Precisely because of capitalism's invasive impact, female slaves were increasingly differentiated from and dominated by males, even as slaves of both genders moved together into routinized plantation work and more highly rationalized relations with slaveholders" (x). Morrissey concludes that "women's treatment differed from men's on both physical terms and in reference to the qualitatively determined areas now under heavy scrutiny—food, shelter, clothing, housing, provision grounds, and the like" (15). However, Hodge's resistance to the idea of Caribbean women as ideologically excluded with respect to the specific circumstances and character of their participation in history, calls attention to the way that concepts of "selves in hiding" can be manipulated within a colonial and postcolonial framework.[11]

Though complicitous in the silencing and at times unsympathetic representation of the female subject, the idea of "selves in hiding," or, for that matter, Mary Mason's grounding of women's autobiography in "identity through relation to the chosen other" (210), is readily applicable to strategies of self-representation in the autobiographical narratives of male Caribbean writers, among them, George Lamming, Derek Walcott, C. L. R. James, and V. S. Naipaul.[12] For these writers the burden of defining and sustaining cultural difference and literary authority in metropolitan centers on both sides of the Atlantic occasions a high degree of erasure, obliqueness, and inventiveness in their manipulation of the genre, but this does not preclude a marked pattern of gender discrimination in their texts. In fact, it is fair to say that gender discrimination is an intrinsic part of their strategies of self-erasure or, for that matter, "the grounding of identity through relation" (Mason 210). In respect to the life stories of white women born and raised in the Caribbean, for example, Jean Rhys's *Smile, Please* (1979) and Yseult Bridges's *Child of the Tropics* (1988), both published posthumously, the phrases "selves in hiding" and "identity through relation" speak directly to an acute defensiveness about race, class, and gender in the colonial Caribbean. Gayatri Spivak's views on "witting and unwitting lapses" or "sanctioned ignorances" in contemporary historiography are pertinent here; she equates "cognitive failure" with "success-in-failure" and "sanctioned ignorances" with colonial domination and patriarchal domination (*Other Worlds* 199). In either case the innate circumspection of autobiography is a self-selecting process that lends itself to strategies of creative misperception.[13]

In practice the cult of domesticity both rationalizes the exclusion of women of color from the sphere of privileged womanhood and exposes fissures in the gender dynamics of the colonial project.[14] Conversely, the visible strengths and strategic resistances registered by women like the Hart sisters, Prince, and Seacole are skewed to the recognition of their ritual debasement and negation within the cult of domesticity. The iconography of familial and domestic space becomes a contested site in all kinds of ways, whether it be the Harts' attempt to rescue black women from sexual exploitation or their marriages to resistant, politically active white men; or Mary Prince's detailed memory of the physical and emotional abuse heaped on black women, men, and children by entire families—masters, mistresses, and children—in the pursuit of propertied power, family decorum, and visible signs of class status; or Mrs. Seacole's reversal of the cult of domesticity in sanctioning herself as Mother Seacole at the boundary of empire. If, as McClintock concludes, the family trope is important to colonialism in that "it offers a 'natural' figure for sanctioning national *hierarchy* within a putative organic *unity* of interests" (357), these narratives' conscious manipulation of the trope is worth noting. The situation of black women at the outer limits of sanctioned "domesticity" within the colonial hierarchy is precisely what constitutes in varying degrees the impetus and theme of their agency.

In "Sex and Gender in the Historiography of Caribbean Slavery," Hilary Beckles distinguishes two parallel epistemological traditions that are of interest here, that of the rebel woman and that of the natural rebel:

> By necessity, the rebel woman is the "special" central figure whose transformative powers are embodied in her singular capabilities. She can be replaced, but the apex remains. She leads those below but her powers and system of organization are from above. The power she has is used for the liberation of the community of the enslaved, but it is not derived from it. In essence, it is an elitist leadership in the tradition of divine authority, and therefore not reproduced within the context of popular social change.
>
> The "natural rebel," however, is your typical "woman in the fields," who possesses no claim to distinct individuality and is therefore one of the masses. . . . The everyday experience of her enslavement represents the basis of a culture of refusal and resistance through which she claims a "self" and an "identity." (136–37)

Though a useful tool for categorical analysis, the dichotomy does not do justice to the overlap or coincidence of apparently antithetical subjectivities represented in these women's texts. Thwaites, Gilbert, Prince, and Seacole may be exceptional women, but their narratives make clear that their resistant spirits were not formed in one camp or the other but in knowledge gleaned in association with both an "elitist leadership" and the oppressed communities of enslaved and colored classes in the colonial Caribbean.[15] Their narratives reveal fluctuating levels of contact and interaction across the boundaries of race, class, and gender in the heyday of nineteenth-century colonial culture that illuminate tensions, contradictions, and interpenetrations between the dominant culture and subordinate or emergent cultures.

Given the explicit generic functions of the narratives of Gilbert, Thwaites, Prince, and Seacole—church history, slave narrative, and travel narrative—self-representation takes predictable directions. These women are discernibly preoccupied with the project of cross-cultural translation in a power-charged situation. They are acutely aware that they will be read as women who have stepped out of their place at the margins of the British Empire. They address an English audience within the conventions of nineteenth-century literary practice in order to challenge the parameters of female subjectivity in relation to race, language, desire, and power.[16] However, a pattern of accommodation does not negate what these texts reveal about the gendered subculture of Caribbean womanhood and its subtexts. Given their slave and colonial subject status at the time that they wrote and published their narratives, their work intersects in the most interesting ways, illuminating the inner directives of resistant women who negotiate the boundaries of language and power and, in the process, demarcate trajectories of self-inscription that persist in the twentieth century. From the Hart sisters to Mary Seacole these narratives illuminate specific historical and intellectual practices that are usefully integrated into any map of Caribbean subjectivities or projection of Caribbean aesthetics. Their empirical base enables a comparative analysis of specific practices of personhood in different race- and class-based life worlds in respect to gender relations, levels of integration and differentiation, metropolitan alliances, travel and dwelling, literary production, and women's agency.

1

Testing and Testifying

The Hart Sisters

Elizabeth Hart Thwaites (1772–1833) and Anne Hart Gilbert (1773–1834) of Antigua were pioneering educators and social workers on their native island. Born into a black slaveholding family, they were devout Methodists who worked to redefine the status of free blacks and slaves in Antigua. Reverend Richard Pattison, an English missionary stationed on the island of Nevis, asked both women to write separate accounts of the rise and progress of Methodism in Antigua. Both complied in 1804, each writing a brief "History of Methodism." Their narratives differ in tone and content, and this is perhaps reflective of their different status and personality. Yet their narratives are complementary in their functional aspects; each is exemplary spiritual autobiography as well as church history and women's history. Anne's narrative focuses on the religious project in its historical aspects and her activism on behalf of Methodism and the women and children of Antigua, while Elizabeth's is a more personal account of the process of conversion and the sisters' commitment to personal salvation, church ministry, and social reform.

As converts to Methodism, the sisters had direct access to influential metropolitan-based organizations ideologically and actively opposed to slavery and the plantation system.[1] While their conversion to Wesleyan Methodism in 1786 and subsequent religious and social activism deepened the process of acculturation in the African Caribbean community, Methodism gave them a legitimate alternative institutional base for organized resistance to an oppressive colonial system. Moira Ferguson concludes: "Their role as

21

religious educators offers them an important status and public voice in Antigua and simultaneously allows them a cover of sorts for abolitionist and emancipationist activities" (*Colonialism and Gender* 3).

As the daughters of Barry Conyers Hart, a free black who reportedly agonized about his role as plantation owner and slave-holder (Ferguson, *Hart Sisters* 5), Anne and Elizabeth were educated according to their privilege and status. They were well positioned to assume leadership roles in the Methodist Church in Antigua. Their status afforded them a certain measure of protection, and their color gave them access to free and enslaved blacks of all classes. Anne Hart Gilbert writes that on her arrival in English Harbor "my complexion exempted me from those prejudices and that disgust which the instability of their white Bretheren had planted in their hearts & they tremblingly ventured to receive us as friends" (Ferguson, *Hart Sisters* 72). As Methodist converts, preachers, teachers, and writers, the Hart sisters asserted their independence as free black women working for the social betterment and spiritual uplift of free and enslaved Africans. They cultivated liberal metropolitan alliances and assumed leadership roles in an alternative community that challenged the ideology and practice of colonial slavery.[2]

Anne Hart Gilbert and Elizabeth Hart Thwaites were a formidable pair. They repeatedly challenged social and political conventions of plantation society, first by converting to Methodism on an island where the white ruling class was largely Anglican and hostile to the spread of evangelical Christianity; by marrying white men of influence in Antigua and in the Methodist Church in Antigua; and by embarking on a program of preaching, teaching, and good works with the explicit intention of changing the image and status of free and enslaved Africans in general and women in particular.[3] In the face of concerted opposition from friends and the ruling elite, the sisters worked for the spread of Methodism among Africans and in the process helped to establish an ideological alternative to the antispiritual, anti-intellectual materialism of the plantation system. They offered religious instruction to slaves and free blacks and taught them to read. Thanks to their energetic intervention, the rituals of church membership generated a new basis for self-definition and with it a new sense of community grounded in spiritual difference and church-sanctioned assembly (Ferguson, *Hart Sisters* 43, 44). The plantation hierarchy had to contend with organized resistance facilitated by the rise of a black and colored church leadership that traveled from plantation to plantation and an influential and powerful founder in Nathaniel Gilbert.[4]

The sisters' stalwart Methodism was not without its downside. Their Methodist devotion to the Bible as sacred text and to literacy inevitably deepened their psychological and cultural dependence on England and gave new impetus to Europeans' sweeping rejection of African and African Caribbean cultures as pagan and barbaric. If the African convert was the equal of the European in the new religious order, ancestral Africa and African-derived customs were rejected as signs of ungodliness, ignorance, superstition, and sin (Ferguson, *Hart Sisters* 58–60). The ensuing tension between an African spiritual base and a European one continues unabated in our time, but what the Hart sisters exude in their lives and their works is the zealous pursuit of social and political change. Piety and patriotism, salvation and emancipation are intertwined in their work and writings.[5] If the acculturative, assimilative disposition of the Methodist Church and its puritanical values were antithetical to an existing slave culture of survival, the Hart sisters nonetheless make a strong case for racial equality, for the empowerment of women, for a developing sense of native community, and for Christianity as a site of resistance.[6] As Moira Ferguson concludes: "By thematizing their concerns as black Antiguans while foregrounding the occupiers' religion, they established a specific black Antiguan cultural identity" (*Hart Sisters* 47). Both women had a highly developed sense of racial solidarity and of Antigua as their native land. In their writings the drama of the antislavery movement is located in Antigua, and they are center stage of their own volition.

The histories of Anne Gilbert and Elizabeth Thwaites, short as they are (eighteen pages and seven pages, respectively), bear explicit resemblance to nineteenth-century African American spiritual or conversion narratives.[7] As church historians, the Hart sisters control the substance of the ensuing discourse though not the circumstances of their literary production. Their narratives testify to their spiritual and ministerial experiences as dedicated members of the Methodist Church in Antigua, and each is written in the form of a letter to Pattison.[8] The letters bring the sisters together in a common agenda, yet their individual histories are different in style and content. They diverge along the lines of private and public, personal and historical. The sisters worked so closely together and their individual histories are so sharply divergent in function that it is easy to suspect collusion. In some respects Anne Hart Gilbert and Elizabeth Hart Thwaites appear to be mirror images of each other. Born one year apart, they died one year apart. Both converted to Methodism at the same time, made radical changes in their lifestyle, and worked closely together with their white husbands on projects that had a dramatic influence on Antiguan life. Working together, the sisters established the first Sunday school in the West Indies in 1809 and founded the Female Refuge Society of Antigua in 1815; in the absence of Anne Hart Gilbert, who had returned to St. John's with her husband when his position at the naval base in English Harbour was eliminated, Elizabeth Hart Thwaites oversaw the girls' department of English Harbour Sunday School. Pattison asked the sisters to write him a letter "regarding the rise and progress of Methodism in Antigua" (Ferguson, *Hart Sisters* 57), and both complied in 1804, barely a month apart, Elizabeth on May 5 and Anne on June 1. Anne wrote that she had done this once before, in 1790.

Their individual histories negotiate very different territory. In Anne Hart Gilbert's "History" personal narrative is subsumed in her account of the religious-historical project. Anne's history details crises and successes in the Methodist program for religious conversion and social reform and her concerns as an activist, teacher, and preacher's wife. She documents instances of superstition and ignorance among slaves, free people of color, and "those called white people" alike (Ferguson, *Hart Sisters* 59–60). Hers is the impassioned discourse of a "full heart" (66), the emotional centerpiece of which is a brief ecstatic affirmation of her personal salvation

(65–66). She inscribes herself with some effort at humility as a model of nineteenth-century Methodist womanhood. She makes herself known in protestations of faith and good works, through her championing of black women and children and her denunciation of a corrupt plantocracy. Though she is married at the time and her husband is intimately involved in church activities, she mentions him only casually and makes no mention at all of the public insults that they suffered when they announced their marriage. In *Antigua and the Antiguans* Frances Lanaghan throws some light on the matter:

> In 1798, Mr. Gilbert, (a relation to the Mr. Gilbert, the founder of Methodism in Antigua), for many years the superintendent of his majesty's dockyard at English Harbour, was united in the bands of wedlock to a highly respectable and accomplished coloured lady of Antigua. The *iniquity*! of this action, as they deemed it, was resented by his brother whites; himself and his lady were openly insulted; and some wag of the island, who, with the brains of a calf, fancied himself an Ulysses in wisdom, gave to the world an example of his would-be wit, by painting Mr. Gilbert's office-door half *black* and half *white*. (2:178–79)[9]

In their respective histories the sisters do not refer to such public humiliations; they focus instead on the high drama of the Methodist mission in Antigua.

Elizabeth Hart Thwaites inscribes herself quite differently in her "History." Whereas Anne moves directly to the historical events preliminary to Methodism on the island and the progress of the Methodist ministry in Antigua, Elizabeth gives "more circumstantial detail of my spiritual course" (Ferguson, *Hart Sisters* 89). Anne writes, "The remotest period to which I can trace the Preaching of the Gospel, in these Islands, is in the year 1671" (57), whereas Elizabeth identifies herself by place of birth and parentage:

> I am, as you know, a native of Antigua. My deceased Grandmother, who was converted to God by the ministry of Rev. Francis Gilbert and who died in the Faith, with my Dear Mother (gone to Glory) were united to the Methodists and trained up the younger branches of the Family, myself among them, in the fear of God and the

observance of religious duties. I was also blest with an affection-
ate Father who ever watched with the tenderest solicitude over the
morals of his Children, as did others of our near Relations, who
by their kind attention prevented our feeling the want of Mother's
care after her Death. (89)

She dwells on the intimate details of her spiritual life. Her "full
heart" is a discourse of interiority while Anne's is a passionate discourse of social justice and individual rights. Elizabeth describes
the internal conflict generated by her class and privilege and the
drastic changes in lifestyle that membership in the society brings.
She is in conflict about her love of music, books, and dancing. She
must endure the criticism of friends who find her conversion fool-
hardy: "There were no young persons, that I knew of, who were
in the Society at this time, that were not slaves; on this, and some
other accounts, I proudly held out as long as I could, from wholly
joining them, tho I gained admittance to many of the private meetings" (92). Elizabeth creates a moving portrait of her close relationship with Anne, intimating that not only did they join the
Methodists at the same time but that Anne "was brought to God
in the same way" (92); spiritual autobiography thus doubles as
biography and as conversion narrative. This foregrounding of self,
family, and friends stands in sharp contrast to Anne's foregrounding of the historical project. Between them they reinscribe
black womanhood so as to project both their own sense of innate
value and their social mission in ideal terms.

The Hart sisters seized Methodism with the fervor with which the
Anglophone Caribbean seized upon English cricket and not dissim-
ilarly.[10] The sisters are both possessed by evangelical Christianity and
possess it to their own ends. Twentieth-century texts of Caribbean
cultural and intellectual history have richly explored the ensuing cultural ambiguity and the creative energy that it generated.[11] More
immediately, the effect of their work and influence was discernible
in the community of slaves and free blacks whom they served and
who sought and found in the sisters' resistant brand of evangelical
Christianity strategies for circumventing an oppressive plantation
hierarchy. These Antiguan natives were "outsiders" from birth, but

armed with a Methodist gospel of personal salvation and social reform, they testify to a feminist resistance that reconfigured their relationship to colonial Antigua. Frances Smith Foster's observations about African American women's literature in the antebellum period seem tailored to the Hart sisters: "The imperatives of sanctification led the converted to challenge traditional beliefs and practices. They created a gospel of social reform that included a more secular feminism and the claiming of authority for civil disobedience" (*Written by Herself* 77). In fact, authorities subsequently brought Elizabeth Hart Thwaites before the Antigua Assembly to answer for her antislavery activities. She was allowed to go free but her co-conspirator, Joseph Phillips, was imprisoned and pauperized for his antislavery efforts. James MacQueen, editor of the *Glasgow Courier*, denounced both in the November 1831 issue of *Blackwoods Magazine* as miserable tools of "anti-colonial faction and rancour" (Ferguson, *Colonialism and Gender* 58). In their parallel histories of Methodism the sisters illuminate the shaping influence of religious activism on their developing sense of selfhood and resistant consciousness as advocates of radical social reform.

2

The Heartbeat of
a West Indian Slave

The History of Mary Prince

Mary Prince was born in Bermuda around 1788. She worked as a household slave in Bermuda and Antigua and in the salt mines of Turk's Island under the most brutal conditions. In 1828 she traveled from Antigua to England with her owners, Mr. and Mrs. John A. Wood, and hoped to secure her freedom there and return to Antigua a free woman. England had declared slavery illegal in 1772, but this law did not apply to British slave colonies in the Caribbean, and Prince's owners rejected all attempts to buy Prince's freedom in England.[1] During the ensuing conflict with the Woods in England, she told her story to Susanna Strickland, amanuensis, abolitionist, poet, and a guest of Thomas Pringle, Prince's employer. The resulting manuscript, *The History of Mary Prince, a West Indian Slave, Related by Herself,* was published as an antislavery tract in England in 1831, with supporting documentation provided by Pringle, who served as Prince's editor and publisher and was secretary of the Anti-Slavery Society. Two years after the publication of her book and a brief court appearance, Prince disappeared entirely from the public record in 1833. Her narrative endures as a pioneering effort, both as slave narrative and as autobiography.

The paths of the Hart sisters and Mary Prince intersect in interesting ways. In the case of Mary Prince, literary agency is achieved in exile with the publication of her life story as discourse defining slave narrative. The text is a collaborative venture involving

Thomas Pringle and Susanna Strickland, a recent convert to Methodism, and a number of well-intentioned supporters in Antigua and England. On one level, the process begins in Antigua through the agency of the Antigua Methodist Church and the Moravians. In her narrative, Mary Prince recalls attending "a Methodist meeting for prayer, at a plantation called Winthorps. I went; and they were the first prayers I ever understood" (72). The Winthorps are Methodist and related by marriage to the Gilberts, the family of Anne Hart Gilbert's husband (Ferguson, *Hart Sisters* 58).[2] Moreover, in the November 1831 issue of *Blackwoods Magazine,* James MacQueen named Mary Prince, along with Joseph Phillips and Elizabeth Thwaites, as "tools of anti-colonial faction and rancour" (Ferguson, *Colonialism and Gender* 58). At Thomas Pringle's request, Joseph Phillips wrote a testimonial on Prince's behalf, which was included in Pringle's supplement to the 1831 edition of *The History of Mary Prince.*

Mary Prince's testimony illuminates the coercive and subversive power of the Methodist meeting in a slave society:

> One woman prayed; and then they all sung a hymn; then there was another prayer and another hymn; and then they all spoke by turns of their own griefs as sinners. The husband of the woman I went with was a black driver. His name was Henry. He confessed that he had treated the slaves very cruelly; but said that he was compelled to obey the orders of his master. He prayed them all to forgive him, and he prayed that God would forgive him. He said it was a horrid thing for a ranger to have sometimes to beat his own wife or sister; but he must do so if ordered by his master. (*History of Mary Prince* 72–73)

Prince reports that she was transformed by the experience, and when she returned to town, she joined the Moravian church, where she received religious instruction.[3] Her conversion served her well. Later, while in England with her owners the Woods, she turned to the Moravians and the Methodists for sanctuary and support in her efforts to secure her freedom and return to Antigua as a free woman. It was due to the efforts of Thomas Pringle and

Susanna Strickland, both Methodists, that Prince's oral history was transcribed and edited for publication as a slave narrative.

The History of Mary Prince is remarkable because it both uses and privileges a black West Indian woman's narrative in a legal and literary context at a time when her autonomy was hotly contested. As slave narrative, her history brings together in a collective agenda the two dimensions of personal narrative and historical project. By its very nature it is a site of resistance and collaboration that makes explicit the interculturative processes that characterize literary production in the Caribbean, then and now. The text is a conventional slave narrative in content, theme, and form, and it bears strong resemblance to cases of slave abuse reported in the *Anti-Slavery Reporter* around the time of its publication in London in 1831.[4] Moira Ferguson notes in *Subject to Others* that Prince's narrative "touched on almost every clause included in resolutions drawn up by the Ladies Anti-Slavery Associations around the country" (294).[5] It is also true that Prince's text corroborates and consolidates Anne Hart Gilbert's denunciation of the plantocracy, drunkenness, debauchery, rape, and other forms of physical and emotional abuse heaped on slaves and slave women in particular.

In her role as house slave Mary Prince inhabited white domestic and familial space to expose it as degenerate and un-Christian. She bore witness from childhood to the sadistic rage of the white mistresses, masters, and their progeny; to occasional friendships; furtive and forbidden acts of kindness; to the coercion, acrimony, and physical and mental abuse that followed her from owner to owner and island to island. As a child-nurse, she modeled an incipient motherhood and cross-class, cross-racial sisterhood that suggests an organic unity of interests in the deviant agency of the slave. Later she details what appears to be a spontaneous discovery that productive alliances can be forged where abuse and victimization are shared. When she intervenes to shield the daughter of her master from his physical abuse, Prince wins a measure of protection from his abuse as well: "The people gave me credit for getting her away" (67). This consciousness of how weaknesses in the hierarchy of power might be manipulated points the way to compromise and collaboration in a narrative quest for freedom.

Alliances formed with local and liberal metropolitan-based Moravians and Methodists serve Mary Prince's will to gain her freedom, though they underscore her dependency in that quest.[6] They make her voice as historian of West Indian slavery possible and credible to a British audience. Yet the alliance of the African Caribbean ex-slave with both Methodists and Moravians was double edged. While the Hart sisters did battle in Antigua, Mary Prince subsequently found herself in exile in England, far removed from home and husband. The differences in these women's subject positions are specific to issues of personality and presence as well as caste and class. Mary Prince was a slave in Antigua who surrendered her oral history to an Englishwoman in order to be heard. As free women of private means, the Hart sisters had legal rights to family, marriage, education, and religious activism that Prince did not share. It becomes clear that Prince struggled with her new faith in a way that she did not have to struggle with moral and ethical considerations of slavery and freedom. For her the freedom to return to Antigua remained unaccomplished, and her narrative reveals an acute awareness of the contradictory elements of liberation and containment framed by church teaching. It is a means to an end that assumes a life of its own as an end in itself, and she had to contend with this without the comfort and support of her native community: "I still live in the hope that God will find a way to give me my liberty, and give me back to my husband. I endeavor to keep down my fretting, and to leave all to Him, for he knows what is good for me better that I know myself. Yet, I must confess, I find it a hard and heavy task to do so" (83).

In some respects the narrative of Mary Prince is that of a West Indian slave marooned in England by laws that made slavery illegal in England, while it was still legal in the colonies. *Shipwrecked* may be a more appropriate signifier because *Maroon* in the Caribbean more often than not refers to a reconstituted community of escaped slaves.[7] The material base of her subjugation makes slavery the starting point of her narrative; self-figuration invokes at-oneness with the emancipation of slaves in the Caribbean. In

Prince's narrative primary subject and group identification is with the enslaved and the oppressed in the Caribbean.

In England, Prince's authority is that of the victim and witness who finds her audience with the assistance of a powerful patron, Pringle, and her amanuensis, Strickland. Personal freedom is conceptualized as the moral and legal right to determine one's identity as a birthright. Feeling, imagination, the priority of her allegiance to and affection for her fellow slaves, and her revelations of a nurturing cultural tradition in the harshest of environments are autobiographical values that appear in the work of Claude McKay, George Lamming, C. L. R. James, and Derek Walcott more than a hundred years later.[8] The distancing perspective of exile, the rootlessness and dispossession wrought by capitalism and slavery, the giving of voice in a narrative of self to a Caribbean community of the imagination, all these link Prince's narrative to twentieth-century male texts that are devoid of reference to her resistant, militant spirit.

Issues of voice and identity are complex in *The History of Mary Prince.* The circumstances governing the textual production of Mary Prince's narrative unquestionably altered her individual authorial voice.[9] She dictated her history to Strickland, who was a poet in her own right.[10] Pringle edited the narrative for publication as an antislavery tract.[11] Social and religious prohibitions surrounding sexually explicit material in the nineteenth-century, and legal liabilities attached to the publication of such tracts, placed further constraints on Prince's individual voice. Yet her narrative retains a qualitative uniqueness that is distinctly West Indian.[12]

In her review of the 1987 edition, Jacqui Alexander poses the question of "whether the psychic structures and consciousness of a black slave woman could ever be accurately rendered in a language of domination, a language of power in which the female subject is herself subverted" (159). The question is a fair one, given the form of the slave narrative, tailored as it is to the abolition of slavery, and the mediation of Methodist activists who promise truthfulness but not the whole unvarnished truth of rape, sexual abuse, and forced promiscuity that is the lot of the slave. The gap between experience and the published narrative is a vexing one for those in pursuit of the unexpurgated text and more information about the circumstances of its transcription.[13] No matter how the question is approached, the coercive or collaborative status of Strickland and Pringle is as much a part of the value of the text as the constraints imposed by the genre of the slave narrative itself. The imbalances of race, class, and gender hierarchies are only partly recoverable in the ambiguous politics of the text. The paradox is that even in its mediated form Prince's narrative endures as a testament to her life and struggle and offers rare insight into the formation of selfhood, narrative authority, and social identity among Caribbean slaves.

While Prince's original language is partially, perhaps wholly, lost in translation from an oral to a written text, what remains is an authorial voice that fuses the public self-consciousness of the slave narrative with the private self-consciousness of the slave. The central focus of her narrative is slavery as a lived historical reality, but Prince is as much the subject of her narrative as slavery is. The Mary Prince of the text is no "neutral passive recorder but rather a creative active shaper" of her life story (Olney, "'I Was Born'" 47);[14] the text strains to verify and convince that it is she who provides the information that is then transcribed and edited.[15] The narrative's sharp exterior focus on slavery coincides with a pronounced sense of self-identity, for slavery is represented as a determinant of consciousness and a crucible of conscience in Prince's life. Her individual life story establishes and validates a slave woman's point of view. Through her voice, however muted, the slave narrative, as evidence of victimization and document of legal history, is transformed into a triumphant narrative of emergent West Indian subjectivity in the gendered, racialized space of a black woman and a slave.[16]

The specific historicity of this slave narrative makes it an ideal forum for the public self-consciousness of the West Indian slave. Historical time is localized in details of Prince's birth, her life, and her vision of the future. Her individual life story becomes public, historical, and nationalist. It is shaped in the real historical time of a changing world, and she is in the vanguard of those changes. Her personal story of victimization and survival, the heroic dream of safety for herself and her community, projects an image of the black West Indian emerging in national historical time. Her private biographical future is linked to the historical future of her "own country" (Prince 82). Prince emerges as the new West Indian in a creative enterprise that links her individual fate to the fate of the West Indies. Telling her life story is a civic and political act that links her individual quest for freedom to the revolutionary restructuring of West Indian society: "I have been a slave—I have felt what a slave feels, and I know what a slave knows; and I would have all the good people in England to know it too, that they may break our chains, and set us free" (64). In linking her individual story to the unmaking of slavery and the emergence of a new world, Prince becomes an active agent of her society's transformation.[17]

In the context of the region's historical quest for freedom and independence, her transformed literate voice emerges as a gender-specific, inclusive ancestral voice. Her narrative suggests a profound identification with the West Indies as territorial cradle.[18] The trope of return to one's native land is fully formed here as return to the West Indies, past, present, and future.[19] Her estranged past and necessary future are located geographically and historically in the West Indies. England is a means to an end, not the fulfillment of a dream of freedom, as it is in *The Interesting Narrative of the Life of Olaudah Equiano, or Gustavas Vassa the African* and the "Narrative of Louis Asa-Asa, a Captured African." Bermuda is her "native place" (66, 67). In England, Antigua is "my own country" where "all old friends and connections" are (82), in contrast to her owner's claim that she "is not a native of this country [Antigua], and I know of no relation she has here" (90). Prince's narrative focuses on the West Indies as the necessary site of self-identification and self-fulfillment in anticipation of the historical changes that emancipation will bring. White West Indians who would maintain slavery are "the foreign people" (83), as she presses her competing claim as a black West Indian and slave. To be West Indian in Mary Prince's terms is more than to make your money there or to be born there and long for affiliation with either Europe or Africa. It is to position yourself self-consciously at the juncture of slavery and freedom and to link your individual life story to the emergence of a new world in the Caribbean.

Prince's narrative brings into sharp focus formative issues surrounding subjectivity and the engendering of national identity in preeminent texts of West Indian autobiography. A theory of the self is crafted here that projects the female autobiographical consciousness as historically aware, resistant, and sympathetically engaged with an oppressed slave majority in the region of her birth.[20] It defines female subjectivity in national historical terms. The public self-consciousness of the female slave is not only about the empowering of women; it is also about the liberation of the whole society.[21] Self-consciousness is engendered by consciousness of others. The tortured body of a female slave speaks through and on behalf of the tortured bodies of men, women, and children alike. Old Daniel's sufferings (64) on Turk's Island are as important as old Sarah's (65), pregnant "Aunt" Hetty's (57), and the daily torture of the two little slave boys, the mulatto Cyrus and the African Jack (56). Interiority is expressed in connectedness to the collective human community.[22]

Prince's public accounting of self is distinguished by the degree and quality of its interiority, its attention to the cultural systems that nurture a human community under siege, and her expectations of the West Indies as a place to live and love and work.[23] Mary Prince's narrative modulates between an aggressive assertion of self as an uncompromising arbiter of value on behalf of an oppressed community and a longing for reconnection with an ideal Caribbean community. It is charged with the necessity for radical social change: "I would rather go into my grave than go back a slave to Antigua, though I wish to go back to my husband very much—very much—very much! I am much afraid my owners would separate me from my husband, and use me very hard, or perhaps sell me for a field negro;—and slavery is too bad. I would rather go into my grave!" (86). The slave narrative as autobiography projects a unity of being beyond the marginalization and alienation imposed by slavery and colonialism. Her individual voice refocuses the public debate on slavery in a language specific to herself and to her West Indian world. She adds her speaking voice to the propaganda war being waged in print and records the foundations of a roots-derived national self-consciousness in West Indian autobiography.

Prince's speaking voice, transformed into a literate text, stands at the crossroads of "the black vernacular and the literate white text, of the spoken and written word, of oral and printed forms of literary discourse" (Gates, *Signifying Monkey* 131).[24] It is a site of resistance and accommodation between different traditions, languages, and cultures, between Europe and Africa in the Caribbean and in Great Britain, and between colony and metropolis. The bond of sympathy that engages the polyphonic arrangement of the text is the unmaking of slavery as a legally sanctioned social and economic institution. This is the forum that both defines the limits and gives Prince the freedom to tell her own story. *The History of Mary Prince* privileges a black West Indian speaking voice in a legal and literary context that effectively redefines who and what it means to be West Indian in the production of literature in 1831. It makes explicit the interdependence of consciousness that characterizes the production of written texts of West Indian literature, which is still largely dependent on extraterritorial, metropolitan publishers for publication and distribution.

The History of Mary Prince appears to "follow" James Olney's "Master Plan for Slave Narratives" quite faithfully ("'I Was Born'" 50–51). Mary's name is changed from her slave name—Mary, Princess of Wales—to Mary Prince, her paternal slave name (74).[25] The title page includes the claim "Related by Herself." The preface by Thomas Pringle testifies to the truthfulness and authenticity of the narrative: "The narrative was taken down from Mary's own lips. . . . It was written out fully, and with all the narrator's repetitions and prolixities, and afterwards pruned into its present shape; retaining as far as was practicable, Mary's exact expressions and peculiar phraseology" (Pringle, preface 45). Pringle assumes personal responsibility for the veracity of the narrative. He is explicit about his cross-examination of Mary "on every fact and circumstance detailed" (45) and the methods of external verification that he uses. Mary's narrative is followed by a "Supplement to the History of Mary Prince by the Editor," which summarizes the legal debate and the humanitarian issues surrounding Mary's struggle to be legally free, not only in England but in Antigua. In the supplement and appendixes to the text, the editor provides corroborative evidence from letters, newspaper items, and cases reported in the *Anti-Slavery Reporter,* testimonials, and other documentary material. Pringle even includes the short narrative of Louis Asa-Asa, who was kidnapped, sold into slavery, and brought to England. In a postscript to the second edition, Thomas Pringle solicits funds on Mary Prince's behalf. He reports that her health is failing and that attempts to buy her freedom from the Woods have been unsuccessful. Temporary manumission in England threatens to make her exile from home a permanent condition. In an appendix to the third edition, Pringle's wife, who is identified only as "M. Pringle"; her sister, Susan Brown; Susanna Strickland; and a friend, Martha Browne, offer eyewitness testimony of "the marks of former ill-usage" on Mary's body (119). These heteroglot voices compete with but do not dominate Mary Prince's fully integrated sense of self in relation to the community that engenders her sense of identity.[26]

Prince seems unthreatened by the collective act of telling, writing, editing, and publishing her story, which, in the oral tradition of storytelling, is infinitely repeatable. She entrusts her speaking voice to her white amanuensis in the language of friendship and trust: "I will say the truth to the English people who may read this history that my good friend, Miss S——, is now writing down for me" (84).[27] The power of her words is oral and familial; writing is what other people do. Her narrative reveals none of the preciousness about individual voice that characterizes the professional writer in our time. Her speaking voice has its own preeminent validity. Her narrative is crafted in full self-consciousness that "oral and written traditions comprise separate and distinct discursive universes" (Gates, *Signifying Monkey* 132), and she seizes on the overlap of intention between both worlds as a site of creation.[28]

Though intent on having her story recorded and published, Prince is not in awe of the book as a means of achieving presence and legitimacy. Reverence for the book is reserved for "the word of God," but conversion to Christianity comes late to Prince and is only one facet of self-definition. Typically, she struggles "to know the truth" rather than simply to accept the teachings of Mrs. Pringle and the Reverend Mr. Mortimer, clergyman of the parish (Prince 82–83). Reading and letters are part of the fabric of her "happy" childhood. As an adult, she is eager to attend the Moravian school, where she learns to read. "In this class there were all sorts of people, old and young, grey headed folks and children; but most of them were free people" (73). She emphasizes her own quickness and social interaction in a community of free blacks. Literacy is the privilege of the free and facilitates conversion to Christianity, but Prince's narrative pays far more attention to the economics of buying her freedom than to achieving literacy.[29] In a paragraph that begins "The way in which I made my money was this," she takes time to explain how she earned her money as evidence of her work ethic, her honesty, and her determination "by all honest means, to earn money to buy my freedom" (71). She does not celebrate literacy as having a necessary relation to the desire for freedom in her West Indian world, though her life story is crafted in full self-consciousness of print capitalism as a way of winning English hearts and minds in the struggle to abolish slavery (58, 64, 84).

It is worth noting that voice is already formed within the context of her own expressive culture when Mary Prince asks to have her story written down. There are examples of a sophisticated controlling voice already in place, both in the West Indies and in England. As a child of twelve, she takes her cue from her father, who admonishes her master for his brutality, and she denounces Captain I——— (60). Later, when she returns to Bermuda with Mr. D———, she reprimands him for his violence and indecency and refuses to be his sexual slave any longer (67–68). Her departure from the Woods' household in England is a particularly rich example of her pre-emptive verbal skills:

> Stop, before you take this trunk, and hear what I have to say before these people. I am going out of this house, as I was ordered; but I have done no wrong at all to my owners, neither here nor in the West Indies. I always worked very hard to please them, both by night and day; but there was no giving satisfaction, for my mis-

tress could never be satisfied with reasonable service. I told my mistress I was sick, and yet she has ordered me out of doors. This is the fourth time; and now I am going out. (80)

She seizes on the fact that the Woods ordered her out of their house and repeats and refashions this into a public speech of recrimination and self-justification. She takes their private space and makes it a public space in a speech act that mocks their ownership in a series of verbal assaults. Whether you call this *signifying* (as an African American would) or *ramachez* (as a Trinidadian would), such a speech performance is a ritual feature of black talk, and Prince is a practiced performer.[30] Though print capitalism shapes autobiographical self-consciousness in Prince's narrative, voice and identity are already in place when she decides that she must go public in England with her story.[31]

Whatever the degree of authorial control that Prince exercised over the published narrative, her voice is a privileged one in the text as a whole, and it speaks out of a distinct West Indian particularity.[32] Though her story was first recorded, edited, and published more than a century ago, a West Indian turn of phrase and style of telling a story are still very much in evidence. Beyond this, the structure of the narrative calls attention to the internal dialogism of Prince's discourse on self and slavery, which is responsive not only to scribe and audience but to a chorus of West Indian voices that provides an apperceptive background of understanding within the narrative itself. The force, passion, and craft of Prince's narrative are to be understood in the context of the expressive resources of the black West Indian community at home as well as in the context provided by the generic features of the slave narrative and autobiography.[33]

In a mixture of direct and reported speech she crafts self in dialogue with the voices of fellow slaves and the voices of the world that opposes slavery. The dialogic structure of her narrative is closely intertwined with the performance-oriented, storytelling aspects of her narrative. As in any well-told story, she gives direct speech to her characters to highlight a conflict, to give depth and tone to a character, or for dramatic emphasis.[34] In the case of

Prince I might argue that these narrative techniques are already in place as part of a highly developed oral tradition of storytelling and signifying of one sort or another. Direct speech communicates the calculated cruelty of Captain I——, who whips her to the point of insensibility when she is a child of twelve: "Giving me several heavy blows with his hand, he said, 'I shall come home to-morrow morning at twelve, on purpose to give you a round hundred.' He kept his word—Oh sad for me!" (58). When Mr. Wood hears of her marriage to Daniel James, a free black tradesman, he flies into a rage and sends for her husband. Direct speech also conveys Daniel's provocative use of irony and her pleasure in the memory: "My husband said, 'Sir, I am a free man, and thought I had a right to choose a wife; but if I had known Molly was not allowed to have a husband, I should not have asked her to marry me'" (74–75). Her narrative is replete with emotive and evocative apostrophes, philosophical reflections, and moral lessons that are a feature of the slave narrative and also a dramatic feature of West Indian storytelling: "I lay down at night and rose up in the morning in fear and sorrow; and often wished that like poor Hetty I could escape from this cruel bondage and be at rest in the grave. . . . It was then, however, my heavy lot to weep, weep, weep, and that for years; to pass from one misery to another, and from one cruel master to a worse. But I must go on with the thread of my story" (57–58). The "thread of my story" is not only a convention of English speech but to the West Indian ear evokes Anansi, the spider-hero of the Akans who emerges as trickster-hero and legendary spinner of tales throughout the West Indies. Iteratives like "weep, weep, weep" or "clatter, clatter, clatter" or "work, work, work" appear throughout the narrative and are a distinctive feature of West Indian speech. Turns of phrase characteristic of West Indian speech include, for example, the use of "salt water" for tears: "Oh, the trials! the trials! they make the salt water come into my eyes when I think of the days in which I was afflicted" (54). Despite the limits placed on her individual authorial voice, the text provides ample evidence of the discursive world of the slave community that shapes her sensibility. This gives her public account of self a cultural coherence beyond the verbal and ideological coherence of the text as a whole. Indeed, the use of a modified vernacular that preserves the tone and style of the original is now commonplace in modern Caribbean writing, but in 1831 this represents an extraordinary harmony of intention.

Prince's editors resist the psychic distanciation that William Andrews describes in *To Tell a Free Story* (62–66). Pringle makes no pretense of neutrality. In his supplement he characterizes Mr. Wood as un-Christian and inhumane (Prince 87); he is "unreasonable" (87), "unconscionable" (89), a liar (95–96), and unscrupulous (98). When Pringle points out Prince's faults in the context of a Victorian ideal of true womanhood, they are "a somewhat violent and hasty temper, and a considerable share of natural pride and self-importance" (105). But these observations are minimized and subordinated to her "considerable natural sense" and her "quickness of observation and discrimination of character" (105). A plausible argument would be that the privileging of the voice of Prince in this text is fundamental to the value of the slave narrative as historical document. Pringle does not gratuitously give primacy to the embodied voice of Prince; rather, he undertakes to transform her oral narrative into a written text and to publish it with supporting documents. The text is contingent upon the eyewitness testimony of Prince. The real authority of the text originates here in the autobiographical consciousness of Mary Prince. In the public space of the slave narrative Prince lays bare for public scrutiny the criminality of slave owners and the legal system that endorses their conduct. She does this through self-revelation. The victim of the slave auction, a public space that allows the slave no voice and no privacy, is recast as witness, judge, and evaluator, as well as victim and survivor.[35] The competing public space provided by the slave narrative as autobiography makes audible and visible the essential humanity of the slave who was once relegated to the margins of consciousness in the marketplace.

The configurational and episodic center of Prince's public account of self is the body of a female slave. The body that had been relegated to the margins of consciousness by the institution of slavery now occupies a central place and speaks out of a pronounced sense of ethnic and racial solidarity. The body of the slave once again occupies a public space, but this time it is on Prince's initiative, and the relationship between private and public selves is not the alienation and marginalization of the auction block but the recovery and the re-creation of community. "I was born" is no mere surface formula for testifying to the horrors of slavery; it is the context for knowing and understanding self. Mary Prince shapes her narrative to a pattern of developing public consciousness in a journey from the unconsciousness and illusory happiness of childhood in slavery through a brutal awakening to the realities of slavery, and progressive stages of resistance and redefinition, to temporary manumission and self-definition. Her journey from slavery to freedom, from childhood to womanhood, from Bermuda to England is a journey from the private self-consciousness of a child to the politicized, public self-consciousness of an enslaved woman speaking on behalf of all slaves. It is both linear and cyclic. The journey's end is a return to her West Indian beginnings.

Prince's movement from one sphere of experience to another is represented in a process of growth and development embodied in a sequence of events that simultaneously characterize different aspects of slavery and critical periods of interior growth in her life. Each event adds new dimensions to private and public contexts of her individual story. The episode in which she intervenes to stop Mr. D——, her master on Turk's Island and in Bermuda, from brutally beating his daughter in a drunken fury testifies to the depravity of the slave owner. It also testifies to an increasingly defiant and politically aware Mary Prince, who acts independently and on principle and redefines herself in the process: "The people gave me credit for getting her away" (67). She is no longer a victim struggling to survive mentally and physically; she is a woman with a superior sense of social responsibility who puts herself at risk in an attempt to change the circumstances that oppress the household: "He turned around and began to lick me. Then I said: 'Sir, this is not Turk's Island.' I can't repeat his answer, the words were too wicked—too bad to say. He wanted to treat me the same in Bermuda as he had done in Turk's Island" (67). She takes her principled rebellion a step further when she refuses to bathe Mr. D—— any longer: "He had an ugly fashion of stripping himself quite naked and ordering me then to wash him in a tub of water. . . . At last I defended myself, for I thought it was high time to do so. I then told him I would not live longer with him, for he was a very indecent man—very spiteful, and too indecent; with no shame for his servants, no shame for his own flesh" (68). This is not only a specific example of the sexual abuse and debauchery of the slave owner but evidence of the emergence of a new Mary Prince after her return to Bermuda from Turk's Island.

The new Mary Prince speaks and acts on her own behalf and on behalf of another woman in pain, even though that other woman is a mistress and an oppressor. She thinks and acts out of a set of values different from those sanctioned by colonial slavery and redefines herself in the process. She silences Mr. D—— in her account of the incident: "I can't repeat his answer the words were too wicked—too bad to say" (67). Her authority derives from the high moral ground that distinguishes this victim's eyewitness account. She speaks and acts to silence and curb the actions of a cruel and abusive slave master. She forms new alliances by gaining public recognition. She formulates plans of her own and carries them out. She is the instigator of her own sale to the Woods when she hears that they are going to Antigua: "I felt a great wish to go there, and I went to Mr. D—— and asked him to let me go in Mr. Wood's service" (68). Ten years on Turk's Island clarify and strengthen her political awareness and resistance. She matures into a self-reliant, resourceful, and active agent on her own behalf and on behalf of others. She is intent on changing her relationship to slavery and on changing the way that world operates.

The apparent contradiction between physical enslavement and interior growth in Prince's individual life provides a rhetorical unity beyond the temporal sequence of her narrative. Even on Turk's Island, where the ritual torture of slaves is constant, Prince's interior growth in awareness is an essential aspect of her prolonged ordeal. The interaction of slave and master on Turk's Island is linked to a heightened understanding of the social values engendered by slavery. When Mr. D—— tortures to death Old Daniel, a slave who "was lame in the hip, and could not keep up with the rest of the slaves" (64), she internalizes the experience: "He was an object of pity and terror to the whole gang of slaves, and in his wretched case we saw, each of us, our own lot, if we should live to be as old" (64). In a community of sufferers, everyday use clarifies and strengthens concepts of guilt and innocence, crime and retribution, evil and good. As slavery becomes incrementally more corrupt, the victim grows more discriminating about its ramifications for slave and master.

The oppressiveness of colonial slavery engenders in Prince an increasingly aware and resistant spirit whose growth and development ironically represent the consolidation of values generated in the "idyllic" landscape of her early childhood. The apparent contradiction between linear development in time and cyclic return to received values provides a complex image of the finely tuned balance between self and society in the oppressiveness of a British slave colony. The opening scenes provide an organizing center for point of view, a scale and background for depicting what follows. They tell of continuity between the slave child's ideal world and the free woman's dream of safe return. Consciousness of freedom begins in childhood: "The tasks given out to us were light, and we used to play together with Miss Betsey, with as much freedom almost as if she had been our sister" (48). The illusory happiness of childhood is represented as the nucleus of freedom as a value. Values governing kinship and community formulated in childhood inform Prince's evaluation of episodes that follow, even while she distances herself from the "foolish creature!" (49) that she was. She evokes childhood as an enduring nucleus to which she returns for clarification of the self's true relationship to the world.[36]

The ironies of Prince's childhood happiness establish scales of comparison for the entire narrative. "This was the happiest period of my life; for I was too young to understand rightly my condition as a slave, and too thoughtless and full of spirits to look forward to the days of toll and sorrow" (49). The interplay of two voices, crafted in an awareness of subjectivity as the creation of time and memory in a specific historical situation, is characteristic of the narrative as a whole. It is apparent in the ironic interplay of past and present, of then and now, at the beginning of her narrative. The values of then and now change with growth and development in the course of her narrative. However, at the beginning of her narrative, then is the innocence of childhood experienced as a nurturing community in which the distinctions between slave and owner are blurred, and she remembers the experience of biological and slave family as one of giving and receiving love and affection. Now is the experience of brutal slavery that she consistently describes in the contrasting terms of victimization and abuse and an ongoing violent onslaught on kinship, community, nurturance, and love.

These are the values that dominate the self's ideal relationship to community in Mary Prince's past, present, and future. They are formulated in an environment in which mutual affection and shared experience temporarily mask the horrors of slavery. She and her siblings are raised by their own mother under the direction of a "kind" mistress, Mrs. Williams, who is herself the victim of spousal abuse and neglect: "My poor mistress bore his ill-treatment with great patience, and all her slaves loved and pitied her. I was truly attached to her, and next to my own mother, loved her better than any creature in the world" (48).[37] Prince recalls her acute distress when she is hired out to Mrs. Pruden as a nursemaid at the age of eleven in exchange for food and clothing. "I cried bitterly at parting with my dear mistress and Miss Betsey, and when I kissed my mother and brothers and sisters, I thought my young heart would break, it pained me so" (48). Yet Mary Prince describes her indenture to Mrs. Pruden as an extension of Mrs. Williams's household. She forms deep attachments to the Pruden children in her care while maintaining close contact with her biological and extended slave family. Seemingly, interiority rests on childhood assumptions about reciprocal love, affection, duty, and equality in this nurturing community.

The values of heart are crafted here, heart as the moral and ethical as well as the emotional and physical center of self and community. "My heart always softens when I think of them" (49), she says of the Pruden children. The death of Mrs. Williams disassembles her known world utterly: "When I thought about my mistress I felt as if the world was all gone wrong; and for many days and weeks I could think of nothing else. I returned to Mrs. Pruden's;

but my sorrow was too great to be comforted, for my own dear mistress was always in my mind. Whether in the house or abroad, my thoughts were always talking to me about her" (50). The personal loss she feels is an occasion for further revelations of interiority; the self in dialogue with the self about lost innocence.

Within three months Mary and two of her sisters are sold "to raise money" for Captain Williams's wedding (50). Her "happy" childhood comes to an abrupt and tragic end, but it is not erased as a value in her continuing life as a slave. The auction of Mary and her sisters is crafted as a site of resistance in defeat. It invokes a storm of protest from Mary Prince in retrospect, but, just as important, she records that the sale is resisted vociferously by members of her biological and extended family as a betrayal of the values that govern the community where heart is formed. Memory, in dialogue with the primary voices of community, coalesces here in the recreated childhood of Mary Prince to reveal the substance of a resistant interiority formed in childhood and slavery. However wrong her motives, Miss Betsey denounces her father's decision as illegal and wicked (50). The degree of Miss Betsey's distress identifies a community of sympathy: "She could not bear to part with her old playmates and she cried sore and would not be pacified" (51). Mary conveys her mother's resistance in the memory of her mother's visible and audible expressions of grief. She conceptualizes the sale of her children as death: "The black morning at length came. . . . While putting on us the new osnaburgs in which we were to be sold, she said, in a sorrowful voice, (I shall never forget it!) 'See, I am shrouding my poor children; what a task for a mother!'" (51). She leaves Prince with an indelible sense of injustice done to her and her family: "'I am going to carry my little chickens to market,' (these were her very words) 'take your last look at them; may be you will see them no more'" (51). She recalls her mother's words as a legacy of value that survives the passage of time. Resistance is fixed in memory as an immutable speech act, to which her psyche returns to recover and renew faith in self and community in autobiography as slave narrative.

Prince's account of the auction moves back and forth between the outer and inner aspects of the sale. The auction takes place in the middle of the street in a public market. She is denied all privacy as she is "surrounded by strange men, who examined and handled me in the same manner that a butcher would a calf or a lamb he was about to purchase" (52). Against the public humiliation of being offered "for sale like sheep or cattle" (52), the narrative zeros in on the interior space of her degraded body, in a reflective and evaluative mode.

The site of interiority at this critical moment in her life is heart.[38] "My heart throbbed with grief and terror so violently, that I pressed my hands quite tightly across my breast, but I could not keep it still, and it continued to leap as if it would burst out of my body" (52). Heart is the pulse beat of life itself. It registers grief and terror. It is individual and collective. "The pain that wrung the hearts of the negro woman and her young ones" (52) is felt collectively. In the same narrative moment heart is an alternative to the material measure of the marketplace as a measure of the moral and ethical sensibility that governs the well-being of individuals in society. "They were not all bad, I dare say, but slavery hardens white people's hearts towards the blacks; . . . their light words fell like cayenne on the fresh wounds of our hearts. Oh those white people have small hearts who can only feel for themselves" (52). Slavery hardens white people's hearts and makes them egotistical and unfeeling. Conversely, in Prince's public account of her life as a slave, heart is a center of resistant subjectivity and interiority. It is a specific image of values recovered and reimposed on childhood recollections, which affirm the terms of the self's existence in and beyond time.

Her mother's parting admonishment as she mourns the loss of her children is "to keep up a good heart, and do our duty to our new masters" (53). When she arrives at her new master's house, she receives a similar admonishment from two slave women who work there. "Poor child, poor child!' they both said; 'you must keep a good heart, if you are to live here'" (54). To keep a good heart is to be strong, resistant, and conscious of self-worth in the face of extraordinary torture and brutality; it is moral and ethical conduct in an immoral and unjust world. It seizes the moral high ground. It is an individual and a collective state of mind. It is an ideology of survival and resistance. It is the well of being. It engenders a new literary tradition rooted in the values of a transplanted and transformed African community in the Caribbean.

Heart is a site of resistance specific to the bond of sympathy and solidarity between father and daughter, when Prince's father removes her from the "hole in the rocks" (60) where her mother has hidden her and returns her to Captain I——, the privateer and merchant who had beaten her to the point of insensibility. In a singular act of courage Prince's father censors and admonishes Captain I—— for his brutality: "Sir, I am sorry that my child should be forced to run away from her owner; but the treatment she has received is enough to break her heart. The sight of her wounds has nearly broke mine. —I entreat you for the love of God, to forgive her for running away, and that you will be a kind master to her in future" (60). Her father's act of courage does not soften the hard heart of Captain I——, but the father's words empower his twelve-year-old daughter to speak up on her own behalf: "I then took courage and said that I could stand the floggings no longer; that I was weary of my life, and therefore I had run away to my mother; but mothers could only weep and mourn over their children, they could not save them from cruel masters— from the whip, the rope, and the cow-skin" (60). Following her father's example, she is empowered to speak from a resistant heart as a primary site of self-identification and identification with others. She speaks for herself, her mother, and all enslaved mothers. Her recollections of childhood shape her slave's life to the enduring values of a mother and father's value-affirming love. She recalls mother, father, siblings, and extended family as a permanent, unchanging source of the indestructible values of heart.

Prince's narrative reproduces and revises images of heart in an elaborate pattern of signification that reflects the myriad voices and values of the text as managed elements of her own voice and heart. Her heart resists the slave's status as marketable commodity. "Oh the Buckra people who keep slaves think that black people are like cattle, without natural affection. But my heart tells me It is far otherwise" (61). Her heart is what Mr. Mortimer seeks to capture for his God. "Mr. Mortimer tells me that he cannot open the eyes of my heart, but I must pray to God to change my heart" (83). Mr. Mortimer seeks to change her resistant heart to an accepting one; she protests to the end: "I must confess, I find it a hard and heavy task to do so" (83).

The epic experience of the West Indian slave is compressed in the metaphor of heart. The story of Prince's scarred and broken body is one of humiliation and torment, a testament to the institutionalization of human greed and brutality in the British Empire. It is a body that knows tenderness and affection as well as violation, torture, and abuse. From the age of twelve until she leaves Antigua with the Woods for England about twenty-eight years later, she is repeatedly stripped naked, suspended by her arms, and whipped until blood flows. Her body becomes the repository of the psychosexual neuroses of masters and mistresses alike. Her individual suffering is recorded in the context of similar terroristic acts of torture meted out to men, women, and children who are routinely stripped naked, suspended, and brutalized. The physical and psychological torture of a lifetime leaves her childless, crippled with arthritis, blind, and in exile. But her embattled body is the vessel of a defiant tribal spirit of resistance that she refashions in memory and characterizes as heart. The fashioning of this trope as a center of value in her epic tale of bondage and deliverance is her own act of creative memory; its origins are oral and familial and illuminate the oral beginnings of West Indian culture in a community under siege. The body in pain is only spasmodically unconscious and inarticulate; lost consciousness returns to hone voice and conscience to the achievement of freedom for self and community. In Prince's narrative, conscience and consciousness coalesce in and around the heart. The heart as center of life and value is formulated in childhood. It endures as a self-contained moral guide. It invokes both self-reliance and shared community.

The interplay of memory, heart, and voice in the fashioning of individual and community values is the center of subjectivity and interiority in Prince's public account of self. The major cultural and political issues of West Indian autobiographical writing are inscribed here in core images of cultural and geographical rootedness in the Caribbean. The autobiographical act of self-reading is preeminently a literary act that uses the story of the self to advance social and political change. Interiority, as female subjectivity, is springboard to an empowering resistance that represents the entire community; the essence of self is heart, a drumbeat sounding out of the communal heartland.[39] Prince's autobiography is a precursive ancestral voice that delineates the essential tropes of return and self-parody in images shot through with the dialogic overtones of a community that is fashioning self out of resistance. Individual conscience and consciousness are fused as memory, heart, and voice to the freedom of an emergent West Indian and Caribbean community. Interiority is contingent on recreating the world that fashions consciousness and conscience; self is never more visible than when it represents all.

3

The Enigma of Arrival
Wonderful Adventures of Mrs. Seacole

Wonderful Adventures of Mrs. Seacole in Many Lands is both selective autobiography and travel narrative, one of very few surviving African Caribbean women's narratives of the nineteenth century and invaluable in scoping subsequent developments in Caribbean literary culture. Published in 1857, *Wonderful Adventures* is the autobiography of a remarkable Jamaican woman, the daughter of a free black Jamaican healer and a Scottish soldier, who established herself as an outstanding entrepreneur and "doctress" in England after the Crimean War (1853–1856).[1] Seacole's career began in Jamaica where she ran a boardinghouse and ministered to the British military. After her husband and mother died, she followed her brother to New Granada in 1850. There she established a general store and hotel and almost single-handedly contained a cholera epidemic. Later, tired of life in New Granada and eager for new adventures, she volunteered her services to the British in the Crimean War and was rejected. With characteristic independence and self-assurance, she went to the Crimean war zone on her own, established a general store and hotel between Kadikoi and Balaclava, about a mile from military headquarters, and worked generously and expertly to care for wounded soldiers on the battlefield and in her establishment. After the war she was much celebrated in England for her heroism and extraordinary service in the Crimea.

Liberal, metropolitan alliances that give agency to the Hart sisters and Mary Prince assume different proportions in the postemancipation world of Mary Seacole's *Wonderful Adventures*. She negotiates the distance between the imperial center and the margins of empire differently. In *Wonderful Adventures* Seacole reconstitutes the freedom to possess the Caribbean as native space legally as well as culturally as the freedom to possess the imperial center as a site of self-definition. The freedom to travel, to participate in capitalist enterprise, to define herself professionally in circumstances of her own choosing, whether fighting a cholera epidemic in New Granada or serving the British military in the Crimea, define her movement away from Jamaica as too small a place for her energy and ambition. A discourse of travel and encounter and the heroic accomplishments of a Jamaican "doctress" and entrepreneur who rejects domesticity as frustrating and constricting succeeds Mary Prince's passionate articulation of the experiences of other slaves suffering under British tyranny and her dream of autonomy and domesticity.

Seacole's narrative is not one of victimization, endurance, and survival but of travel and adventure in the pursuit of new experience, new knowledge, and new constructions of self. Travel has a different value in *The History of Mary Prince,* where the traveling subject is a slave and freedom is linked conceptually to domesticity, a liberated native community, and a sense of national belonging; Prince struggles in her narrative with a discourse of power that is contingent on separation and alienation from her native land. Alternatively, the fundamental freedom that Seacole articulates in her narrative is the freedom to be a traveling subject of the British Empire and to be celebrated as an individual who challenges the racial, national, gendered straightjacketing of nineteenth-century British imperialism at home and abroad.[2] In place of the collectivity at the heart of Prince's narrative is the sensuous particularity of an individual life, laying claim to rights and privileges that accrue to a singular British subject.

If *The History of Mary Prince* reflects an embryonic nationalism formed in resistance to slavery, *Wonderful Adventures* reflects an acceptance of colonialism after slavery.[3] Though free blacks in Jamaica were not granted the same civil rights as people born in England until the Disabilities Act of 1830, and civil unrest continued after the slave rebellion of 1830–1832, and after the post-

emancipation period of apprenticeship from 1834 to 1838, Seacole's narrative celebrates her status as the subject of an empire
that she identifies with the freedom to travel and to refashion herself, seemingly at will. The discourse of travel and encounter generates an ideal space abroad for distancing herself from her
exploited and abused native land. That distance established, Seacole is relatively free to construct an identity beyond Jamaica and
to establish her difference as a colonized subject who has acquired
the transforming values of Englishness through travel, knowledge,
and service to common ideals.[4] The image of self is crafted here
in a journey from the perceived margins of civilization to its center. In the course of that journey Seacole graduates from celebrity
status among expatriates in Jamaica as a Creole "doctress" and
notoriety in New Granada as the yellow "doctress" to legendary
status in the Crimea and in Britain as Mother Seacole, guardian
of English values away from England.

In *Wonderful Adventures* Seacole redefines her marginalized
Creole Jamaican self as the celebrated Mother Seacole—Crimean
heroine, healer of Englishmen at home (as in Jamaica) and abroad
(New Granada and the Crimea), and purveyor of English values
at the margins of empire (as universal home).[5] This narrative ploy
suggests a keen awareness of the intricacies of colonial politics in
respect to race, class, and gender and a willingness to manipulate
them to her own ends as traveling colonized subject. As mulatto,
doctor, entrepreneur, sutler, hotelier, traveler, adventurer, a woman
of work, and a widow who rejects the chance of a second marriage and domesticity, Seacole is on one level the embodiment of
racial and cultural "contagion" at the boundaries of the empire,
yet she playfully and purposefully constructs these signs of deviant
agency as an organic constituent of colonial power and her patriarchal inheritance.[6] As mulatto, she is a figure of contagion; as
healer, she conquers contagion and keeps it at bay. She neutralizes
any fear of sexual contagion by doubling as a kind of maternal
essence operating within the colonial iconography of familial and
domestic space. As Mother Seacole, she projects her gender difference in a service that nurtures and sustains Anglo male privilege and does this in a space that is quite distinct from that

occupied by Anglo women as guardians of domesticity and the British civilizing mission. Seacole's self-constitution as emblematic of colonial progress at the boundaries of empire carries with it an assertion of black women's power in the vacuum created by the cult of domesticity; however, it also speaks to an adoption of British colonial culture as a model of authentic being.

In a reconstitution of the liberal metropolitan alliances that aided the historical project and personal itinerary of the Hart sisters and Mary Prince, Seacole allies herself with a relatively liberal British military establishment in Jamaica and abroad. Brathwaite notes the social and economic significance of this in *The Development of Creole Society in Jamaica*: "The markets and the Army camps were the places of interracial concourse, despite efforts by the authorities to uphold the principle of 'apartheid'" (300).[7] Thus cultural resistance and autonomy have a distinct value to the yellow "doctress" from Jamaica, child of a free black Jamaican woman and a Scottish officer, as she is writing her own travel narrative two short decades after the emancipation of slaves in her native land. A pressing issue in Jamaica, even as she writes, is the decision by the British government to institute direct rule by the Crown in place of the system of representative government that had been in existence in one form or another in the British Caribbean since the 1640s; this decision was supposed to help end the slave trade and protect free people of color from island assemblies controlled by planters and slave proprietors.[8] For Seacole, being a British subject carried with it expectations of safety and protection at home in Jamaica and abroad (Brathwaite, *Development* 70). Amy Robinson notes the downside of such expectations from a nationalist point of view: "One of the signal results of the debate over the slave trade is the slaves' successful appropriation of the title of the British subject abdicated by the planter class. But the effect of this appropriation is the dislocation of the West Indies as the defining national context of identity, and the subsidization of Great Britain as the location of the authentic British subject" (22).

Writing from an anticolonial position in *The Pleasures of Exile,* George Lamming links this dislocation, still evident in continuing waves of migration from the Caribbean to England in the midtwentieth century, to the idea of "England's supremacy in taste and judgment: a fact which can only have meaning and weight by a calculated cutting down to size of all non-England" (27). To be a colonial, he argues a hundred-odd years after Seacole's *Wonderful Adventures,* is to be in a state of exile; the colonial "arrives and travels with the memory and habitual weight of a colonial relation" (25) who must prove his worth to the other and "win the approval of Headquarters, meaning in the case of the West Indian writer, England" (24). In *Poetics of Relation* Edouard Glissant makes a distinction between exile and errantry, but the focus of his concern is the same migratory pattern in Caribbean life: "Whereas exile may erode one's sense of identity, the thought of errantry—the thought of that which relates—usually reinforces this sense of identity" (20). What becomes clear in the links established among the preoccupations of Seacole in the nineteenth century, and George Lamming and Edouard Glissant in the twentieth, is how deeply entrenched the union between elsewhere and possibility is in the psyche of the colonial subject and how overdetermined were the conditions of Seacole's wanderlust.

The intersection of travel, adventure, and ordeal as substantive components of Seacole's autobiographical consciousness projects a precursory image of the restless, rootless, wandering West Indian colonial that becomes a distinctive feature of modern and postmodern West Indian consciousness. Travel, adventure, and ordeal give narrative substance to autobiographical values inspired by her expressed desire to shape a life of personal, social, and cultural significance beyond Jamaica.[9] Seacole explicitly addresses her narrative to an English reading public. She invokes the English reader as a civilizing presence whom she seeks to educate about her difference and her value as a contributing agent of the empire. She seeks the recognition of the British and courts their approval. The built-in assumption of this narrative is that it will earn her a place in the "civilized" consciousness of the culture that determines value in her world. The image of self that she crafts here makes this an exemplary text of colonial migration, both as an ideological positioning and as a sociohistorical feature of colonial life. The artistic arrangement of the text reveals who Seacole wants to be as a Jamaican woman in midcentury and, to that extent, who she is at the time of writing. Her narrative makes specific the contradictory values of a colonial woman of color who seeks to legitimize her difference at the conservative heart of empire in an autobiographical reformulation of her life beyond the boundaries of empire in New Granada and the Crimea.[10]

The internalized values of a colonial relationship to Britain, with its assumptions of English "supremacy in taste and judgment," dominates Mary Seacole's public account of herself as Creole doctor, Jamaican entrepreneur, and Crimean heroine. Cultural hybridity surrenders to British imperialism as a civilizing force, though this surrender is not unqualified. Seacole's revolt against the marginalization imposed by race and gender is a qualified revolt against the civilizing values that she professes to honor. She does not challenge the idea of a British empire so much as she struggles to redefine her place in it. The energy of the text as Caribbean autobiography lies here, in the contradictions of resistance and accommodation. The British Empire is a sacred value in her life, whether it represents social and cultural legitimacy at home and abroad or much desired safety from predatory "Yankees" in New Granada. But beyond her devotion to empire, her narrative celebrates her singular status as a Jamaican woman who, at forty-five, defies English-derived social conventions and carves out a new life for herself as an adventurer, entrepreneur, and "doctress" in the Isthmus of Panama and on the battlefields of the Crimea. In the process of telling her story, she self-consciously redefines womanhood around her individual accomplishments as a Jamaican woman of color, blurring conventional distinctions between women who are culture bearers and nurturers and keepers of the hearth and men who make themselves in aggressive encounters with alien and hostile worlds.[11]

In New Granada and the Crimea, Seacole defines herself in terms of race and gender with relative freedom and self-confidence, and she is understandably far more aggressive in highlighting the racism and sexism that she encounters in Central America than the complicity of the British Empire in such discriminatory systems of exclusion. She is critical of the London street boys who poke fun at her and her companion's complexion on her first visit to England (4). But she makes polite excuses for the authorities who laugh at her offer to go to the Crimea as a nurse: "In my country, where people know our use, it would have been different; but here it was natural enough—although I had references, and other voices spoke for me—that they should laugh, good-naturedly enough, at my offer" (78). After she suffers a second and a third rejection, she describes a short-lived crisis of faith in her status as colonial subject: "Doubts and suspicions arose in my heart for the first and last time, thank Heaven. Was it possible that American prejudices against colour had some root here? Did these ladies shrink from accepting my aid because my blood flowed beneath a somewhat duskier skin than theirs?" (79). Whatever the degree of irony and self-parody that she used here, Seacole clearly has no taste for the role of tragic mulatto and quickly recovers her energy and focus. When her wish to be sent to the Crimea as a hospital nurse is denied, she decides that she will go anyway: "I made up my mind that if the army wanted nurses, they would be glad of me, and with all the ardour of my nature, which ever carried me where inclination prompted, I decided that I would go to the Crimea; and go I did, as all the world knows" (76). She resists the racist stereotyping evident in the rejection that she suffers at the hands of the British War Office and Florence Nightingale's screening procedures (79). She does this by falling back on the self-authorization that characterizes her developing sense of mission in Jamaica and New Granada and by forming alliances with English aristocrats and officers in the Crimea, as she had done in Jamaica.

Seacole reserves her diatribes against racism and slavery for white North Americans wherever she encounters them. She describes specific humiliations that she suffers at their hands (57), their cruel pursuit of escaped slaves in New Granada (51–52), and her spirited response to one American's desire to bleach her complexion to an acceptable white (47–48). She consistently contrasts the behavior of the white North Americans whom she meets in New Granada with the conduct of English men and women. She characterizes the Americans as racist bullies, violent and uncivilized, while the English are civilized, restrained, and free of the prejudice that characterizes the conduct of Americans.[12] Seacole is conscious of her prejudice against Americans and, typically, turns her bias into a clarification of her superior judgment and values: "I think if I have a little prejudice against our cousins across the Atlantic—and I do confess to a little—it is not unreasonable" (14). Self-placement is elaborate here as Seacole recognizes Britain's historical relationship with its former colony while identifying her own superior judgment as intrinsically British. Seacole identifies herself as bonded culturally and politically with both the British and the slave, carefully negotiating the ironies built into that historical relationship. She is explicitly British in taste and judgment and explicitly mulatto rather than black, in the parlance of the day. She accedes to class and color distinctions between her sometimes Creole, sometimes yellow, self and "the excited nigger cooks" of Cruces (20) and the "good-for-nothing black cooks" who "laugh with all their teeth" (141). She is uncompromising, however, in her antislavery position.

> I have a few shades of deeper brown upon my skin which shows me related—and I am proud of the relationship—to those poor mortals whom you once held enslaved, and whose bodies America still owns. And, having this bond, and knowing what slavery is; having seen with my eyes and heard with my ears proof positive enough of its horrors—let others affect to doubt them if they will—is it surprising that I should be somewhat impatient of the airs of superiority which many Americans have endeavoured to assume over me? (14)

She uses the language of the antislavery tract and arrogates its high moral tone. However, she makes no specific reference to continuing barbarities that the colonial system inflicted on nonwhites in the West Indies. Everything is less acute in comparison to slavery in the United States. What she recalls is the maxim "that on a slave touching its [English] soil his chains fall from him" (52). England is safety and security to this Creole woman who leaves her native land to seek fame, fortune, and adventure in other lands. Criticism of the racist structure of colonial society is mute and barely visible. The values of the text reveal a strong commitment to the

British Empire as a national context for self-definition that precludes overt criticism. At the end of her narrative she announces herself "ready to take any journey to any place where a stout heart and two experienced hands may be of use" (198) to the British Empire.

The contradictions between Seacole's "feminist" resistance and her commitment to "English" values are discernible; one can only assume some measure of irony in the gap between her experience and her complicity with the project of imperialism.[13] Anne McClintock reminds us that beyond the fissures of formal ambivalence, the politics of agency involves "the dense web of relations between coercion, negotiation, complicity, refusal, dissembling, mimicry, compromise, affiliation and revolt" (15). Seacole's public account of self challenges literary conventions about the essentially private spheres of Victorian womanhood at the time that she was writing. She defines herself in action and acts to affirm her sense of herself as a self-made woman. She makes it clear that after the death of her husband, she remains a widow and "an unprotected female" by choice (8); she chooses to do battle with the world on her own. She is unafraid of competing with men, especially if they happen to be "the Spanish doctor, who was sent for from Panama" (27), or the French chef and "great high priest of the mysteries of cookery, Mns. Alexis Soyer" (149). She feels valued for what she can do and that can be "woman's work" (153) or "the work of half a dozen men" (149). Even though her personality and her exploits are in sharp contrast to "the housebound, man-dominated Victorian woman" (Middleton 4), Seacole invokes the conventions of Victorian womanhood in writing about herself, using the comparative framework that enables her deployment of Victorian values. She complains about women in New Granada who dress in trousers and ride "their mules in unfeminine fashion" (20); she scoffs at "those French lady writers who desire to enjoy the privileges of man, with the irresponsibility of the other sex" (20); and she repeatedly calls the reader's attention to her own womanly attire, even when the inappropriateness of it strikes her as amusing, for example, when she is clambering up a steep and muddy incline in New Granada (13). When tending to the sick and wounded in Balaclava, her feminine attire is explicitly a sign of her womanly mission in a man's world (97).[14]

In her account of her life and work in the Crimea, Seacole represents her bold adventuresome spirit as the embodiment of womanly love and duty to the warhead of empire. She substitutes service for submission as the hallmark of true womanhood and seeks to legitimize her presence in the Crimea "as doctress, nurse, and 'mother'" (124). She is the "right woman in the right place" (76) and creates a distinguished role for herself as patron of the war effort and mother of English "sons" away from home. Her adulation of the British military and her aggressive involvement in the war are characterized as patriotic fervor and evidence of her committed Englishness. But no matter how Seacole configures her relationship to the military and her active role in the Crimea, her unabashed exhilaration in the war effort constitutes a serious assault on gender binaries. Her use of a maternal narrator challenges the conventional dichotomies associated with respectable Victorian womanhood and with war. When Mother Seacole insists that the battlefield is her rightful place, she is demolishing the boundaries between the home front and the battlefield. Her British Hotel, established with her own money in Spring Hill, was a commercial and humanitarian enterprise: general store, restaurant, hotel, and health clinic, furnishing the essentials of English at-homeness to officers and enlisted men who could afford to pay for these services. She was celebrated by the British public during and after the war for her heroic initiative on behalf of the officers and enlisted men stationed there. Because volunteers were expected to pay their own way, and she lost her capital investment at the end of the war, she can claim a certain disinterest in her efforts to sustain "that dream of home in this world" in English fathers, husbands, sons, and brothers (99). Her figuration of the mother on the battlefield is distinct from the stereotype of the saintly nurse popularized in the figure of Florence Nightingale.

In "Arms and the Woman" in their book of the same title, Helen M. Cooper, Adrienne A. Munich, and Susan M. Squier explore the culturally repressed themes of war and writing in the works of Elizabeth Barrett Browning. Of particular interest is their attention to

Elizabeth Barrett's literary representation of herself as "mother arming her sons" (15). As they point out, her figuration of the sword-bearing mother mythologizes a repressed source of female power in epic tradition (13). In this sense Mother Seacole is also a reconfiguration of Jamaican Nanny of the Maroons as "doctress" and maker of magic on the battlefield. Seacole does not lead maroon guerrillas into battle against British soldiers, rather she ministers to Nanny's one-time enemy.[15] While it is fair to say that Seacole's rebellious, independent, competitive, Jamaican spirit Creolizes and feminizes the European male space that is the Crimean war zone, her achievements are represented as individual accomplishments that celebrate service and devotion to patriarchal authority and empire as embodied in the British military.

The war zone of the Crimea is where Seacole achieves the authority and recognition from which to launch her autobiography, conceptualized as a celebration of heterogeneous empire and of her individual Jamaican woman self: "I shall make no excuse to my readers for giving them a pretty full history of my struggles to become a Crimean heroine" (76). *Wonderful Adventures* is a success story; who Seacole struggles to be is who she becomes. She strives to become a heroine and to be perceived as one by the English. Her ambitions impel her to the site of heroic action in the Crimea, to take her place among the pantheon of heroes there.[16] Attentive to the self-promotion that characterizes her narrative, Mary Seacole explains that she must sound her own trumpet, that it "will be more satisfactory to the reader" (124). She includes an array of testimonials to her heroic service "for the simple reason that they strengthen my one and only claim to interest the public, viz., my services to the brave British army in the Crimea" (124). What saves Seacole from charges of unmediated parasitism and naive individualism is the care with which she establishes her devotion to the British military and her professional interest in medicine as a legacy of her childhood nurtured over a lifetime. She is the inheritor of a native tradition of healing that provides her with a valuable means of economic and personal independence in nineteenth-century Jamaica (Alexander and Dewjee 13–14, 42 n8).[17] She eagerly learns from her mother and from the doctors with whom she works. Her medical knowledge and entrepreneurial skills give her the power to create a community around her wherever she goes. The point of this public account of her travels and adventures is how she comes to choose service to the British military in the Crimea as a context for self-fulfillment, as self-appointed nurse-mother and hotelier-sutler to the British military camp in the Crimea at midcentury. This is not a conversion narrative; Seacole does not change so much as become more experienced and well known. She moves from anonymity to public acclaim. She re-creates her life to reflect the legendary figure of a marginalized black woman who wins fame and, ultimately, fortune within the empire that colonized her history, through her heroic service to English national heroes of the day.

Seacole's self-portrait as Crimean heroine projects a theory of self that sharply contrasts with that implicit in Mary Prince's slave narrative. In the latter the autobiographical self is both solitary and representative of a community at home in the West Indies; self-representation locates the autobiographical subject in the heart of a collective West Indian community of slaves. Seacole's narrative disengages the autobiographical subject from the Jamaican community and repositions her in the metropolitan heart of empire. The public and political event that gives her written life meaning is the Crimean War, not the crises of community that afflict Jamaica. Her past, present, and future are subsumed in the heroic values of empire and the battlefield. She stands alone as a celebrated black woman in a community of white men, as one heroic Jamaican woman among heroic English men.[18] She leaves the Crimea regretfully, claiming that she has "no home to go to" (192).[19] She identifies herself as the rootless traveler who comes home to the value-defining space that she makes for herself in service to the British military. She devalues significant spheres of her Jamaican identity to project herself ultimately as the facilitator of male privilege and empire. Anthony Trollope unintentionally makes this point in *The West Indies and the Spanish Main* (1859), when he invokes Seacole's name in his account of his stay in Jamaica: "I took up my abode at Blundle Hall, and found that the landlady in whose custody I had placed myself was a sister of the

good Mrs. Seacole. 'My sister wanted to go to India,' said my landlady, 'with the army you know. But Queen Victoria would not let
her; her life was too precious.' So that Mrs. Seacole is a prophet,
even in her own country" (6). The rugged individualism that characterizes her successful exploits in the "frontier" territory of New
Granada invokes patronage as a strategy of self-definition in metropolitan Europe. This appears to have little to do with home-
lessness and everything to do with colonial desire.

Seacole's organization of autobiographical time communicates
little about her everyday life in Jamaica up to the age of forty-five
and a great deal about her heroic adventures after that. She devotes
one short chapter to her childhood; her travels as a young woman
to London, New Providence, Haiti, and Cuba; her married life;
and widowhood (1–6). She spends another three pages on the
death of her mother and her growing skill and reputation as a doctor in Kingston (6–9). The next sixty-three pages are organized
around her adventures in New Granada between 1850 and 1854
as a doctor, merchant, hotelier, and gold seeker (9–72). She organizes the rest of the narrative around her exploits in the Crimean
war zone, where she establishes the British Hotel (72–200).

Seacole begins her public account of self conventionally: "I was
born in the town of Kingston, in the island of Jamaica, sometime
in the present century" (1). While this self-placement identifies the
connectedness of origins, it does not suggest belonging in the sense
of nation, home, community.[20] The organizing center for seeing and
depicting, the scales of comparison, the approaches and evaluations
that determine how her experiences in New Granada, Panama, and
Europe are to be seen and understood are not located "at home"
in a Jamaican social reality but "at home" in post-Crimean England.[21] Mary Seacole may be rooted in Jamaica, but her narrative
is written for an English audience. Perhaps the persistent fact of
her marginality is what makes her authenticating devices—name
dropping, documents, letters—necessary in her public account of
self. She was never a slave, but her perceived need of patronage
recalls the authentication strategies of the slave narrative.

Seacole self-consciously constructs her narrative around a series
of events and experiences that explain and contextualize her heroic

work in the Crimea. The form and values of her narrative are interchangeable. They reflect her love of adventure, the desire to perform heroic national service, and her eagerness to receive the recognition that is her due in England, the center of civilizing values in her world. Thus her narrative focuses on the adventures of heroic Mother Seacole in the Crimea as fulfillment of a destiny shaped in childhood in Jamaica, a destiny that the four years she spends in and out of New Granada codify to the point of an obsession. Her pre-Crimean life emerges as both necessary precondition and preamble. She situates the inner values of her Jamaican self within the network of civilized values that shaped the British Empire. Her Jamaican identity acquires the weight and authority of empire. She admits no conflict of interest; to be Jamaican and to be a British subject are culturally interchangeable. She projects a rare harmony of inner and outer being in a narrative of extraordinary silences and omissions.

The multifaceted world of Seacole's Jamaica is the most obvious of these omissions. Jamaica is not recalled here except to establish that the primary initiative in her heroic adventurous life belongs to Seacole herself. The antecedent center of her psyche is Jamaica distilled into the briefest sketches of her parents, her patron, and her childhood. Her destiny as an adventurous Creole "doctress" is rooted in a few facts of her multiracial, multicultural origins in Jamaica. "My father was a soldier, of an old Scotch family; and to him I often trace my affection for a camp-life, and my sympathy with what I have heard my friends call 'the pomp, pride, and circumstance of glorious war'"(1). To him she attributes her "energy and activity which are not always found in the Creole race" (1). She identifies her mother as a Creole who ran a respectable boardinghouse in Kingston and "an admirable doctress" (2). Seacole attributes her talents as an entrepreneur and a doctor to her mother's influence. "It was very natural that I should inherit her tastes; and so I had from early youth a yearning for medical knowledge and practice which never deserted me" (2). She specifically names her mother as a role model for her professional undertakings: "I saw so much of her, and of her patients, that the ambition to become a doctress early took firm root in my mind" (2). She says little else of substance about her parents or about the "old lady, who brought me up in her own household among her own grandchildren" (2).

She characterizes her childhood and youth in Jamaica exclusively in terms of her ambition to become a "doctress" and her desire to travel. She briefly describes the solitary games that she played as a child in imitation of her mother, using first her doll, then dogs and cats, and finally herself to practice medicine on (3). At twelve she begins to assist her mother in running her boardinghouse and attending to invalid British officers and their wives who were stationed in Jamaica (3). As she matures, her desire to travel coalesces around England and the longing to escape Jamaica. "I was never weary of tracing upon an old map the route to England; and never followed with my gaze the stately ships homeward bound without longing to be in them, and see the blue hills of Jamaica fade into the distance" (4). The dynamic of her life is located here in a few facts of her birth and her young life. She reimagines her childhood as she fulfills her ambitions and establishes continuity between the Jamaican child and the Crimean heroine.[22] She erases Jamaican social reality outside the bare facts of her relationship with the British military, their families, and visitors to the island, and the omission is deliberate: "It is not my intention to dwell at any length upon the recollections of my childhood" (2).[23] She is just as cryptic about her adult working life in Jamaica. "How slowly and gradually I succeeded in life, need not be told at length" (7). She is self-conscious but unapologetic about these omissions. Beyond the bare facts of her birth and parentage, she establishes that she fulfilled her womanly obligations willingly and well. She loved her husband, her patron, and her mother and mourned their deaths. She is industrious and successful in her business undertakings and has the will and energy to chart her own recovery from disaster. She writes pointedly, in three casually delivered sentences, about grave personal danger and the loss of her establishment in the great fire of 1843: "As it was, I very nearly lost my life, for I would not leave my house until every chance of saving it had gone, and it was wrapped in flames. But, of course, I set to work again in a humbler way, and rebuilt my house by degrees, and restocked it, succeeding better than before" (7). This does not become an occasion to say anything about the cause of the great fire in Kingston or civil unrest in Jamaica or the status of Creole women. She carefully avoids the politics of colonialism as a lived reality in the Jamaica of her day. Instead, she establishes her long-standing relationship to the British military and briefly sketches aspects of her character and personal values. She prizes happiness over money; she is a woman of action and is optimistic in the face of misfortune: "Although it was no easy thing for a widow to make ends meet, I never allowed myself to know what repining or depression was, and so succeeded in gaining not only my daily bread, but many comforts besides, from the beginning" (6–7). Her tone is mature, reflective, and self-confident. She is a woman of experience and discretion.

Mary Seacole calls the reader's attention to other conscious omissions and casually or carefully explains them. In one instance she explains that she does not want to weary the reader with details of her voyage to Constantinople, because that voyage "is already worn threadbare by book-making tourists" (82). Later she explains her philosophical reasons for not focusing on "the nameless horrors" of the spring of 1855 in the Crimea; it is contrary to the veterans' code of conduct to dwell on the horrors of the battlefield (136), and it is not part of her narrative design as "the historian of Spring Hill" (146). The details of Mary Seacole's Jamaican life are not privileged in the same way. In her narrative she detaches the image of self that she crafts from the Jamaican landscape without explanation. Her property and business are left in the care of a female cousin. What is essentially Jamaican in her skillfully crafted self-image is embodied in her traveling person. With her expertise in caring for the sick comes an expertise in running an establishment that is at once a boardinghouse and clinic. This expertise is portable. It is not tied to a cultural context or to a landscape. It facilitates her love of travel, her thirst for adventure, her professional ambitions, and her desire to define herself in alternative social and geographical spaces. Seacole erects rhetorical barriers between her Jamaican origins and her public image, between the very idea of an organic, collective Jamaican community and her identity as loyal British subject.

Despite the carefully contrived harmony of inner and outer being that Seacole writes into her narrative, the rhetorical arrangement of the text suggests unidentified areas of conflict between the Jamaican core of her fate and personality and her struggle to become a Crimean heroine. As Simon Gikandi observes: "To be a colonial subject in the nineteenth century, then, is to exist in a cultural cul-de-sac: you cannot speak or exist except in the terms established by the *imperium*; you have to speak to exist, but you can utter only what the dominant allows you to utter; even when you speak against the culture of colonialism, you speak its language because it is what constitutes what you are" (142). Despite the "friendly and confidential" (8) tone that Mary Seacole assumes with her readers and her philosophical interludes, her story takes shape as an entirely public account of self. She reveals nothing of herself that might not be the substance of conversations with others. She erases interiority along with Jamaica. The preexisting public image of Seacole as Crimean heroine shapes her autobiographical self-consciousness. Her life story is skewed to public approval and public patronage. Seacole is a much celebrated public figure when she returns to England from the Crimea, thanks to the reporting of William Howard Russell (1820–1907), special correspondent for the *Times* during the Crimean War (Alexander 28 n25). Everything that she mentions is indicative of her preformed character and her heroic destiny. Travel and adventure are more a question of self-positioning than interior development. Her self is formed in Jamaica, and it is represented through accomplishments in New Granada and the Crimea.

The revelation of Seacole's character and personality begins in earnest in the New Granada section of her narrative. Seacole follows her brother Edward to the Isthmus of Panama in 1850, driven by "my reviving disposition to roam" and the desire to "be of use to him" (9). In fact, Seacole goes in search of adventure and new economic opportunities. In Cruces and Gorgona her economic ventures acquire an overlay of civilizing mission. She describes Panama as a lawless place under the "weak sway of the New Granada Republic" and inhabited by "the refuse of every nation" (10). She not only makes money in Cruces and Gorgona but she performs a vital function as a medical practitioner. She is "pleased and gratified" when she recalls her efforts in caring for the sick and dying during an outbreak of cholera in Cruces (25–26). Her speculative ventures are represented as bastions of "civilized" values, in places where civilization does not yet rule. She establishes standards of conduct and value and guards these fiercely. England is consistently her frame of reference: English rivers (15), "the English at home" (40), "any Englishman" (41), "as is the case in civilized England" (44), and always the ideal English reader, sympathetic, understanding, and prejudiced against Americans, Spaniards, Spanish Indians, Greeks, Turks, Maltese, and Catholics.[24]

Seacole uses New Granada to establish who she is on her own terms, that is, on the basis of her experience in negotiating chaotic social situations, whether because of a cholera epidemic, the lack of basic amenities, or the ability to impose English standards of value in the most unlikely settings. Details of Seacole's everyday life in New Granada establish the virtues and values of Mother Seacole in the Crimea at every turn. Her experiences in New Granada directly anticipate her experiences in the Crimea, from dealing with thieves, hiring help, erecting a physical plant from very little, and creating a center of order and social comfort to dispensing medical services. She gives elaborate details of her material circumstances, how she establishes her medical practice, how she treats cholera and conducts a postmortem examination, how she builds and runs her stores and hotels. She fully particularizes here her professional self-consciousness as a "doctress" and businesswoman, which she had briefly introduced as the substance of her adult life in Jamaica. In the freedom of frontier towns like Cruces, Gorgon, and Escribanos, she acquires new knowledge and new skills; she tends to knife and gunshot wounds and stitches back slit ears (16–17).

The temporal and spatial values of Seacole's adventures in New Granada reveal her worthiness as a British subject in terms that preclude the contentiousness of West Indian colonial politics in midcentury. In New Granada, Seacole can be historically and politically aware without having to be critical of the way the empire does its business. She expresses her opinion on a wide range of concerns, from the construction of the Panama Canal to the superiority of black slaves who had fled south and settled there to Catholic practices. She is acutely aware of how power functions and is forthright about how she negotiates corruption, racism, and male dominance in a frontier environment. Her travels and adventures provide a context for self-definition that minimizes ancestry and emphasizes experience, knowledge, and practice. She creates an image of self in foreign lands that is concrete and substantial. She travels to fulfill her sense of adventure and to make money. Seacole is no polite observer or passive recorder of exotic, alien worlds. In New Granada she participates fully in "frontier" life as a businesswoman and a doctor. The biographical values established here—initiative, intelligence, chastity, courage, fearlessness, physical and emotional strength, entrepreneurial and nursing skills, and fidelity to the "civilizing" values of the British Empire—take rhetorical precedence over the long years spent establishing a reputation as a businesswoman, "doctress," and loyal colonial subject in Jamaica. They affirm her identity and her preparedness for her Crimean initiative without reference to the social and political conflicts of her life in colonial Jamaica.

The tone of Seacole's public account of self changes from New Granada to the Crimea. She accomplishes the dramatic unfolding of her multifaceted and unconventional character in an exotic environment. She presents herself in the Crimean episode as a known entity. The rubric of self-revelation in new and unexpected situations degenerates into a rubric of glorification and heroization. Her public image as a Crimean heroine, and her expressed gratitude for the honors and the patronage she has received, coopts the vitality of the ideal antecedent self that she constructs in the neutral territory of New Granada. Her rhetorical strategy progresses from self-glorification to an extravagant uncritical glorification of everything English, from "the English boy, in all his impudence and prejudice" (106) to Lord Raglan, whose tragic death becomes a testament to her influence with his attendants and survivors, and the distribution of the Order of Bath awards: "I was anxious to have some personal share in the affair, so I made, and forwarded to head-quarters, a cake which Gunter might have been at some loss to manufacture. . . . I received great kindness from the official at the ceremony, and from the officers—some of rank— who recognized me; indeed, I held quite a little levee around my chair" (168–69). Little in the lengthy Crimean section of the narrative fosters autobiographical expression of Seacole's private self-consciousness. Self-representation grows stilted and stereotyped and a process of ossification sets in. She totally invests her individual success, happiness, and merit in the glorification of the imperial warhead. What is vital and dynamic about Mary Seacole in New Granada becomes predictable in the Crimea as she assimilates and internalizes military codes of conduct, values, and responses. The "first woman to enter Sebastopol from the English lines" (173) must have her mementos of the conquest and, like any stout English lad, thrashes an American sailor, who has her arrested as a Russian spy, while French soldiers hold him down. She renders her descriptions of battle scenes with no perceptible difference in sensibility. As "kind-hearted officers" make time to bid her good-bye at the end of the war, she observes, seemingly without a trace of irony, that "war, like death, is a great leveler, and mutual suffering and endurance had made us all friends" (191). Formal issues affecting the public performance of self-consciousness qualify the expression of private self-consciousness, as in the case of Mary Prince. The details of Seacole's everyday life in the Crimea, evidence of her heroic service, say little about Seacole's inner core; what she does and says is who she is. Even when she complains, as the British army withdraws, that she has no home, or smashes cases of expensive cheeses with an axe rather than let the Russians have them inexpensively, her mounting frustration reflects a longing for reconnection rather than disillusionment and doubt. Self-imaging is observably tied to patronage and courts recognition.

She particularizes her preformed public image as a woman who serves the needs of England's fighting men in her British Hotel and on the battlefield as an elaborate and heartfelt gesture of love and devotion to her English "sons." Whether she is making cakes and lemonade from temporary quarters in an ammunition ship in the

Black Sea (101) or supplying the comforts of home from the British Hotel (138–40), the descriptor that she most favors is Mother Seacole. She organizes her autobiographical self-consciousness around an organic connectedness to the heroic possibilities of military life. She redefines her professional self-consciousness as a "doctress" and businessperson in the context of honorable camp follower and sutler.

Seacole instantiates a West Indian psychology that puts Mary Prince's peasant rootedness at a distance. Seacole's *Wonderful Adventures* extols the colonizing authority of metropolitan culture. It is a direct and sharp contrast to viewing one's own story as a return to the African and peasant heart of the Caribbean, as a coming home to a New World identity. What is especially compelling and unusual about Mary Seacole is that little is weak and self-effacing about her life and actions. Paradoxically, even as she embraces British colonial values, she exerts a powerful, muscular energy that forces new parameters on her status as colonial.

Part 2

The Estranging Sea

The autobiographical narratives of Claude McKay, George Lamming, C. L. R. James, and Derek Walcott extend and develop the tropes of departure and return, travel and encounter that are so clearly demarcated in the narratives of Mary Prince and Mary Seacole. Though the arrangement and process of narration are markedly different in each case, the repetition of these tropes (with variations reflective of the individual identity of the autobiographical subject) suggests areas of continuity regarding interests and capacities, as well as relationships with the world, that distinct Caribbean communities may share, despite being widely separated in time. On the other hand, this comparative framework also exposes the degree of women's alienation in Caribbean literary culture for the better part of the twentieth century. This alienation of erasure and misrepresentation went largely unchallenged until writers like Jean Rhys, Phyllis Shand Allfrey, Merle Hodge, Erna Brodber, and Jamaica Kincaid both initiated a process of recuperation and reversal through the substance and quality of their literary production and made issues of male dominance visible.

In *Whispers from the Caribbean* (1991) Wilfred Cartey theorizes that the paradigm of departure and return in Caribbean literary culture is a movement from personality to presence: "*Personality* . . . evokes the person as affected by the combined forces of colonialism, of economics, of historical imperialism and Great Power rivalry. *Presence* is a cultural or spiritual term; it suggests the person in his own spiritual interiority, his selfhood as bestowed on him by his own people, their values, their worldview, their mores. Both *personality* and *presence* are in a constant state of tension and interaction" (xii–xiv). Cartey writes with a regional nationalist agenda in mind, seeking "prescriptions for a cohering social reality, unified by a dynamic indigenizing of social, cultural, and political elements, an indigenizing with its prognosis of a holistic Caribbean society" (xiv). He assumes a teleology of origin-return that transcends decentered lateral connections.[1] In Cartey's thinking, transnational culture making uncovers a specific and local sense of identity formed around a unique multicultural root.

In *Black Women, Writing, and Identity* Carole Boyce Davies is less prescriptive about the outcome and more attuned to the limitations of nationalist discourse in mapping transoceanic cultures. The trope of departure and return does not anticipate sociocultural homogeneity so much as a coexistent plurality that continually redefines itself: "The Caribbean Sea is therefore a site of dissemination of a variety of socio-cultural processes, a site of continuous change and the ongoing questioning of self, origin, direction" (13). According to Davies, decentered lateral connections coexist with a teleology of origin-return, and she identifies these as important prerogatives of women in quest of personal fulfillment and economic stability. She argues a point central to this study: that women incorporated similar structures of awareness through travel and transforming encounters with other worlds, though they could not and did not deploy them in similar ways. Nomadism in the Caribbean, however circumscribed by restrictive contingencies, is gendered primarily in the specific bias of its representation.[2] Davies describes the sociocultural phenomenon as intraterritorial and extraterritorial, regional and global in its character, and bases her study on a hybridized but persistent foundational kinship with Africa.

The narratives of Claude McKay and George Lamming introduce with great complexity the centrality of Africa and the black
Atlantic diaspora to the Caribbean experience of journey, migration, settlement, and resettlement. For Claude McKay, who emigrated to the United States in 1912 and made his permanent home
there, black nationalism was both ontological and strategic,
embroiled in and transcending national politics.[3] He articulated a
passionate Afrocentrism and with it the ambivalences built into a
diverse black Atlantic diaspora. In his autobiography, *A Long
Way from Home*, Claude McKay relishes the black fellowship that
he found in multicultural Marseilles after a long sojourn in Russia, Germany, and Paris: "It was good to feel the strength and distinction of a group and the assurance of belonging to it" (*Long
Way* 229). He records that in Paris he felt precisely the opposite
among white American expatriate writers and artists: "Color-
consciousness was the fundamental of my restlessness. And it was
something with which my fellow-expatriates could sympathize but
which they could not altogether understand. For they were not
black like me" (*Long Way* 245). His visit to Morocco adds yet
another dimension to issues of racial identification as he records
a sense of being at one in a culturally diverse yet traditional North
African culture, where class, color, and colonialism combine to
affirm an innate sense of well-being: "For the first time in my life
I felt myself singularly free of color-consciousness. I experienced
a feeling that must be akin to the physical well-being of a dumb
animal among kindred animals, who lives instinctively and by
sensations only, without thinking. But suddenly I found myself
right up against European intervention and proscription" (*Long
Way* 300). In Claude McKay's Morocco the diasporan themes of
race, nation, and exile come to an uneasy rest politically and
philosophically in a colonial culture that cannot be reduced to any
single national or ethnic tradition.

Subsequently, the African Barbadian historian and poet Edward
[Kamau] Brathwaite would map a different route to a different
Africa, from Barbados to England to Ghana, pressing the genealogical connection with Africa to its inescapable conclusion. In his
autobiographical essay, "Timehri" (1974), Brathwaite models a

process of healing the fragmented, rootless, black West Indian subject exemplified in Claude McKay's *A Long Way from Home:*

> Slowly, slowly, ever so slowly; obscurely, slowly but surely, during the eight years that I lived there [Ghana], I was coming to an awareness and understanding of community, of cultural wholeness, of the place of the individual within the tribe, in society. . . . I came to a sense of identification of myself with these people, my living diviners. I came to connect my history with theirs, the bridge of my mind, now linking Atlantic and ancestor, homeland and heartland. When I turned to leave . . . I came home to find that I had not really left. That it was still Africa; Africa in the Caribbean. (33–34)

Africa emerges as a desired but obstructed future, illuminating but not resolving the discrepant temporalities of a fragmented and differentiated Caribbean subject.[4]

The anticolonial diasporic base of racial identification in Claude McKay and the restorative values of physical and spiritual reconnection with Africa in Brathwaite take their place in a full-blown discourse of departure and return, travel and encounter, errantry and exile. Like Claude McKay before him and Kamau Brathwaite who came after, in *The Pleasures of Exile* George Lamming frames these issues in terms of a cultural alienation and wanderlust generated by slavery and colonialism: "I am still young by ordinary standards (thirty-two, to be exact), but already I feel that I have had it (as a writer) where the British Caribbean is concerned. I have lost my place, or my place has deserted me" (*Pleasures* 50). In *The Pleasures of Exile* the writer and intellectual is part of a West Indian community on the move, discovering nuances in filiation and affiliation that, in Lamming's case, crystallize around a compulsion to travel beyond the Caribbean to England, Africa, and the United States. The black Atlantic emerges as distinct, diverse, and foundational but is ultimately displaced as a master trope in the competing diasporic claims of the Caribbean's multiethnic, multiracial populations.

In *Coming, Coming Home* (1995) Lamming reexamines the evolution of transnationalism within and beyond the archipelago as a universal feature of Caribbean life, as part of an ongoing economic compulsion and an important contributor to a process of regional cultural integration on a variety of levels:[5]

> From the middle of the nineteenth century to the second decade of the twentieth century, Barbados provided over fifty thousand workers to Guyana and Trinidad. The population of Trinidad and Tobago doubled in forty years between 1844 and 1881 as a result of this movement of peoples from St. Vincent, Grenada, and as far as St. Martin in the northeast. . . . During the first two decades of this century, more than one hundred and twenty thousand Haitians and Jamaicans became a resident force of labor in the Republic of Cuba. A morning's walk around Santiago de Cuba, is hardly distinguishable from a view of the cosmopolitan complexions of downtown Port of Spain. (33–34)

Lamming focuses on intraregional migration as part of a process of cross-fertilization and reciprocity that underpins and sustains the "Caribbean nature of our relation to the world, at the material and cultural levels of negotiation" (*Coming* 24). Thirty-odd years after the publication of *The Pleasures of Exile*, Lamming's representation of the Caribbean—as a "nation that is not defined by any particular boundaries" (*Coming* 32)—emphasizes the *presence* of a multiply centered Caribbean culture rather than the questing errant *personality* of the earlier text.

Lamming's later emphasis on a Caribbean root, on a sense of identity inscribed in territorial as well as racial origins, finds a correlative in Edouard Glissant's conception of the "open boat" of Caribbean consciousness: "We know ourselves as part and as crowd, in an unknown that does not terrify. We cry our cry of poetry. Our boats are open, and we sail them for everyone" (*Poetics of Relation* 9). Lamming's emphasis on a Caribbean presence—community in territory—as a place of return, of homecoming, that maintains itself in the face of continuing errantry, points to the genesis of a counterculture that reconstructs its own critical, intellectual, and moral genealogy.[6] Glissant's open boat similarly sidesteps regional-territorial boundaries in an "errant" quest for "totality," an imaginary that he is careful to differentiate from a totalitarian universal: "Errant, he challenges and discards the universal—this generalizing edict that summarized the world as something obvious and transparent, claiming for it one presupposed sense and one destiny" (*Poetics of Relation* 20).[7] Whereas Lamming refers to José Martí (1853–1895), hero of the Cuban War of Independence from Spain, to represent the "singular importance of the Caribbean external frontier" to patriotic consciousness in the region (*Coming* 44–45), Glissant uses Frantz Fanon's journey from colonial Martinique to the Algerian Revolution as an example of the quest for an identity that is beyond the territorial root (*Poetics of Relation* 18). The internationalist subtext here has everything to do with the politics of location and the related but different subject positions of Glissant and Lamming as mediators of the Caribbean imaginary at home and abroad.[8] The discourse of errantry and exile, migration and journey shifts back and forth, illuminating the variables of cultural rootedness, territorial possession, and overlapping interwoven practices of nationalism and internationalism in the Caribbean at the end of the twentieth century. There, Glissant's Martinique is a part of the European Common Market as an overseas department of France, and Lamming's newly independent Barbados fashions itself as part of Caricom, the British Commonwealth of Nations, the Organization of American States, and the United Nations.[9] Both Martinique and Barbados are constituent parts of a coexistent Caribbean plurality and have a distinct place in the intellectual and cultural history of the region.

In the space fashioned by autobiographical practice, a linked nationalist-internationalist discourse articulates specific local and global attachments.[10] The narratives of Claude McKay, C. L. R. James, Lamming, and Walcott under consideration here engage questions of language, cultural authority, gender, and location in ways that subvert fixed categories of identity. They also invite a reading of the Caribbean as a geographical and cultural construct that frames an eccentric quality of consciousness, shaped and reshaped by the cumulative effect of shifting regional, hemispheric, and global networks of community. A paradoxical sense of cultural belonging that does not necessarily coincide with a specific site of dwelling, or even a sense of territorial at-homeness, shapes self-consciousness and self-representation in all these texts. This is traceable to a variety of economic and political circumstances, shifting affiliations, and social relations. As much as anything else, the pace of intraregional and extraregional migration and cultural exchange nurtures a dynamic of differentiation that systematically redefines, if not subverts, the nationalist project in the twentieth century in all its phases—prenationalist, nationalist, extranationalist, and so forth.

The problem of time and time consciousness as a constitutive element of progress and social development comes to an uneasy rest in the tropes of departure and return, travel and encounter, grounded as they are in a material and cultural phenomenon that links here and there, past and present in a community of interchangeable travelers and dwellers, islanders and exiles.[11] Estrangement from native landscape on a variety of levels is written into the narratives of the Harts, Prince, and Seacole and is extended and developed as a major project of self-writing by Claude McKay, C. L. R. James, Lamming, and Walcott. The authors of the narratives included in this study construct identity multiply as a natural artifact and a conscious choice, a deeply embedded historical formation, and a cultural invention. The two autobiographies of Claude McKay are a case in point, organized as they are around a deployment of the departure-return trope that reverses the values of personality and presence that Cartey ascribes to it.

The spatial and cultural disjunction of the Jamaican poet in the United States reveals yet another axis of otherness in an unfolding matrix of associations. Seacole's feminine deployment of the Ulysses paradigm is repeated in Claude McKay's *A Long Way from Home* and is fundamentally altered in the transposition to McKay's distinctive needs as a male bisexual professional writer and by the emergence of the heterogeneous United States as a competing metropolitan power with colonizing cultural imperatives of its own. In the context of Seacole's affiliative identification with the British Empire, Claude McKay expresses cultural resistance in the rejection of British colonial authority and the pan-Africanist public image that he crafts for himself as internationalist and bad nationalist who seeks affiliation with black America.

Though Claude McKay belongs to a different generation, Lamming's observations in *The Pleasures of Exile* about the United

States, as opposed to England, as a site of maturation are worth considering here, because Claude McKay as a Jamaican North American decenters both African Americanist and colonial-anti-colonial discourses with his autobiographies: "If the West Indian writer had taken up residence in America—as Claude MacKay [*sic*] did—his development would probably be of a different, indeed, of an opposed order to that of a man who matured in England" (*Pleasures* 25).[12] Claude McKay's narratives throw light on the discrepant temporalities of black Atlantic and Caribbean diasporas in relation to burgeoning race-based and territorial nationalist discourses. What remains unaddressed is the cross-cutting sexuality of bisexual Claude McKay, who masks his homoerotic quest in a vaguely framed pitch for the free play of sexuality. The link between Claude McKay's sexual nonconformity, his political radicalism, and his restless wanderings remains the work of literary scholars and critics like Wayne F. Cooper, who writes that McKay's "sexual orientation is much more than clear-cut. Although McKay had sexual relations with women, he also had many homosexual affairs, particularly in the United States and Europe. The evidence indicates that his primary orientation was towards the homosexual" (*Claude McKay* 30).

In *A Long Way from Home* Claude McKay writes his bisexuality out of the script. He displaces issues of sexual identity onto a defensiveness about black masculinity and an observed prurient interest in racist sexual stereotypes: "Maybe I was not civilized enough to understand why the sex of the black race should be put on exhibition to persuade the English people to decide which white gang should control the coal and iron of the Ruhr. . . . I think the Anglo-Saxon mind becomes morbid when it turns on the sex life of colored people" (*Long Way* 75–76).[13] Claude McKay's repressed bisexual narrative is expressed in an uncentered, vagrant desire. The unexpected appearance of his Jamaican wife, of whom his companions are unaware, leaves him feeling exposed and longing to escape: "I had married when I had thought that a domestic partnership was possible to my existence. But I had wandered far and away until I had grown into a truant by nature and undomesticated in the blood. . . . I desired to be footloose, and felt impelled to start going again. . . . Go, better than stand still, keep going" (*Long Way* 150). The impulse to escape takes him to Russia and a twelve-year sojourn abroad. However, Claude McKay's subversive and defensive strategies of self-representation expose gaps in the narrative, where unnamed restrictive contingencies threaten to disrupt the vagabond troubadour persona he creates for himself and with it related Caribbean theories of nomadism, migration, and pleasurable exile.

In hindsight the suppression of homoerotic expression compresses rather than erases kinship with the mainstream of Caribbean literary culture, taking us deeper into the mystery of the root. As Edouard Glissant reminds us: "The founding books have taught us that the sacred dimension consists always of going deeper into the mystery of the root, shaded with variations of errantry. In reality errant thinking is the postulation of an unyielding and unfading sacred" (*Poetics of Relation* 21). To read Claude McKay in the context of such Caribbean-centered theoretical formulations is to reckon with the price that Caribbean intellectual history has had to pay for the repression of the homoerotic. In "Critics in the Dark" Ian Smith argues this point: "The critical geography seems to have no place to situate sexuality, specifically the homoerotic within a postcolonial discourse, replicating an imperial dislocation, a tendency that can be described as a neocolonial sexual semiotics" (4). In this context one might argue that the denial of the homoerotic destabilized West Indian literary and critical practice in the reenactment of a colonial practice that strove to erase and/or demonize the homoerotic, as in the case of an Oscar Wilde or a D. H. Lawrence.[14] Frantz Fanon's *Black Skin, White Masks* is another case in point. Not content with erasure, Fanon models a heterosexual masculinist siege mentality that displaces his own rebellious racialized colonial ambivalence onto women and homosexuals (*Black Skin* 158, 180).

At this juncture it is worth noting that Audre Lorde's quasi-Caribbean lesbian text, *Zami: A New Spelling of My Name* (1982), highlights an implicit rejection in the sequence of the Claude McKay texts, of the linear progressivist narrative of the nation-state. Problems of nationality, location, sexual identity, and

historical memory shadow the quest for "new forms of community, co-existence, pleasure" that both writers share (Foucault,
Power/Knowledge 120).[15] Claude McKay's idylls of Jamaica in
My Green Hills suggest an obstructed, pained yearning for reconnection, as does Lorde's fetishizing of Carriacou in *Zami,* appro-
priately published as "a biomythography by Audre Lorde." In
Black Women, Writing, and Identity, Davies identifies three levels of reconnection with the Caribbean for Lorde, the African
American daughter of Grenadian American immigrants: "first, the
parental home, the Caribbean homeland occupying the secondary
level, and at the tertiary level the African identification" (17).
Davies observes the discrepant temporality of Lorde's reconnection with "revolutionary Grenada (not colonial Grenada) and the
sense of possibility and challenge it held" (122). As is the case of
Claude McKay's *My Green Hills,* Lorde's highly selective reconnection in *Zami* is as much a rejection as a reconnection: "Once
home was a long way off, a place I had never been to but I knew
out of my mother's mouth. I only discovered its latitudes when
Carriacou was no longer my home. . . . There it is said that the
desire to lie with other women is a drive from the mother's blood"
(255–56). What is available to Lorde and politically unavailable
to Claude McKay is an explicit sexual recentering of the
Caribbean as a locus of identification. To Lorde sexual specificity
is everything, and the level of invention with respect to the
Caribbean as "home" is high.

The aesthetic paradigm of departure and return in Claude
McKay is a primary organizing value in the transformation of
autobiographical form from the studied vagrancy of Claude
McKay's *A Long Way from Home* to the utopian *My Green Hills
of Jamaica.* The contours of the movement away from home as
unfolding destiny are reversed in Claude McKay's symbolic return
to his Jamaican youth as an idealized space shortly before his death
in *My Green Hills.* Edward Said's nationalist anti-imperialist phase,
followed by a liberationist anti-imperialist resistance beyond
nationalism, has a different chronology in the unfolding drama of
Claude McKay's autobiographies (Said, "Yeats" 82). The so-called
nativist enterprise is a race-based subtext in *A Long Way from*

Home; in *My Green Hills* it is rooted firmly in the geopsychic space of Claude McKay's Jamaican beginnings.

Written in the United States after the extraordinary success of Richard Wright's *Black Boy* (1945), *My Green Hills,* with its crude ironies of utopian "green" beginnings, is a disjunctive moment in African Caribbean autobiography, largely because of the way it idealizes Claude McKay's colonial childhood. More typical is his representation of the departure of a talented son for the wider horizons of the United States as the fulfillment rather than the betrayal of native origins, a subtext with variations in Lamming's *In the Castle of My Skin* and *The Pleasures of Exile,* C. L. R. James's *Beyond a Boundary,* and Walcott's *Another Life.*[16] In *In the Castle of My Skin* Lamming gives a distinctly antipastoral thrust to native space that he conceptualizes as a colonial creation, while C. L. R. James resists this characterization of native space altogether, and Walcott is at some pains to distinguish between the artistic personality and landscape as colonial creation and the natural landscape in which the creative sensibility renews its sense of alterity in native community.

By midcentury the Anglophone Caribbean's steady progress toward independence of Great Britain, the Cuban Revolution of 1959, the civil rights movement in the United States, and the liberation of the African colonies were increasing the pressure to produce a counterdiscourse displacing colonialism's dominative system of knowledge.[17] Inevitably, literary culture is engaged in the combined deconstructive-reconstructive process. The evolution of anticolonialist discourse is powerfully instantiated in the negritude of Aimé Césaire's *Notebook of a Return to the Native Land* and later in his *Discourse on Colonialism.* As in the case of Claude McKay, the alienation of the black intellectual finds radical activist expression with the publication of such works as Jean Price-Mars's *Ainsi parla l'oncle,* C. L. R. James's *The Case for West Indian Self-Government* and *The Black Jacobins,* Nicolas Guillen's *West Indies Ltd.,* Eric Williams's *Capitalism and Slavery,* Fernando Ortiz's *Cuban Counterpoint: Tobacco and Sugar,* Alejo Carpentier's *The Kingdom of This World,* and Frantz Fanon's *Black Skin, White Masks.* The pressure to produce a counterdiscourse can be measured in part in the elaborate architecture of many of the autobiographical texts under scrutiny here.[18]

In the narratives of Claude McKay and Lamming, and also of C. L. R. James and Walcott, the creative writer's contradictory sense of difference from and at-oneness with the group from which he is born is predictably in tension with the pressure to locate that contradictory sense of difference in the spirit of the group.[19] Cartey's regional nationalist ideal of an increasingly holistic society attempts to anchor the discernible restlessness and tension between home and elsewhere that is evident in narratives like these. George Lamming's autobiographical novel of colonial childhood and adolescence, *In the Castle of My Skin,* is a useful point of departure for studying the elaborate architecture of this burgeoning nationalism.[20] In *In the Castle of My Skin* Lamming juxtaposes first-person with omniscient narrative and in the process subsumes self-revelation in larger issues of cultural identification and appraisal. The limited understanding of youth is ironically highlighted by the omniscient narrative, which is in turn enjoined as an extension of the autobiographical pact.[21] The fragmented structure of Lamming's *The Pleasures of Exile* extends the autobiographical pact even further. The sporadically autobiographical first-person narrative in *The Pleasures of Exile* anchors wideranging essays on cultural and political decolonization. The author is both witness and participant, and the target is British colonial authority. The ending of *The Pleasures of Exile* coincides with the ending of *In the Castle of My Skin,* leaving little doubt that these works are complementary, mutually illuminating narratives. Lamming links the trope of departure and return with that of travel and encounter as an inevitable process of alienation that is rooted in a colonial childhood.

In his preface to *Beyond a Boundary* C. L. R. James makes his lifelong obsession with cricket the substance of and the occasion for intellectual history and cultural assessment: "This book is neither cricket reminiscences nor autobiography" (n.p.). His theme, he explains, is the genesis of the West Indian personality, Caliban's attempt to establish his own identity. However, despite the author's protestations, the autobiographical frame that he uses registers the ensuing narrative as an autobiographical space, and tropes of departure and return, travel and encounter mingle comfortably as noncompetitive elaborations of each other. The distancing modernist perspective of exile that Lamming projects in his narratives is transformed in C. L. R. James's *Beyond a Boundary*, which projects a harmonious unity of being in the sociological contours of a colonial sensibility. It progresses logically to nationalist consciousness in the idealized figure of the cricketer as, alternatively and in combination, Caribbean native, African prince and warrior, Victorian gentleman, traveler, and dweller.

The studied rootedness of Walcott's autobiographical poem *Another Life* illuminates the ironies of C. L. R. James's self-celebratory nationalist odyssey in *Beyond a Boundary*. Walcott, like Lamming and C. L. R. James before him, stresses a value other than autobiography. In describing the genesis of the poem, he states that in *Another Life* he abandoned autobiography for elegy and intellectual history, which I interpret as an invitation to read his autobiographical poem against the C. L. R. James and Lamming texts as the deepening and broadening of a common autobiographical root.[22] That root is variously defined in the press of migration within and beyond regional boundaries. In *Another Life* Walcott organizes it around departure and return in a continuing rhythm of reengagement with native space, primarily demarcated as St. Lucia and extended to include his life in Trinidad. Historical time is localized in the details of Walcott's growth and development as an artist in St. Lucia and a renewed commitment to the Caribbean as territorial cradle, a geopsychic self-positioning prefigured earlier in the narratives of the Hart sisters and Mary Prince.

Claude McKay's *A Long Way from Home* and *My Green Hills*, Lamming's *In the Castle of My Skin* and *The Pleasures of Exile*, C. L. R. James's *Beyond a Boundary*, and Walcott's *Another Life* are radically different texts, yet a distinctive pattern emerges. All engage directly with the social and political issues that preoccupied preindependence and postindependence cultures and societies in the region for the better part of the twentieth century, with a few alarming exceptions. One of these is women's oppression within the liberating parameters of nationalist discourse. In *Making Men* Belinda Edmondson makes an important point about male-authored "revolutionary" discourse in the region: "I argue that the traditional, male-authored representations of revolution and revolutionary discourse are tied to the image of men negotiating over the 'body' of the land. The men in this tableau are, on the one hand, the English colonizer, on the other, the oppositional black male subject" (12). Claude McKay, C. L. R. James, Lamming, and Walcott, in their very different narratives, are all preoccupied with defining a cultural and political reality in the gendered terms of male privilege and dominance.[23] The individual predicament of the writer as autobiographical subject projects a collective predicament in the ideal terms of a masculine self-positioning that is fundamentally nationalist-internationalist and Afrocentric in its representation of Caribbean space.

4

"The Traveling Ulysses Scene"

Claude McKay's *A Long Way from Home* and *My Green Hills of Jamaica*

The two autobiographies of Claude McKay encapsulate contrasting tropes of migration and return as distinct autobiographical modes. *A Long Way from Home* (1937) is the autobiography of the Jamaican writer as expatriate, negotiating a place for himself in the literary establishment of post–Renaissance Harlem after twelve productive years as a black writer in Europe and North Africa.[1] He gives his Jamaican origins only passing reference. In contrast, *My Green Hills of Jamaica* (published posthumously in 1979) is the autobiography of McKay's Jamaican childhood and youth.[2] Written in 1946 while he was receiving treatment in Albuquerque, New Mexico, for a chronic heart ailment, *My Green Hills,* Claude McKay's autobiography of return, encapsulates his Jamaican rather than his "American beginning" (*Long Way* 1). This artifice imposes a peculiar strategy of splitting or shadowing of the autobiographical subject in each autobiography. In *A Long Way from Home* "home" is New York; cultural identity is a willed repositioning of self on the basis of race, proven talent, and ambition, "a matter of 'becoming' rather than 'being'" (S. Hall, "Cultural Identity" 70). It is premised on the rejection of Jamaica as a delimiting native space: "Jamaica was too small for high achievement. There one was isolated, cut off from the great currents of life" (*Long Way* 20). However, in *My Green Hills* "home" is the mythicized Jamaica of his vanished childhood; it is the inspiration and foundation of self and art. Self-identification is premised on a specific landscape, a racial history,

87

and a culture that have fixed value over time. Self-identification is as much an essence as a positioning.[3]

The two autobiographies split Claude McKay's New World African psyche into two beginnings: one black American and one Jamaican. In *A Long Way from Home* he founds his cultural legitimacy and authenticity on his performance as a writer and traveler in the United States, Europe, Russia, and North Africa from 1918 to 1934. In *My Green Hills* he establishes his cultural legitimacy and authenticity by the facts of his birth and cultural connectedness to family and native community in Jamaica. The apparent contradiction between the performance-driven migratory values of *A Long Way from Home* and the received values of native community in *My Green Hills* illuminates the complexities of cross-cultural identity within the diaspora and the "new" internationalism of postcolonial migrations. The Jamaican immigrant's double vision inhabits an intervening space at the crossroads of history and literature.[4] The journey from Jamaica to the United States is a journey from country to city, from "colonial backwater" to metropolitan center; it is a journey across national boundaries from one diasporan space to another. Frantz Fanon writes: "In the world in which I travel, I am endlessly creating myself" (*Black Skin* 229). In this context the precursory *A Long Way from Home* is a celebration of journey and quest as a refashioning of self; the writer as "a troubadour wanderer" (*Long Way* 354) inscribes alternative strategies of black selfhood—singular and communal—that locate the Jamaican migrant as outsider at the creative juncture of diasporan identities and aesthetics in the United States.

In *A Long Way from Home* Claude McKay links his representation of self and creativity ideologically to his peasant origins in colonial Jamaica but not in a productive, transformative way. He links the values that organize the narrative to achieving credibility as a cultural presence in the United States, rather than in Jamaica: "I had no desire to return home. What I had previously done was done. But I still cherished the urge to creative expression. I desired to achieve something new, something in the spirit and accent of America. Against its mighty throbbing force, its grand energy and power and bigness, its bitterness burning in my black body, I would raise my voice to make a canticle of my reaction" (*Long Way* 4). The migrant's press for recognition and acceptance is pluralistic rather than totalizing. Autobiographical unity is the anticipated unity of successful relocation in black America. "As soon as I *desire* I am asking to be considered," writes Fanon, ". . . I demand that notice be taken of my negating activity insofar as I pursue something other than life; insofar as I do battle for the creation of a human world—that is a world of reciprocal recognitions" (*Black Skin* 218). Anticipating recognition and reconnection, Claude McKay allows memory of his Jamaican past to be eclipsed by memory of his black American future.[5]

In *My Green Hills* the reverse is true; Claude McKay represents memory of the past as an aestheticized fragment. The present and future that engender the text lack narrative substance. References to his life after Jamaica are few, and references to the historical changes that transformed Jamaica in that time are virtually nonexistent. Claude McKay renders his Jamaican childhood as a world sufficiently complete to ensure its continuance as a model of human relationships in the New World: "In spite of its poverty, my island of Jamaica was like a beautiful garden in human relationships" (*My Green Hills* 46). Claude McKay celebrates the enduring reverberations of his Jamaican childhood and youth as emblematic of the agricultural, familial, and distinctly black Jamaican folk roots of his ethical and aesthetic being.[6] The ideological assumptions underlying Claude McKay's elaboration of a myth of childhood suggest a cultural core that endures the vagaries of time and travel and persists as a site of strength and also of vulnerability in his reconstitution as black American. Jamaica as heartland is a race, a class, and a cultural orientation; it is a network of values from which Claude McKay emerges fully formed as peasant farmer, agricultural student, and folk poet.

A Long Way from Home and *My Green Hills* enact distinct worldviews, yet cross-referencing makes explicit the ways in which the language of personhood in each shadows the other.[7] The worlds of home as native space and of home as metropolitan crossroads reflect contradictory values and ideals. In *My Green*

Hills he fetishizes Jamaica-as-native-space as a nurturing, stable environment that privileges family and agricultural community as the nucleus of being.[8] Yet paradoxically, departure is the premise of Claude McKay's individual future; the autobiographical hero's emergence into manhood fulfills a growing alienation from the constriction of island life.[9] In *A Long Way from Home* the values of native space are eclipsed by the values of the road as a reputation-gathering, achievement-oriented, adventure-driven space that precludes domesticity and acceptance of traditional social roles. In *The Man-of-Words in the West Indies* Roger Abrahams draws broad distinctions between the values of respectability and reputation embodied in Yard and Crossroads, Household Rites, and Road Festivities (151–55) that clarify certain behavioral and conceptual differences underlying autobiographical self-imaging in the Claude McKay texts.[10] Claude McKay structures the ordered world of *My Green Hills* around the multigenerational, vertical organization of the family as opposed to the horizontal male world of mobility and friendship networks in *A Long Way from Home*.[11] The tension between domesticity and mobility does not threaten the status quo in *My Green Hills*, where these alternative lifestyles coexist in culture-defining tension. In *A Long Way from Home* the vagabond cuts loose from the vertical (traditional) contexts for self-representation. Claude McKay redefines *home* as the migrant culture of Harlem, where geographical and social mobility energizes cultural transition from the South to the North and a parallel migration from the Caribbean to the United States.[12] In *A Long Way from Home* Claude McKay draws the contested cultural and ideological space of the metropolitan crossroads along class as well as racial lines; he represents the troubadour vagabond as expatriate and as "at home" wherever he goes among the black working class and as an outsider among the class-conscious black Harlem elite.[13] Yet after twelve years abroad, the vagabond troubadour is an outsider even to the black working class.

The inversion in the sequence of the narratives, which first erases and devalues, then restores and celebrates ancestral beginnings, dramatizes the different artistic-autobiographical values governing the texts. In *A Long Way from Home* self-imaging is contingent on the myth of the politically and intellectually free man; it lacks the unity of an organic connectedness to community. In the absence of a self-defining ancestral landscape, Claude McKay uses as an image of identity the mask of a wandering minstrel "on the American stage" (*Long Way* 3) and around the world. Stephen Butterfield takes note of Claude McKay's use of the minstrel show (*Long Way* 145) as an image of white America haunted by the presence of "blackface, great, unappeasable ghost of Western civilization" (Butterfield 143). As a version of the minstrel mask, the mask of the troubadour wanderer generates its own dialectic of connectedness to and distance from the community.[14] As prequel, *My Green Hills* locates the vagabond troubadour in the contradictory impulses of Claude McKay's peasant and African beginnings in Jamaica. Jamaica generates both the need and the wherewithal to travel and grow beyond the boundary of a colonial culture on a small island in the Caribbean. As a site of identification, Jamaica, like the United States, is a space of psychic doubling for the Jamaican writer on the move; it is what Homi Bhabha describes as "a doubling, dissembling image of being in at least two places at once" (*Location of Culture* 44).

In the light of *My Green Hills,* the mask of minstrelsy that Claude McKay assumes in *A Long Way from Home* can be read as the mask of the displaced folk poet of *Songs of Jamaica* (1912) and *Constab Ballads* (1912), both of which were published before his departure for the United States. In *A Long Way from Home* Claude McKay transforms the folk poet, as "articulate consciousness" of the Jamaican peasant (13), into the "peasant and proletarian aspirant to literary writing" (139) whose primary affiliation is with the working class everywhere. The folk poet emerges sporadically in *A Long Way from Home* in the pastoral values of poems like "Flame-Heart" (73–74) and "The Tropics in New York" (116) and in the sixth and last section of the book, called "The Idylls of Africa."[15] The latter makes brief but pointed reference to Claude McKay's three-year sojourn in Morocco in a classic African Caribbean evocation of Africa as a place of retreat and renewal. The pastoral vision of "The Idylls of Africa" restores the vagabond troubadour to the ancestral landscape and values that

Claude McKay celebrates in *Gingertown* (1932) and *Banana Bottom* (1933) and anticipates the pastoral tone and cultural specificity of his later autobiography of boyhood and youth in Jamaica. However, these elements are muted in *A Long Way from Home*, where the folkloric hero as vagabond and troubadour wanderer privileges the political and intellectual independence of the outsider over ancestral rootedness.

In the light of veiled references to his homosexual preference, Claude McKay's mask of minstrelsy can also be read as the mask of a displaced sexuality subsumed in the mask of the troubadour wanderer who is nourishing himself "on the poetry of existence" (*Long Way* 354). In the context of the notorious masquerade balls that were fashioned around the free play of sexuality in McKay's Harlem, the mask of the minstrel as vagabond troubadour readily lends itself to such a reading (Garber 324; Chauncey 228–67). Writing about Oscar Wilde, Jonathan Dollimore observes that "a non-centred or vagrant desire is both the impetus for a subversive inversion, and what is released by it" (14). He notes that in Wilde's writings inversion works on a series of nature-culture binaries that throw some light on the contradictory identifications of vagrant desire and ancestral rootedness that govern Claude McKay's two autobiographies. Dollimore observes that in Wilde's works, "deviant desire rather than creating a new integrity of the self, actually decenters or disperses the self, and the liberation is experienced as being, in part, just that" (14). Dollimore's theories of sexual dissidence lend credence to a reading of *A Long Way from Home* as, in part, an attempt to escape the repressive ordering of colonial Jamaican society as well as the repressive ordering of a race- and class-conscious Harlem intelligentsia. This escape is marked in *A Long Way from Home* by "an inversion of the binaries on which that ordering depends" (Dollimore 14) while maintaining an identification with the romantic racialism of nationalist discourse. The subtext here is the convergence and apparent irreconcilability of Claude McKay's homosexual preference and dominant racial and national discourses in the Caribbean and in the United States.

In *Gay New York* George Chauncey documents Harlem's homophobia and the explicit link between homosexuality in

Harlem and the corrupting presence of bohemian whites from Greenwich Village (260). In 1926 W. E. B. Du Bois was actively promoting an African American art that reflected the values of the black community's conservative, educated middle class.[16] Later, Harold Cruse would link the ambivalences and ambiguities of Claude McKay's relationship to the United States and to the Harlem intelligentsia to a historic "dis-ease" between West Indians and black Americans in the United States and to Claude McKay's refusal to commit himself wholeheartedly to anything other than his own art (Cruse 47–48). Cruse characterizes Claude McKay in fixed terms as "the critical outsider looking in, the objective traveler passing through on his way to the next adventure or attraction" (48).[17] Cruse's discourse of cultural difference sidesteps Claude McKay's sexual difference, though it is interesting that Cruse identifies McKay's cultural-sexual difference as a site of artistic creation. Claude McKay assimilates such grudging recognition of his creative difference in the role of troubadour wanderer, or "vagabond with a purpose," that he so carefully crafts for himself in A Long Way from Home.[18] The poet as vagabond takes his position as outsider and celebrates it, with some self-mockery, as a site of cultural authority and creation. He repeatedly calls attention to the "play" of difference and marginality as a carefully constructed dimension of autobiographical self-imaging in A Long Way from Home.[19]

"There is nothing quite like the idea of play to get us into a muddle," writes Susan Suleiman (1).[20] Vagabond is a generic mask that essentializes and parodies the shifting positions from which Claude McKay views life and from which he makes his life public. The mask of the vagabond, like the mask of the troubadour wanderer, becomes functional only in motion. As iconoclast and man of the road, Claude McKay uses the generic function of the rogue, the clown, and the fool to lay bare the fatuousness of any sort of conventionality that challenges his "personal freedom" (Long Way 314). Harassed by the British in Morocco, Claude McKay identifies himself with characteristic vagabond flair: "I said I was born in the West Indies and lived in the United States and that I was an American, even though I was a British subject, but I preferred to think of myself as an internationalist. The *chaoush* said that he didn't understand what was an internationalist. I laughed and said that an internationalist was a bad nationalist" (*Long Way* 300). As troubadour wanderer, he goes on the offensive, celebrating his estrangement from home as Jamaica and from home as New York as a privileged vantage point. The troubadour wanderer is a poet and player on "the American stage" (*Long Way* 3) and on the world stage. He is the ambitious expatriate "gripped by a lust to wander and wonder" (*Long Way* 4). He travels in Europe and Africa, goes native in Morocco, is lionized in Russia, and is hounded by the British for working with Sylvia Pankhurst on the Marxist weekly *Workers' Dreadnought*. His marginal status as Jamaican African American writer gains in heterogeneity from his travels and wide-ranging experience of oppressed, black, and minority groups in other places, but this does not translate into cultural authority in nationalist black America.

In *A Long Way from Home* Claude McKay's primary concern appears to be the restoration of his public image as a black writer in the United States after years abroad. After the publication of his first novel, *Home to Harlem* (1928), which Claude McKay wrote in Marseilles, James Weldon Johnson urged him "to return to America to participate in the Negro renaissance movement" (*Long Way* 306). Participation meant negotiating a productive, transformative relationship with a community that he had fled about six years earlier: "But the resentment of the Negro intelligentsia against *Home to Harlem* was so general, bitter and violent that I was hesitant about returning to the great Black Belt. . . . I knew that if I returned I would have to find a new orientation among the Negro intelligentsia" (*Long Way* 307). As Wayne F. Cooper makes clear in *Claude McKay*, McKay's homosexual preference is coded in references to white radicals and a bohemian lifestyle in Russia, France, and Germany as well as in the United States. When he returns to the United States in 1934, the task of finding "a new orientation among the Negro intelligentsia" remains to be accomplished. He envisions his autobiography as an opportunity "to clarify his social, political, and artistic evolution and current convictions as a black writer" (W. Cooper 306). True to Claude McKay's intentions, *A Long Way from Home* is conceptualized in part as an apologia, selectively explaining his motives, actions, convictions, and "errors" in taste and judgment since his arrival in the United States in 1912: "I will confess that I may fall short of that degree of civilization which perfects the lily-white state of mind of the gentle southern lady. And that was why as a creative writer I was unable to make nice distinctions between the carnal and the pure and happened perhaps to sin on the side of the carnal in *Home to Harlem*" (*Long Way* 346).

Claude McKay gropes toward restoration of his public image through a nonconsensual race-based affiliation and an extraordinary record of individual accomplishment, rather than through a projection of being ideologically at one with the Harlem intelligentsia. In the absence of a cohesive interiority that is built by and reflected in a narrative of interior growth and development, the mask of the wandering minstrel is unable to speak authoritatively to "the spiritual consolidation" of the race.[21]

Travel, adventure, and artistic history are interlocking narrative and compositional elements of the vagabond and troubadour wanderer in *A Long Way from Home*. While artistic autobiography is an important organizing element, travel and adventure give specific values to Claude McKay's glamorization of his accomplishments as expatriate writer. The title of the autobiography calls attention to "the chronotope of the road" (Bakhtin, *Dialogic* 243) as an organizing motif and actual itinerary in the text.[22] The titles of the six parts of the autobiography emphasize an actual course of travel to the United States, Britain, Russia, Western Europe, and North Africa. "American Beginning," "English Inning," "New York Horizon," "The Magic Pilgrimage," "The Cynical Continent," and "The Idylls of Africa" fuse the life of the autobiographical subject to an actual spatial and temporal course. In each section Claude McKay establishes a direct link between his travels and his developing career as a black writer. He gives an account of his poetry and fiction, their genesis, their themes, the circumstances under which they were published, the amount of money he was paid, and the public reaction to their publication. He traces his career as a journalist and editor. He gives a catalogue of famous people met, honors received, humiliations suffered, places visited; he defends his reputation as a black writer and intellectual and even explains personal failings and inappropriate conduct—all in the interest of characterizing himself as one who is passionately committed to writing as a way of life and ideologically committed to writing the black experience.

From the outset Claude McKay identifies himself as a man of motion. His first chapter, "A Great Editor," begins with his working as a waiter on the train between New York and Philadelphia; he has just received an invitation from Frank Harris that will launch his career as a writer in the United States. The furtive flight on the freedom train is reconfigured in the railroad worker as migrant and aspiring poet. The Jamaican man of words is a traveling man. Exhilarated by the prospect of an American audience for his work, much as Mary Seacole was by the prospect of an English audience for hers, Claude McKay identifies with the sound and movement of the "rushing train and whistle": "Roar louder and louder, rushing train and whistle, beautiful engine whistle, carry me along, for I myself am a whistle tuned to the wind that is blowing through me a song of triumph" (*Long Way* 5). Despite the similarities, this is not the image of the West Indian as rootless drifter that one finds in Edward [Kamau] Brathwaite's *Rights of Passage*, nor is this George Lamming's uprooted West Indian colonial as Caliban laying claim to his difference in *The Pleasures of Exile* as the vantage point of the migrant's double vision, or even V. S. Naipaul's quest for a place of identification. Claude McKay prefigures their sense of cultural displacement, but his inscription of journey as site of identification is distinctly celebratory.

The chronotope of the road creates a space that is ideally suited to fashioning images of self in the adventurous mock-heroic vein of the troubadour and vagabond who fills in the details of his nomadic life as he goes along. Claude McKay locates himself in the tradition of the poet as wanderer, "the man who moves through the ruins of great civilizations with all his worldly goods by caravan or pack mule, the poet carrying entire cultures in his head, bitter perhaps but unencumbered" (Walcott, "Muse of History" 3). Claude McKay calls attention to his "eclectic approach to literature" and his "unorthodox idea of life" (*Long Way* 28). As vagabond, Claude McKay identifies himself as an iconoclastic folk hero. He seeks to win acceptance and influence through his reputation as an accomplished writer with an international reputation, rather than as a purveyor of traditional values. He mocks the formalities of social intercourse among the black bourgeoisie, declaring his independence of them and asserting his right to cultural dissensus and alterity. Embarrassed by Harlem Eclectic Club members for appearing before them in inappropriate dress, he repays their intolerance with insult. "I admire women in bright evening clothes. But men! Blacks in stiff-arched white facades and black uniforms like a flock of crows, imagining they are elegant—oh no!" (*Long Way* 115). Claude McKay positions himself beyond the boundary of their cultural values as a vagabond, identifying himself with an array of characters and values that are clearly intended to be antagonistic and conflictual. As Bhabha puts it, in the poetics of exile "the boundary becomes the place from which *something begins its presencing*" (*Location of Culture* 5). Claude McKay allies himself in a qualified way with the radical white literary establishment, radical black movements, the black working class, and also with gamblers, pimps, and prostitutes; he makes a major issue of his friendship with a down-and-out white thief. Yet he remains fiercely protective of his independence and qualifies all these alliances at one point or another, from Frank Harris to his buddies on the railway. His praise is usually followed by criticism or assertion of difference. He is the outsider as poet, as parvenu, and as black expatriate whose value is projected not in terms of original and initial subjectivities but in terms of performance on the road and a series of collaborative and conflictual, even hostile, relationships with a broad network of friends, acquaintances, and famous people.

In the absence of native space, each encounter and each reference testifies to heterogeneity of being and historical presence. Claude McKay identifies himself with Langston Hughes's "primitive Negro poems" in an attempt to explain the black intelligentsia's hostility to *Home to Harlem* (*Long Way* 322). Claude McKay also identifies selectively with Ernest Hemingway, Frank Harris, Hubert

Harrison, George Bernard Shaw, and many others, either directly or through praise of their work, their character, or values. Conversely, he readily distances himself from them with derogatory remarks or critical appraisal. He carefully distinguishes himself from Stanley Brathwaite (*Long Way* 26–28), the American expatriate crowd in Paris (*Long Way* 243), and Gertrude Stein (248, 265). He admires Du Bois's *The Souls of Black Folk* but is disapproving of his coldness and establishment demeanor (*Long Way* 109–11). Claude McKay defines himself in exilic space by establishing similarity and difference with others, partially through parasitic attachment to famous names and personalities and partially through gossip.[23] The nature of the vagabond precludes participation in the stabilizing rituals of community, and this militates against the stabilizing values of home that might serve as an organizing center for point of view, scales of comparison, approaches, and evaluations (Bakhtin, *Dialogic* 103) and might root the narrative in the United States as "native space" by choice.

In a conversation with Robert Stepto, Toni Morrison captures something of the motion-as-energy-as-creation that characterizes Claude McKay's self-portrait: "The big scene is the traveling Ulysses scene, for black men. . . . It is the Ulysses theme, the leaving home. And then there's no one place that one settles. . . . Go find out what that is, you know. And in the process of finding, they are also making themselves" (226). The creative energy that Morrison ascribes to black American geographic and social mobility is a dramatic point of cross-cultural connection between black American and a black Jamaican masculinist discourse in *A Long Way from Home*. It also clarifies the subversive dimensions of Claude McKay's self-characterization as vagabond. In Claude McKay's case the Ulysses theme appears inimical to the cultural consolidation at the heart of classic black American autobiography as both solitary and representative of the group.[24] Moreover, the image of self as vagabond is preformed; it is the idealized image of the writer in self-imposed exile, for whom self-definition is journey and achievement and empowerment is performance. Self-consciousness is organized around a public record of words, deeds, and acts. It does not represent an observable growth in character, only changes in status. As a representation of self, the text comes full circle: Claude McKay is troubadour wanderer and vagabond at the beginning and at the end. The mask is fixed for the duration of the performance with few missed cues. As Henry Louis Gates, Jr., observes of the "mask-in-motion" in "Dis and Dat": "Mask is the essence of immobility fused with the essence of mobility; fixity with transience; order with chaos; permanence with transience; the substantial with the evanescent" (89). The troubadour wanderer endures changes in fortune marked by a series of journeys and meetings, but he remains essentially the same. Maturity is accomplished in the transition from colonial Jamaica to the United States before the sequence of the narrative: "When I was a lad I wrote a rhyme about wanting to visit England and my desire to see the famous streets and places and the 'factories pouring smoke.' . . . Now that I had grown up in America and was starting off to visit England, I realized that I wasn't excited any more about the items I had named in my juvenile poem" (*Long Way* 59). Claude McKay conceals childhood and youth behind the mask of an accomplished state of being. In lieu of the interiority that might accrue from the evolution of being through childhood, adolescence, and young adulthood, self gains in complexity and substance through myriad encounters and a host of references to famous and little-known characters.

As an expatriate exercise, *A Long Way from Home* repeats and revises the Ulysses theme that Seacole inscribed in *Wonderful Adventures of Mrs. Seacole in Many Lands*. Both Claude McKay and Seacole are Jamaicans in quest of alternatives to a delimiting island environment. Once they abandon native space for a journey into the unknown, fame and fortune are a matter of survival. Seacole's narrative is organized around her accomplishments as a "doctress," while Claude McKay's narrative is organized around his accomplishments as a writer. In both cases the writers are pleading their case in an "alien" landscape and culture. Their record of service is both genuine and "illegitimate." The British War Office and Florence Nightingale's staff reject Seacole's offer of service in the Crimea. The black literary establishment denounces Claude McKay's most popular novels as politically incorrect (W. Cooper 244–45). Both are heavily dependent on white patronage and connections with the rich and famous as a way of establishing legitimacy and gaining acceptance. Though they recognize and honor Jamaica as originary space, their narratives celebrate departure and opportunities for self-fulfillment that are not available at home. Home as Jamaica is a value orientation, the nucleus of being and a point of departure. Though talents and ambitions are shaped in Jamaica, fulfillment is not linked to native community but to journey and relocation. Beyond issues of gender, class, and professional interest, a major point of difference in these texts published eighty-one years apart is in the relationship to the United States. In 1857 Seacole looks on the United States with justifiable horror as a slave society and feels grateful for the protection that her status as a British subject affords her. In 1938 Claude McKay is impatient with British colonialism and the brand of racism that he finds in England: "For England is not like America, where one can take refuge from prejudice in a Black Belt. I had to realize that London is a cold white city where English culture is great and formidable like an iceberg. . . . It was not built to accommodate Negroes" (*Long Way* 304). The United States remains Claude McKay's preferred home despite its history of racism and its continuing exploitation of its black citizens. The "Negro pale of America" acquires the matrix of meanings that Claude McKay associates with a sense of racial and cultural connectedness: the joy of being "just one black among many" in the shadows of Harlem (*Long Way* 95–96); the relief of living "in among a great gang of black and brown humanity" in Marseilles (*Long Way* 277); or feeling himself "singularly free of color-consciousness" in Morocco (*Long Way* 300). To the expatriate as troubadour wanderer, home is recoverable in black communities everywhere that Claude McKay feels "the strength and distinction of a group and the assurance of belonging to it" (*Long Way* 277).

Claude McKay carefully constructs a sense of being at home in New York as a site of rebirth and meaning-governed future. Returning to Harlem after a couple of years in England, Claude McKay describes the exhilaration of his homecoming in tribal terms: "At first I felt a little fear and trembling, like a stray hound scenting out new territory. But soon I was stirred by familiar voices and the shapes of houses and saloon, and I was inflated with confidence. A wave of thrills flooded the arteries of my being, and I felt as if I had undergone initiation as a member of my tribe" (*Long Way* 95). Claude McKay emphasizes a passionate attachment to New York's cityscape and allies himself organically with the black working class there. He selectively introduces his sense of otherness in the United States as class or ethnic conflict with the Harlem intelligentsia or the white literary establishment or his working-class buddies:

> I did not come to the knowing of Negro workers in an academic way, by talking to black crowds at meetings, nor in a Bohemian way, by talking about them in cafes. I knew the unskilled Negro worker of the city by working with him as a porter and long-shoreman and as a waiter on the railroad. I lived in the same quarters and we drank and caroused together in bars and at rent parties. So when I came to write about the low-down Negro, I did not have to compose him from an outside view. (*Long Way* 228)

Stating the case for cultural autonomy among Caribbean writers in *The Pleasures of Exile,* Lamming observes that a peasant and proletarian sensibility is the foundation of the new West Indian literature (38–39). Claude McKay's creative impulse is similarly driven by race, class, and his roots in the soil; however, in *A Long Way from Home* this does not foster Caribbean nationalism but a racial identification that transcends national boundaries. As it evolves, a compelling motivation of the text is the will to graft his distinctive cultural ethos onto the spirit and accent of black America.[25]

In *A Long Way from Home* Claude McKay's wandering comes to an end in North Africa. Morocco fulfills a personal quest for the meaning and value of race and class in the heterogeneous United States that grounds the troubadour wanderer; it signals the end of a journey that begins with Claude McKay's expatriate expectations of being at home in the United States. Claude McKay's quest for self-defining value beyond native space is linked from the outset to the relative values of race in personal and social relationships in the United States and in Jamaica. In the part called

"American Beginning" this is a point of discordance around which Claude McKay constructs an elaborate defense of his white friends that is authorized by no less a person than his Jamaican father, whose social relationships, as the author explains it, are governed by a keen sense of social justice and morality rather than race (*Long Way* 37–38). When Claude McKay leaves the United States for Russia in 1922, he describes the journey in terms of a quest for knowledge and freedom: "What could I understand there? What could I learn for my life, for my work? Go and see, was the command. Escape from the pit of sex and poverty, from domestic death, from the cul-de-sac of self pity, from the hot syncopated fascination of Harlem, from the suffocating ghetto of color consciousness. Go, better than stand still, keep going" (*Long Way* 150).

In differentiating himself from the white American expatriates in France, Claude McKay explains that unlike the others, "color-consciousness was the fundamental of my restlessness" (*Long Way* 245). In Fez he experiences complete freedom from race consciousness for the first time in his life (*Long Way* 300). When he "goes native" in Morocco, Claude McKay does not simply take up temporary residence in an alien and exotic landscape, because in Morocco he consciously goes home to Jamaica, racially and culturally. As he recounts in "The Idylls of Africa," his autobiographical quest ends there. Cultural heterogeneity acquires new meaning in Casablanca, when he finds Jamaican myalism reproduced in the social function of the "Guinea sorcerers (or Gueanoua), as they are called in Morocco" (*Long Way* 296).[26] Marrakesh is "like a big West Indian picnic, with flags waving and a multitude of barefoot black children dancing to the flourish of drum, fiddle and fife" (*Long Way* 304). The physical and psychic affinity that he feels with "the native element" clarifies the values of *native* as it is used throughout the narrative as a racial and group identification.

In Morocco he reactivates his relationship to the Jamaican landscape and people.[27] While living in Tangier, he begins writing *Gingertown,* a collection of stories set in both Jamaica and Harlem, and he finishes it in Xauen. He writes *Banana Bottom,* a classic novel

of return to the agricultural heartland of Jamaica, in Tangier in circumstances that reproduce the peasant rhythms of his life in
Jamaica.[28] He rents a dilapidated structure on more than an acre
about three miles outside town and settles down to the business of
subsistence farming and writing, with views of the sea and the
mountains of Spanish Morocco (*Long Way* 331; W. Cooper 274).
Claude McKay makes the house habitable and hires domestic help.
In keeping with his carefully constructed vagabond image as a man
who loves women and loathes domesticity, in *A Long Way from
Home* he glosses over the rhythms of his daily life in Tangier and
anything that might confirm his homosexual preference. Claude
McKay spends more time explaining the vagaries of his liaison with
"Carmina" than on the degree to which he "went native" in
Morocco while writing *Banana Bottom*. He is quite explicit about
the nature and fulfillment of his quest, but he remains secretive in
A Long Way from Home about the transformation of his values that
occurs in Morocco. In a mock-messianic voice in the final chapter,
"On Belonging to a Minority Group," Claude McKay delivers a
stern message of "group spirit and strong group organization" (350)
and makes playful reference to Marcus Garvey to underscore his
point about the cultural authority of the West Indian in the United
States: "A West Indian charlatan came to this country, full of anti-
quated social ideas; yet within a decade he aroused the social consciousness of the Negro masses more than any leader ever did"
(*Long Way* 354). This is both a disclaimer and a competitive self-
positioning. The troubadour wanderer has a new sense of purpose.
He plans to make the case for a "new" attitude toward group consciousness among black Americans, the fruit of a personal quest that
Claude McKay imbues with relevance for all of black America.[29]

In *My Green Hills* Claude McKay reverses the mask of the vagabond as troubadour wanderer, with its fundamental disregard for
national boundaries and native space as a way of inscribing self;
here he inscribes self in native space in the fixed terms of a vanished childhood and youth. Though the narrative ends with Claude
McKay's departure for the United States at the age of twenty-two,
the world he leaves behind remains intact; the departure of a
favorite son or Jamaica's emergence in national-historical time

does not threaten its continuance. The axiological center of the narrative is praise of an ancestral landscape that is peasant and New World African. The autobiographical hero is of idyllic descent. His childhood and youth are inscribed in the idyllic space of family and agricultural community. Despite the documentary quality of its emphasis on everyday life, Claude McKay's vision of the past is elemental. History surrenders to myth in a narrative of a childhood and youth that celebrates wisdom, goodness, justice, love, labor, and the harmonious condition of man and society in an idealized past.[30]

In *My Green Hills* the future intrudes minimally, with occasional references to the United States as time present, but these references all serve to enrich the past, to weight it with value. Describing the Madras handkerchiefs of village women, Claude McKay explains: "Some of them were knotted upon their heads in the kind of turban that is so fashionable in America today, and others were tied under the neck like American school girls wear them" (*My Green Hills* 1–2). Later, he compares mosaics in the old plantation houses to mosaics in Morocco, but the scales of comparison favor his Jamaican past rather than his mainland present: "Years later in Morocco I ran into some mosaics which reminded me of these old homes in Jamaica" (*My Green Hills* 57). Even more to the point, when Claude McKay makes a connection between his mother's premature death and his own, he establishes generational precedence; the past gains authority over the present and the future. "I never thought that in three decades I'd be laid low with the same disease" (*My Green Hills* 65). He portrays an event that belongs to the future as something that belongs to the past. After thirty-four years abroad, Claude McKay straightens the line of his destiny in an imaginative rerooting of self in the Jamaica of his childhood and youth. *My Green Hills* is a narrative of place as well as of childhood and youth. Every geographical, economic, and sociopolitical concretization roots the autobiographical hero in his native world. There is an organic grafting of self onto Jamaica as native place. The unity of the narrative is the unity of self and place. Native space is idealized space in autobiographical time; it transcends time as organizing center of value and essence of being.

The dimension of other in a harmonious childhood and youth that exists in the re-creation of a vanished place and time combines multiple pastoral paradigms and displacements, among them, the child cult, the proletarian cult, the folk cult, and the cult of the primitive (Ruhe 131, 133). Claude McKay evokes the pastoral values of innocence, simplicity, and nostalgia and the search for the primal in a constellation of pastoral images (McCleod 245–46, 253). Yet autobiographical values in the text are at odds with the spirit of the pastoral. The counterpastoral elements are most in evidence in the artistic autobiographical values that root the text in the real life events of family and agricultural community, however idealized and sublimated. Despite the pervasive garden imagery and the myth of an original innocence and harmony with nature and community, the title suggests that the author's alienation in the United States is double edged. There is alienation as well from "the clean green high hills of Jamaica" (*My Green Hills* 66), referenced in *A Long Way from Home* as a site of naiveté and expectations formed in ignorance of a wider world.

Claude McKay's combination of the agricultural and family idyll as a context for the elaboration of a myth of childhood and youth has a real Jamaican boyhood as its model. In his observations about the idyllic chronotope, Bakhtin differentiates between the agricultural family idyll and the conventional pastoral: "This form comes closest to achieving folkloric time; here the ancient matrices are revealed most fully and with the greatest possible actuality. This is explained by the fact that this form of the idyll uses as its model not the conventional pastoral life (which, after all, exists nowhere in such a form) but rather draws upon the real life of the agricultural laborer" (*Dialogic* 227). Claude McKay's positioning of self as peasant farmer, folk poet, and student is not merely ideological; it is profoundly spatial and concrete. The happy childhood of Claude McKay's Jamaican "Black Boy" stands in marked and perhaps calculated contrast to Richard Wright's record of childhood and youth published in 1945, the year before McKay began *My Green Hills*. Claude McKay is born into a landowning peasant family in Sunny Ville, a "sparsely populated village" of "about twenty-one families" in "the heart of the peasant farming district" (*My Green Hills* 1, 23). Claude McKay stresses the remoteness of the village, the fertility of the land, its abundance, its lushness, the rhythms of peasant life, the centrality of children, his family's rootedness in that life, and a harmonious relationship with the island as a whole.[31] He gives his family members heroic stature in the village, not simply because of their relative wealth as small landowners but because of their productive relationship with the village. They exist entirely and fully in the village; they are identical with the people and the place. Family lore has it that his father is Ashanti and his mother is Madagascan. He is Justice; she is Goodness (*My Green Hills* 61). These values are evident in their everyday engagement with each other and with the community. His brother, U'Theo, is educated in Kingston. He is a man who moves comfortably at all levels of society yet remains a man of the people. His education does not lead to expatriation but to renewed commitment to the land and community. He is not only the village teacher; he leases the nearby Palmyra estate from its English absentee owner and reclaims it as a productive village enterprise. His father runs a small sugar mill, but mechanization in the hands of his father, like U'Theo's education, does not disrupt the harmony of village life or its organic link with nature.

Natural disasters like flooding are temporary setbacks; they do not signal the breakdown and reconstruction of the society as in George Lamming's *In the Castle of My Skin*.[32] To Claude McKay disasters are elemental and strengthen community ties. Disruption and conflict, where they occur, are a direct result of British colonial mismanagement in the form of agricultural inspectors who give bad advice and missionaries who threaten to transform the religious faith of the community into religious intolerance. These negatives are transformed into positives in the towering figures of his father, mother, and brother. His father's sternness and strictness, though attributed to his Presbyterian upbringing, ultimately sustain family and community. Harmony of being is achieved through the rhythms of collective life and labor. When his mother dies, the grief is felt individually and in the community as a whole. While the death of his mother marks the end of Claude McKay's childhood in a formal sense, the harmony of life is restored in the rituals and customs of community. The village marks the occasion with an elaborate funeral and wake. She is buried on family property, "close to an orange tree, just a few paces from the house" (*My Green Hills* 64).

The organizing values of the narrative are the agricultural base of Claude McKay's life and his art as folk poet and narrator of this autobiography of childhood and adolescence. He downplays his beginnings as a poet to chart the peasant rhythms of his Jamaican life. Though autobiographical time traces the development of the barefoot peasant boy into folk poet and agricultural student, the progression of his life is framed by a collective life of labor and production. The mask of the troubadour wanderer is not yet formed. Claude McKay leaves Jamaica at the end of the narrative, but the general expectation is that he will return as an agricultural instructor. The final words of the text subvert this expectation, but Claude McKay describes his departure as an individual act and does not link it to disruption in collective life. In fact, in Sunny Ville his impending departure is a village event. Once his plans are set, Claude McKay returns to Sunny Ville to prepare for his departure: "Meanwhile I did a lot of planting. With the help of the peasants I planted yams and conga peas, black-eyed peas and red peas as well as sweet potatoes, yams and like things. There were about eight months before I would be ready to sail for America, so the peasants gave many tea meetings for me" (*My Green Hills* 83).

His departure is as much a collective event as his mother's funeral or preparing one's land for planting. "It was a kind of community work. Today one peasant was helped by the other peasants and the next day it was another peasant. So it went round and round until every peasant had his land cleared" (*My Green Hills* 29). Each departure from Sunny Ville in some way returns Claude McKay to the collective work-oriented base of the Jamaican peasantry. As a child of six, he moves to Montego Bay with U'Theo but returns seven years later to plant and harvest alongside his brothers and his father. Claude McKay leaves for Kingston with a view to cultivating the patronage of Walter Jekyll, an English gentleman living in Jamaica who had a keen interest in the music and stories of the Jamaican peasantry. Jekyll tutors Claude McKay in languages, literature, and philosophy and educates him to an appreciation of the folk base of Jamaican culture. Acting on Jekyll's advice, Claude McKay creates a series of poems in Jamaican dialect about the life of the island's urban and rural poor that are collected and published in Kingston as *Songs of Jamaica* and in England as *Constab Ballads,* in the year of his departure.

Claude McKay's focus on self as emergent folk poet is contextualized by native space, youthful innocence, and naiveté; by environment rather than horizons; by Jamaican life and culture rather than individual psychology and ambition. Despite intrusions of death, violence, and natural disasters like the great earthquake that struck Kingston in 1907, the Edenic image persists in retrospect. "The people of Jamaica were a curious lot—as if God had planted a lovely garden of humanity there. The greatest drawback in the island was its extreme poverty. Otherwise the different races of people lived very happily together" (*My Green Hills* 71–72); "then we also had Chinese and Indians, Hindus and Mohammedans, who married our native women and had beautiful children. As I have said, the people of Jamaica were like an exotic garden planted by God" (*My Green Hills* 72). The ideological underpinnings of this garden as a model of interracial and interclass harmony are markedly different from those of other gardens in the literature of Jamaican girlhood and adolescence, notably Erna Brodber's in *Jane and Louisa Will Soon Come Home,* Jean Rhys's in *Wide Sargasso Sea,* Margaret Cezair-Thompson's *The True History of Paradise,* and Patricia Powell's *The Pagoda.* In all these, images of entrapment and frustrated life menace the security and beauty of the garden. Fashioned from memory after more than thirty years abroad, Claude McKay conceptualizes his Jamaican garden as idyllic space. Its otherworldliness is fixed conceptually to the dimension of other in childhood and youth and in native space as an absolute ideal past.

In *My Green Hills* the mask of childhood and youth is a naive mask that facilitates the representation of self as living intensely and productively within a collective community. He gives childhood and youth archetypal value as a primal space of growth and renewal. Self is the creation of family and community. Together they represent the axiological thrust of the narrative. As Jamaican youth, the autobiographical hero gains substance through his participation in community life. Though the hero's difference is established, it is as a boy embarrassed by the talents that separate him from the other boys and later as a young man from his friends in the police force. Autobiographical values of this text seek identification with community rather than to memorialize the self's individual contribution to community. Claude McKay's stress on a happy childhood emphasizes the creative possibilities of the community as well as the exceptional child. *My Green Hills* clarifies the value of childhood as an image of identification. Parents, siblings, friends, patron, school, work, play, language and learning, sex and death—he evokes all the archetypal experiences of childhood. Childhood is a primal space that charts original landscapes of being. "In our reveries toward childhood, all the archetypes which link man to the world, which provide a poetic harmony between man and the universe, are, in some sort, revitalized" (Bachelard, *Poetics of Reverie* 124). In a national cultural context a harmonious Jamaican childhood and youth conceived within the matrixes of the agricultural and family idyll charts the rituals of survival and creation in an impoverished outpost of the British Empire. The narrative of liberation acquires new meaning in Claude McKay's willingness to reinscribe an idealized and sublimated Jamaican boyhood and youth as internal to his black American identity.

A Long Way from Home and *My Green Hills* are a lively contrast in autobiographical forms and values. One is premised on journey and quest and probes the roots of heterogeneous community beyond fixed cultural imperatives. The other is premised on reconnection with primordial beginnings in a vanished childhood and abandoned native space. Read as an autobiography in two parts, what begins as a physical journey in quest of knowledge, fame, and fortune in foreign lands ends in a mental journey of reconnection with an ancestral landscape and original state of being. In *A Long Way from Home* Claude McKay's vagabond troubadour, like Edward Said's traveler, is an archetypal wanderer who "crosses over, traverses territory, and abandons fixed positions" (Said, "Identity" 18). In *My Green Hills* the limitations of the vagabond as a sign of identification become explicit; Claude McKay abandons the carnival space of the crossroads in favor of native space as imaginative home and enabling ground. The journey back to the beginning is a springboard to one's ancestors; the journey's end is ultimately the consolidation of an ancestral landscape across diasporan time and space. The inversion of autobiographical values in the two narratives illuminates the ambivalence occasioned by the overlap and displacement of cultural difference. The affirmation of identity in each text enacts a transformation of the autobiographical subject, an illusory presence that is spatially split at the site of identification. Whether the site of choice is Harlem or Jamaica, the doubling, dissembling image of identity signals absence and loss and a longing for reconnection at the heart of the autobiographical process.

5

Blurred Genres, Blended Voices
George Lamming's *In the Castle of My Skin*

In the Castle of My Skin re-creates the author's childhood and adolescence in Barbados from the age of nine to the eve of his departure for the neighboring island of Trinidad when he was seventeen.
The narrative is both singular and collective; it is about one boy
among other boys and Creighton's Village, the village community
in which they grow up. The parallel that Lamming establishes
between one boy's childhood and the community that constitutes
it transforms that childhood into a symbolic embodiment of
Caribbean culture and society in the last stages of colonialism.
From the outset Lamming links his personal history to major
upheavals in the community that are cumulatively of disastrous
proportions: a devastating flood on his ninth birthday, an island-
wide strike and riots not long after, and the sale of the village land
to speculators shortly before he leaves his mother and friends for
his first job in Trinidad.[1] He sustains the parallel between the
child's world and the world of Creighton's Village unevenly to the
end; he links autobiographical time to village and island history
both embryonically and anagogically. The village is dismantled just
as he leaves the island. Though the autobiographical narrative is
by its very nature open ended, the boundaries of childhood and
adolescence give a certain degree of structural and thematic closure to the text's quest for self and artistic perspective in a vanished past.[2]

Lamming's autobiographical novel of childhood and adolescence is written against the anonymity and alienation from self and
community that the author experienced in London when he was

twenty-three. This narrative of reconnection and repatriation positions the written self as a developing sensibility within his native community. Lamming reconstructs the world of his childhood from the mixed perspective of the writer in exile and the child's understanding of his world: "In the desolate, frozen heart of London, at the age of twenty-three, I tried to reconstruct the world of my childhood and early adolescence. It was also the world of a whole Caribbean reality" (*Castle* xxxviii).[3] In this highly politicized narrative the past is situated in a network of values that project the sociocultural processes of the colonial Caribbean as facets of a childhood and, by the same token, give that childhood mythic status as evidence and example of those sociocultural processes at work. The elaboration of a myth of childhood reveals the underlying attitudes, thought systems, and ideals of a whole society. Childhood is "a destination in art arrived at by way of art."[4] It is a Bachelardian place of writing and renewal where artistic consciousness and historical conscience are formed.

Lamming's choice of genre suggests reservations about autobiography as the appropriate vehicle for reconstructing the vanished world of his childhood and adolescence. The autobiographical novel (as opposed to autobiography) signals a conflict between the author as subject and as creator of the narrative. A complex rhetorical design sustains the contradictory impulses of this self-conscious and self-celebrating text. Lamming's strategy is to split the narrative into contrastive but complementary first-person, omniscient, and dramatic modes of narration that blur the boundaries between author and authorial persona, and between the constitutive parts of the authorial persona. The first-person narrative is primarily the autobiographical account of a childhood filtered through memory and imagination, a portrait of the artist as a young man. The omniscient narrative is concerned with the problems of the community as others, adults and children, experience them, whether the child or adolescent could have perceived or understood the problems or not. The dramatic modules constitute an entirely different mode as they mime the speech of villagers—adults and children—in ironic encapsulation of facets of village life and the protagonist's consciousness, if not his experience.

Lamming identifies himself with the first-person narrator by giving the protagonist and narrator a designation that resembles his own name. Using "G." makes it clear that the protagonist is "other than" the author and serves an allegorical as well as autobiographical function within the narrative. Author and persona merge tentatively to acknowledge a coincidence in person between the two and also to establish the limits of self-equivalence. G. is clearly not the author at the time of writing, but their separate worlds coincide; the values that Lamming invests in the recreated world of his childhood and adolescence shape and form G. His fluid position at center and periphery of the text, as author and protagonist of an autobiographical fiction, is sustained and validated by the parallel and overlap between the narrative modules that share a common axiological center. The fluidity and reciprocity of narrative modes have the effect of fusing author and protagonist to a specific Caribbean reality.

Though each narrative mode has distinct functions, Lamming does not sustain clear-cut boundaries between them. The overlap of voice and function is evident early in the text. In the first chapter the first-person narrative moves casually between the alternative dimensions of childhood recreated, adult reflection, and ironic self-assessment. In the second chapter the focus of G.'s narrative shifts abruptly from the intimate details of a child who is interacting with his mother and neighbors to a sweeping characterization of the village community and the child's place in it: "Miss Foster. My mother. Bob's mother. . . . It seemed they were three pieces in a pattern which remained constant. The flow of its history was undisturbed by any difference in the pieces, nor was its evenness affected by any likeness. There was a difference and there was no difference" (*Castle* 24).

Immediately after this characterization of G.'s world as typical of a wider order, a depersonalized narrator, using signposts such as "one gathered" and "one could see" (*Castle* 25) to establish collectivity, delivers an authoritative political analysis of the feudal structure of village life (*Castle* 25–29).[5] G.'s village is reimagined with irony as a miniature Barbados, "the oldest and least adulterated of British colonies" (*Castle* 25). The transformation of G.'s village into symbolic British colony endows G.'s singular childhood with broad social significance: G. is a colonial child. By the end of the chapter the narrative returns to the pattern of everyday life in Creighton's Village, to recording the rituals of the public baths, of boys flattening pins and nails into blades on the railroad tracks, of Miss Foster, Bob's mother, and G.'s mother conversing under a cherry tree, "not thirteen, not thirty, but three" (*Castle* 33). There is little difference tonally in the narrative shift in focus from the feudal structure of Creighton's Village to the Queen's Birthday celebrations at Groddeck's Boy School [*sic*], where omniscient narrative ranges freely from the summary of conversations among the boys to the objective rendering of their conversations and lengthy stream-of-consciousness passages that reveal the inner turmoil of the headmaster.

The intertwining and overlap of distinct narrative modes intensify the ironic contrast, for example, between the self-referential quality of the first-person narrative and the broader social, historical, and cultural contexts of the omniscient narrative. The charged political consciousness of the omniscient narrative serves as a constant reminder of the difference between the alternative dimension of G.'s developing sensibilities and the author as creator of the text. As child and adolescent, G. is only partially aware of the constituents and situations of the world that encompasses him. As the imperfectly constituted hero and subject of his own narrative, G.'s individual life is validated and extended in the reciprocal narrative of the omniscient narrator, even as the distinction between the two spheres is neutralized in the metaphysical and artistic whole that is Lamming's autobiographical fiction. In the world of childhood re-created, each dimension of consciousness becomes a facet of Lamming's fully empowered imagination, imposing form and meaning on a life transformed into a symbol of the sociocultural processes of a specific time and place.

The multifaceted relationship between the contrastive and complementary modes of narration illuminates a dynamic relationship between writing and place, place and childhood. As subject of his own narrative, G.'s relationship to his village as a child and adolescent is passive and essentially filial. He listens, observes, and records. The house that he shares with his mother in the village is one of many. It embodies a common heritage. It provides the window that situates the eye and ear of a ballad memory. In the opening chapter G. is literally peering through the window or peeping through the jalousies (*Castle* 9, 22). The consonance between the inside and outside of G.'s village home represents the center and circumference of his vision. He is the creation of his colonial village, and its boundaries inscribe his sensibility. The entries in his diary in the last months before he leaves home confirm this (*Castle* 258–60). Yet G. is weakly assimilated into the collective community that constitutes his lived experience. His "love for the sprawling dereliction of that life" (*Castle* 224) is in conflict with a cultivated sense of difference, so that on the eve of his departure he feels no solidarity with his friends. The last entry in his diary reveals a deeply felt alienation: "When I review these relationships they seem so odd. I have always been here on this side and the other person there on that side, and we have both tried to make the sides appear similar in the needs, desires and ambitions. But it wasn't true. It was never true" (*Castle* 261). An ontological fear of self-revelation is linked to his deep-seated alienation from family, school, and community.[6]

The impersonal vision of the omniscient narrator replaces G.'s ontological fear with an overarching ideological identification with the plight of the villagers.[7] Autobiography is depersonalized and the "solitary" life of a child gains in coherence and intelligibility from the stories of Ma and Pa (his godfather) and from the stories of others, whether it is the story of the boy who is victimized by the headmaster's savage whipping or the story of Mr. Slime (the schoolteacher turned labor leader and land speculator) or the shoemaker. In the context of *In the Castle of My Skin* as a whole, the alternative consciousness of the omniscient narrator signals the development of a specific race and class consciousness in the author that is only marginally present in the developing subjectivity of G., by implication the author as a young man. This consciousness effectively transforms G.'s retreat from family, friends, and community as an adolescent hiding somewhere in the castle of his skin (*Castle* 261) into a retrospective that locates native community and territorial history at the axiological center of the autobiographical text.

Lamming resolves the problem of alienation by writing the essential unity of his life into a record of his childhood and youth; the act of writing identifies an essential link between origins and creative vision. The process of change begins in the Caribbean but is not resolved there. Before he leaves, his mother overhears him reading and rereading 14 John: "I go to prepare a place for you. And if I go and prepare a place for you, I will come again and receive you unto myself; that where I am, there you may be also" (*Castle* 280). Citing 14 John suggests that migration and return form a single arc in the thought-world of G. On the eve of his departure, though, this remains undeveloped in a text with an acute sense of a passing social order and the contradictory impulses that make his departure a necessary precondition of growth. Migration fulfills a process of colonial alienation, a young man's longing to escape, to establish a new identity (*Castle* 260). Return is the culturally symbolic act of the young writer who rejects the premise of starting "with a clean record" in another place (*Castle* 260) and self-consciously links the individual destiny of the writer in exile to native community.

During his interview by Kent, Lamming identified Richard Wright's *Black Boy* as an antecedent text that affects his understanding of the "backward glance" as a trope of migration and return:[8] "Speaking of Wright, the other day I came across an exercise book I used as a young boy . . . which would probably have a date like 1948, and I found pages and pages of *Black Boy* written out in ink. I remember very well this very long section where Wright is reflecting about leaving for the North" (96–97). Even a cursory reading of both texts illuminates the ideological underpinnings of *In the Castle of My Skin* as an autobiographical novel of return and reconnection. Lamming repeats and revises many tropes and rhetorical strategies that Wright used in representing a reality that is historically different from that of *Black Boy*. Whereas Wright leaves "without a qualm, without a single backward glance" (281), Lamming's protagonist-narrator is characteristically "takin' a last look at the place" (*Castle* 302) in the days before he leaves. Where Wright is confident, G. is full of apprehension, despite his desire to leave and shape a new identity (*Castle* 260).[9] Where Wright stresses books as the key to his survival and passion for life, Lamming privileges the oral traditions of his native community in his written record of childhood and youth. Whereas Wright's use of fictional techniques strengthens rather than mutes the narcissism inherent in autobiography, Lamming's blend of autobiography and fiction reconceptualizes the values of Wright's "exceptional Black Boy" to emphasize the collective experience rather than the individual predicament.

As in *Black Boy*, Lamming's primary concern with a developing male sensibility and evolving historical conscience calls attention to the gendered space of the text. Lamming rarely mentions girls, and, except for the prostitute, he associates women with domesticity. He characterizes the relationship between village mothers and sons as a struggle for parental control undermined by absent, irresponsible, or abusive fathers. Nameless schoolboys speculate that mothers are "stupid, that's why most of us [are] without fathers" (*Castle* 46). The devotion of these mothers is not questioned but their authority and guidance is. Lamming associates them with a religious and political conservatism in the society. As culture bearers they tend to the colonial hearth. Their creativity is the creativity of sexual reproduction and nurturance within a colonial system of values. G.'s mother raises him to advance within the colonial hierarchy of power, not to challenge it. Miss Foster is hostile to the overseer and worshipful of the landlord. Ma cannot accept social change that is not explicitly sanctioned by God and the landlord. As the embodiment of an ancestral colonial landscape that is both nurturing and delimiting, G.'s mother's influence is radically curtailed by an ongoing process of individuation and by her own limited comprehension of colonial politics. Lamming strives for a fine balance between the process of individuation that drives a wedge between G. and his mother and the bonds of mutual affection and appreciation that he memorializes in the text as a whole. However, the question of sexual difference is foreclosed when, as in this case, the autobiographical subject is male and the contradictions of colonialism converge on the maternal as polluting agent.[10] In the case of the prostitute who intercepts G. just before his departure for Trinidad (*Castle* 261), Lamming represents the feminine other as a radical evil that G. vehemently rejects.[11]

In *Reminiscences of Childhood* Richard N. Coe states the case for the autobiography of childhood and adolescence as an autonomous genre with "its own rules and its own inner structural laws, which are quite distinct from those of standard autobiography; it has its own archetypal patterns, its uniquely-delineated heroes and heroines, its experiences and motivations" (1). The entanglements of G.'s consciousness at various stages reveal an overarching concern with the ideas, attitudes, and values behind the archetypal experiences and encounters of his Caribbean boyhood, among them, uncelebrated birthdays, school, forbidden adventures at the beach and at an open-air prayer meeting, stealing into the landlord's compound, the strike and riots, and departure from home.[12] Each experience reveals something about systems of thought and value in the culture that engendered him; the archetypal figures of childhood and village life—mother, head teacher, fisherman, preacher, overseer, landlord, politician, the ancestral figures of Ma and Pa—emerge from these experiences. Each is a point of access in the process of recovering and memorializing the origins of selfhood in a vanished community.

Though the novel begins and ends with domestic scenes involving G. and his mother, the intervening text reveals G.'s interactions with boyhood friends and gives voice to a chorus of village boys who illuminate the world of other children in the village. G.'s individual predicament merges with that of other village boys and the adult world of social and political relations of which the child has only partial awareness. This is the technical cunning of Lamming's beginning. The flood that spoils G.'s hopes for a birthday celebration causes widespread destruction in the village. The parallel establishes individual difference and shared predicament. The fragility of the village outside parallels the fragility of G.'s family situation in the absence of an extended family. The flood invades G.'s house and the roof leaks. His mother reproaches him for his tears of disappointment and frustration: "I was wrong, my mother protested: it was irreverent to disapprove the will of the Lord or reject the consolation that my birthday had brought showers of blessing" (*Castle* 9). The details of a nine-year-old's disastrous birthday and his mother's attempts at comforting him with conventional Christian wisdom illuminate the text's ideologizing function. The flood is a direct link to the wider reality of the feudal structure of life in the village. The repairs to the village roads are the responsibility of a reluctant landlord who, the overseer's brother reports, cries "buckets of drops" (*Castle* 97) when he has to spend money developing and maintaining the village's infrastructure. The landlord and his family inspect the damage, and their privileged position in the village is internalized in the children's games: "When the carriage disappeared with the landlord and his family, small boys came out to rehearse the scene" (*Castle* 28). The white landlord is established as a dominant cultural influence in shaping village values and customs. When the lights are turned off at the great house, the villagers below receive it as a signal to do the same: "A custom had been established, and later a value which through continual application and a hardened habit of feeling became an absolute standard of feeling. I don't feel the landlord would like this. If the overseer see, the landlord is bound to know. It operated in every activity" (*Castle* 29).

The shift from standard English to Creole ("if the overseer see") makes multiple levels of irony clear. Lamming is linking the child's world to the world of colonial culture and politics, and the discontinuities in this linkage underscore his criticism of the mechanics of cultural production in Creighton's Village. The components of Lamming's vision of childhood are endowed with a series of precise significances that illuminate the child's world and the adult world that circumscribes it. The hierarchical and sequential linkage that Lamming establishes between school, church, and empire parodies the school ethos of classic texts of English childhood such as Thomas Hughes's *Tom Brown's School Days* (1858) and Rudyard Kipling's *Stalky and Co.* (1899). The occasion is the annual celebration of Queen Victoria's birthday with speeches, parades, and mindless displays of rote learning, followed by the annual distribution of pennies to the children. The English school inspector's speech reveals a fundamental conflict of interest: "The British Empire, you must remember, has always worked for the peace of the world. This was the job assigned it by God, and if the Empire at any time has failed to bring about that peace it was due to events beyond its control" (*Castle* 38). The speaker condemns the system in the act of praising it; linking the school's performance with the civilizing mission of the British Empire rings hollow in its parodic excesses and more so as the narrative unfolds. Lamming represents the archetypal figure of the great headmaster as a toady who guards his privilege as "village overseer" with smiles and fawning in his dealings with the English school inspector and with sadistic violence in his dealings with the schoolboys. The unfolding sequence of the education narrative intertwines the fixed values of the school inspector's sense of divine mission with the uncertainty of the boys, who ask key questions about Queen Victoria, slavery, freedom, and the minting of pennies and construct their own fanciful answers from a variety of contradictory sources. The paradox of the school is that it perpetuates ignorance and confusion among the children. Lamming's method of intertwining the contrasting preoccupations and levels of consciousness among the school inspector, the teachers, and the children places as much emphasis on how the village school culture functions as part of the colonial enterprise as on the effects of that culture on the socialization of the children.

The archetypal experiences of childhood are all charged with anticolonial sentiment. The day that G. spends at the beach with his friends is framed by their growing awareness of race, color, and class differences. G.'s imaginative reading of the clouds as social text reflects this. His mother's ambitions have already marked him as different from the other boys, and G. and Bob are surprised into a recognition of their growing mistrust of each other (*Castle* 110). From their curiosity about crabs mating to King Canute and an observed conflict between weddings and family life in the village, the boys are obsessed with language as a mechanism for explaining and understanding their environment. It is the basis for games and metaphysical inquiry. The boys are aware that words and experience are different dimensions and that understanding and negotiating the world are linked to one's facility with language on multiple levels. A reflective G. intervenes to put the boys' obsession with language in perspective: "Perhaps we would do better if we had good big words like the educated people. But we didn't. We had to say something was like something else, and whatever we said didn't convey all we felt" (*Castle* 154). The perceived conflict in values between the formal language of the educated colonial and the intuitive, creative, secret language of the boys signals the text's concern with language as cultural agency and with the foundational values of an oral tradition.

The boys' struggle to name and communicate their own reality occurs in a context quite distinct from those of school and home. The day at the beach opens up new horizons; it is a magical space away from the rituals of rote learning and colonial indoctrination: "We didn't notice it then, but when something bigger appeared like the sea and sand, it brought with it a big, big feeling, and the big feeling pushed up all the little feelings we had received in other places" (*Castle* 153). The beach is a site of discovery and magical transformations. The giant of a fisherman becomes a man: "Contact had made him human. Now he was like us. He was only big and strong, as we would say in the village, but he was like us" (*Castle* 153). They encounter and assimilate the awesome otherness of adult maleness as village giant. The fisherman's angry intolerance of their play is linked enduringly to his maleness, his blackness, his beauty, and his physical strength.

The distinction between myth and reality is difficult to maintain in a reconstruction of the vanished and essentially otherworldly past of a childhood. In Coe's study of autobiography and the experience of childhood, *When the Grass Was Taller,* the elusive borderline between the autobiography of childhood and the novel is a recurring point of reference:

> In the first place, the Childhood, like the traditional novel, is clearly structured with a beginning, a middle, and an end, and, as in the Aristotelian ideal of tragedy, the end is implicit in the beginning. In the second place, the balance between literal and symbolic truth is shifted in the direction of the latter. Incidents are given weight

in straight autobiography according to their factual significance; in the Childhood, more often than not, according to their emotional, imaginative, or metaphysical significance. (79)

In Lamming's novelization of childhood, G.'s development to maturity follows the autobiographical norm. G. is first seen with his mother, and he is operating within the confines of the immediate neighborhood. Later, as a boy among boys, there are secret excursions in which they scout and test the boundaries of the village on a forbidden beach and within the walls of the landlord's enclave. Finally, he is a young man among men on the eve of a momentous break with the circumscribed existence and understanding of a village youth. The process of individuation is the basic schema of childhood narratives as different as Richard Wright's *Black Boy,* James Joyce's *A Portrait of the Artist as a Young Man,* and Camara Laye's *L'Enfant noir.* Like each of these writers, Lamming alters literal facts in order to clarify the essential truth of his childhood as he understood it as an adult writing in England. In *In the Castle of My Skin* these changes accentuate rather than diminish the experiential archetypes of childhood even as these archetypes are recombined in patterns specific to his Caribbean experience.

In *In the Castle of My Skin* G. is organically connected to a concrete geographical and historical reality in specific references to the great flood, the strike and riots of 1937, and to World War II. These references, among others, locate G.'s mythical village in a real world in real time. Personal history is conceptualized as the foundation of and inspiration for autobiographical myth. Literal truth is sacrificed to symbolic truth but remains a visible, verifying context within the text itself. In *On Autobiography* Philippe Lejeune reflects on the issue of autobiographical verisimilitude in the ironic narrative of childhood:

In the classical autobiographical narrative, it is the voice of the adult narrator that dominates and organizes the text; although he stages the perspective of the child, he hardly lets him speak. This is completely natural: childhood appears only through the memory of the adult. . . . To reconstruct the spoken word of the child, and eventually delegate the function of narration to him, we must abandon the code of autobiographic verisimilitude (of the "natural") and enter the space of fiction. So it will no longer be a question of remembering, but of making up a childlike voice, this dependent on the effects such a voice can produce on a reader rather than on a concern for fidelity to a childlike enunciation, that, in any case, has never existed in this form. (53–54)

Lamming has been forthcoming about some of the liberties that he has taken with the factual circumstances of his life in writing *In the Castle of My Skin* (Paquet, *Novels* 13–14). In *The Pleasures of Exile* he writes that Pa's forced departure from the village actually occurred when he was about twelve and not when he left for Trinidad, as he says in *In the Castle of My Skin* (226). Lamming also acknowledges that Pa's house was moved to another village and that he was not sent to the almshouse, as in *In the Castle of My Skin*. Furthermore, Creighton's Village is actually a composite of two villages that he knew intimately as a child, Carrington's Village and St. David's (Munro and Sander). In yet another telling instance, Lamming chooses not to identify the role of his stepfather in his childhood. In each case, however, the novelization of childhood in *In the Castle of My Skin* does not represent a radical departure from the autobiographical norm.

The erasure of a stepfather underscores the myth of the male child "fathered" by a passionate, ambitious, and articulate mother and the ensuing anxieties and tensions of a maturing male subjectivity in the absence of grandparents, siblings, and other relatives: "My birth began with an almost total absence of family relations. My parents on almost all sides had been deposited in the bad or uncertain accounts of all my future relationships, and loneliness from which had subsequently grown the consolation of freedom was the legacy with which my first year opened" (*Castle* 12). A child's blank memory engenders loneliness and inquiry. The adult quest for self and community begins in the curiosity of a lonely child and continues in the broader theme of cultural orphanage that is the legacy of colonial history throughout the text. The absence of fathers measures an imbalance waiting to be corrected. One might argue that what matters here is not the historicity of autobiographical detail but the value that Lamming ascribes to his individual childhood as the key to a wider Caribbean reality. Novelization of the author's childhood gives the written text the self-sustaining integrity of a fictional life, condensed and controlled by an elaborate design. Creighton's Village is no static re-creation of a "typical" village. It celebrates and critiques the underlying unity of native space and mythicizes Lamming's authorial obsession with defining key features of the community that engendered him and his altered relationship to that community at the time of writing.

The polyphonic design of *In the Castle of My Skin* underscores ironic distance in Lamming's novelization of childhood and autobiography. The contrastive juxtaposition of first-person and omniscient narrative modes dominates the structure of the novel, but their authority over the narrative as a whole is muted by a host of village voices that complement and compete with the dominant discourses. Both the self-discursive G. and the omniscient narrator repeatedly defer to a chorus of village voices that name their own reality.[13] The oral traditions of the village are given qualified authority, from the child's fantastical reconstruction of social reality to Pa's dream vision (*Castle* xxxvi). Lamming casts G. as a listener as well as an observer.[14] Whatever G.'s motivation in keeping silent, his mother's words dominate their last supper together. G. spends that day at the beach with Trumper, Boy Blue, and Bob, and the other boys have a lot to say. G.'s narrative voice is reflective and descriptive, but he defers to the voices of the other boys, who narrate their own anxieties and speculations within the text, often with the minimum of intrusive commentary. The undiluted egotism of the child who expects his mother to produce a birthday cake while a flood is raging outside merges with the selves of others.

The same is true of the omniscient narrative. The anonymous narrator is at times intrusive and domineering, as in the description of the head teacher and the school inspector on the occasion of the Queen's Birthday (chapter 3) or in the description of the hierarchical structure of village life in which the overseer is given mythical monster value as an agent of colonial power (chapter 2).

On other occasions this authoritative voice surrenders to a villager's voice, most notably Pa's or Ma's or the shoemaker's, or the boys in Groddeck's Boy School. These characters are named allegorically according to their function in the village and in the text. Ma and Pa are the oldest inhabitants in the village and are barometers of different attitudes toward the fundamental changes occurring there. The boys are named simply First Boy, Second Boy, Third Boy, and the victim. Though depersonalized by their symbolic designation, their voices communicate directly and powerfully the individually and collectively felt cultural core of village life. In the process the village projects an autonomous life of its own that is independent of the values generated by the contrastive juxtaposition of the first-person and omniscient narratives that name and interpret the villagers and their world; these narratives also provide an occasion for them to express their own humanity. As facets of the written self, the villagers are given authority and interpretive power over the unfolding historical and political events that dominate their lives. The paradox of these village voices—natives of the split authorial persona—is that they lack the artist's perspective that would give their experiences the overarching significance that the author inculcates into the whole narrative: "The three were shuffling episodes and exchanging the confidences which informed their life with meaning. The meaning was not clear to them. It was not their concern, and it would never be" (*Castle* 25). The carefully constructed dialogue of characters like Ma and Pa, the shoemaker, and the boys and their mothers not only communicates an immediate sense of community with a vibrant moral and philosophical base but calls attention to the rich range of oral traditions that shape and sustain the community's questing spirit. The poetic tradition begins here in "the regular pattern of talk that filled the villager's life" (*Castle* 92).[15]

The individualized voices of the village introduce a folkloric content that humanizes and intensifies native space and affirms its underlying unity in a national-historical context.[16] Pa and Ma introduce a generational time that is epochal. Pa's dream vision of the enslavement and forced resettlement of Africans in the New World is a memory that he struggles to retrieve in a self-induced hallucinatory state; it is not an operative part of village consciousness. At the other end of the time continuum the children signal a changing village consciousness. They shock their mothers with their mockery of the "white gentl'man": "Look, look what fowlcock do,/Look what fowlcock do to you" (*Castle* 21). Many years later Trumper returns from the United States with a new idiom of race consciousness and political activism that is different from the values that Pa developed during a comparable stint of migrant labor in Panama many years earlier. Where Pa dream-speaks the fragmented psyche of the New World African whole, the post-America Trumper articulates it in casual conversation.

The village voices are different, but they share common preoccupations about their changing world. Apart from Brother Dickson, they use a common language, what [Edward] Kamau Brathwaite calls the nation language of a submerged/emerging culture (*Roots* 261, 266).[17] This emphasizes the personal-historical gap between the split authorial persona and the villagers. However, the centrality of a wide range of village voices speaking in their own language also emphasizes the underlying bond of sympathy and appreciation that links the split authorial persona in exilic space and time to native space.[18] The line of demarcation between the split authorial persona and the author in *In the Castle of My Skin* might be compared with the collapsing fence between G.'s yard and Bob's (*Castle* 16–17). The ideological foundations of this tripartite sensibility are clarified by an interpretive model that Lamming provides subsequently, in *The Pleasures of Exile*:

> The West Indian novel, by which I mean the novel written by the West Indian about the West Indian reality is hardly twenty years old. . . . The education of all these writers is more or less middle-class Western culture, and particularly English culture. But the substance of their books, the general motives and directions, are peasant. . . . It is the West Indian novel that has restored the West Indian peasant to his true and original status of personality. (38–39)

Lamming treats the West Indian novel as a cultural icon, evidence of a specific class consciousness and cultural practice.[19] These values dominate the autobiographical essay that concludes *The Plea-*

sures of Exile. In "Journey to an Expectation" Lamming invades the self-regulating aspect of *In the Castle of My Skin* with an auto-biographical tribute to Papa Grandison, who died shortly after *In the Castle of My Skin* was published. In the process Lamming clarifies the ideological underpinnings of his use of autobiography in *In the Castle of My Skin.* He gives a short interpretive account of what Papa Grandison meant to him as a child and explains the expulsion of Papa Grandison from their village as the compelling motivation behind the writing of *In the Castle of My Skin* (*Pleasures* 228). Lamming quotes the last page and a half of the text and represents the ending as a colonial manifestation of race and class consciousness.

Independent of the retrospective intervention of "Journey to an Expectation," the last pages of *In the Castle of My Skin* provide several clues that Pa/Papa is a privileged ancestral other in this narrative of the fatherless child. Not only does Pa's "last look at the place" coincide with G.'s departure from the village but at their last meeting it is Pa who names the situation: "'We both settin' forth tomorrow,' he said. 'I to my last restin'-place before the grave, an' you into the wide wide world'" (*Castle* 302). Pa names the structure of *In the Castle of My Skin* "before" it is written. Speaking in folkloric time of major upheavals—of floods, riots, and landlessness—the old man observes that the sale of the village lands and the forced relocation of many villagers was implicit in the devastating floods that spoiled G.'s birthday (*Castle* 303). The ideological value of G.'s sympathetic identification with Pa as "a colonial symbol of traditional man" (*Pleasures* 229) is implicit in the form of the text. However, Lamming's retrospective intervention reiterates autobiographical discourse as an aspect of the text's ideologizing function. The denial of authorial ego implicit in the elaborate architecture of *In the Castle of My Skin* might be described as "a natural-naive isolation, a relative isolation, and not an isolation in principle, not an aesthetic isolation" (Bahktin, *Art* 165). In its rhetorical design, *In the Castle of My Skin* represses autobiography, but Lamming's retrospective commentary emphasizes the author's wish to root the text in personal-historical experience. The commentary provides interpretive cues for a reading of the form and the content of the text that calls attention to its autobiographical center.

The relationship between autobiography and fiction is as fluid as the relationship between narrators in the text. In his introduction to the 1983 Schocken edition of *In the Castle of My Skin*, Lamming reverses his emphasis on autobiography in "Journey to an Expectation," which appeared in *The Pleasures of Exile*. He represents collectivity as both the form and the substance of the text as autobiographical novel: "The book is crowded with names and people, and although each character is afforded a most vivid presence and force of personality, we are rarely concerned with the prolonged exploration of an individual consciousness. It is the collective human substance of the village that commands our attention. The Village, you might say, is the central character" (*Castle* xxxvi). Here Lamming changes his emphasis on the rhetoric of autobiography in "Journey to an Expectation" to the rhetoric of collectivity, from a personal gesture to a meditation on the process of meaning production and on his own changing values. The discourse shifts from the authorial subject as survivor and living witness to the typicality of the narrative, from the "me" in the text to the "me" writing and reading the text. Thus he treats his decision to leave G.'s mother nameless in the text as an example of the symbolizing process at the heart of *In the Castle of My Skin*: "The mother of the novel is given no name. She is simply G.'s mother, a woman of little or no importance in her neighborhood until the tropical season rains a calamity on every household; and she emerges, without warning, as a voice of nature itself" (xxxvi). Authorial ego is sacrificed in a self-celebrating creativity. G.'s mother is transformed into a symbol of community when she initiates the pattern of call and response, when her particular voice prompts a chorus of other voices in recognition of their shared plight.

Lamming characterizes the book that he published thirty years earlier and offers the reader guidance about the right way to read it. He uses his 1983 introduction to *In the Castle of My Skin* as the occasion to restate a theory of the Caribbean novel that he had conceptualized in *The Pleasures of Exile*:

The Novel has a peculiar function in the Caribbean. The writer's preoccupation has been mainly with the poor; and has served as a way of restoring these lives—this world of men and women from down below—to a proper order of attention; to make their reality the supreme concern of the total society. But along with this desire, there was also the writer's recognition that this world, in spite of its long history of deprivation, represented the womb from which he himself had sprung, and the richest collective reservoir of experience on which the creative imagination could draw. (*Castle* xxxvii)

This emphasis on the specific ideology of his art as generic Caribbean writing is a conscious attempt to encode his artistic intent, just as he had done in *The Pleasures of Exile*. He calls attention to the conditions of writing in the Caribbean, both in terms of the writer's relationship to his native space as threshold to community and creativity and also to his changing values and his changing audience.

Lamming's changing emphasis from one retrospective commentary to another appears relative to the material circumstances of the publication. *The Pleasures of Exile* was published first in England in 1960, while Lamming's introduction to *In the Castle of My Skin* was published first in the United States in 1983. In the latter Lamming adds a new catalogue of concerns about the ideological underpinnings of the text. He reflects "on the role which America was to play in shaping the essential features of the novel" (xl). He clarifies Trumper's sojourn as a migrant laborer in the United States as a salutary one, to the extent that he returns with a new understanding of the political and cultural significance of race and "with a political experience which the subtle force of British Imperialism had never allowed to flourish in the Islands" (xli). These themes are explicit in *In the Castle of My Skin*, but Lamming places new emphasis on them in the 1983 interpretive retrospective.

Lamming's anxieties about how the text is read reveal an interesting autobiographical twist. Having made a case for *In the Castle of My Skin* as a generic Caribbean text, Lamming subverts the privilege that he claims for the text-context relationship by questioning the method and ideology that shaped the text. He enters into a dialogue with himself about the artistic integrity of his portrayal of the 1937 riots in Barbados. It is both defense and critique: "The novelist does not only explore what had happened. At a deeper level of intention than literal accuracy, he seeks to construct a world that might have been; to show the possible as a felt and living reality. So for a long time I remained haunted by the feeling that the white landlord should have been killed; even if it were presented as the symbolic end of a social order that deserved to be destroyed" (xl).[20] In *In the Castle of My Skin* the dialectics of fiction and autobiography do not exist as simple reciprocity. Like Bachelard's dialectics of inside and outside, "they are always ready to be revised, to exchange their hostility" (Bachelard, *Poetics of Space* 218).

In the Castle of My Skin is a modern Caribbean classic.[21] Not only does it contain valuable insights about childhood and society in the colonial Caribbean at midcentury but the elaborate and unconventional structure of the narrative provides an interpretive framework for investigating the text in its own historical moment and in ours as well.[22] Lamming's choice of genre reveals an author who is skeptical about unmediated autobiography. The splitting or doubling of the authorial persona into lyrical voice and collective chorus makes autobiographical discourse the subject matter and content of the text. The limitations of G. as a maturing sensibility suggest the limitations of the lyrical hero as narrating consciousness. However, *In the Castle of My Skin* is fundamentally celebratory of self and community in the link that it establishes between origins and artistic vision. G.'s departure is prelude to reconnection and return. The autobiographical novel is a narrative space that fuses artistic consciousness to the symbolic native space as imaginative home and enabling ground that "the castle of my skin" suggests.

In *In the Castle of My Skin* Lamming reconceives the literary topos of the castle in the gothic, or "black," novel as a metaphor for the reclamation and restoration of his New World African

Caribbean village ancestry. He converts the "castle," or plantation great house, as an image of feudal domination into a metaphoric space that privileges the village's history, its dynastic primacy, family archives, ancestral portrait gallery, legends, and traditions.[23] In the narrative space of Lamming's black "castle," autobiographical return is rendered obliquely as an autobiographical novel of childhood and adolescence, and the authorial "I" is suppressed and circumscribed as narrator of his own story.

6

Autobiographical Frameworks
and Linked Discourses

George Lamming's *The Pleasures of Exile* and C. L. R. James's *Beyond a Boundary*

George Lamming replays the autobiographical and elegiac under-pinnings of *In the Castle of My Skin* in a different key in *The Pleasures of Exile*, which ends with a retrospective of *In the Castle of My Skin*, quoting in full the last page and a half of the autobiographical novel. Cross-referencing and retelling the story of the callous eviction of his late godfather, Papa Grandison, from his home as an old man, Lamming rewrites the autobiographical pact: "The meaning of Papa's departure is the story of *In the Castle of My Skin*" (*Pleasures* 228).

> Papa was a colonial; so am I; so is our once absolute Prospero. For it is that mutual experience of separation from their original ground which makes both master and slave colonial. To be colonial is to be in a state of exile. And the exile is always colonial by circumstances: a man colonised by his incestuous love of a past whose glory is not worth our total human suicide; colonised by a popular whoredom of talents whose dividends he knows he does not deserve; colonised by an abstract conscience which must identify its need with another's distress through a process of affection called justice; colonised by the barely liveable acceptance of domestic complaint; colonised, if black in skin, by the agonising assault of the other's eye whose meanings are based on a way of seeing he vainly tries to alter; and ultimately colonised by some absent vision

132

which, for want of another faith, he hopefully calls the Future. (*Pleasures* 229)

Out of this memorial to Papa Grandison, Lamming fashions a renewed commitment "to change the meaning and perspective of this ancient tyranny" (*Pleasures* 229). To this end he fashions a dialogue with classic texts of imperialism and decolonization, Shakespeare's *The Tempest* and C. L. R. James's *The Black Jacobins*, quoting liberally from both and creating a countertext of his own in the process.[1]

The Pleasures of Exile incorporates the memoirs of Lamming's life as a young writer in self-imposed exile in England and his travels in the Caribbean, West Africa, and the United States in a series of interrelated essays on cultural politics. Like Edward Said's traveler on a ceaseless quest for knowledge and freedom, Lamming occupies different geographical and cultural spaces, uses different idioms, assumes a variety of disguises, masks, and rhetorics (Said, "Identity" 18) in a shifting combination of playfulness and seriousness, irony and commitment. In this respect *The Pleasures of Exile* anticipates the postcolonial critic's preoccupation with the politics of migration, cultural hybridity, and the prerogatives of minority discourse. Beyond this, the politicized, self-celebrating subjectivity of the author as traveling writer and resistant colonial subject clarifies issues around the mediation of literary production in postcolonial discourse. In *The Pleasures of Exile* Lamming conjures up a specific subjectivity, his own, as evidence and example of a wide range of intellectual, psychological, and cultural responses to colonialism. He self-consciously renders the text as an alternative discourse with an ideological bias specific to his experience as colonial subject and calls attention to its own artfully rendered ideological bias as part of a dynamic process of cultural production and consumption in a period of decolonization.

As intellectual history, *The Pleasures of Exile* is specific to the colonial Caribbean; it also illuminates the coercive, transgressive processes of meaning production in colonial societies everywhere. Underlying the text is a theory of language, discourse, and representation that transforms the author as colonial subject and consumer of British intellectual and cultural history into a self-conscious producer of alternative discourses. Lamming calls attention to the performative function of the text, to its autobiographical framework and its dialogic intent. His goal is "the dismantling of a colonial structure of awareness" (*Pleasures* 36). With the assumed authority of a transgressive cultural presence, he critiques British cultural institutions from Shakespeare to the Institute of Contemporary Arts, the BBC, the *Times Literary Supplement,* and the *Spectator.* Lamming names an alternative hierarchy of values that is rooted in his childhood, the Caribbean of the Haitian ceremony of the souls, C. L. R. James's *The Black Jacobins,* and a community of writers from the colonial Caribbean.

Anticipating challenges to his alternative discourse, Lamming plays with assumptions of cultural authority as an artifice to which he, and others like him, are also entitled: "It will not help to say that I am wrong in the parallels which I have set out to interpret; for I shall reply that my mistake, lived and deeply felt by millions of men like me—proves the positive value of error. It is a value which you must learn" (*Pleasures* 13). His dissenting voice is personal and collective.[2] As colonial subject, Lamming offers himself as a representative text to be read and as a privileged interpreter of his own historical moment. The form and value of his organizing and legitimizing presence in the text lies in the relationship between self-reflection and the performance of critical reading. He is observer of his own experience and of a wide range of experiences within his cultural domain as colonial subject. Self acquires meaning and value as part of a pattern of Caribbean migration, Caribbean writing, colonial servitude, and a tradition of resistance and revolt. The controlling "I" of this multivoiced text is a plurality of texts, generating a multiplicity of meanings that determines the text's shifting value as method and document of cultural and intellectual history.

The very title of the text, *The Pleasures of Exile,* suggests the paradox and ambiguity of spatial and psychic disjunction wrought by the whole etiology of the Caribbean as a colonial enterprise that took on a life of its own as a distinct cultural entity while still subordinate to, and dependent on, the discourses of empire for self-definition. The pleasure of the text lies in its play on the para-doxical and unorthodox.[3] Exile is a site of both alienation and reconnection:

> This may be the dilemma of the West Indian writer abroad; that he hungers for nourishment from a soil which he (as an ordinary citizen) could not at present endure. The pleasure and the paradox of my own exile is that I belong wherever I am. My role, it seems, has rather to do with time and change than with the geography of circumstances; and yet there is always an acre of ground in the New World which keeps growing echoes in my head. I can only hope that these echoes do not die before my work comes to an end. (*Pleasures* 50)[4]

The writer in exile is the subject and vehicle of Caribbean cultural and intellectual history here; the value of his individual life is embedded in a productive, transformational relationship to the Caribbean as a point of origin. Cultural ambiguity is evidence of both cultural resistance and synthesis.[5] The writer as traveler and expatriate links his destiny to the circumstances of his birth and his history as a necessary beginning.

The ideological "I," distinctly committed to the new world of the Caribbean as a decolonized space, takes precedence as the foundation of self and discourse: "I do believe that what a person thinks is very much determined by the way that person sees. This book is really no more than a report of one man's way of seeing, using certain facts of experience as evidence and a guide" (*Pleasures* 56). Perspective is expressive of resistance, commitment, and self-celebrating creativity. It emphasizes the substance and method of the writer's calculated decentering of colonial discourse as the exclusive privilege of British intellectuals and institutions. In "What the Twilight Says" Derek Walcott writes about "the learning of looking" that restores the subject colonial writer to the original space of his birth and his personal history as a necessary begin-ning: "My generation had looked at life with black skins and blue eyes, but only our own painful, strenuous looking, the learning of looking, could find meaning in the life around us, only our own strenuous hearing, the hearing of our hearing, could make sense of the sounds we made" (9).[6]

In *The Pleasures of Exile* Lamming demystifies perspective as an intellectual process that resituates the colonial writer as an active agent of decolonization. Lamming makes his way of seeing the subject and method of the text. He reconstitutes the idiosyncrasies of his writerly disposition, chance encounters, and unusual events as representative of the sociocultural processes of colonialism in his own time. Each fragment, each shift in the dialogic mode of discourse, each new combination of description, reflection, and analysis reveals or confirms some facet of the author's personal experience as evidence and example of the cultural conditioning of British colonialism and his commitment to dismantling "the colonial structure of awareness which has determined West Indian values" (*Pleasures* 36). The discursive space of the text is a self-authorizing, self-interrogating space that rejects the cultural authority of the Institute of Contemporary Arts, the BBC, the *Times Literary Supplement,* or the *Spectator* over the apportionment of value in the Caribbean and in the world.

Autobiography might seem incidental in such a politically charged text, yet its framework is fundamental to the occasional nature of the text and to the task of dismantling a colonial structure of awareness as Lamming conceptualizes it. There is no troubling delay between the moment of critique and the activity of political resistance. Lamming calls attention to the autobiographical framework of the text in chapters such as "The Occasion for Speaking," "Evidence and Example," and "A Way of Seeing." He represents himself as both witness to and participant in a great collective movement. He constructs the prototypical paradigm of the colonial exile around his own high degree of historical awareness and resistant consciousness as a Caribbean writer. The author as narrator and subject of the text is a highly visible and audible presence. The narrating "I" is authoritative, combative, and judgmental and is identified with the author quite explicitly. Self-imaging is skewed purposefully to personal reminiscences as method and substance of a self-authorizing Caribbean intellectual history: "In order to take you on the inside of what I know, I shall have to draw on what an older man would justly call his reminiscences" (*Pleasures* 24). Self-focus enhances rather than diminishes authority; it serves to establish the author's credibility in a cultural space of his own creation.

In *The Pleasures of Exile* Lamming locates himself in autobiographical time and space as a Caribbean writer in self-imposed exile in London at the age of thirty-two (*Pleasures* 50), without committing himself to an account of his life in England. The discursive space of the text shifts continually from multiple sites of marginality—London, Africa, the Caribbean, and North America—contesting old notions of self and story and destabilizing generic margins. Yet Lamming struggles to stay rooted in his original space, the activating dynamic of his writerly resistance. His voluntary exile is not the alienation of "the neurotic intellectual," alone and rudderless (152); he identifies with a historically aware, resistant community of creative writers, scholars, and activists from the Caribbean and the greater Americas "that started as an alternative to the old and privileged Prospero, too old and too privileged to pay attention to the needs of his own native Calibans" (152). His dialogue with C. L. R. James, identified as an inspirational fellow traveler, models an intellectual community: "There was neither master nor slave, but two West Indians sprung from two different islands of the Caribbean, separated by some twenty-five years, talking from two different generations, talking always about their world, and talking, therefore, about a world infinitely wider than their islands; for the new world of the Caribbean is, in the time sense of the world, the Twentieth Century" (*Pleasures* 152). The two share a perspective but see differently. Conversation among equals supersedes the colonizing imperative of the teacher as master.

Throughout his extended dialogue with C. L. R. James's *The Black Jacobins*, Lamming's persona identifies him with a tradition of resistance and lays claim to the Haitian Revolution as a facet of his New World African Caribbean identity on behalf of the whole Caribbean. In West Africa and in the United States the authorial persona is the traveling colonial who measures the meaning of his condition in alternative contexts for self-definition. Whether he is covering the funeral of King George VI for the BBC, driving from Kumasi to Zaria, or exploring Harlem, the sense of contributing to a Caribbean destiny is pronounced (*Pleasures* 50). The narrator's pervasive sense of participating in a great historical moment determines the autobiographical values; his valuable life surrenders its meaning in a gesture of collectivity.

In the shifting symbolic codes that Lamming uses in his introduction, he is prosecutor, defense counsel, witness for the defense and for the prosecution, and hangman (10–12). In addition to these interpretive cues for reading the self's place and importance in the world, Lamming sketches in an interactive theoretical framework that roots the ideological position of the author in his exemplary flawed status as colonial. The dominant contexts for ideological positioning are the Haitian ceremony of the souls, *The Tempest,* and *The Black Jacobins.* Lamming uses them to situate his personal experience as evidence and example of colonial alienation and exile transformed into a site of liberation. The shifting frames of identity in *The Pleasures of Exile,* from "the field of vision to the space of writing," from personal experience to public debate, is a disputed colonial space that spans Africa, the Americas, and Europe, geographically and culturally, and anticipates many of the arguments regarding the Barthian Deep Me, the Written Me, the Subaltern and Postcolonial Subject in postcolonial discourse (Bhabha, "Interrogating Identity" 6).

Lamming repeatedly calls attention to the dialogic nature of the text, to the "I" that writes out of the oppositional space of otherness as a way of dismantling the monologic imperative of colonial history: "This book is based upon facts of experience, and it is intended as an introduction to a dialogue between you and me. I am the whole world of my accumulated emotional experience, vast areas of which remain unexplored. You are the other, according to your way of seeing me in relation to yourself" (*Pleasures* 12). Lamming's emphasis on dialogue contextualizes the aggressive intent of the text, in which dialogistic and conversational overtures periodically assume the contentiousness of a public trial.

In a discursive shift from one cultural context to another, Lamming uses *The Tempest* to schematize the terms of dialogue: "It is my intention to make use of *The Tempest* as a way of presenting a certain state of feeling which is the heritage of the exiled and colonial writer from the British Caribbean" (*Pleasures* 9).[7] Though the narrator identifies himself as a descendant of both Prospero and Caliban, his sympathetic identification is with Caliban in the oppositional discourse that follows. Lamming wraps himself in the plural symbolic cultural codes of Caliban "as a landscape and human situation" (119) and tailors his self-image as cultural historian and critic to a Caliban who never loses "the spirit of freedom" or "his original sense of rootedness" (101), who "keeps answering back" and refuses to be silent (102). Transformed into a twentieth-century cultural icon, Lamming's Caliban recognizes and uses his enslavement by Prospero as a transformative juncture: "Caliban had got hold of Prospero's weapons and decided that he would never again seek his master's permission. That is also my theme: a theme which embraces both literature and politics in our time" (*Pleasures* 63). Caliban's wide-awake resistance is a calculated response to oppression, evil, and mystification. Caliban as symbol of ignorance and savagery in Shakespeare's imperialist discourse is refashioned in Lamming's liberationist discourse as symbol of heroic resistance. In the nineteenth-century Caribbean, Caliban is Toussaint L'Ouverture, architect of the Haitian Revolution. In 1938 he is C. L. R. James celebrating Toussaint's military victory as a Caribbean epic in *The Black Jacobins*. In 1960 Caliban is the historically aware resistant colonial writer from the British Caribbean.

The verbal aggressiveness of Lamming as latter-day Caliban carries something of an apocalyptic threat: "The time is ripe—but may go rotten—when masters must learn to read the meaning contained in the signatures of their former slaves. There may be more murders; but Caliban is here to stay" (*Pleasures* 63). The stridency of tone that characterizes the book as a whole and the invective that Lamming reserves for the "colour-baiters" and "culture-vultures" of the Institute of Contemporary Arts (83), and for the reviewers of the *Times Literary Supplement* and the *Spectator* (28–29), illuminate another facet of exemplary flawed self-imaging in the text. The authorial persona, as Caliban, creates multiple spaces for the frank expression of personal bitterness, distrust, cynicism, irony, defiance, and jubilation in the text's characterization of self as colonial other, writing himself and his Caribbean reality into existence at the heart of empire.[8]

Lamming's appropriation of Caliban as exemplary flawed revolutionary hero who models the ambiguities of the resistant liberationist spirit of his time and place initiates a text-based counterdiscourse around *The Tempest* in the modern Caribbean that incorporates complex issues of identity, authority, and freedom.[9] Lamming uses the facts of his own migration to London, as part of a larger migrating labor force from the Caribbean after World War II, to investigate issues of cultural and psychological dependence that O. Mannoni and Frantz Fanon had explored in regard to Madagascans and Antilleans. In contrast to Mannoni's use of Caliban to demonstrate his theory of the dependency complex of colonized peoples, Lamming creates a different set of values around Shakespeare's fictive Caliban and stakes out his own position on Caribbean language and culture in the process: "The old blackmail of Language simply won't work any longer. For the language of modern politics is no longer Prospero's exclusive vocabulary. It is Caliban's as well; and since there is no absolute from which a moral prescription may come, Caliban is at liberty to choose the meaning of this moment" (*Pleasures* 158). While Lamming's observations on cultural dependency in the British colonies of the Caribbean complement Fanon's in *Black Skin, White Masks,* Lamming stresses the difference between language as agent of colonization and that language rechristened as the product of Caribbean endeavor, between the language of Shakespeare and the language of C. L. R. James: "This gift of Language is the deepest and most delicate bond of involvement. It has a certain finality. Caliban will never be the same again. This gift of Language meant not English, in particular, but speech and concept as a way, a method, a necessary avenue towards areas of the self which could not be reached in any other way. Caliban's future . . . the very name for possibilities—must derive from Prospero's experiment" (*Pleasures* 109). In *The Pleasures of Exile* this gift of language is an ambiguous space that can fertilize and extend the resources of human vision beyond the colonizing process.

Though intended as a prison of service and measure of superiority, language is created anew in the Caribbean (*Pleasures* 110–11, 119). If language as education is "the first important achievement of the colonising process" (109), a colonial "education" paradoxically nurtures historical awareness and a spirit of resistance in the case of Toussaint L'Ouverture and of C. L. R. James, Lamming, and a community of named Caribbean writers. *The Pleasures of Exile* is evidence and example of this paradox at work.

In "Caribbean and African Appropriations of *The Tempest*," Rob Nixon notes the double incongruity of Caribbean and African intellectuals' use of a canonical European text like *The Tempest*, "given Shakespeare's distinctive position as a measure of the relative achievements of European and non-European civilizations" (560). Roberto Fernández Retamar calls it "an alien elaboration, although in this case based on our concrete realities" (16). The perceived incongruity of the Caribbean intellectual's use of the play models the process of assimilation and transformation that C. L. R. James describes in *Beyond a Boundary* as the genesis of a Caribbean-based regional identity. In C. L. R. James's classic text a passion for Thackeray nurtures a spirit of liberation, a model British public school education in Trinidad produces a pan-Africanist and nationalist, Caribbean mastery of English cricket transforms a ritual of colonial dominance into a ritual of resistance and national pride.[10] Within the contradictory legacies of colonialism, genius subverts and transforms the structures that were meant to confine it. The perceived incongruity in fact models an ideological and aesthetic resolution of the historical and cultural contradictions of the multiethnic, multiracial, polyglot Caribbean. Lamming's ideological and aesthetic commitment is to the production of the culture of a new society after centuries of colonial rule; the migration of themes from one era to another is dialectical.[11]

Lamming's selective reading of *The Tempest*, followed by an equally selective reading of *The Black Jacobins*, demonstrates this creative process at work in the colonial Caribbean. The emerging discourse invests specific cultural authority in the written word as agent of colonization and also of decolonization. Richard Hakluyt's *The Principal Navigations, Voyages, Traffiques, and Discoveries of the English Nation* (1598–1600) and *The Tempest* are identified as complementary pre-texts that reveal the centuries-old process by which Europe laid the foundations of its colonizing mission on the fictions of explorers, travelers, and adventurers. Lamming elaborates a comprehensive argument about the specifically ideological content of the European book as purveyor of cognitive codes of cultural superiority and a civilizing mission. The complicated relationship between literature and history in sustaining the apparatus of empire and, conversely, in dismantling that apparatus and constructing alternatives permeates the self-conscious design of this multifaceted text.

In *The Tempest* Prospero's power and authority derive from magical books, which are his exclusive property. In *The Signifying Monkey* (127–69) Henry Louis Gates, Jr., examines the trope of the magical Talking Book in the narratives of James Gronniosaw, John Marrant, John Jea, Ottobah Cuguoano, and Olaudah Equiano. The authority of the book as insignia of authority in the colonization of the New World has even wider significance, as Nathan Wachtel demonstrates in *The Vision of the Vanquished*. Atahuallpa's failure to recognize the significance of the Bible that Pizarro hands him as a test of fealty leads to his prompt arrest and execution and the collapse of the Incan Empire (Wachtel 14–15). The significance of this historic event is heightened once it is understood that Pizarro is himself illiterate.[12] The book as fetish and insignia of authority problematizes the relationship between the written word as cultural artifact and the conquest of the New World. The substance of the book and its use are distinct spheres of value that are nonetheless intimately related.

In *The Pleasures of Exile* Lamming targets the myth-making value of the book as a literary and political phenomenon that links Hakluyt and Shakespeare to the destiny of the modern Caribbean. Lamming, as traveler to the native land of Hakluyt, Hawkins, and Raleigh, reverses the journey and the intention of their travel narratives. The dialogic intention of his text not only reverses the colonizing intention of the imperial monologue but also takes as its first casualty the mythical character of European constructions of alterity. The book as fetish and insignia of authority is reconstituted as a site of transgressive appropriation.[13] If Prospero's magic resides in his books, they hold the key to his undoing. Prospero's books become a necessary site of contention in the struggle to redefine and reorder colonial reality.

Lamming challenges the privilege of the English text by offering his own unorthodox evaluation of the thought systems, values, and ideals in *The Tempest* as evidence of a pervasive decadence and corruption in colonialism from its inception. Using *The Tempest* to clarify his ideological position, Lamming directly challenges Shakespeare's authority over Caliban's cultural space as a misrepresentation of Caliban's reality. He uses C. L. R. James's *The Black Jacobins* to name an alternative reality, "Caliban as Prospero had never known him" (*Pleasures* 119). His use of Caliban as emblematic of creative and persistent resistance rather than a brutish child of nature iterates both the arbitrariness of critical theory as an intellectual exercise and its usefulness in the creation of alternative liberationist cultural codes.

"West Indians first became aware of themselves as a people in the Haitian Revolution," observes C. L. R. James in his appendix to the 1963 edition of *The Black Jacobins* (391). The gap between Shakespeare's Caliban and the resistant spirit of the African slave in C. L. R. James's *The Black Jacobins* marks the difference between a European and a Caribbean mythology. Nixon concludes that the value of *The Tempest* for Caribbean and African intellectuals "faded once the plot ran out. The play lacks a sixth act which might have been enlisted for representing relations among Caliban, Ariel, and Prospero once they entered the postcolonial era" (576). That remains to be seen in the Caribbean, where Caliban has been reinvented as a spirit of revolt, as a landscape and a human situation with creative resources not envisioned in Shakespeare's play. Unlike Jean Rhys's fictional reconstruction of Charlotte Brontë's Jane Eyre in *Wide Sargasso Sea*, Lamming's use of *The Tempest* in *The Pleasures of Exile* and in *Water with Berries* is unconstrained by the play's plot. Lamming's use of the play, like Césaire's *Une Tempête*, Edward Kamau Brathwaite's "Caliban, Ariel, and Unprospero," and Retamar's "Caliban" in *Caliban and Other Essays*, gives Caliban a mythical life of his own as "a possibility of spirit" (*Pleasures* 107) whose future is unrealized in Shakespeare's play.

When Lamming made C. L. R. James's text a focal point of his literary and political discourse in *The Pleasures of Exile,* James's pioneering Caribbean-centered history was out of print and neglected. Lamming might have celebrated Toussaint L'Ouverture's singular achievement without reference to *The Black Jacobins,* but he chose to identify a culture of resistance already in place in the Caribbean that binds the literary endeavors of C. L. R. James, the self-taught historian, to Toussaint, the soldier and revolutionary (*Pleasures* 148). Lamming's tone is celebratory as he illuminates cultural connections that nurture a regional culture of resistance and nationalism: "And it is wonderful that this epic of Toussaint's glory and his dying should have been rendered by C. L. R. James, one of the most energetic minds of our time, a neighbour of Toussaint's island, a heart and a desire entirely within the tradition of Toussaint himself, a spirit that came to life in the rich and humble soil of a British colony in the Caribbean" (*Pleasures* 150). Furthermore, it is "[C. L. R.] James more than any man I know" who rouses Lamming to a similar sense of responsibility as a writer and intellectual (151–52).[14] In the interest of an evolving Caribbean-centered, text-based discourse, Lamming self-consciously models literary production based on formal lines of continuity among Caribbean texts. He reads, repeats, and revises C. L. R. James's text and, in the process, links his own text to James's as a necessary beginning.

The Pleasures of Exile charts the events of a ten-year period, beginning with Lamming's arrival in London in 1950, but only in one chapter, "The African Presence," does Lamming include notes ostensibly written while traveling in West Africa and visiting friends in New York. The text is usefully compared with Claude McKay's *A Long Way from Home* as a self-study of the Caribbean writer as traveler and expatriate. Unlike Claude McKay, however, Lamming remains heavily invested in defining the parameters of the Caribbean experience. The center of the expatriate's world remains the colonial Caribbean and the writer's mission of ideological demystification. The lives of Caribbean expatriates in West

Africa and in the United States are more important than any objective account of those places and their people. The Caribbean as cultural cradle remains the text's organizing center for seeing and depicting the world.

Africa is not the same quality of beginning for Lamming in *The Pleasures of Exile* as it is for Brathwaite, writing in 1970 after eight years of living and working in Ghana ("Timehri" 33–34). Lamming's reclamation of Africa for all the Caribbean is part of the text's program of ideological demystification, part of a necessary rounding out of the New World African writer's perspective. West Africa, like black America, is both familiar and strange to the Caribbean writer. In both he discovers a colonial relation that strengthens his original perception of a colonizing European presence and of a shared relationship to that presence. In a startling replay of Claude McKay's encounter with the colonial Jamaica of his childhood in Casablanca and Marrakesh (*Long Way* 297, 304), Lamming sees himself in a troop of Boy Scouts assembled at the airport in Ghana to welcome a colonial dignitary: "It was a profound experience, for I was seeing myself in every detail which they lived. . . . This experience was deeper and more resonant than the impression left by the phrase: 'we used to be like that.' It was not just a question of me and my village when I was the age of these boys. Like the funeral ceremony of the King, it was an example of habits and history reincarnated in this moment" (*Pleasures* 161–62). In the United States he measures the supremacy of the white standards against a similar structure of values in the Caribbean: "To be accepted on merit as a worshiper in that great Cathedral [the *New York Times,*] where taste is supposed to be no respecter of complexions, is not unlike the West Indian's delight with the prim-lipped approval of the *London Times*" (*Pleasures* 202). "The African Presence" is a formal act of reconnection after the violent dispossession of slavery and colonialism, but the writer's destiny is linked to the elaboration of a Caribbean reality.

According to Brathwaite, *The Pleasures of Exile* belongs to the age of the emigrant: "The West Indies could be written about and explored. But only from a vantage point outside the West Indies" ("Timehri" 32–33). In fact, *The Pleasures of Exile* provides a culture-specific context for understanding the relationship between exile and the narrative imagination from Mary Prince to Jamaica Kincaid, continuing patterns of migration from the Caribbean, as well as the potency of self-identity in mapping the shifting ground of Caribbean cultural identities.

Despite the complexity of the text, resistance and liberation are a male enterprise in *The Pleasures of Exile*. The autobiographical framework generates a self-conscious, self-celebrating male paradigm that goes unchallenged in the text. In *The Pleasures of Exile* Caliban, like Melville's Ishmael, is left alone; creation is a male enterprise. Miranda shares Caliban's creative potential to the degree to which she shares his innocence and ignorance of Prospero's magic, though their difference in status turns their common experience into an oppositional space: "In some real, though extraordinary way, Caliban and Miranda are seen side by side: opposite and contiguous at the same time. They share an ignorance that is also the source of some vision. It is, as it were, a kind of creative blindness" (*Pleasures* 115). Sycorax, as symbol of a landscape and a changing human situation, is a memory, an absence, and a silence. In "Beyond Miranda's Meanings," her afterword to Carole Boyce Davies and Elaine Savory Fido, eds., *Out of the Kumbla*, Sylvia Wynter makes a strong case for the insufficiency of *The Tempest* as a theoretical interpretive model that silences and erases the "native" woman in liberationist discourse. In Lamming's corpus, altering the male paradigm of resistance and liberation requires a shift in genre. In Lamming's *Season of Adventure*, a novel published in the same year as *The Pleasures of Exile*, the central character is a woman who has a pivotal role in the revolutionary restructuring of corrupt neocolonial rule in a fictive Caribbean republic. But Lamming's emphasis is on the transformation of a male-directed society, not on the liberation of women as a distinct social category. Not until *Water with Berries* and *Natives of My Person* did the existence of an obsessive-compulsive male paradigm of achievement become the subject of investigation.[15]

In his introduction to the 1984 edition of *The Pleasures of Exile*, Lamming emphasizes the value of the text as a document of intellectual and cultural history, even as he distances himself from it in time and tone: "Much has changed in the fate and names of places; but the central issues have remained the same. Some of the judgments on people and events may have seemed extravagant and provocative, but these may also serve as reliable evidence of a particular way of seeing" (n.p.). Lamming mediates the value of his own text as evidence of a specific consciousness and practice. Twenty-four years after it was first published, he stresses the sincerity, authenticity, and truthfulness of the text as evidence of its singular value. He reminds the reader of the time and place of the text's creation to locate its value for the reader in 1984; the self-conscious self-criticism of the author in 1960 has value as social text in the decades that follow.

Despite the distance that the author places between himself and the text in his role as mediator of its value, the dynamics of the original text are restated. It stands as a record and reminder of his personal development as a Caribbean writer and of the sociocultural dynamics of the colonial and postcolonial Caribbean: "*The Pleasures of Exile* was intended to be read as a writer's extended notes on the themes which had appeared and would persist in a body of novels. The voice was not only personal in tone. It registered a collective experience of the period, and sought to reflect and interpret the anxieties and aspirations of a Caribbean sensibility at home and abroad" (introduction, n.p.). The codes of value established in the text of 1960 are reaffirmed as representative of a specific consciousness and practice that are celebratory of the writer's productive, transformative relationship to his society in a period of revolutionary social change. In the 1984 retrospective Lamming invites a historical reading of the text. He calls attention to a changing social reality that is directly reflected in the text, to its value as a subtext to his fiction, and as a frame of reference for readers in and out of the Caribbean "who were born after 1960."

The dialogue with C. L. R. James that Lamming initiates in *The Pleasures of Exile* continues in *Beyond a Boundary* with James's invocation of the thematics of Caliban that Lamming had entertained at some length in *The Pleasures of Exile* and in James's verification of many of Lamming's perceptions about colonial levels of awareness, for example:

> It was only long years after that I understood the limitation on spirit, vision, and self-respect which was imposed on us by the fact that our masters, our curriculum, our code of morals, *everything* began from the basis that Britain was the source of all light and leading, and our business was to admire, wonder, imitate, learn; our criterion of success was to have succeeded in approaching that distant ideal—to attain it was, of course, impossible. Both master and boys accepted it as in the very nature of things. . . . And, as for me, it was the beacon that beckoned me on. (James, *Beyond a Boundary* 38–39)

> This is what I mean by *myth*. It has little to do with lack of intelligence. It has nothing to do with one's origins in class. It is deeper and more natural. . . . This *myth* begins in the West Indian from the earliest stages of his education. . . . It begins with the fact of England's supremacy in taste and judgment: a fact which can only have meaning and weight by a calculated cutting down to size of all non-England. The first to be cut down is the colonial himself. (Lamming, *Pleasures* 26–27)

This is not to suggest that the two men think alike on all issues; in fact, Lamming takes issue with C. L. R. James on his "relation to a colonial bureaucracy" (*Pleasures* 47), and indeed James positions himself quite differently in relation to that bureaucracy. The point is that a culturally specific dialogue is underway that contributes in no small way to the foundations of a distinctly Caribbean discourse. As Lamming does in *The Pleasures of Exile,* C. L. R. James uses an autobiographical framework to ground theoretical discourse in a lived colonial experience. The autobiographical framework of *The Pleasures of Exile,* with its calculated historical specificity, anticipates C. L. R. James's use of autobiography as an intellectual and cultural framework in the preface to *Beyond a Boundary*: "The autobiographical framework shows the ideas more or less in the sequence that they developed in relation to the events, the facts and the personalities which prompted them.

If the ideas originated in the West Indies it was only in England and in English life and history that I was able to track them down and test them. To establish his own identity, Caliban, after three Centuries, must himself pioneer into regions Caesar never knew" (*Beyond a Boundary* n.p.). Thus C. L. R. James appears to accept the designation of Caliban but substitutes Caesar for Prospero, extending the historical and cultural frame of reference to suit his own purposes.

In both *The Pleasures of Exile* and *Beyond a Boundary,* the autobiographical framework grounds intellectual and cultural history in an experience that is lived passionately. Self is problematized in relation to observed complexities of the historical moment, but the illocutionary center of the text remains stable.[16] Deeply interactive with the anti-imperialist imperative of nationhood, the author as colonial subject abandons the curriculum vitae biographical model in favor of autobiography as the foundation of an evidential and critical method (as in Lamming's "experience as evidence and guide") of cultural assessment.[17] The author's writerly disposition becomes an index of the defects and possibilities of his historical moment.

After the discontinuities of narrative sequence and competing foci of attention in *In the Castle of My Skin* and *The Pleasures of Exile, Beyond a Boundary* appears to be direct and calculated in its use of autobiography, self-consciously isolating and hierarchizing the complex, shifting relationship between the rebel C. L. R. James, cricket, and colonial culture. Written entirely in the first person, *Beyond a Boundary*'s authoritative voice is the voice of the mature C. L. R. James, recalling the past selectively and evaluating it in the context of the zeitgeist of cricket, the barometer of an evolving nationalism. Here the fractured consciousness and split sensibility of Lamming's *In the Castle of My Skin* is made whole, though this is arguably a matter of rhetorical strategy that signals the text's debt to *In the Castle of My Skin* and *The Pleasures of Exile* and issues its corrective. The difference in form marks a change in tone and values. The discontinuities of narrative perspective, of individual and communal destiny, family and village life in *In the Castle of My Skin* are reconstituted as the reverse. In lieu of the devastating flood and subsequent erasure of the village community in *In the Castle of My Skin,* C. L. R. James, the world traveler, celebrates rootedness and continuity:

> In the turmoil around me, my family fascinated me as never before. On that spot from which I looked through the window at Matthew Bondman and Arthur Jones succeeding generations of the James family have lived in direct descent for over 150 years. . . . Some members of the family must have helped to build the Church of the Good Shepherd where I memorized the chapters and verses of the lessons so as to look them up in the Bible, where the last rites were said for my father. When he was married in 1900 my great grandmother presented him with a mahogany table and wardrobe which had been given to her at her wedding 120 years ago. They are still in use. (*Beyond a Boundary* 246)

C. L. R. James's insistence on continuity in a time of radical social and political change repeats and revises the "hail and farewell" at the end of *In the Castle of My Skin* and *The Pleasures of Exile.* In lieu of a childhood marked by loss as in *In the Castle of My Skin,* C. L. R. James's childhood home remains intact, and continuity with his idiosyncratic childhood is assured. Thus the source of the narrator's self-knowledge is relocated within native community, and his colonial childhood is less harshly represented than in *In the Castle of My Skin.* C. L. R. James's youthful passion for cricket and literature coincide with the adult's passion for cricket, literature, and politics in what appears to be a natural progression, linking childhood experience with the adult's perception of the truth.[18]

At issue here is the way that autobiographical discourse diffuses and modifies without displacing the original text, in this case Lamming's *In the Castle of My Skin,* in an expanding continuum of seemingly endless possibilities. For example, on the first page of *In the Castle of My Skin* Lamming situates G. at a window from which he looks out on the annual floods raging around him: "From a window where the spray had given the sill a little wet life I watched the water ride through the lanes and alleys that multiplied behind the barracks that neighboured our house" (9).

C. L. R. James emphatically reclaims the window trope in *Beyond a Boundary,* where the first of seven parts to the text is titled "A Window to the World," and the titles of each of its three sections replay motifs in Lamming's *In the Castle of My Skin*: "The Window," "Against the Current," and "Old School-Tie." C. L. R. James's persona is not nine but six, and his window does not look out on a raging flood but a recreation ground. Inside, the C. L. R. James cottage is safe and dry, though it is the rainy season; here G.'s mother is reconfigured as three (the multiplication is also a motif in Lamming's *Castle*)—the six-year-old's grandmother and two aunts—and books are within easy reach:

> By standing on a chair a small boy could watch practice every afternoon and matches on Saturdays. . . . From the chair also he could mount on to the window-sill and so stretch a groping hand for the books on top of the wardrobe. Thus early the pattern of my life was set. . . . When I tired of playing in the yard I perched myself on the chair by the window. I doubt if for some years I knew what I was looking at in detail. But this watching from the window shaped one of my strongest early impressions of personality in society. His name was Matthew Bondman and he lived next door to us. (*Beyond a Boundary* 13)

The vista changes and with it the situating of narrative perspective and the structuring of content. The self-parody inherent in an autobiography that traces a pattern of growth and development is smoothly integrated here. Published when he was sixty-two, *Beyond a Boundary* records C. L. R. James's personal development, from British intellectual to West Indian nationalist, and provides him and his readers with a means of understanding the social, political, and cultural transition from colonialism to independence. With all the authority and persuasiveness that he can funnel into his first-person narrative, C. L. R. James parallels his personal development with that of the growth of cricket, from a ritual of colonial dominance into ritualized resistance and, ultimately, a ritual celebration of independent selfhood. C. L. R. James's tone is confident and celebratory of West Indian selfhood beyond the conflicting legacies of colonialism: "What interests me, and is, I think, of general interest, is that as far back as I can trace my consciousness the original found itself and came to maturity within a system that was the result of centuries of development in another land, was transplanted as a hothouse flower is transplanted and bore some strange fruit" (50). Genius subverts and transforms the structures that were meant to confine it. The evidence lies in the double text: C. L. R. James's subversion of a model British public school education into an instrument of revolutionary social change from colony to nationhood and the cricketer's subversion of cricket into an instrument for the assertion of national spirit.

Like *The Pleasures of Exile, Beyond a Boundary* is explicitly autobiography in the service of something other than the story of a life and deeds done. It begins as a journey back into childhood and village community, the cultural act of the self reading the society that engendered him. In the preface and in the text itself C. L. R. James explains exactly what he is not doing: "This book is neither cricket reminiscences nor autobiography" (n.p.). Actually, he is doing both things simultaneously and something more. His theme is social relations, politics, and art according to C. L. R. James. The subject of his text is as much C. L. R. James as it is James's analysis of cricket in the West Indies. Autobiography is a necessary framework for his ideas about the growth of nationalism in the colonial Caribbean, ironically, nurtured by the very structure of values that Britain used to impose its colonial will. Thus *Beyond a Boundary* is about the genesis of West Indian identity gleaned through years of participation in, and observation of, the game of cricket, a popular national sport in its country of origin, Great Britain, and in the West Indies, formerly colonial territories of Great Britain. C. L. R. James accomplishes this by integrating two levels of experience, the public and the private. The public arena is the cricket field: "a stage on which selected individuals played representative roles which were charged with social significance. I propose now to place on record some of the characters and as much as I can reproduce (I remember everything) of the social conflict" (72). The private arena is C. L. R. James's own intellectual development up to the time of writing, from child prodigy to political activist and committed nationalist: "A British intellectual before I was ten, already an alien in my own environment among my own people, even my own family. Somehow, from around me I had selected and fastened on to the things that made me whole" (28).

As with *In the Castle of My Skin,* the autobiographical framework of *Beyond a Boundary* serves a double function. For while autobiography personalizes history and politics, autobiography is depersonalized when individual experience is identified as part of a cultural pattern. The individual predicament merges with the collective, and self-definition is achieved in representative terms. C. L. R. James writes himself into the text as witness and participant. His primary concern with the self as autobiographical subject is with the self as an authoritative and reliable way into the collective experience, and the reverse.[19] He continually reidentifies himself in the text as exceptional and, paradoxically, as representative colonial and thus one of the populace.

Philippe Lejeune's observations about the games that writers (specifically, André Gide and François Mauriac) play with autobiography seem appropriate here as a measure of the ways in which writers like Lamming and C. L. R. James manipulate the autobiographical pact to their own ends. By choosing to write incomplete or fragmented autobiography, as Lejeune observes, they "designate the autobiographical space in which they want us to read the whole of their work." "Indeed," he continues, "they establish the nature of the ultimate truth to which their texts aspire. In these judgments, the reader forgets all too often that autobiography is understood on two levels: at the same time it is one of two *terms* of the comparison, it is the *criterion* that is used in the comparison" (27). In *In the Castle of My Skin* and *The Pleasures of Exile,* as in *Beyond a Boundary, Another Life, Finding the Center, A Way in the World, Smile Please, The Zea Mexican Diary, My Brother,* and others, one observes a self-conscious manipulation of autobiographical space to a variety of ends. In each, autobiography is devalued or denied as the preferred discourse, yet in each autobiography is deployed, establishing the importance of the autobiographical project to the fashioning of a distinctly Caribbean literary discourse.[20]

7

Poetic Autobiography
Derek Walcott's *Another Life*

Another Life is a long autobiographical poem in which Derek Walcott re-creates his childhood, adolescence, and growth to maturity as a Caribbean poet. The first three parts—"The Divided Child," "Homage to Gregorias," and "A Simple Flame"—are organized around shaping influences in his childhood and adolescence in St. Lucia, among them his tutor and mentor, Harold Simmons, his friend and companion Dunstan St. Omer, and his teenage sweetheart, Andreuille Alcée. The fourth part, "The Estranging Sea," is set in Trinidad where the poet has settled with his family, and it reflects on changes in the social and political landscape after colonialism and on his parallel development as an artist.

Published ten years after C. L. R. James's *Beyond a Boundary* and twenty years after George Lamming's *In the Castle of My Skin*, *Another Life* is yet another reformulation of the distinctive nexus between self and colonial history that is at the core of the Lamming and C. L. R. James texts. All three use the autobiographical self as a vehicle for exploring the collective dilemma: "Our generation found its metaphor of the cycle of colonialism and self-government: our maturity, our self-discovery coincided with the externals of independence, in the self-liberation of the colonial world" (notebooks Aug. 65). In *Another Life* the developing artist-poet's self subsumes and is subsumed in the complexities of regional cultural development. Walcott reconceives autobiography as the story of others who, conversely, acquire emblematic value not only as aspects of the environment but as aspects of the self. In this process the individual is defined and subsumed in others, in a

gesture of indebtedness to and connectedness with the circumstances of a childhood.[1]

In *Castle* Lamming describes self and society in seemingly tan-
gential episodes like the stories of Bots, Bambi, and Bambina
(133–41) and Jon, Jen, and Susie (122–25). C. L. R. James identifies the stable center of his childhood in heroes like Matthew
Bondman and Arthur Jones—how these men "ceased to be merely
isolated memories and fell into place as starting points of a connected pattern" (*Beyond a Boundary* 17). The same is true of Walcott's cameo portraits of Castries folk from Ajax to Zandoli and
his retelling of "The Pact" (*Another Life* 3.ii, 4). On one level self
acquires meaning through the scenes and conditions of childhood,
and in the process a wider social reality is transformed into autobiographical myth. In *Another Life,* through careful selection of
events and the comments of the narrator, personal history makes
concrete the spiritual history of the region: "So, from a green book
held in the hands of an astigmatic master, in those mornings of
my life when I imagined myself a painter, the spiritual history of
this region begins" (notebooks Nov. 65).

The divided child of Lamming and C. L. R. James reappears in
Walcott's *Another Life* in a shared quest for coherence, reconciliation, and affirmation of purpose. Walcott charts a different course
in his memories of childhood when he makes poetry the stable center of his identification with native place and community and the
prime instrument of self-knowledge: "Let me believe . . . I was right
to be a poet" (notebooks 7).[2] Walcott's choice of poetry is what
sets *Another Life* apart. As he said in his Nobel lecture, "Poetry
. . . combines the natural and marmoreal; it conjugates both tenses
simultaneously: the past and the present, if the past is the sculp-
ture and the present the beads of dew or rain on the forehead of
the past" (*Antilles* n.p.). As in *Beyond a Boundary,* the narrator
retraces his life from a time when he could not see the warring fragments of his life. Understanding is linked to the poetic form and
autobiographical quest; the task of autobiography and poetry are
one and the same. Poetic truth coheres in the autobiographical
events, the life experiences through which the emerging aesthetic
personality is rendered. Walcott's childhood and adolescence are

the medium through which the shape of his life as poet is mani-
fested, linking poet and poetry to place, people, culture, and history. The text is designed from the outset as autobiography that
will serve the multiple functions of poetic self-realization.

Like C. L. R. James, Walcott takes the reader into his confidence
about what he is doing. In *Another Life* Walcott as narrator-
protagonist casts himself in the role of reader of his booklike life,
a life that is as complex and mysterious as the sea:

> Verandahs, where the pages of the sea
> are a book left open by an absent master
> in the middle of another life—
> I begin here again,
> begin until this ocean's
> a shut book, and, like a bulb
> the white moon's filaments wane. (5)

From the outset the narrator asserts his authority over the text and
frees himself to function openly as reader of the book of Caribbean
life.[3] The narrator acknowledges the limitations of his recollections
in tranquility, of memories shaped by artistic vision:

> They have soaked too long in the basin of the mind,
> they have drunk the moon-milk
> that x-rays their bodies,
> the bone tree shows
> through the starved skins,
> and one has left, too soon,
> a reader out of breath. (11)

Walcott makes the nature of his authorial voice, the authority he
assumes, and its limitations part of the text that he is reading:

> three lives dissolve in the imagination,
> three loves, art, love and death,
> fade from a mirror clouding with this breath,
> not one is real, they cannot live or die,
> they all exist, they have never existed (109)

Having drawn attention to the nature of the text, Walcott registers shifts in perspective and autobiographical function by changing narrative point of view at will, moving from first to third person and from past to present tense. The manipulation of point of view gives Walcott the freedom of a third-person narrator to characterize his childhood in the broad cultural and political terms of colonial servitude. This element of self-parody, as in Lamming's text, dramatizes the autobiographical text as the self in dialogue with earlier versions of the self. For example, in part 1 Walcott can be "the student" or "the child" or "I" or "we." Thus Walcott, as reader and writer of the book of Caribbean life, is able to bridge the gap between the different points of view that fracture *In the Castle of My Skin* and to sustain this unity of vision through the four parts of *Another Life*.

This process is facilitated by the lyric organization of observation, thought, memory, and feeling as part of a single process. Walcott's assertion that in *Another Life* he abandoned autobiography for elegy and intellectual history appears to be the logical outcome of the merging of lyrical and autobiographical modes. In fact, when Walcott abandoned the original prose narrative inspired by "Leaving School," the value of the autobiographical "I" changed radically. The shift from prose to verse in the merger of lyrical and autobiographical modes creates an ideal textual environment for both using and transcending the autobiographical self as subject. It reconceives the lyrical voice of Lamming's G. structurally and tonally. Walcott's lyrical voice, like C. L. R. James's, has final authority over the text. Its pastoral and elegiac values are pronounced as Walcott shapes the text to mourn the suicide of his mentor, Harold Simmons, a representative West Indian artist and intellectual in whom "the fervor and intelligence/of a whole country" is found (127). C. L. R. James had shaped his text to honor Frank Worrell, the victorious first black captain of a West Indian cricket team, at its conclusion. C. L. R. James's joy is untempered by the bitterness that Walcott feels about the neglect that artists in the Caribbean suffer. This bitterness is nonetheless quite distinct from the anguish and uncertainty that characterizes G.'s farewell at the end of *In the Castle of My Skin*.

Another Life makes explicit a continuing dialogue among West Indian writers who seek to establish the foundations of their selfhood in a Caribbean reality.[4] Theirs is the privilege of naming a world in terms that identify its deprivations, humiliations, and limitations and also its creativity. "To understand the West Indian expression one must know how thoroughly it has educated itself beyond the primary challenges it was offered," writes Walcott (notebooks Aug. 65), which I understand to mean that the creative imagination of the poet and visionary, literate or not, outstrips history. When Lamming referenced a youthful Walcott's definition of West Indian selfhood in the title of *In the Castle of My Skin,* he made it clear that his autobiographical fiction was intended as a critique of Walcott's definition of self in relation to a "brittle china shepherdess," in *Epitaph of the Young:* "You in the castle of your skin, I the swineherd" (6). In *The Pleasures of Exile* Lamming misquotes Walcott's line: "You in the castle of your skin, I among the swineherd" (228). Lamming substitutes *swine* for *swineherd* (228) and effectively rewrites young Walcott's line of verse. C. L. R. James continues this autobiographical discourse on West Indian selfhood by critiquing Lamming's text and, by extension, Walcott's early poem, in an authoritative definition of West Indian selfhood as a blend of African and European cultures embodied in C. L. R. James himself and in West Indian cricket. The great cricketer Learie Constantine is a prince on the cricket field (107). Frank Worrell is "crowned with the olive" (251). Walcott's *Another Life* reenters the discourse to state the case for the interdependence of the artist and community.

Between 1970 and 1974 Derek Walcott published several essays on Caribbean literary culture: "What the Twilight Says: An Overture" (1970), "Meanings" (1970), "The Caribbean: Culture or Mimicry" (1974), and "The Muse of History" (1974). These essays articulate an overarching set of philosophical and methodological considerations that are central to any discussion of a modern Caribbean aesthetic and sensibility and are central to an understanding of the aesthetic personality that Walcott creates in *Another Life,* published in the same period. In *Another Life,* one of the great archetypal poems of the polyglot Caribbean, Walcott creates a prototype of the Caribbean poet as possessor and trans-

mitter of knowledge about his culture.[5] The poem and essays together constitute an integrated poetic vision, a kind of cultural
manifesto, in which Walcott determines his own legitimacy as
Caribbean poet and, by extension, affirms the authenticity of Caribbean literary culture.

The overarching themes in all these works are the New World
themes of a new civilization and a new poetic tradition that bind
the disparate elements of an evolving society into a moral and artistic whole. The Caribbean poet is not just a creature of language but
the creator of a language that illuminates the regional quest for identity.[6] To name the new world of the Caribbean is to share in the
drama of its creation. These themes are central to Walcott's art; they
are perhaps central to the self-definition of all New World peoples
who seek to transcend the authority of European cultural traditions.
These themes are not new, but Walcott writes with the energy and
vigor of a modern Caribbean poet in whom the distinctive poetics
of Walt Whitman, Pablo Neruda, Aimé Césaire, and St. John Perse
are reconceived with a freshness and clarity that illuminate core values of a distinctly Caribbean sensibility ("Muse" 2–7).

Walcott's vision of the Caribbean is essentially Adamic ("Muse"
2–3; "Caribbean" 13). He defines Caribbean man, regardless of
ancestry, in elemental terms of transformation and rebirth.[7] In Walcott's New World mythology the soldering of Africa and Europe
in the American archipelago led to a new beginning that is sym-
bolized for Walcott in the Creole languages that proliferated in the
Caribbean and in the indigenous folk cultures that sprang up
around them.[8] In 1979 Walcott told the interviewer Edward
Hirsch: "It was the experience of a whole race renaming something that had been named by someone else and giving that object
its own metaphoric power" (287). The genesis of Creole languages
was a primal act of self-identification, an original scripting of cultural values that forms the basis of modern Caribbean culture.[9] It
was an elemental process of dismantling and reconstitution, the
genesis of a second Eden without any pretense of innocence or
naiveté: "The apples of its second Eden have the tartness of experience. . . . There is a bitter memory and it is the bitterness that
dries last on the tongue. It is the acidulous that supplies its energy"

(Walcott, "Muse" 5). Reconstruction of self and society was not only a social necessity but the foundation of a new cultural tradition that required "the recreation of the entire order, from religion to the simplest rituals" (5).

Walcott's celebration of his Caribbean roots, of his beginnings "on a small island, a colonial backwater" ("Twilight" 14), is the foundation of a distinctly Caribbean sensibility that links him functionally to Césaire and Guillén on one hand and to continental poets like Whitman and Neruda on another. Walcott's celebration of the Caribbean landscape as a site of creativity and renewal is an affirmation of the uniqueness of the culture that produced him. But in the 1970s this had the added significance of ferreting out and legitimizing the pervasive African influence on the culture in contradistinction to the European. In a 1979 interview, Walcott told Hirsch: "Our music, our speech—all the things that are organic in the way we live—are African" (285).[10] Cultural and poetic synthesis in the modern Caribbean is not a sign of cultural degeneracy spawned by colonialism but a creative enterprise initiated by Africans in an oppressive and hostile environment. Walcott aspires to nothing less than the spirit and tone of the "new naming of things" ("Muse" 13) that gave the region its peculiar cultural momentum and uniqueness.[11]

In "What the Twilight Says," Walcott describes the process by which African slaves laid claim to the New World and, in so doing, devises an inspirational model that shapes his own poetics:

> What would deliver him [the New World Negro] from servitude was the forging of a language that went beyond mimicry, a dialect which had the force of revelation as it invented names for things, one which finally settled on its own mode of inflection, and which began to create an oral culture of chants, jokes, folk-songs and fables; this, not merely the debt of history was his proper claim to the New World. For him metaphor was not symbol but conversation, and because every poet begins with such ignorance, in the anguish that every noun will be freshly resonantly named, because a new melodic inflection meant a new mode, there was no better beginning. (17)

In the framework of the Antillean quest for identity and cultural authenticity, the rebirth of tradition in this new naming of things is not mimicry but metamorphosis. To fashion one's own mask, the mask through which one may speak to and for the gods, is to move beyond mimicry, to speak with God's tongue, and to find one's own voice in turn.[12]

The metaphor of the mask is appropriate to both the search for voice and the achievement of voice in the Caribbean. At Trinidad's Carnival, masquerade is an image of mimicry on one level and, on another, an original reconstitution of European and African cultural traditions.[13] Since its inception in 1783, Trinidad's Carnival has functioned as one of the few reliable keys to the evolution of Trinidad's moral and artistic identity. It is a cultural phenomenon that fuses disparate cultural elements of island life into an artistic whole that is peculiar to itself. The fusion is myriad and the ensuing "chaos" ritualized and repeated in self-conscious celebration of the spiritual forces shaping the culture.[14] In its various manifestations—the steel drum, calypso, and carnival costume—Carnival becomes for Walcott the embodiment of art forms "originating from the mass, which are original and temporarily as inimitable as what they first attempted to copy" ("Caribbean" 9).

In "The Caribbean: Culture or Mimicry?" Walcott observes that "like America, what energizes our society is the spiritual force of a culture shaping itself, and it can do this without the formula of politics" (4). He told Hirsch in 1979 that the recognition of authoritative cultural voice in indigenous cultural traditions provides him with an effective counterbalance to the colonizing influence of European culture: "What I have tried to do . . . is combine my own individual poetic sensibility with the strength of the root, the mass racial sensibility of expression" (287–88). Voracious about art and culture in their myriad forms,[15] Walcott has something more in mind than reproducing the Creole languages of the Caribbean, something more than mimicking folk cultural forms: "It did not matter how rhetorical, how dramatically heightened the language was if its tone were true, whether its subject was the rise and fall of a Haitian king or a small-island fisherman, and the

only way to re-create this language was to share in the torture of
its articulation. This did not mean the jettisoning of 'culture' but,
by the writer's making creative use of his schizophrenia, an elec-
tric fusion of the old and new" ("Twilight" 17).

These values engage Walcott directly in the critical debate surrounding ancestry, colonial history, cultural diversity, and assimilation in Caribbean literature. Walcott's position is diametrically
opposed to the terms of V. S. Naipaul's rejection of the Caribbean
in *The Middle Passage* for the Caribbean's multiracial, multiethnic character and for its alleged lack of history: "Racial equality
and assimilation are attractive, but only underline the loss, since
to accept assimilation is in a way to accept permanent inferiority"
(*Middle Passage* 181). Naipaul's rejection of cultural assimilation
as a creative process is reinforced by his equation of "history" with
creativity: "History is built around achievement and creation, and
nothing was created in the West Indies" (29). Though much
bandied about in Caribbean discourse since it was first published
in 1969, *The Middle Passage* raised questions about Caribbean culture as a conceptual need. Walcott responds by creating the counterdiscourse of a new and authentic Caribbean cultural identity
engendered by the place and the people: "You build according to
the topography of where you live. You are what you eat, and so
on; you mystify what you see, you create what you need spiritually, a god for each need" ("Caribbean" 12).[16] If there is a failure of creativity in the region, it is the failure of colonialism:
"Nothing was created by the British in the West Indies," Walcott
told Hirsch in 1986 (213). Walcott argues that "for the colonial
artist the enemy was not the people, or the people's crude aesthetic
which he refined and orchestrated" ("Twilight" 35), but "shame
and awe of history" ("Muse" 2). He rejects "the idea of history
as time for its original concept as myth, the partial recall of the
race" (2). Caribbean man is "a being inhabited by presences,"
rather than "a creature chained to his past" (2). This shift in focus
from past to present is not seen as acceptance of defeat but as deliverance from servitude to colonial history, a strategy for survival
that is the beginning of a new poetic tradition:

The slave converted himself, he changed weapons, and as he adapted his master's religion, he also adapted his language, and it is here, that what we can look at as our poetic tradition begins. Now began the new naming of things.

Epic was compressed in the folk legend. The act of imagination was the creative effort of the tribe. Later such legends may be written by individual poets, but their beginnings are oral, familial, the poetry of the firelight which illuminates the faces of a tight, primal hierarchy. ("Muse" 13)

Walcott argues here that cultural assimilation was not surrender to bondage but a victory of epic proportions for the New World African. The interpenetration of conflicting and apparently irreconcilable cultures shaped a new moral and artistic imperative in the Caribbean.[17]

This is Walcott's lifeline as a Caribbean poet whose sensibility bridges Africa, Asia, and Europe in a Caribbean setting. Walcott accommodates a plurality of cultures in a poetic tradition that evolves from the epic experience of African slaves in the Antilles, and he locates that tradition in the larger context of a New World experience: "It is this awe of the numinous, this elemental privilege of naming the new world which annihilates history in our great poets, an elation common to all of them, whether they are aligned by heritage to Crusoe and Prospero or to Friday and Caliban" ("Muse" 5). Walcott rejects colonialism, an act of empire, as the beginning of the modern Caribbean in favor of "the new naming of things": "The shipwrecks of Crusoe and of the crew in *The Tempest* are the end of an Old World" ("Muse" 6). The reconstitution of community in the Caribbean begins with the reconstitution of language in that place; the new language is the beginning of a new way of life for an entire community. The poet's task, as it emerges in this period of Walcott's development, is to continue this process of creation, to remain faithful to the moral and cultural imperative initiated as a collective enterprise by our African ancestors in the New World. The colonizing imperative meets its end here; selective assimilation signals metamorphosis as cultural process rather than historical event. In his essays and in numerous interviews that he gave during this period, Walcott engenders a concept of Caribbean culture that legitimizes the range and depth of his own literariness and in the process validates the authenticity of Caribbean literary culture. In the terms dictated by his essays, Walcott is most Caribbean when he lays claim to the artistic traditions of the world as his legitimate sphere of influence. Rei Terada calls the creative process Walcott's Creole poetics: "We find creole and classical, native and foreign, individual and communal, singular and multiple, doubled one within the other; as a result, we have to see all of Walcott's poetry as creole poetry, for it incorporates myriad idiolects, glimpses of private language, and glimpses of universal language alike into a creole of creoles" (118). Yet in Walcott's concept of Caribbean culture, the authorizing, validating presence is autochthonous, telluric, and oral in its outward manifestations. Walcott's ideal of the good man is of "a man who is dependent on the elements, who inhabits them, and takes his life from them. Even further, the ideal man does not need literature, religion, art, or even another, for there is ideally only himself and God" ("Caribbean" 12); the ideal man's wisdom owes no necessary debt to the ideal of reading and writing that is the poet's medium. Walcott's poet is possessor and transmitter of this ideal knowledge as he traverses the world. The ambiguity is ultimately without crisis because he remains rooted in the "oral, familial, the poetry of the firelight" ("Muse" 13).[18]

The relationship between Walcott's essays and *Another Life* exemplifies the way that personal, even private, details in Walcott's works are linked to a more encompassing poetics. The ordeal of memory has its correlative in the exile's ordeal of distance and return to a truer vision (Echevarria 10). The poet's life as written becomes a repository of cultural signification. If culture originates in nature, it is embedded in collective memory and in the idiosyncrasies of the individual poet's life and language. In *Another Life* the ideal poet is the creation of the collective community:

People entered his understanding
like a wayside church,

they had built themselves.
It was they who had smoothed the wall
of his clay-colored forehead,
who made of his rotundity an earthy
useful object
holding the clear water of their simple troubles,
he who returned their tribal names
to the adze, mattock, midden and cookingpot. (*Another Life* 127)

Walcott implants himself as authoritative cultural source, as the one who both validates and is validated by the collective culture. The autobiographical mode that Walcott uses identifies him as an insider and allows him to define the relationship of self to culture in ideal terms. If culture is embedded in memory, and memory is rooted in language, the process of literary self-constitution in *Another Life* locates the poet at the creative center of community and authorizes him to speak of and for the collective. The poet and his art merge in a cluster of tropes around self and collective culture that privileges the poet as authentic and authoritative cultural voice. In the four parts of *Another Life* Walcott loosely organizes his memories into epochs and historical changes. Idiosyncratic personal experiences are fashioned as a repository of signification for the metaphorical transformation of life into art and the poet's narrative into the narrative of an entire people within his lifetime. In the process the poet is transformed into cultural archetype, and poetic autobiography gains credence as both the lived historical reality and the myth generated by that experience.

In *Another Life* the process of becoming a Caribbean poet is narrated as the resolution of cultural conflicts engendered by European settlement of the Caribbean islands through plunder, genocide, slavery, and indenture. It is a process of simultaneous dismantling and self-constitution in the aftermath of empire. In "Meanings" Walcott describes himself as "a kind of split writer; I have one tradition inside me going one way, and another tradition going another. The mimetic, the narrative, and dance element is strong on one side, and the literary, the classical tradition is strong on the other" (48). In *Another Life* Walcott emerges from such conflicts as the unifier that he described in "Muse": "carrying entire cultures in his head, bitter perhaps, but unencumbered" (3). Like the steel band member who listens assiduously to Beethoven as he refines Ogun's instrument in a Trinidad "panyard," Walcott places himself at the meeting point of the different cultural traditions of Europe and the Third World in the Caribbean, in a passion for creation that rejects inherited antipathies for a New World identity "in which all our races are powerfully fused" ("Necessity of Negritude" 22).[19]

What *Another Life* details is that the poet's growth to this maturity of vision, his recovery of cultural values that would allow the warring parts of himself and his culture to interact creatively, was an exhilarating though painful experience begun in his childhood.[20] Walcott records that his learned appreciation of the folk life and folklore of St. Lucia provided the necessary counterbalance to European culture in his formative years. His passion for the people and the landscape of St. Lucia, nurtured variously by Harry, Dunstan, and Andreuille, the three figures around whom parts 1, 2, and 3 of *Another Life* are organized, initiated his recovery from a boyhood sense of cultural orphanage and prompted him to reject the history and rhetoric of empire, of conquest and defeat, to recover another way of seeing himself in the world. The urge to be the legitimate heir to Marlowe and Milton ("Twilight" 31) dissolves before the momentousness of "Adam's task of giving things their name" (*Another Life* 145).

Harry Simmons, Walcott's mentor, teacher, and an authority on local folklore, first showed the poet the way out of his childhood perceptions of himself as "a prodigy of the wrong age and color" (*Another Life* 7). The poet discovers through Simmons another way of seeing himself and his landscape in the works of the Jamaican poet George Campbell, who appropriates Blake to his own ends. Walcott quotes Campbell selectively:

> "Holy be
> the white head of the Negro,
> Sacred be
> the black flax of a black child . . ."

And from a new book,
bound in sea-green linen, whose lines
matched the exhilaration which their reader,
rowing the air round him now, conveyed,
another life it seemed would start again. (*Another Life* 7)

Inspired by Simmons and the different sense of values that pervades Campbell's poetry, the young poet's passion for art intensifies as a passion for the St. Lucian landscape and people. In his notebooks Walcott notes the process of apprenticeship initiated by Campbell: "The black poems owed their power to Blake, but in their anger, forgiveness or despair they envied nothing" (7).[21]

Schooled in the heroes of Greek and Roman myths, in Charles Kingsley's *The Heroes* and Nathaniel Hawthorne's *Tanglewood Tales* (*Another Life* 17), the mature poet identifies cultural equivalents in the rhythms of life around the child. He devises another mythology that places the St. Lucians around him at the center of his creative impulse. In chapter 3 of *Another Life* the poet sketches some of them in a series of cameo portraits: Ajax, Berthilia, Choiseul, Darnley, Emmanuel, Farah and Rawlins, Gaga, Helen, Philomene, Ligier, Midas, Nessus, Submarine, Uncle Eric, Vaughan, Weekes, Xodus, Zandoli: "These dead, these derelicts, / that alphabet of the emaciated, / they were the stars of my mythology" (22). The portraits are revealing in their swift characterization of aspects of folk life in St. Lucia and what they say about the poet's developing sensibility. The divided child walks with Homer and Milton and Methodism among a people rooted in a culture of their own making and their own language, French Creole. It is a mythology that, in a colonial context, is perceived as antithetical to the tone and spirit of Western culture because it is oral and African and because it exists outside the school syllabus and church dogma. The poetic impulse is to unite both traditions in a primal act of self-identification.

The "dry rocks" (*Another Life* 23) of an English-derived Methodism invite the divided child to become a preacher and writer of great hymns on its behalf. But this child is rooted in a framework of African Caribbean belief that some call "devil-worship" and

others "superstition," which the poet recognizes as the spiritual life
and creative resource of his community.

traumatic, tribal,
an atavism stronger than their Mass,
stronger than chapel, whose
tubers gripped the rooted middle-class,
beginning where Africa began:
in the body's memory. (*Another Life* 24)

The poet's childhood absorption in folk beliefs and the rituals
around him, and his keen sense of their creative power, their independent life in his community, provide him with a counterbalance
to the classics of European culture. Chapter 4 indicates that the
mature poet clings to the folk songs and tales and rituals of St. Lucia
as an essential part of his creative impulse. In this chapter he
recounts a story from his childhood that he calls "The Pact." It is
the story of Auguste Manoir, "pillar of business and the church"
(*Another Life* 25), who also practices obeah. "The Pact" is tonally
true to the folk tales of its type and a highly accomplished narrative poem in itself. But Walcott's debt to the folk imagination goes
beyond the literary applications of folklore. In "What the Twilight
Says" Walcott writes about the influence of songs and tales that he
heard as a child: "All these sank like a stain. And taught us symmetry. . . . It had sprung from the hearthside or lamplit hutdoor in
an age when the night outside was a force, inimical, infested with
devils, wood-demons, a country for the journey of the soul, and
any child who has heard its symmetry chanted would want to recall
it when he was his own story-teller, with the same respect for its
shape" (24). Walcott identifies himself as the inheritor of a living
tradition of folk belief and custom and with it a way of seeing the
world and his place in it. In "Meanings" Walcott makes it clear
that for him the landscape and the people of St. Lucia are a singular inheritance: "There is a geography which surrounds the story-
teller, and this is made physical by things like mist or trees or
whatever—mountains, snakes, devils. Depending on how primal the
geography is and how fresh in the memory, the island is going to
be invested in the mind of the child with a mythology which will

come out in whatever the child grows up to retell" (50). Walcott's lifelong efforts to keep at bay the weight of history and the authority of a European classical tradition in a small British colony rest here, in the landscape and people of the Caribbean. The poet stays rooted spiritually and geographically while, Januslike, he gazes in different directions, assimilating different cultural traditions without uprooting himself.

Another Life is expansive in its connections, patterns, metaphors, themes, and resonances. Walcott uses St. Lucian folklore as he uses myriad references to the classical traditions of Western Europe, as a way into himself, as a way of tracing the growth of his aesthetic personality across cultural boundaries that are national, racial, and class derived. It is a way of approaching himself, of defining his artistic sensibility in the elemental terms of "a being inhabited by presences, not a creature chained to his past" ("Muse" 2).

Walcott's intimate revisiting of his native landscape in part 1 of *Another Life* culminates in a moment of intense lyricism and reverence for the people and the place, a moment of dedication in which the poet surrenders to his vocation. When the poet is just fourteen, he loses himself in a trance one afternoon as he wanders alone on the hills overlooking a coastal village:

> I drowned in laboring breakers of bright cloud,
> then uncontrollable I began to weep,
> inwardly, without tears, with a serene extinction
> of all sense; I felt compelled to kneel,
> I wept for nothing and for everything,
> I wept for the earth of the hill under my knees,
> for the grass, the pebbles, for the cooking smoke
> above the laborers' houses like a cry,
> for unheard avalanches of white cloud. (*Another Life* 41–42)

The poet's dedication to art assumes an intensely felt geographic and spiritual context: "The body feels it is melting into what it has seen. This continues in the poet. It may be repressed in some way, but I think we continue in all our lives to have that sense of melting, of the 'I' not being important," he told Hirsch in 1986

(203). The achievement of voice begins for the poet in the merging of self with the social reality around him: "I have felt from my boyhood that I had one function and that was somehow to articulate, not my own experience, but what I saw around me" (210). In *Another Life* the mature poet remembers and renews his identification with the social and objective world embodied in St. Lucia, then and at the time of writing:

> For their lights still shine through the hovels like litmus,
> the smoking lamp still slowly says its prayer,
> the poor still move behind their tinted scrim,
> the taste of water is still shared everywhere,
> but in that ship of night, locked in together,
> through which, like chains, a little light might leak,
> something still fastens us forever to the poor. (*Another Life* 42)

The poetic impulse is inextricably linked to the landscape and the people of St. Lucia.

Walcott's passionate attachment to his native landscape is given a new context in part 3 of *Another Life* in which he explores his love for Andreuille, his love for St. Lucia, and the nature of his own art: "The disc of the world turned / slowly, she was its center" (*Another Life* 83). Walcott projects the transforming power of an imagination nourished by "the literature of Empires, Greek, Roman, British, through their essential classics," as he says in "What the Twilight Says" (4). The apparent betrayal, as he describes it in "The Muse of History," lies in the nature of art, in the distinctive life of the imagination that exists independently of actual experience and yet exists simultaneously with it: "There is a memory of imagination in literature which has nothing to do with actual experience, which is, in fact, another life" (25). By the same token, in *Another Life* Andreuille is transformed by the literary imagination into Anna, an aesthetic object: "The hand she held already had betrayed her / then by its longing for describing her" (90). Walcott makes a Kantian distinction between the realm of the mind and the world. Anna "already chosen / as his doomed heroine" speaks on her own behalf in the poem: "I became a metaphor, but / believe me I was unsubtle as salt" (*Another Life*

92, 109). Anna the material object and Anna the aesthetic object, though distinct, are linked in the poet's art. The transforming power of the imagination is linkage. The dualism that characterizes the poet's aesthetic sensibility is only superficially betrayal. It is characteristic of the spiritual forces shaping the culture of the region from Haitian Vodou to Rastafarianism, from "The Pact" to *Another Life*:

> No metaphor, no metamorphosis,
> as the charcoal-burner turns
> into his door of smoke,
> three lives dissolve in the imagination,
> three loves, art, love, and death,
> fade from a mirror clouding with this breath,
> no one is real, they cannot live or die,
> they all exist, they never have existed: (*Another Life* 109)

In *Another Life* the search for some ancestral tribal country ends where it started in the Caribbean (41), in a dramatic shift in focus away from ethnic ancestral homelands to New World beginnings.

As Walcott describes it in *Another Life,* the process of discovering his voice as a Caribbean poet was a struggle for the fourteen-year-old, who was searching for a way to resolve the cultural conflict between Europe and Africa in colonial St. Lucia. In this context Walcott describes his youthful fascination with British history and how it contributes to the conflict within him. The conflict is embodied in the mutually exclusive claims of two grandfathers, one white and one black, one European and one African, one prompting him to follow in the footsteps of European masters, the other rooted in the landscape of his birth.[22] The young poet grows frustrated with the pressure to choose, to accept and reject. He registers his anger and impatience in Creole:

> But I tired of your whining, grandfather,
> in the whispers of marsh grass,
> I tired of your groans, grandfather,
> in the deep ground bass of the combers,
> I cursed what the elm remembers,

I hoped for your sea-voices
to hiss from my hand,
for the sea to erase
those names a thin,
tortured child, kneeling, wrote
on his slate of wet sand. (*Another Life* 64–65)

One end to the conflict is erasure and new beginnings. Ultimately, the poet rejects servitude to the muse of history as essentially uncreative: "The truly tough aesthetic of the New World neither explains nor forgives history. It refuses to recognize it as a creative or culpable force" ("Muse" 2). He claims the freedom to shape the meaning of his inheritance anew, to create his own context for being. At the end of "The Muse of History" Walcott addresses his two grandfathers, prototypical ancestors, black and white, in a spirit of independence and gratitude: "I accept this archipelago of the Americas. I say to the ancestor who sold me, and to the ancestor who bought me I have no father, I want no such father, although I can understand you, black ghost, white ghost, when you both whisper 'history,' for if I attempt to forgive you both I am falling into your idea of history which justifies and explains and expiates, and it is not mine to forgive, and I have no wish or power to pardon" (27). The poet substitutes dialogue for servitude and veneration. He cuts himself loose from the enervating bonds of history and redefines the terms of his relationship to the past and the future.[23]

In the final part of *Another Life* the poet as traveler arrives in Rampanalgas. It is a place of rest, Resthaven. "Rest, heaven. Rest hell" (*Another Life* 138). He remains firmly rooted in the Caribbean landscape, unworried by its lack of ruins and monuments, by its lack of "history." He rejects the inherited conflict of colonial history for the child's clean slate of wet sand: "They will absolve us, perhaps, if we begin again, / from what we have always known, nothing" (*Another Life* 137). Naipaul's sardonic view of a place with no history, the scourge of a colonial sensibility, is laid to rest in a different truth. The absence of history is a new world. As Walcott says in "What the Twilight Says," "If there is nothing, there is everything to be made" (4). In *Another Life* "nothing" is "the loud world in his mind" (141). Refashioned in a language beyond mimicry, it has the force of revelation, of veritably new names for all things. The poet emerges as keeper of the faith, with his revolutionary embrace of "no history" as a blessing, as the chance to begin anew.[24] History as the ultimate cultural mask is a Carnival throwaway.[25] The ritual divestment is renewal, an act of faith.

Walcott's Caribbean poetics rests on rethinking history, time, and traditional concepts of the self. Walcott's primary point of cultural identification is the "New World Negro" who, in a language of his own creation, embarked on a new naming of things: "My real language, and tonally my basic language, is patois," he told the interviewer Robert Hamner (417). The advent of being in the modern Caribbean is the invention of a new language, the word incarnate. It follows that Walcott's archetypal "hero" is a poet. His prototypical Caribbean man is a conjurer of words who creates new contexts for being and keeps alive the original quest for identity in the New World of the Caribbean. The aesthetic personality of *Another Life* articulates a Caribbean aesthetic for life and for art, for a life other than that of the region's Old World forebears. Within the autobiographical framework of *Another Life*, poetry emerges as instrument of self-inquiry and a source of healing self-knowledge that Walcott describes much later in *Antilles*: "There is the buried language and there is the individual vocabulary, and the process of poetry is one of excavation and self-discovery."[26]

Part 3

Birthrights and Legacies

The autobiographical discourses of Claude McKay, George Lamming, C. L. R. James, and Derek Walcott evoke the concept of a black Atlantic as a racialized, foundational master trope in the staging of individual and collective identity. Edward [Kamau] Brathwaite's early essays on a West Indian "sense of rootlessness, of not belonging to the landscape" are a case in point ("Timehri" 29). In "Sir Galahad and the Islands," an essay in *Roots* that Brathwaite first published in 1957 and revised in 1963, the poet, critic, and cultural historian argues that two main types make up the West Indian sensibility, the emigrants and the islanders: "I want to suggest, in this essay, that whether we think it desirable or not, the migrant has become a significant factor on the literary scene and is, in fact, a product of our social and cultural circumstances. I want to submit that the desire (even the need) to migrate is at the heart of the West Indian sensibility—whether that migration is in fact or metaphor" (7). Brathwaite regards migration as inevitable, given the material and cultural poverty of the islands.[1]

He argues subsequently in *Roots* that this migratory impulse is "a spiritual inheritance from slavery," that it is essentially African and "a permanent part of our heritage" (30, 29).[2] Brathwaite is aware of the competing diasporic claims of non-African Caribbean populations to the same condition, but his African-centered cultural base and orientation privilege the intercultural penetration of the African experience.[3]

A similar bias of racial self-consciousness is evident in the auto-biographical narratives of C. L. R. James, Claude McKay, Lamming, and Walcott, whose different identifications with the Caribbean as native space preclude any significant reference to a sizable though marginalized community of immigrants from India in Trinidad, Guyana, and Surinam and to a lesser degree in Claude McKay's Jamaica and Walcott's St. Lucia. Among these writers, it is left to Lamming in *The Pleasures of Exile* to identify the Indian population in the Caribbean as a significant presence. But the truth is, as *In the Castle of My Skin* indicates, Indians were not a formative part of his life while he was growing up in Barbados. Within the framework of Caribbean autobiographical discourse, group identification is insistently parochial in respect to race, class, and ethnicity. In full self-consciousness of the implications of this bias in the construction of self-identity, in *Coming, Coming Home* Lamming laments the marginalization of Indians in the Caribbean (39–42) and the alienation of the European Creole (24) in African-centered Caribbean institutions and consciousness. In Walcott's *The Antilles* a similar lament names "the chained Cromwellian convict and the Sephardic Jew, the Chinese grocer and the Lebanese merchant" (10–11), as well as the Carib, the Aruac, and the Taino: "I am only one-eighth the writer I might have been had I contained all the languages of Trinidad" (7).[4] But these sentiments, genuine as they are, do not reflect the disposition of autobiographical practice, which tends to cultivate marks of difference within the contours of a singular group identity with a distinctive teleology and ethos.

It is left to consider how concepts of group identification and cultural localization are played out in the autobiographical narratives of V. S. Naipaul and Anna Mahase, Sr., as well as those of

Jean Rhys and Yseult Bridges. As gendered ethnic and racial subjects, these writers, the first two of Indian and the latter two of
European descent, male and female, remind us that Caribbean
autobiographical discourse, with its deep and multiple genealogies,
is not about cultural homogeneity. The Caribbean writes in a
range of competing voices, and autobiographical discourse, insofar as it is preoccupied with racial, ethnic, gender, and national
distinctions, embodies these differences in socially and spatially distinct communities. Thus autobiographical discourse is both eman-
cipatory and adversarial in its capacity to turn representations of
native space into a staging ground for diverse conceptions of group
identity.

Given the multidimensionality of Caribbean native space, each
of these narratives contrasts and competes with the others in mapping important distinctions in cultural development and orientation. At issue here are conflicts and differences of race, class, and
ethnicity and the ways in which these narratives relate to established autobiographical conventions of self-identification and
self-preservation in the African Caribbean cultural base of the
Anglophone Caribbean. Each narrative reconstitutes different centers of orientation in the preoccupations and dimensions of the
autobiographical act. All are significant in the way that they
demonstrate disjunctive attitudes and expectations in Caribbean
communities and in the insight that they provide into the nature
of autobiographical discourse as a producer of local subjects as
well as the localities that contextualize these subjectivities.[5] As an
archive of lived actualities, it would seem that autobiography
speaks to a cultivated sense of difference and diversity. In the context of Arjun Appadurai's observation that "culture is a dimension of human discourse that exploits difference to generate diverse
conceptions of group identity," it might be argued that in
Caribbean literary culture, autobiography has emerged as "a device
for talking about difference" and "for the mobilization of markers about group difference" (13, 15). The narratives of Naipaul,
Mahase, Bridges, and Rhys illustrate this point.

The complexities of cultural localization in the Caribbean are
reconfigured yet again in Naipaul's *Finding the Center* and *A Way*

in the World. As with C. L. R. James, Lamming, and Walcott before him, the autobiographical imperative appears to lie in the creation of a fictional-factual context for self-representation as the old colonial framework steadily collapses. Much in these narratives suggests that Naipaul is writing out of an ontological need similar to that of Claude McKay, C. L. R. James, Lamming, and Walcott. In the case of Naipaul, differences in narrative form and content revolve around assertions of Indian otherness and the trauma of racial self-consciousness in the absence of clear-cut social and cultural indexes for enacting and locating his sense of cultural difference. The autobiographical act unfolds as a quest for the familial and ethnic roots of his creativity in colonial Trinidad. It can be argued that in *Finding the Center,* Naipaul, like C. L. R. James, Lamming, and Walcott, is staking his individual ethnic claim to an autobiographical space occupied by Claude McKay and subsequently by Lamming, C. L. R. James, and Walcott as an African Caribbean cultural space that effectively, however unintentionally, erased Naipaul's constitutive ethnic presence as an Indian born and raised in colonial Trinidad. This thematic is also a subtext of Naipaul's *A Way in the World,* which makes the case for contrasting varieties of subjectivity and identification in the intellectual and cultural history of the Caribbean, where a foundational kinship with Africa is represented as one among others.

What remains unchanged in the Naipaul narratives is the epistemological issue of defining manhood and ethnicity within the parameters of colonial history and the subordination of women to an undisturbed sense of male privilege. Negotiating autobiographical space for his distinctive ethnicity does not extend to women. Yet discursive boundaries have shifted for Indian women as well as Indian men in the Caribbean, as recently published personal narratives of Indian women in Rosanne Kanhai's *Matikor* confirm. The narratives suggest a multiplicity of cultural components in the Indian woman's experience, and Mahase's autobiography, *My Mother's Daughter,* is but one narrative among others that might be constituted quite differently. In *My Mother's Daughter* the social construction of Caribbean identity is filtered through the dynamic relationship of an Indian immigrant minority to the

Canadian Presbyterian Mission in Trinidad. Writing late in life, with a keen sense of achievement in her personal and professional undertakings, Mahase positions herself as an active agent of social change in a narrative that is grounded in the alternative Indian Caribbean reality of the Christian convert, as opposed to that of the Hindu woman transformed and displaced by migration and indenture. Not only does Mahase have little to say about the Hindu experience as a part of her subjective experience but her narrative is devoid of reference to the plantation-owning class to which Bridges and Rhys belong.[6] In fact, Bridges and Mahase were born in Trinidad a decade apart, in 1888 and 1899, respectively. The island is small by any standards, the population limited in size, yet the sense of place and community in their respective narratives could hardly be more different. Structures of feeling, interest, and intimacy are embodied in sharply differentiated social groups that provide a highly localized sense of belonging to community and place. For her part, Mahase constructs a framework for self-definition that effectively displaces local white authority, even as it displaces Hindu authority as arbiter of her Caribbean autonomy. Her patrons are officials of the Canadian mission, and support from within the British colonial administration comes from African Trinidadian educators working their way up through the ranks.

In "Text, Testmony and Gender" Bridget Brereton examines, among others, the autobiographical narratives of Bridges and Mahase. Brereton concludes: "These female-authored texts do not provide a consistently gendered testimony, nor do they always bring a clearly feminine perspective to bear on the Caribbean societies with which they deal. The author's ethnicity and class, the values and limitations of the societies and eras to which they belonged, make this inevitable" (90). Given the range of ethnic and class diversity in the Caribbean, and the mechanisms of cultural localization available to each through personal narratives, it is perhaps not all that surprising that the autobiographies of Rhys and Bridges are also sharply differentiated in form and function.

On one level Rhys's *Smile Please* and Bridges's *Child of the Tropics* register a familiar trajectory of spatial and cultural localization preliminary to emigration. As in other autobiographical narratives of childhood in this book, in particular, Claude McKay's and Lamming's, a sense of Caribbean beginnings is created and preserved in the representation of childhood as a site of displaced dwelling, an enduring marker of birthright and cultural inheritance. The Caribbean is registered as a concrete place of childhood dwelling; it encompasses growth, self-awareness, personal and cultural competencies in respect to flora, fauna, food, politics, government, roads through towns and wilderness, and extended family. As Kwame Appiah observes in respect to such narratives: "The accumulation of detail is not a device of alienation but of incorporation" (71). A person out of place can thus be represented in place, inheritance as prelude rather than destination. The Trinidad-born Bridges and Dominican-born Rhys are rooted in the European Creole class/caste in both islands by several generations.[7] Yet despite observable conjunctures between the life-worlds of Rhys and Bridges, their autobiographical narratives are in several respects contradictory representations of the values that organize the European Creole's relationship to the Caribbean as native space and in marked contrast to the ontological values of the Indo-Trinidadian Mahase, who shapes her narrative subjectivity without reference to the exclusive world of the European Creole.

Discernible class, caste, and race-based cleavages of interest evident in narratives like these are the subject of ongoing analysis by literary critics and cultural historians of the Caribbean, among them Kenneth Ramchand, Edward Kamau Brathwaite, and Evelyn O'Callaghan. For example, in a pioneering study, *The West Indian Novel and Its Background* (1970), Ramchand adapts the phrase "terrified consciousness" from Frantz Fanon's *The Wretched of the Earth* (1965) "to suggest the White minority's sensations of shock and disorientation as a massive and smouldering Black population is released into awareness of its power" in the Caribbean (223). In *Contradictory Omens* Brathwaite takes Ramchand's psychosocial analysis a step further. He distinguishes the ideological underpinnings of the Euro-Creole upper class to which Bridges and Rhys belong in terms that are in marked contrast to his own African-centered concern to reverse the historical elision of the culture of the majority ex-African population of the Caribbean:[8]

"Cohesiveness and direction came not from the internal connection between classes (there was no mediating 'middle'), but from a sense of being 'European,' derived from their metropolitan origin or memories; and a sense of being white, 'civilized' and superior, derived from the 'philosophy' elaborated to justify slavery" (32). The cultural contribution of this group therefore was essentially structural-functional and materialistic in quality. Its objective was to perform well within the "raw materials" sector of the mercantilist framework. Its great achievement was the plantation and the evolution of highly efficient political assemblies. Its aesthetic achievement was the great house and the "'civilization of the wilderness'" (32).

In a brief but pointed reference to Wally Look Lai's analysis in "The Road to Thornfield Hall" of Rhys's *Wide Sargasso Sea* (1968) and Ian McDonald's *The Hummingbird Tree* (1969), Brathwaite concludes: "White creoles in the English and French West Indies have separated themselves by too wide a gulf and have contributed too little culturally, as a group, to give credence to the notion that they can, given the present structure, meaningfully identify or be identified, with the spiritual world on this side of the Sargasso Sea" (*Contradictory Omens* 38). Evelyn O'Callaghan takes issue with Brathwaite in *Woman Version* (1993), arguing for the social relevance of these "outsiders' voices," whatever the degree of their alienation from and hostility to the black majority: "It is useful to read texts from the colonial period from a particular gender perspective in order to see how patriarchy in the imperial project was constructed" (22). But she succumbs to the argument that they are indeed outsiders. It is left to consider how these issues are registered in the Bridges and Rhys autobiographical texts and where these texts might be situated individually and collectively in respect to the constitutive relationship of autobiography and self-representation to the multidimensionality of the Caribbean as native space.[9]

Like their nineteenth-century antecedents, these women's narratives illuminate specific historical and intellectual practices peculiar to their class and ethnic orientation and their individual identity. In *Woman Version* O'Callaghan's emphasis on "the dynamic of *interrelating* sources and influences" in lieu of "the roots of the version" (13) is problematic to autobiography, if only because that *dynamic* is so inextricably linked to a discernible *root* in each of the narratives. In Caribbean women's autobiography, as in Caribbean autobiography generally, the discursive production of identity generates disparate, contradictory, and at times mutually exclusive fables of identity.[10]

8

Fragments of Epic Memory
V. S. Naipaul's *Finding the Center* and *A Way in the World*

Finding the Center brings together V. S. Naipaul's two previously published personal narratives, "Prologue to an Autobiography" and its companion piece, "The Crocodiles of Yamoussoukro," with a brief foreword by the author.[1] The first narrative is an autobiographical account of his beginnings as a writer, with particular attention to the role of his father in that process. The second is a personal essay about his visit to the Ivory Coast. In his foreword Naipaul contextualizes and interprets both essays as examples of the writing process. As an autobiographical text in three parts, *Finding the Center* is fragmentary and discontinuous. It has three distinct voices, each reflecting a different facet of the author's quest for historical self-knowledge and artistic self-realization. In each the problematics of reflective autobiography without the chronology of traditional biography occasions the quest for new forms of self-inscription.

Sara Suleri observes that in Naipaul's career, "autobiography is a highly overdetermined category: *An Area of Darkness* clearly demonstrates the degree of narrative concealment represented by the ostensibly autobiographical mode" (165). Yet in a text like *Finding the Center*, the autobiographical mode is so central and determining an element that it invites an autobiographical reading of all its parts.[2] Like C. L. R. James before him, Naipaul uses the foreword to disavow autobiography and call the reader's attention to it at the same time: "'Prologue to an Autobiography' is not

183

an autobiography, a story of a life or deeds done. It is an account of something less easily seized: my literary beginnings and the imaginative promptings of my many-sided background" (vii). Yet like C. L. R. James's *Beyond a Boundary, Finding the Center* is autobiographical, with specific references to family, friends, places, and events that locate the author-narrator's need or quest for a fixed personal center in an ever changing and expanding reality. It appears that what is being rejected here is the biographical model, and in its place Naipaul proposes a different kind of autobiographical project, one that privileges the genesis of his own distinct aesthetic personality in the specific circumstances of his origins in colonial Trinidad.

Naipaul stresses "the process of writing" (*Finding the Center* vii) as a rationale for publishing "Prologue to an Autobiography" and "Crocodiles" as one text, but that in itself calls attention to the autobiographical values that underlie a text in which writing is the key to self-knowledge and self-knowledge is subject to the vagaries of quest and invention. The self-portrait engendered is racialized, politicized, and professional in its orientation. As author-narrator-protagonist, Naipaul makes himself known as the son of indentured immigrants; following in his father's footsteps, he chooses the role of the errant writer as a site of self-definition and empowerment. This choice and its fallout constitute a central and defining dilemma of the three parts of *Finding the Center*.

In his foreword Naipaul writes about the nature of his life and his life's work as facets of a single personality: "an account, with the understanding of middle age, of the writer's beginnings" (viii). Despite the radical difference in form, the autobiographical pact that he proposes is not dissimilar to Walcott's in *Another Life*: "If I were a poet the impulse might have produced a poem. To a prose writer, though, the impulse by itself was nothing. It needed a story, and I could think of none for some years" (Naipaul, *Finding the Center* vii). In "Prologue to an Autobiography" the author-narrator's quest for historical self-knowledge and artistic self-realization returns him to a landscape that is familial, ethnic, and colonial. In "Crocodiles" the narrator as traveling writer takes his confession of identity beyond the autobiographical framework described in "Prologue to an Autobiography" to the Ivory Coast, where he measures his racial-ethnic angst against that of African West Indians he meets there: "The people I found, the people I was attracted to, were not unlike myself. They too were trying to find order in their world, looking for the center" (ix). "The Crocodiles of Yamoussoukro," Naipaul explains in the foreword, complements "Prologue to an Autobiography" in that it shows "this writer, in his latest development, going about one side of his business: traveling, adding to his knowledge of the world, exposing himself to new people and new relationships" (viii). Again, the self-referential frame is explicitly invoked; his travel to the Ivory Coast is represented as a specific biographical event that illuminates his quest for the true form of his life and his life's work as an East Indian West Indian writer.

Naipaul's foregrounding of the writer as traveler brings a particular stress to his quest for "the story that would do the narrative binding—gather together all the strands of my background—and achieve the particular truth I had in mind" (vii). For the traveling writer, observes Edouard Glissant, consciousness of lineage inscribed in territory must go "beyond the pursuits and triumphs of rootedness required by the evolution of history" (*Poetics of Relation* 16). For Naipaul, errantry is deployed as an interpretive figure in the writer's quest for narrative emplotment; the writer travels to England, India, Trinidad, and Venezuela on one phase of his quest for self-knowledge and to West Africa on another. In lieu of the chronology imposed by territorial rootedness is the chronology dictated by the nature of his quest for "the particular truth I had in mind" (*Finding the Center* vii): "A writer after a time carries his world with him, his own burden of experience, human experience and literary experience (one deepening the other); and I do believe—especially after writing 'Prologue to an Autobiography'—that I would have found equivalent connections with my past and myself wherever I had gone" (ix). In *In the Castle of My Skin* Lamming locates the center of reality, in the Spengemann sense, in the fictionalized village of his childhood and adolescence (Spengemann 77). In *Beyond a Boundary* C. L. R. James locates his manifest personal destiny in the zeitgeist of cricket; he first intuits this destiny on the playing fields of Trinidad when still a boy and nurtures the thought through adolescence and adulthood. In *Another Life* Walcott prefigures his destiny as a poet in the scenes and conditions of his boyhood and adolescence in his native St. Lucia. Naipaul's *Finding the Center* raises questions about territorial rootedness in the shifting ground of the autobiographical project, in the idea of a "prologue" to autobiography that traces territorial lineage in the vagaries of his father's efforts to be a writer in colonial Trinidad, which is in turn contextualized in the tentativeness of the Indian immigrant experience. Naipaul locates the mystery of the Caribbean root in the very quirkiness of quest through the contradictions of history and memory and in the process challenges the "nationalist" imperative of the C. L. R. James, Lamming, and Walcott narratives that privilege territorial rootedness as a value in the engendering of the self.

In "Prologue to an Autobiography" narrative concealment is represented as both his peculiar inheritance and a problematic of autobiography in the absence of family history.[3] Both are contextualized as the encumbrances of colonial migrations that leave the protagonist with two disparate perceptions of time and history: "I grew up with two ideas of history, almost two ideas of time. There was history with dates. That kind of history affected people and places abroad, and my range was wide. . . . But Chaguanas where I was born, in an Indian-style house my grandfather had built, had no dates. . . . About our family, the migration of our ancestors from India, I knew only what I knew or what I was told. Beyond (and sometimes even within) people's memories was undated time, historical darkness" (*Finding the Center* 46). Migration destroys one time line and opens the door to another. A new sense of continuity emerges at the end of a year of travel in India in 1962: "Two ways of history came together, two ways of thinking about myself" (*Finding the Center* 47). The quest for self-knowledge that is a quest for narrative binding is in part the invention of a cumulative line of development outside the normal boundaries of time and history: from the Freelance's room in London to his father's life and career as a journalist in Trinidad to Bogart in Venezuela to family history gleaned in Trinidad and India. The quest for a narrative binding is the quest for a symbolic frame that can contain a developmental continuum outside chronological time.

In "Prologue to an Autobiography" Naipaul states his claim to a specific geographic and cultural landscape: "To become a writer, that noble thing, I had thought it necessary to leave. Actually, to write, it was necessary to go back. It was the beginning of self-knowledge" (34). The return to his beginnings in the Caribbean, beginnings that are circumscribed by the conditions of his upbringing and the legacy of his father, is an arduous physical and mental journey. Naipaul locates his destiny as a writer in his father's desire to be a writer. Self-definition is made contingent on knowing more about his father's world; thus Naipaul's account of his beginnings as a writer is subsumed in links to his father's life and the circumstances of his family's migration from colonial India to the British colony of Trinidad and Tobago, where his relatives were settled as indentured laborers. Naipaul names that historical reality, given only passing mention in the C. L. R. James, Bridges, Lamming, and Walcott texts examined here, as he must in order to recover the boyhood models that prefigure his destiny as a writer. While the self is not projected as representative of the ethnic experience, Naipaul's experience of that world becomes a point of access into the ethnic experience of several generations. This is accomplished by naming his ancestry insofar as he is able in the absence of adequate written records and a clear-cut chronology. He is both subject of this text and vehicle for narrating the experience of others. His individual experience as a writer acquires meaning in the context of the collective experience of Trinidad's East Indian community. Naipaul uses his extended family to represent the necessary background to the Indian experience of immigration, settlement, and return and subsequent migrations, and he uses his father to establish the precedent or basis for his own neurosis as a colonial writer from Trinidad. The logical order of the narrative returns him to Trinidad and to his father as the origin of his life as writer.

Naipaul's quest for healing self-knowledge and artistic self-realization is necessarily an attempt to discover self in community and thereby to know himself in the stories of others, but he calls attention to its being a highly selective, even fictional, process when even the immediate past is imperfectly known. For example, his search for a narrative strategy coheres in the story of Bogart, a peripheral figure in his extended family, who subsequently emigrated to Venezuela and was the inspiration for his first book, *Miguel Street*. As an interpretive figure, Bogart provides Naipaul with a key to the enigma of Indian arrival, in which the clan is not a site of identity consolidation so much as a launching pad to unscripted cosmopolitan experiences and subsequent migrations.[4] Naipaul recovers Bogart from the shifting sands of isolated memories as a link between personal history and the true form of his life as a writer: "For all its physical wretchedness and internal tensions, the life of the clan had given us all a start. It had given us a caste certainty, a high sense of the self. Bogart had escaped too soon; still passive, he had settled for nullity" (*Finding the Center* 44). Telling Bogart's story becomes a focal point for restarting a narrative of return that Naipaul had begun eight years previously and abandoned: "My narrative ran into the sands. It had no center" (vii). Naipaul finds a moment of epiphany in Bogart, in the gap between fact and fiction, the known and the unknown that Bogart's migrations illuminate.

If the story of Bogart provides narrative binding, his father's story proves to be the symbolic center of the son's life as a writer. Recognition turns on elegiac identification as Naipaul makes himself a kind of double or shadow of his dead father. For example, in "Prologue to an Autobiography" Naipaul identifies a fear of extinction as something he inherited from his father, who at one point was unable to see his reflection in a mirror:

"What form did my father's madness take?"

"He looked in the mirror one day and could not see himself. And he began to scream."

The house where this terror befell him became unendurable to him. He left it. He became a wanderer. (*Finding the Center* 70)

Naipaul makes a connection between his father's neurosis and his own connected obsessions with writing and traveling. The end is in the beginning. His spiritual and imaginative quest comes to rest in the figure of his father as pundit turned writer and reformer: "And what is astonishing to me is that, with the vocation, he so accurately transmitted to me—without saying anything to me about it—his hysteria from the time when I didn't know him: his fear of extinction. That was his subsidiary gift to me. That fear became mine as well. It was linked with the idea of the vocation: the fear could be combated only by the exercise of the vocation" (*Finding the Center* 72). Colonial alienation could hardly be more critical; writing out of such an acute sense of historical displacement carries the weight of a pioneering literary project. In this context the self-authenticating, self-defining function of *Finding the Center* is focused on the genesis of an aesthetic personality that can transform the existential angst of father and son by writing their shared sense of loss and alienation into existence. In the marvelous economy of this father-and-son narrative, the son literally bears the mark of his father in the scar above his right eye (26).

Suleri writes that "the idiom of trauma itself requires a reformulation that can provide a language for the slippage of trauma from apocalypse into narrative" (5). For Naipaul it may be that the narrative reformulation required is autobiography, or as close to it as he can get. In "Prologue to an Autobiography" Naipaul speculates on what might have kept his father from writing his own autobiography when urged to do so by his son: "His early life seemed an extension back in time of my own. . . . When I was at Oxford I pressed him in letters to write an autobiography. This was to encourage him as a writer, to point him to material he had never used. But some deep hurt or shame, something still raw and unresolved in his experience, kept my father from attempting any autobiographical writing" (*Finding the Center* 49–59). The son's quest for originality and origination in his father's narrative reformulation is denied, and in the absence of such a defining representational image Naipaul reports the story of his father's illness and profound anxiety about cultural location. By the same token, it may be that for Naipaul the cultural landscape of the East Indian West Indian colonial writer endures in images of cultural dislocation and erasure so acute that errantry becomes a strategy of survival as well as an avenue of escape. The idea of autobiography as prologue captures some of the complexity of the task that Naipaul set for himself. It suggests a preliminary discourse on autobiography and also that autobiography will follow.[5] Like the text's title, *Finding the Center,* this promise of autobiography proves to be an ironic commentary on both the nature of autobiography and the autobiographical pact implied. "It represents my full intention," Naipaul observes in the foreword (viii), having structured his retrospective around a parallel between the process of writing and autobiographical self-inscription.

In the foreword Naipaul uses the metaphor of shipwreck, of running "into the sands," to describe a narrative without a center, a failure of creativity that is an absence of perspective. At the end of "Crocodiles" Naipaul embellishes sand as a metaphor for his own continuing sense of cultural insecurity as a colonial from Trinidad, where the ancestral connection is fragile and imperfectly known. The existential void of a New World identity is a recurring theme in Naipaul's work, and in "Crocodiles" the travel narrative reflects and validates the existential angst of the writer as autobiographical subject and author in its cultural specificity:

> I said, "Arlette, you make me feel that the world is unstable. You make me feel that everything we live by is built on sand."
>
> She said, "But the world is sand. Life is sand."
>
> I felt she was saying what Hindus say as a doctrinal point, and feel as a truth in times of crisis: that life is illusion. But that was wrong. Ideas have their cultural identity. . . . The Hindu's idea of illusion comes from the contemplation of nothingness. Arlette's idea of sand came from her understanding and admiration of a beautifully organized society. (*Finding the Center* 174–75)

The overlapping themes of cultural difference and the contradictions of postcolonialism nurture a subtext of racial and ethnic differentiation that went unexamined in "Prologue to an Autobiography." Arlette is a black West Indian from Martinique who has settled into expatriate status in the Ivory Coast; the narrator is a Hindu from Trinidad. Racial passion among Africans in the

Caribbean as a site of Hindu displacement and alienation is pursued obliquely at a discrete distance. Travel permits a level of self-erasure that makes autobiography impossible except as intellectual and cultural history. In the terms proffered, the writer is a mental traveler and an aesthetic construct to be explained, discovered, or expressed.

If "Prologue to an Autobiography" situates the writer at "home" in the mixed legacy of his father, "Crocodiles" situates the writer in his uprootedness, traveling and writing in an ongoing quest for healing self-knowledge and artistic self-realization. While "Crocodiles" might be read as political journalism or a travelogue, the narrative foregrounds the author's subjectivity in an extended analysis of traveling and writing as a sustainable creative process in personal and professional terms. Cultural rootedness is pushed into the background in this traveler's quest for new experiences of places and people and new forms of knowledge and consciousness. In "Crocodiles" the cultural root is a frame of reference, a way of looking, that seeks and gains clarification in the Ivory Coast among expatriates—travelers and dwellers alike—who are black, white, and racially mixed, European, American, Caribbean, and African. The writer makes up the script as he goes along: "It is a writer's curiosity rather than an ethnographer's or journalist's. So while, when I travel, I can move only according to what I find, I also live, as it were, in a novel of my own making" (*Finding the Center* 90). As exemplary travel narrative, "Crocodiles" returns the author as narrator to the world of writing as site of self-definition. Self-creation is an ongoing process that is realized in the ritual act of writing. The author-narrator is a colonial by birth and education, one whose heightened understanding of his Caribbean beginnings brings a measure of self-acceptance and fuels his quest for self-knowledge and artistic development. The culture of travel, as Naipaul describes it, facilitates the reinvention of an aesthetic self in alternative historical and geographical sites: "It became the substitute for the mature social experience—the deepening knowledge of a society—which my background and the nature of my life denied me. My uncertainty about my role withered: a role was not necessary. I recognized my own instincts as a traveler and was content to be myself, to be what I had always been, a looker. And

I learned to look in my own way" (*Finding the Center* x). In a replay of Lamming's "one man's way of seeing" in *The Pleasures of Exile* (13), Naipaul differentiates his role as a traveling writer from that of his father, for whom writing "was a version of the pundit's vocation" (*Finding the Center* 54).

Naipaul's emphasis on looking situates him in a colonial tradition of travel writing that was constructed on observed, qualitative differences between the colonizer and the colonized. Mary Louise Pratt coins the terms *anti-conquest* to describe strategies of representation that are intended to suggest innocence within the project of empire and *seeing-man* to describe the protagonist of anti-conquest: "The main protagonist of the anti-conquest is a figure I sometimes call the 'seeing-man,' an admittedly unfriendly label for the European male subject of European landscape discourse—he whose imperial eyes passively look out and possess" (*Imperial Eyes* 7). According to Pratt, the "postcolonial adventurer" reinvents the role of seeing-man by inverting key rhetorical strategies of their earlier explorer forebears: "The impulse of these postcolonial writers is to condemn what they see, trivialize it, and dissociate themselves utterly from it" (*Imperial Eyes* 217). In "Crocodiles" Naipaul is careful to resituate himself as postcolonial visitor, traveler, and observer. He uses a coterie of informants, native and expatriate, to explain the significance of what he observes and does not understand.[6] He questions and contextualizes his authority as seer and quotes his sources extensively, seemingly to underline the dialogic structure and scope of his engagement with the place and people. The cult of the seeing-man as arbiter of value seemingly dissolves in confessions of ignorance, incomprehension, and bias. But these strategies of innocence are located within another meaning-making apparatus that is deeply engaged with the ideological project of colonialism: "I travel to discover other states of mind. And if for this intellectual adventure I go to places where people live restricted lives, it is because my curiosity is still dictated in part by my colonial Trinidad background. I go to places which, however alien, connect in some way with what I already know" (*Finding the Center* 90).

The cultural and intellectual authority of Naipaul as postcolonial traveler and observer is continually qualified by self-irony, but what remains in place here is a binary epistemology that constructs oppositional scales of value around Europe and Africa, Arlette and Andrée, French Africa and African Africa, light and dark, day and night, and so on. At one point he invokes the twin reality that links the world of African slaves in colonial Trinidad to postcolonial contradictions of the Ivory Coast:

> In the slave plantations of the Caribbean Africans existed in two worlds. There was the world of the day; that was the white world. There was the world of the night; that was the African world, of spirits and magic and the true gods. . . .
>
> Something of this twin reality existed at Yamoussoukro. The metropolis, the ruler's benefaction to his people, belonged to the world of the day, the world of doing and development. The crocodile ritual—speaking of a power issuing to the president from the earth itself—was part of the night, ceaselessly undoing the reality of the day. (*Finding the Center* 149)

Naipaul's use of a binary epistemology to reenact colonial stereotypes is constructed as an enduring facet of his colonial background in Trinidad. It links his inherited fear of annihilation to an African presence that is perceived as resistant, if not impervious, to Western systems of thought and social organization. It is crystallized in the narrator's nightmare of a collapsing bridge and his anxieties about safe passage. He concludes: "The buildings of Abidjan, seen in the morning mist of the lagoon, seemed sinister: proof of a ruler's power, a creation of magic, for all the solidity of the concrete and the steel: dangerous and perishable like the bridge in my dream" (*Finding the Center* 155). The comparative framework that he uses enables the insertion of his cultural difference as a sign of authority, just as the insertion of his dream reintroduces old anxieties about the writer's cultural location.

Self-writing is problematized by traveling as opposed to dwelling in "Crocodiles," and by making "the clan" a site of displaced dwelling in "Prologue to an Autobiography." The autobiographical act emerges of necessity as a lonely act of self-definition and self-affirmation that performs its own distinctive mediation of Trinidadian Indian otherness in the colonial and postcolonial Caribbean. Travel and quest are explicit themes, a rhetorical strategy, and an instrument of self-inquiry and artistic self-realization. Thus in *Finding the Center* Naipaul combines the quest for historical self-knowledge and artistic self-realization and in the process makes a case for alternative forms of subjectivity and identification in the intellectual and cultural history of the Caribbean. As self-inscribed postcolonial adventurer, Naipaul transposes the existential angst of his own historical situation, as delineated in "Prologue to an Autobiography," in the linked performance of travel and narrative. The autobiographical act ends here, as it must, in the persona of the writer at work.

The fictiveness of autobiography that is a subtext in *Finding the Center* is also the thematics of Naipaul's *A Way in the World,* alternatively subtitled *A Novel,* and *A Sequence.*[7] Here the distinction between fact and fiction, recollection and invention, blurs to irrelevance. *A Way in the World* begins as an autobiographical narrative of childhood and adolescence and develops into a meditation on colonial history as a sociological and spiritual conditioning through accounts of Sir Walter Raleigh's final expedition to the Americas, Francisco Miranda's ill-conceived attempt to invade Venezuela in the eighteenth century, and Foster Morris's narratives of travel to the region in the middle of the twentieth century, among others. As in *Finding the Center,* Naipaul maintains a narrative connection with extraliterary autobiographical experiences while rejecting the traditional chronological form of autobiography. By designating the narrative a "sequence" and then a "novel," Naipaul appears to mock the erratic, eclectic nature of a creative process that explains a life and a life's work as facets of the same quest. Read in conjunction with *Finding the Center, A Way in the World* resituates the autobiographical discourse of the earlier text, combining the quest for historical self-knowledge and artistic self-realization in a multiform narrative that coheres around the writer at work in different settings: an aesthetic personality in whom autobiographical recollections, musings, and inventions mark different stages in self-awareness and in artistic development.

In fact, portions of the author's foreword to *Finding the Center* read like an interpretative key to *A Way in the World*: " Both pieces are about the process of writing. Both pieces seek in different ways to admit the reader to that process" (*Finding the Center* vii). About "Prologue to an Autobiography" Naipaul writes: "It is not an autobiography, a story of a life or deeds done. It is an account of something less easily seized: my literary beginnings and the imaginative promptings of my many-sided background" (vii). In "Crocodiles of Yamoussoukro" he privileges "one side of his business," that of the travel writer: "traveling, adding to his knowledge of the world, exposing himself to new people and new relationships" (viii). In *A Way in the World* these different dimensions—the process of writing, literary beginnings, intellectual and cultural history, the writer as traveler—are threaded together in a fashion that resembles the self-referential posture of Lamming's *The Pleasures of Exile*, though the differences are acute, as they must be, since Naipaul maps the genesis of a distinct aesthetic personality writing out of a different time, place, and ethnicity. The problematic of autobiography that they share is posed by the intrusive presence of the author-narrator in a retrospective that rejects the biographical paradigm in favor of intellectual and cultural history.

By foregrounding travel and migration as universal cultural practice, Naipaul illuminates complex issues of intercultural identity in the post-Columbian Caribbean. He analyzes the dynamics of travel through autobiographical and fictional narratives, journals, diaries, letters, historical documents, oral histories, and performance traditions. As Edward Baugh observes in "Travel as Self-Invention," this is not new in Caribbean writing. But there is something distinctive about the way that Naipaul uses travel to inscribe a self-referential methodology for cultural analysis. In the gendered space of *A Way in the World* travel is construed as a universal trope: a discourse, a genre, and a basis for comparing the different cultures that traverse and constitute the Caribbean. Native place is a site of arrivals and departures, of local-regional-global encounters

involving domination, resistance, commerce, intercultural penetration, and ideological appropriation.[8] The native traveler leaves
home and returns in ongoing interaction with a variety of different cultures. He is islander and exile, dweller and traveler; in him
the intercultural figure of the native and the intercultural figure of
the traveler overlap and intertwine.

In *A Way in the World* the delimiting self-other binaries of
"Crocodiles" have given way to an urbane at-homeness and free
play of self-invention so willful and overdetermined as to dissipate
the earlier text's preoccupation with the logic of origins and colonial-postcolonial discursive paradigms, for example: "We all
inhabit 'constructs' of a world. Ancient peoples had their own. Our
grandparents had their own; we cannot enter absolutely into their
constructs. Every culture has it own; men are infinitely malleable"
(159). Another example is his often-repeated assertions about the
unreliability of recorded impressions and even an observed distinction in the quality of first and second memories: "The second
memory is probably satirical and mischievous" (33). Naipaul's ex-
centric native traveler seems like a contradiction in terms, but this
is part of the playfulness of his changeable writer-narrator, whose
personal history matches Naipaul's precisely from time to time,
despite the disavowals of subtitles like *A Novel* or *A Sequence*.[9]
The writer-narrator is a complex historical subject, in the tradition of George Lamming's ex-centric "native" cosmopolitan traveler in *The Pleasures of Exile*, C. L. R. James's in *Beyond a
Boundary*, and Claude McKay's in *A Long Way from Home*, and,
gender aside, Seacole's in *Wonderful Adventures*. Naipaul's insular base is constructed as a site of explorations, migrations, settlements, and transforming encounters.[10]

Naipaul's organizing tropes are familiar to readers of Caribbean
literature. Predictably, in the Caribbean travel as exploration and
transforming encounter turns on the quest for El Dorado, the lost
world, the aboriginal landscape, identity, origins, ancestry, psychic
reconnection, and rebirth. *A Way in the World* is replete with the
overlapping tropes of return to one's native land and quest for an
aboriginal landscape ("an aboriginal Indian place," "the aboriginal island," "the untouched aboriginal island," "a crowded abo-

riginal Indian island," "a fabulous aboriginal landscape") in a tropological refashioning of a Caribbean myth or desire for psychic integration. For Antonio Benítez-Rojo this is a plus: "The ordinary thing, the almost arithmetical constant in the Caribbean is never a matter of *subtracting*, but always of *adding*, for the Caribbean discourse carries, as I've said before, a myth or desire for social, cultural and psychic integration to compensate for the fragmentation and provisionality of the collective Being" (189).

In *A Way in the World* Naipaul begins by challenging this assumption in the elegiac introductory "Prelude: An Inheritance," which registers the loss of ethnicity in the "bizarre" eclecticism of Leonard Side, whose creativity finds expression in his work as an undertaker, a floral arranger, and maker of dainty cakes. Leonard Side is invoked as an Indian and Muslim who, in the absence of discrete social and cultural markers, and in ignorance of his ancestry, has lent his creativity to the vagaries of the cultural moment: "He knew he was a Mohammedan, in spite of the picture of Christ in his bedroom. But he would have had almost no idea of where he and his ancestors had come from" (*Way in the World* 10). Beyond this, Naipaul's attention to detail fixes on a displaced homosexual decorum in Leonard Side that generates fear and unease: "He would have been used to people treating him in a special way: the women in the classes clapping him, other people mocking him or scorning him, and people like me running away from him because he frightened us. He frightened me because I felt his feeling for beauty was like an illness; as though some unfamiliar, deforming virus had passed through his simple mother to him, and was even then—he was in his mid-thirties—something neither of them had begun to understand" (*Way in the World* 9–10).

Naipaul speculates that Leonard Side would have had to migrate to come to terms with his sexual difference. By the end of the opening chapter, "Prelude: An Inheritance," Side emerges as a figure of ethnic and cultural displacement whose quest is unknowable, either in the circumscribed space of his native island or in his unrecoverable ethnic identity. But the angst of this is recorded as the feelings of the narrator as a child, "in a time of fever" (*Way in the World* 4). By chapter 7 the enigmatic narrator claims to be a

New Man: "I had arrived at a way of looking that contained both the fabulous past and the smaller scale of what I had grown up with" (224); and later, situating himself in relation to the Spanish American revolutionary Miranda, he says: "I feel now that I was carried away by a private idea of ancestry, and overlooked too much of what was obvious" (252).

Naipaul's enigmatic Leonard Side is prelude to a narrative quest for forms of identification with which to circumnavigate the enigma of racial and cultural inheritance, a quest that reconfigures the rational framework of chronologies by making chronological time captive of the space that his narrator chooses to occupy. Given the proliferation of spatial references, the crossing and recrossing of physical and conceptual boundaries in *A Way in the World,* it comes as no surprise that the narrator's quest for aboriginal space penetrates the poetic space of El Dorado. The poetics of landscape merges with the poetics of El Dorado in an elaborate pattern of intratextual and intertextual parodic signification that assumes the form of a free-ranging critical discourse on travel as a discursive framework for multicultural identity.[11] Naipaul's use of the tropes of return and quest are so pervasive, so self-referential and complex, that they are repeated in every chapter in a deepening pattern of repetition and revision, linking each to each, the beginning with the ending. The narrator returns to his quest and, at different points in *A Way in the World,* so do Columbus, Sir Walter Raleigh, Miranda, Sorzano, and Blair. Every repetition entails a difference, and repetition works against closure, even in the death of Blair, whom Naipaul returns to Trinidad in a coffin. In the final chapter, "Home Again," the narrator writes an obituary for Blair that might be the narrator's own and is a replay of Level's "little formal farewell speech to Miranda" (*Way in the World* 348) that, with characteristic flourish, is also a replay of Biswas's "Daddy Comes Home in a Coffin" in Naipaul's *A House for Mr. Biswas.*

By linking return and quest, Naipaul signals a conceptual link with the quest for El Dorado as a mythical historical enterprise pervading a distinctly Caribbean cultural geography. Together these tropes articulate a cross-cultural poetics that resists a nationalist, ethnic, racialist quest for unique origins. Aboriginal space puts precursors before ancestors, displacing ancestral desire for organic cultural differentiation with a cultural chronotope that privileges a poetics of landscape in a quest for "the beginning of things" (*Way in the World* 218) and a discourse of travel as a way of inscribing cultural flux as an identity marker. For Glissant "the *poetics* of landscape, which is the source of creative energy, is not to be directly confused with *the physical nature* of the country. Landscape retains the memory of time past. Its space is open or closed to its meaning" (*Caribbean Discourse* 150).

In *A Way in the World* the intertwining, overlapping tropes of return and quest are managed by a narrator who, as traveling native, is something of a shape shifter, assuming a series of interrelated roles as the returning native, world traveler, native informant, writer-inscriber, reader, researcher, quester, and native dweller. In fact, he invokes the confidence man to describe the Venezuelan Miranda, who is represented as an early version of himself, a precursor of sorts (252).[12] His psyche is split into then and now, child and adult, narrator and character in a parodic replay of the often reiterated quest for psychic reintegration. Driven by the narrative's interior logic, native space is multidimensional as a frame of reference for such a disconcertingly hybrid native traveler. It is identified as the island of Trinidad expanded to include its hinterland-heartland refashioned as Guyana, Venezuela, Brazil, and Columbia. The idea of national boundaries becomes meaningless as a way of mapping native space because this is actually determined by the narrator's conception of return and the nature of his quest for aboriginal space: "Over a number of journeys I began to think of Venezuela as a kind of restored homeland" (220). Given the narrator's level of sophistication in respect to the historical density of place, native space extends to the most widely separated transhistorical boundaries, even as they are sublimated in the transhistorical codes of nature as aboriginal landscape.

Naipaul's foregrounding of culture as travel discourse resituates culture as a site of dwelling in the representation of native space.[13] Cultural dwelling is perceived as subject to ceaseless cultural transformation. He notes that the Mohammedans are now squatting where, hundreds of years before, there had been "Cumucurapo, an aboriginal Indian place" (*Way in the World* 40); new immigrants from the smaller islands gathering near a disused lighthouse, with its 1897 inscription of Queen Victoria's Diamond Jubilee, which is also the centenary of the British Conquest of Trinidad, at Point Galera, a promontory named by Columbus, now another aboriginal place "cleansed of its past" (*Way in the World* 76); Woodford Square, where East Indian derelicts have been replaced by Africans, and the site of tumultuous political changes (31); and Cedros, where once "aboriginal Indians were masters of these waters. They no longer existed; and that knowledge of currents and tides had passed to their successors . . . descendants of agricultural people from the Gangetic Plain" (223). Considered in specific historical relation to travel, cultural dwelling assumes the transitional quality of travel encounters.

Reinforcing this representation of native space in *A Way in the World* is the inscription of cosmopolitan native travelers who parallel, anticipate, and critique through repetition the narrator as excentric native. The most obvious of these are Lebrun, a Marxist writer and revolutionary on the run, whom the narrator identifies as a precursor; Blair, another traveler for whom the ethnocentric, race-based quest for identity dead ends in East Africa; and Sorzano, the East Indian from Trinidad who has acquired "a new land, a new name, a new identity, a new kind of family life, new languages even" (228) in Venezuela and who makes a pilgrimage to Trinidad for special prayers from the Hindu scriptures for a son in trouble. The terrain of return in *A Way in the World* is replete with markers that conceal as much as they illuminate. By focusing on hybrid cosmopolitan experiences that intersect with his own history of travel, displacement, and quest, the narrator creates a self-referential space for the portrayal and understanding of related concepts of culture and of travel.

Naipaul's narrator returns to native space as one who has inscribed its particulars and his relationship to its various parts in any number of books of history, fiction, and travel. The territory to which he returns was crisscrossed in previous journeys exten-

sively inscribed in a series of widely read texts. He returns to this
space again, pen in hand, to retrace previous journeys and to reinscribe his relationship to native space from a different perspective.
For example, while *A Way in the World* covers much of the same
territory as *The Loss of El Dorado,* it explicitly embraces what
the earlier history would not, in this case, ambiguity and alarm:

> Port of Spain was a place where things had happened and nothing
> showed. . . . History was a fairytale about the strange customs of
> the aboriginal Caribs and Arawaks; it was impossible now to set
> them in a landscape. History was the Trinidad five-cent stamp:
> Raleigh discovering the Pitch Lake. History was a fairytale not
> so much about slavery as about its abolition, the good defeating
> the bad. *It was the only way the tale could be told. Any other ver-
> sion would have ended in ambiguity and alarm.* (*Loss* 375; empha-
> sis added)

In lieu of the younger writer's linear, hierarchical vision of a single history in *The Loss of El Dorado* is the intricate performance
of Naipaul as he reconstructs his public persona as traveling writer,
splitting his public image into "then" and "now" and seductively
modeling for the reader the act of reading new meaning into
antecedent texts, his own and others. *A Way in the World* is,
among other things, a rereading of a range of earlier Naipaul texts,
including *In a Free State, The Loss of El Dorado,* and *The Middle Passage,* but *A Way in the World* ranges widely across the
entire body of his work.[14] The trope of return fashions an alternative "way of looking that contained both the fabulous past and
the smaller scale of what I had grown up with" (*Way in the World*
224). By implication this alternative liberates the author from the
apocalyptic postures he had assumed in the earlier text.[15]

The tendency to self-parody is everywhere in evidence in *A Way
in the World.* Self-parody is so sustained as to make it an impossible exercise to name more than a few instances here without sac-
rificing analysis to annotation. Suffice it to say that the reader must
supply the literary models, or narrative elements of parody and
hidden polemic will be obscure. For example, the culture shock
that the narrator experiences when he "was writing a book of

history" in London and studying the historical documents of the region is clearly a reference to *The Loss of El Dorado* (213); the account of his first visit in January 1961 to the highlands of what was then British Guiana can be read against an account of Naipaul's visit there in *The Middle Passage* (1962). Self-parody is part of a sustained attempt to critique the discursive practices of native and non-native travelers through parody and pastiche. Historical narratives generated by Columbus, Raleigh, and Miranda, Picton, Hislop, and Level de Gorda are identified as literary historical markers that both obscure and illuminate native space. These markers are so compromised as historical documents that the narrator rewrites his earlier use of them in three sections of *A Way in the World* that he designates an act of unwriting: "New Clothes: An Unwritten Story," "A Parcel of Papers, a Roll of Tobacco, a Tortoise: An Unwritten Story," and "In the Gulf of Desolation: An Unwritten Story." In these sections the narrator critiques travel as a discourse and a genre and perhaps his earlier failure to recognize the limitations of genre.

In "New Clothes" Naipaul splits the narrator's voice so that one bears an ironic relationship to the other. The twinning of the narrator as he penetrates the hinterland by boat parodies the figure of the divided self in Wilson Harris's Donne and his twin the Dreamer in *The Palace of the Peacock,* warring facets of a single persona who journeys upriver toward death and psychic integration. The subjective musings of one voice critique the narrative strategies of the other. Historical ironies proliferate in references to Malcolm X in 1971, the last of the Frank James gang, African runaways, Amerindian bounty hunters, the Czechs, and of course the narrator himself: "So for this narrator—who is more than a traveller looking for new sights—everything seen on the river has many meanings" (*Way in the World* 48).

In "A Parcel of Papers" a case might be made that Naipaul is signifying upon Lamming's *Natives of My Person* in the extended dialogue between "the old man" and "surgeon" as their ship is becalmed in the Gulf of Paria. The intertextuality is not unfriendly in that this "unwritten story" is a rigorous critique of Raleigh's "lies," his willful misrepresentation of what he saw and experienced, and by implication Naipaul's use of Raleigh's narrative in the past. It does not take much to see that Naipaul is parodying intertextuality in the surgeon's extended cross-examination of Raleigh that recalls Benítez-Rojo's ferreting out of the uncanny in Las Casas's "Plague of the Ants" (*Repeating Island* 85–111).

"In the Gulf of Desolation" self-parody doubles as an act of criticism and interpretation as the narrator mocks his own failure of vision by identifying Miranda quite explicitly as a mirror image of his immature self: "I too, but in my own way, thought of him as a precursor. I saw him as a very early colonial, someone with a feeling of incompleteness, with very little at home to fall back on, with an idea of a great world out there, someone who, when he was out in this world, had to reinvent himself. I saw in himself some of my own early promptings (and the promptings of other people I knew)" (*Way in the World* 252). In this chapter Naipaul takes parody a step further by amplifying the foregrounding in tropological revisions of all three "unwritten" stories, decentering the revisionary transformative narrative of return and quest even further.

> At one time I thought I should try to do a play or a film—a film would have been better—about the Gulf. I saw it as a three-part work: Columbus in 1498, Raleigh in 1618, and Francisco Miranda, the Venezuelan revolutionary, in 1806: three obsessed men, well past their prime, each with his own vision of the New World, each at what should have been a moment of fulfilment, but really near the end of things, in the Gulf of Desolation. Separate stories, different people, changing style of clothes, but the episodes would have developed one out of the other, as in a serial. (*Way in the World* 246)

As Naipaul maneuvers his narrative with great deftness through shifting paradox and ongoing translation, it becomes clear that *A Way in the World* is about writing itself, its possibilities and its limitations, and that the rage and anger about origins and the annihilation of collective memory that characterize *The Loss of El Dorado* have been rendered inoperative, at least for the duration of this text.

One might say that in *A Way in the World* Naipaul is floating free at last in a radical reversal of the *maronnage* and shipwreck that he projects in "Passenger: A Figure from the Thirties" (chapter 4): "We didn't have backgrounds. We didn't have a past. For most of us the past stopped with our grandparents; beyond that was a blank. If you could look down at us from the sky you would see us living in our little houses between the sea and the bush; and that was a kind of truth about us, who had been transported to that place. We were just there, floating" (81). Or it may be that the narrative's final return to Parry's funeral parlor, where it began, signals yet another reenactment of "In the Gulf of Desolation," where the written record, subject as it is to invention, resists the annihilation of time. The enigma of the ending derives in large part from the insistent fictiveness of self-representation throughout and the extended revisions of previously written texts, suggesting that historical biography is inadequate and insufficient to the task of self-writing, which begins and ends in the act of writing and rewriting against the fear of extinction: "It was linked with the idea of the vocation: the fear could be combated only by the exercise of the vocation" (*Finding the Center* 72).

9

Maternal Bonds

My Mother's Daughter: The Autobiography of Anna Mahase Snr., 1899–1978

V. S. Naipaul's place in this study lies not only in his innovativeness and creativity but in the different racial-ethnic space that he occupies in Caribbean literary discourse. The complexities of cultural localization are evident in Naipaul's acute awareness of the disrupting, transforming experience that an Indian ethnicity brings to the literary culture, displacing established binaries of master and slave, European and African. What Naipaul has left unchallenged is the gendered bias of these binaries. In this context *My Mother's Daughter: The Autobiography of Anna Mahase Snr., 1899–1978* assumes special significance. Mahase's short narrative is not only historically grounded but it is grounded in an alternative Indo-Caribbean reality in part because she is a woman and also because she is a convert to Christianity and self-consciously roots her narrative in the nationalist discourse of the postcolonial Caribbean.

My Mother's Daughter was published posthumously in 1992 (she died in 1978) with an epilogue by her daughter, also Anna Mahase, and various authenticating appendixes, including the brief "Autobiography of Kenneth Emmanuel Mahase" (1893–1955) by the husband of Anna Sr., two poems in praise of the Canadian Presbyterian Mission and Trinidad by Anna Sr., tributes to the achievements of her husband and children, a map showing Canadian mission districts and the railway lines on which they relied, and a series of family photos. Writing plainly and purposefully, Anna Mahase links her ethnic identity as an Indian woman of high caste on the one hand and the child of Indian immigrants who converted to Christianity on the other to her multifaceted life in Trinidad as a committed Christian woman and social activist, a trained teacher in the Canadian mission schools, and a devoted wife and mother. This is not a narrative of childhood but the summation of a life, sustained, practiced, and recreated at "home" in Trinidad. Mahase demonstrates a conscious effort to establish a legacy of belonging to her Caribbean home and of interconnectedness with a wider world that includes the Americas and Europe as well as India.

In *Roots* James Clifford observes in respect to the representational challenge of cultural localization: "Some strategy of localization is inevitable if significantly different ways of life are to be represented. But 'local' in whose terms? How is significant difference politically articulated and challenged? Who determines where (and when) a community draws its lines, names its insiders and outsiders?" (10). In Caribbean autobiographical practice these lines are drawn discursively around specific sites of dwelling and travel, illuminating transnational, political, economic, and cultural forces that traverse and constitute local and regional worlds. Identity markers within the texts under scrutiny here characteristically extend beyond a highly localized site of dwelling to regional and global encounters, coproductions, dominations, and resistances (Clifford 24); each specifies a distinct center of value that contextualizes the others in respect to the patchwork process of identity formation in the greater Caribbean.

Anna Mahase was born in 1899 into an ethnic Indian community that was much besieged by the host community's general perception of Indians as exotic and who were marginalized by differences of language, religion, and custom.[1] Negative stereotypes proliferated: Indians could be prone to violence or passive and docile, depending on the bias (Bridges 185, 195). Among the most injurious was the often repeated statement that the Indians had no real commitment to life in the colony: "The Coolie is notoriously *with* us only, but not *of* us. He gives nothing for what he takes, and thus contributes but little to the wealth of the country. He hoards his treasure to take it back to his native land, and while

among us, consumes hardly anything of our imports."[2] Anna
Mahase was also born into a Christian family, which made her a
distinct minority within the Hindu and Moslem Indian community. Moreover, she was Canadian Presbyterian in a British colony
where the Christian majority was predominantly Catholic, and the
British administration was "officially" Anglican. Beyond this,
Anna lost the support and intimacy of family life when her parents split up in 1910. Before departing for British Guiana (Guyana)
in search of work, her father left Anna, eleven, and her sister, Dor-
cas, thirteen, in the care of the Canadian mission's Iere Girls'
Home at Princess Town, "to be trained to be good housewives,
who would and should be leaders and examples wherever they
went" (Mahase 26). Later that year her mother returned to India
with her youngest daughter, Hannah, and found work with the
American mission there; she left her two young sons in the care
the Reverend Morton, a missionary working to educate and convert Indians in Trinidad.[3] After their father found work in Guyana,
the Reverend Morton sent the boys to him. For Anna the rhythm
of displacement and dispossession ended with her marriage to
Kenneth Mahase when she was twenty.

In "Prologue to an Autobiography" Naipaul explores as ontological desire and irrecoverable loss the Indo-Trinidadian quest for
community after the disruption and threat of the indenture experience: "This was what my father passed on to me about his family and childhood. The events were as dateless as the home events
of my own confused childhood. His early life seemed an extension back in time of my own; and I did not think to ask until much
later for a more connected narrative. . . . But some deep hurt or
shame, something still raw and unresolved in his experience, kept
my father from attempting any autobiographical writing" (*Finding the Center* 49–50). Much later Naipaul recoups what he can
from his father's sister, then on her deathbed and sharply focused
on what is to be her legacy. Communication is strained because
she still speaks little English: "But her talk to me was serious. It
was of caste and blood. . . . She wanted me to know now, before
the knowledge vanished with her, what she—and my father—had
come from. She wanted me to know that the blood was good"

(52). As Naipaul records, she says nothing about the wretchedness of work on the sugar estates, life in the barracks, and the
abuses of contract labor (53). The erasure is willed; the legacy is
pride in blood and caste.

In the space of such irreparable loss and longing for at-oneness,
My Mother's Daughter only partially fills the breach in community
and ancestry engendered by the loss of India as original space. The
sugar estates, the barracks, and contract labor are not Mahase's lot,
and she does not name them as part of her experience; in this
respect she repeats the elision of Naipaul's aunt. However, Mahase
records her loss and struggle for survival in terms of the specific
historical, cultural, and intellectual practices that shaped the
momentous transition from India to the Caribbean. Hers is the
legacy of a self-inscribed pioneer, who is about the business of
claiming and defending the New World of Trinidad as a homeland.
In *Routes* James Clifford asks, "What does it take to define and
defend a homeland? What are the political stakes in claiming (or
sometimes being relegated to) a 'home'?" (36). Anna Mahase's
autobiography responds to both questions; at stake are spiritual and
physical survival and the values by which she secures these.

In the opening chapter, named for her mother, Rookbai, she
begins by claiming authorship: "I began writing my story in April
1935. I stopped and began again in 1945. Then again in 1956"
(1). After this she methodically names herself in specific sequence:
Her father is head teacher of the Guaico Canadian Mission Indian
School; he is an India-born Hindu convert to Christianity who
came to Trinidad with his brother and widowed mother as a child;
her mother is an India-born Brahmin who ran away to Trinidad
at the age of twelve after she was taken to her new husband's
household, and she was also a convert to Christianity. First,
Mahase invokes her mother in the title of the chapter, then she
names her father's profession, his race and ethnicity as a Christian Indian, and her place of birth, then her mother's race, caste,
and ethnicity as a convert to Christianity. They lived in one of several settlements built by Indians who settled in Trinidad after
indenture, where the Canadian Presbyterian Mission established
a ministry and a school.[4]

Within these ontological configurations of family, faith, time and place of birth, race and ethnicity, home and belonging are mapped discursively across four generations—parents, siblings, children, and grandchildren—in a social space that expands geographically and experientially to include those places lived in, visited, and traveled through.[5] She traverses the island terrain by foot, donkey, train, and taxi. The boundaries of community are constituted ontologically and by use.[6] Belonging is established by dwelling and familiarity. Dwelling is not immobility or fixity so much as the practice of crisscrossing the terrain, building alliances with different communities, and in the process generating a discrete sociology of claiming and defending a homeland that is hers by historical and political circumstances but remains to be possessed discursively and corporeally as a context for self-representation. In these contexts she articulates the political stakes of claiming a "home." "I feel myself a real 'Son of the Soil'" (51), Mahase asserts at a particular point, registering her birthright across race, gender, and faith.

Mahase's strategies include the discursive competence of the local historian and native informant; it is unapologetically the personal narrative of the social activist, the partisan chronicler, and the keeper of family, community, and national records. For her, narrative operates on all three levels simultaneously. She records the numerous ways that she challenges community boundaries through the manipulation of her appearance, active intervention, cultivation of alliances, and sanctioned resistances. For example, she recalls that on her first teaching assignment, she trades in her Canadian mission attire for traditional Indian dress and greets the community in Hindi when she rounds up the neighborhood children at the start of the school day. The Reverend Morton seeks and obtains a special exemption from the director of education so that she can continue teaching after she is married: "When I was to be married I was almost out of the teaching profession, because the then code of regulations said 'No married woman is to be retained on the staff of any Government or Assisted Primary School in the Colony'" (46). She carefully records that Charles Solomon, the African Creole school inspector and father of Dr. Solomon, the current minister of home affairs, actively encourages her to retake her Third Class Teachers' Examination after failing it, thereby establishing her ties with influential people outside her ethnic group, church, and village community (42). Conversely, she exercises her ethnic authority when she takes time in her narrative to critique "corrupt" naming practices in the local Hindu community or to describe the "unique" Hindu traditions and customs that her mother practiced "though a Christian and the wife of a preacher" (12).

Not only does Mahase focus on the Canadian mission–Hindu alliance as a productive context for sustaining, practicing, and reinventing "home" but she foregrounds gender as center of consciousness. This begins with the identification of Rookbai as educated according to Hindu custom and an independent-minded and rebellious twelve-year-old who steals the money she needs to run away from an arranged marriage and who makes the long arduous journey by boat from Calcutta to Trinidad on her own. Mahase is emphatic about her mother's leadership qualities and the gender hierarchy that oppresses her spirit: "*My mother was a born leader of women and children*. But the only one she could not lead was my father. He always had his way, and it seems to me that events took place and changes in their own attitudes towards each other began. Misunderstandings I say, because as children, we noticed the change of behavior between them" (13). Her pride in her mother as an independent person with a will of her own is undiminished when her parents split up, and her father gives Anna and her sister into the care of the Canadian mission to be educated and in time married to suitable Christian Indian men. Mahase is critical of the arrangement as a marriage brokerage, which is not surprising, given her admiration of her mother's independent spirit: "The intention was good but did not prove satisfactory in many cases" (27). When her father goes to Guyana to look for work and her mother returns to India, Mahase couches these events in terms of her mother's expressed desire and an implicitly stated source of conflict between her parents: "My father went to British Guiana, and at the end of that year 1910, my mother with my youngest sister six years old, went to India, *which had always been her desire*" (20; emphasis added). Mahase values the letters and gifts that she receives from her mother from India. We are told that Rookbai found work with the support of the Canadian mission. There is a measurable continuity of value between the mother in India and her daughter in Trinidad.

In numerous instances Mahase's independent spirit shapes her destiny, and this is nowhere more evident than in the way that she circumvents the authority of the Canadian mission and social convention in her courtship with Kenneth Mahase and her subsequent marriage to him out of mutual love and commitment rather than by an arrangement between guardians. A successful marriage of her own choosing is a point of pride in Mahase's narrative, as are her education and her training as a teacher. She teaches alongside her husband until her retirement and contributes financially and intellectually to her family life. She represents this as a shared responsibility. The turning point in her life, as she describes it, is her high school education and training at a teachers' college. Mahase's emphasis on education as agency is not surprising, given that education is represented as her life's work. In "Midnight's Children and the Legacy of Nationalism," Patricia Mohammed reminds us that education was an important "means to personal and social recognition, allowed mobility for the individual and family, and brought economic rewards" (746). To support her point Mohammed quotes an Indian girl's statement about the importance of passing her examinations in Vera Rubin and Marisa Zavalloni's remarkable study *We Wish to be Looked Upon*: "We wish to be looked upon. I hope the examination would be a further step in my achievement of being someone to be looked upon" (67). This quest for recognition in the larger community, to cross the barriers that alienate and marginalize, dominates Mahase's narrative. It is a form of self-credentialing for fuller participation in the national community.

In *My Mother's Daughter* Mahase is conscious and celebratory of her pioneer status in *"the Nucleus of the Women's Section of the Naparima Training College for Teachers"* (33; emphasis in original). In a chapter entitled "A Worthy Pioneer," she reiterates this point of pride in personal achievement: "My teaching career began on May 1, 1917, *I being the first East Indian Assistant*

Teacher to be employed in an Assisted Primary School in North Trinidad, and later on, in 1919, the first East Indian qualified female teacher in the Island" (38). She elaborates on her pride in her accomplishments many years later: *"I am happy that I was able to blaze a trail, the result of which can be well satisfying to those who have continued and brought knowledge to the entire East Indian womanhood in Trinidad.* Thanks to the Canadian Mission" (38). She is careful to situate her sense of personal achievement ahead of the Canadian mission and later to characterize her active participation in many spheres in a similar way. She concludes: "My whole life was and has been one of continued activities in many spheres of life, teaching as a career, housekeeping and seven children, gardening as a hobby, poultry rearing, Child Welfare League and Child Welfare Weekly Clinic at the school, the W.M.S. of our church, Christian Endeavor Society, a regular Sunday School Teacher, an organist of our church for a long time" (92–93). Interiority is evident in the grief of an eleven-year-old child left with strangers and in a habitual pattern of reflection, but Mahase's autobiography turns on the reinvention of community as a public performance that engages the individual passionately in an interactive process that generates the necessary spiritual sustenance. Though Mahase does not travel outside the island, her parents, siblings, and children do, and through them she extends levels of cultural interaction with Canada, the United States, and Britain, even as she maintains contact with relatives in Guyana and reestablishes contact with her sister's children in India.

In *My Mother's Daughter* the discursive space of autobiographical narrative produces yet another configuration of Caribbean womanhood that constitutes itself at the expense of other worlds within her small and highly circumscribed island community, whether it is that of Hindu and Muslim Caribbeans, African Caribbeans, or white Creoles. Mahase, like the other writers in this study, chooses the constituency that best serves her purposes. Autobiographical agency pits her "I" against the others in what can be read as a radical act of appropriation and distancing. The vision of Christian womanhood inscribed by Mahase is strongly oriented toward the domestic roles of wife and mother;

however, she also pioneers a new role for Indian Caribbean women as a trained teacher who works alongside her husband as teacher and social activist. Mahase's brand of Christian womanhood is a blend of complicity and resistance, resisting as she does the arranged marriages of the Canadian mission while embracing their style of egalitarian marriage. By dedicating herself to an active and productive community life, Canadian mission–style, she carves out a distinctive space for Indo-Caribbean women that is a marvel of selection and erasure.

Like the Hart sisters, Anna Mahase allies herself with a transnational, metropolitan-based religious organization that is both liberating and alienating in the new forms of consciousness and the feminist activism that they bring to the lives of these island dwellers. Across the span of a century and a half, the empirical base of these narratives evidences a clear movement from the preoccupations of a slave colony to a modern nation-state, but a pattern persists in the enduring if reconstituted framework of transnational links and aspirations, unrestrained by ideas of spatial boundaries and territorial exclusiveness. From the Hart sisters to Mahase, identity is linked incontrovertibly to transforming transnational and transcultural influences and alliances with people, lands, and cultures beyond their Caribbean homeland.[7]

10

Colonist and Creole
Yseult Bridges's *Child of the Tropics* and Jean Rhys's *Smile Please*

In the wake of Claude McKay's pastoral exuberance in *My Green Hills of Jamaica,* and the studied melancholia of George Lamming's *In the Castle of My Skin,* the works of Jean Rhys and Yseult Bridges reconfigure yet again the values of a Caribbean childhood. Born within a couple years of Claude McKay, both creative writers revisit their Caribbean childhoods in narratives that are sharply differentiated despite observable conjunctures in status and privilege. McKay was born in Jamaica in 1890, the same year that Rhys was born in Dominica, and two years after Bridges was born in Trinidad. Claude McKay left Jamaica to study in the United States in 1912, while Rhys left Dominica for England in 1907, and Bridges left Trinidad even earlier, perhaps in 1902. It seems pointless to seek further parallels because the quality and character of their lives are so different, except that they all revisit their Caribbean childhoods in intimate interactions of memory and place. The result is a rooting of the writer's sensibility in a native Caribbean landscape that in effect reengineers the values of their original departure and subsequent errantry in gestures of filiation. What persists across the distance of time and space in these childhoods revisited is the lack of narrative connection among their different life-worlds, even where race, caste, and ethnicity are roughly equivalent, as in the case of Rhys and Bridges. Edouard Glissant observes that the commonality of errantry and exile is that "in both instances the roots are lacking" (*Poetics of Relation* 11).[1] Thus we have the paradox

214

of these narratives of childhood in their discernible, even passionate, gestures of rerooting and also their lack of correlation. In each case the dominative system of organization in the narrative is ideological rather than a sense of shared experience.

Rhys's *Smile Please* is in part a series of loosely connected autobiographical sketches of her childhood and adolescence in Dominica that are fraught with unease about her family's status on the island. On the other hand, Bridges's *Child of the Tropics* is a more conventional narrative of a privileged and happy childhood and adolescence. It is perhaps emblematic of the transgressive nature of the autobiographical narratives of Bridges and Rhys that, even though rooted in a conservative Victorianism, both *Child of the Tropics* and *Smile Please* may be read as postcolonial texts. Rhys's penetration of Caribbean literary consciousness does not occur until the publication of *Wide Sargasso Sea,* which preceded the dictation of her unfinished autobiography by several years. Similarly, Bridges's citing of a passage from Eric Williams's *Inward Hunger* (1969) marks *Child of the Tropics* as a narrative informed by postcolonial consciousness. However, while Rhys's *Smile Please* is discernibly in conflict with the formal structures of autobiography and its ideological assumptions of unitary being, Bridges uses them to advantage in the reification of the white Creole class to which she belongs and to that extent widens the gulf that Edward Kamau Brathwaite decries. For example, her use of the Caribbean Trinidadian nationalist Eric Williams as a referent and historical authority is offset by her use of Charles Kingsley, whom Eric Williams mocks in *British Historians and the West Indies* for his ideological inconsistencies.[2] Evelyn O'Callaghan argues that texts like these reveal much about the relationship between the European cult of domesticity and the patriarchal-colonial enterprise. Certainly, some abiding conflicts of colonial feminism are made explicit as Bridges and Rhys negotiate issues of race, class, gender, and sexuality in their narratives.

Yseult Bridges's *Child of the Tropics* was edited by Nicholas Guppy, her nephew and a writer and ecologist. Guppy introduces her as a successful writer and amateur ethnographer and testifies to the authenticity and veracity of the text as a "settler" narrative:

"It depicts the rich and fascinating life of English and French set-
tlers in the Caribbean in their Victorian heyday. Perhaps in fiction
Patrick Leigh-Fermor in *The Violins of Saint-Jacques,* or George
W. Cable in *Madame Delphine* and *Old Creole Days* have captured
some of the feeling of that vanished world" (9).[3]

On one level *Child of the Tropics* is an insider's portrait of the
manners and customs of a class at a specific time and place, and
as such it assumes the ideological contours of a normalizing discourse.[4] In this case the normalizing discourse of manners and customs is integrated with the nostalgic narrative of a happy childhood.
One result is the projection of childhood innocence and otherworldliness onto a historical epoch and the displacement of the
latter onto the exclusive, self-regulating world of a childhood that
ends when she leaves Trinidad for England at the age of fourteen.
Within the constraints of the autonomous autobiography of childhood, historical time is transmuted, the distinction between myth
and reality is blurred, and settler-colonial space is valorized as a
utopian space.[5]

Bridges's narrative immersion in the flora and fauna of Trinidad
(her father was a well-known English paleontologist who settled
in Trinidad) begs the question raised by Brathwaite, that this
knowledge and love of the landscape never extended beyond the
concern for what was being created in a "superficial, economic
sense" (*Contradictory Omens* 33). In this vein it might be argued
that the narrative framework of an idealized happy childhood
that is at one with place sidesteps issues of displacement and
accountability that surface in Rhys's *Smile Please.*[6] One context
for negotiating Brathwaite's charge in Bridges's case might be to
substitute Gaston Bachelard's notion of reverie as a descriptor for
autobiography and memoir: "There are reveries so deep, reveries
which help us descend so deeply within ourselves that they rid us
of our history. They liberate us from our name" (*Poetics of Reverie*
99). But this would be to emphasize the narcissistic-mythical elements in this carefully detailed exotic fantasy at the expense of its
more aggressive didactic-interpretive elements.[7]

In "The Other Question" in *The Location of Culture,* Homi
Bhabha invokes Jacques Lacan's schema of the Imaginary to explain

the close relationship between narcissism and aggressivity in colonial discourse; an application of Lacan also illuminates the psychosocial resonance of a colonial childhood in Bridges and Rhys.

> The Imaginary is the transformation that takes place in the subject at the formative mirror phase, when it assumes a *discrete* image which allows it to postulate a series of equivalencies, samenesses, identities, between the objects of the surrounding world. However, this positioning is itself problematic, for the subject finds and recognizes itself through an image which is simultaneously alienating and hence potentially confrontational. This is the basis of the close relation between the two forms of identification complicit with the Imaginary—narcissism and aggressivity. (77)

Following this line of thought, narcissism and aggressivity in the Bridges and Rhys narratives of childhood project overlapping and contradictory ideologies that are complicitous in imperial myth making and also facilitate the unmasking of such myths.

Bridges's *Child of the Tropics* is predictably a fence-building exercise, marking as it does the exotic boundaries of a colonial identity grounded in the preservation of French Creole and English colonial social, cultural, and economic interests in postemancipation Trinidad.[8] She gives a fund of information about the manners and customs of her class, the landscape and living conditions she and her neighbors enjoyed, the flora and fauna that caught their attention.[9] She describes the warmth, the richness, and the intricacy of caste-class relationships and loyalties as she experienced them as a child; in short, this can be read as a loving memorial to the safety, security, privilege, and European promise of her tropical childhood. It follows that this narrative is heavily invested in the house and garden or plantation as a psychic space that may be threatened periodically from within (Aunt Nini's meanness or a thieving black servant) but remains a safe harbor for daydreams and play and for the subsequent assumption of an English identity that conforms to the ideals of nineteenth-century Englishness as Simon Gikandi describes them: "a patriarchal domestic space, a harmonious social order, and psychological restraint" (105).

Bridges describes herself as shaped primarily by her renowned English father's intellectual and scientific interests and distances herself selectively from her French Creole mother's domestic authority and social aspirations. She may criticize her mother's sister, Aunt Nini Rostant, but she is careful to celebrate values of the Rostant clan as a whole, praising them as model plantation owners whose slaves chose to stay with them after emancipation and who are much loved by their pensioners and other dependents. The narrative indicates that she conforms to her mother's domestic authority reluctantly as a child and even pokes fun at her mother's colonial obsession with high fashion and culture, though this does not preclude conformity at the age of fourteen to the expectations of parents, family, and class that she don "the conventional summer attire of an English schoolgirl" on her departure for England (203).[10] Female agency is allied to the English side of the family, where women were professionally active and dared to be unconventional without loss of status, at least in a remote corner of the British Empire. We are told that her paternal grandmother, Amelia Parkinson (1808–1886) of Kinnersley, Herefordshire, was a painter who, in 1871, at the age of sixty-three went on an expedition into the upper reaches of the Orinoco and was gone for more than a year. Bridges recalls that she had a wealthy English aunt who wanted to adopt her and make her sole heir to a considerable fortune. It comes as no surprise that, when she was nine and on a visit to England with her parents, Bridges knew England to be her home and destiny: "As I kneeled on the carriage seat gazing out of the window a strange feeling came over me: I *knew* that this was my country: I *knew* that however much I loved Trinidad here only could my home ultimately be; that whatever fate might take me in the days to come, the roots of my being were deeply implanted here—and would eventually pull me back" (172).

The comparative colonial framework of "home" and "abroad" has been internalized not only as a value but as a birthright. Thus her narrative of childhood, despite the high degree of intimacy with place and people, is devoid of interest and attachment to Trinidad beyond her immediate home and family. Most tellingly, England ("Land of My Fathers") enables identity differentiation from the narrow sphere of her mother's world in Trinidad; it is, however, a differentiation that her mother endorses because she has herself shifted her cultural allegiance to England during the course of her marriage.

Though her English grandfather (Robert Guppy) and her English father (Lechemere Guppy) are actively engaged in politics and in the colonial administration of Trinidad, and Bridges describes herself as intimate with her father's considerable library, his workshop, and later the daily routines of his estate in Santa Cruz, though she has read and cites Eric Williams's autobiography *Inward Hunger,* Bridges's memoir is structured strictly within the conventions of stereotypical racial discourse. For example, the world of the Indian indentured immigrant is relegated to the periphery of Bridges's autobiographical consciousness, almost as an afterthought: "How little thought we gave to such poor creatures in those days! Yet there were scores like him—and there are to this day in many countries. Homeless, they slept under a tree or on a public bench. Unemployed, they were thankful to earn a couple of cents carrying a load for an able-bodied negro, who bullied and derided them, and not infrequently cheated them out of even this pittance" (62).[11] Though Indians work the Guppy estate under an African overseer, and the household includes a feudal-style retinue of black servants, protégés, and retainers, Bridges's adult consciousness of the island's majority African and Indian population conforms to the stereotype.[12] Colonial fantasy clarifies her racial difference and theirs as part of a visible and natural order. Later, at Glenside, the Guppy estate in the Santa Cruz valley, Bridges is defensive about the impoverished and much beleaguered Indian agricultural laborer: "These were all East Indians, and they lived in such neat little whitewashed houses built of mud and thatch, and set amidst the plots of land from which they earned their livelihood. . . . They were orderly, civil and hardworking. They did not pilfer from the estate, which was the invariable practice of the negroes: and they possess dignity and grace; the young men were unusually handsome and the girls exceedingly pretty" (185).[13]

Her "insider" knowledge of racial difference rationalizes and reinforces colonial privilege as part of a visible and natural order of things, seemingly at every turn.[14] If East Indians are fetishized as agricultural laborers, the "negro" occasions a distinct chain of stereotypes. Not surprisingly, intimacy with black people is one-sided and stereotyped by their functional relationship to the family.[15] Household servants function as an extension of parental authority and protection; they serve principally as gate keepers and boundary markers.[16]

Unsupervised excursions outside the domestic sphere engender fear and danger. On one occasion Bridges ventures out on her own to meet her parents on their arrival from England and finds herself surrounded by black men, women, and children: "They gaped and jabbered, and the smell of their unwashed skin and clothes was rank and nauseating. My knees went weak, my stomach seemed to cleave to my spine. With all my heart I longed for Estelle [her black nanny]" (112).[17] She is rescued from racial and sexual terror by a passing Englishman, reaffirming the bias of racial and cultural stereotypes in which "white heroes and black demons are proffered as points of ideological and psychical identification" (Bhabha, *Location of Culture* 76).[18] This account of the lurking menace of black people outside the garden walls, and others that voice a fear and scorn of the lugubrious and thieving mulatto (55, 57), not to mention the intrusive "besmirching" intimacy of a wealthy Portuguese merchant class girl whom she encounters at school (120), are all represented as actively menacing to an idyllic girlhood and intimate a Caribbean subjectivity in flight from "degenerative" interculturative processes that are under way.[19] The resistant consciousness here is sensitive only to issues of gender discrimination and is peripherally so.[20] Agency for Bridges is the freedom to be her Creole mother's daughter and to experience firsthand her father's world of books, scientific inquiry, and estate production and to claim his English identity as her own.

In comparison, Rhys's *Smile Please* is not only oppositional; it is transgressive. Her subversive "unfinished autobiography," dictated to the English novelist David Plante, edited by him under her supervision, and further subjected to Diana Athill's editorial authority before publication in 1979, suggests that Rhys is at odds with the way she is defined, as a white Creole and a colonial, by the dominant ideology of an Edward Long or a Trollope or a Froude or a Kingsley or a Yseult Bridges.[21] The episodic and eccentric manner of her dictation to Plante challenges the Bridges style of caste consolidation; in fact, *Smile Please* tells a destabilizing story that challenges many assumptions that shape the Bridges narrative. This shift in values is located in the form and substance of the vignettes that encapsulate the contradictions and ambivalences of her Dominican childhood in *Smile Please*.

I am concerned here with the first section of Rhys's unfinished autobiography, which she titled "Smile Please," rather than with the second section, "It Began to Grow Cold." As her editor, Diana Athill, explains in an editor's note, Rhys did not consider the material in the second section finished work, and some of it is little more than notes.[22] The first section, by contrast, is thematically and structurally complete as a narrative of childhood, ending as it does with leaving home in excited anticipation of life in England: "I was on my way to England. . . . Already all my childhood, the West Indies, my father and mother had been left behind; I was forgetting them. They were the past" (76). Bridges's narrative of childhood ends at a similar point, though in a different vein: "But I knew with a clear, nostalgic certainty that now, in that very instant, I was bidding farewell to my childhood; that though I should see these familiar scenes again, and see them with a happy heart, yet never should I see them with the same untrammeled rapture, the same pure, unsullied joy" (205).[23] Intimations of return and reconnection are absent in Rhys; in their place is the finality of a much desired ending to an unstable childhood. If *Child of the Tropics* can be described as an exotic-didactic-interpretive childhood, then *Smile Please* is thematically and structurally an exotic-schizophrenic childhood, described by Richard N. Coe as "an experience of the past self, in which two incompatible cultural backgrounds clash . . . violently" (228).

This violence to the psyche is apparent in the fragmentary, episodic nature of Rhys's autobiography.[24] It is also there in a recurring thematic of "terrified consciousness." The sense of legitimacy, of safety and security, that constitutes the psychic space of home and family in *Child of the Tropics* is absent in Rhys, and this may have been fueled by the family's shrinking financial resources and relative loss of privilege. In Rhys's Dominica the family compound is vulnerable to attack by rioting black Dominicans, which she describes in "Black/White" (37–38). Not only is her mother's ancestral home, the Geneva house, "burnt down two, or was it three, times" (29) but her parents are alienated from family members who reside there, and visits stop abruptly when she is still quite young. Moreover, there is social exchange between Rhys's mother and Mrs. Campbell, a colored woman married to a white man, and Rhys implies the kind of intimacy between them that allows her mother to express her fear of financial ruin and weep in anticipation of it within her daughter's view. This kind of fissure in the hierarchy of race and class is not possible in Bridges's representation of Alice Guppy's household, where the socially acceptable "colored" woman simply does not exist. The mulatto Lizzie Waldron, who is called in to pawn valuable items when Alice needs cash for some foible, generates fear and unease in the child Yseult, who is conditioned to see the mulatto woman's presence as intrusive and menacing (57–58).[25]

In *Smile Please* the instability of social values and institutions, public and private, is linked in highly focused fragments to a corresponding psychic instability so that the child appears to be the hapless victim of social and political circumstances in which she shares yet for which she bears no responsibility because she is a child. For example, she links her childhood fear of losing her mother's love to a childhood desire to be black because she thinks that her mother prefers black babies; in the process Rhys constructs her whiteness as a kind of original sin and occasion for rejection. Envy and fear, love and hatred of black people coexist without resolution in the sensibility of the child. The child's innocence and vulnerability are recorded in each failed attempt to change her relationship to her social environment. Her overtures of friendship to a colored girl at school are rebuffed: "This was—hatred impersonal, implacable hatred. I recognised it at once and if you think a child cannot recognise hatred and remember it for life you are most damnably mistaken. . . . I never tried to be friendly with any of the colored girls again. I was polite and that was all" (30).

This reverses the representation of a cross-class/color gesture of friendship among schoolgirls in *Child of the Tropics,* when Bridges is offended by the presence in Miss Bunkle's once exclusive school of "Portuguese, Venezuelan, Lebanese, Syrian and Greek girls as well as English and French; and some of them to my innocent eyes were odiously precocious" (120). When Mina, the daughter of a wealthy Portuguese, tries to establish a friendship with Yseult by giving her a silver thimble, then inviting Yseult to her birthday party and giving her a kiss on the lips, Yseult is revolted: "Suddenly she slipped an arm around me and kissed me on the mouth. I went hot and cold. I was horrified and oddly revolted, but had not the courage to move" (121).

In *Smile Please* there are instances when Rhys tries to help the cook in the kitchen, or to teach the overseer how to read and write, that end in failure due to an observed hostility among the colored and black population to her interventions, which they correctly interpret as marks of difference and superiority that reinforce a hierarchical relation between white and black, mistress and servant. But Rhys's ambivalence about race comes to rest in her representation of black women as debased and malignant.[26] She describes her black nurse Meta, as "the terror of my life" (22) and blames her for generating an enduring fear and distrust of black people in her as a child (24). A similar pattern is repeated when the overseer's wife registers her disapproval of the teenage Rhys's teaching her husband to read and write in their home: "I think it was the fifth time I went there that we were interrupted by someone laughing very loudly in the doorway. I looked up and there was John's wife, just come in from work on the estate. She was a very big woman, much bigger than John himself. Her skirts were girded up far above her knees and she had a cutlass in her hand. The sharp edge looked blue" (69). Standing in the doorway, John's wife clearly occupies that dangerous threshold zone, "where the public world of propertied power and the private world of familial decorum met their conceptual limit" (McClintock 119). The teenage Rhys acknowledges defeat and withdraws resentfully and petulantly. Liberation from the constraints of class and privilege appears to be a childish fantasy; agency is limited finally to flights of the imagination into the immensities intuited in language, books, religion, and nature and her eventual "escape" to England with her aunt at the age of sixteen.

Rhys's narrative design retreats from intimations of unitary being across the racial and cultural divide generated by the brutal hierarchies of slavery and colonialism. Her subversive choice of form suggests Wilson Harris's "exciting pathways into the reality of traditions that bear upon cross-cultural capacities for genuine change in communities beset by complex dangers and whose antecedents are diverse" (Harris, Womb xv). Her choice of vignettes gives anecdotal coherence to the child's contradictory subjectivities as an inescapable condition of being Jean Rhys in that place at that time and for all time. The fragmented narrative structure projects no resolution; on the contrary, it appears to mark Rhys's psychocultural plurality as permanent and the nucleus of her creativity.27 It is also a narrative form that refuses to take "Reveries toward Childhood" in the Bachelardian sense of a sacred communion with a primal self too seriously (Poetics of Reverie 99–141). Vignettes like those in the chapter titles for Smile Please— "Smile Please," "Facts of Life," and "The Religious Fit"—are ironic commentaries on childhood autobiography. For example, "Smile Please" summons up a photo session when Rhys was six, locates the gap between her memory of the occasion and the photo that keeps the memory alive, and also serves as a material and imagined measure of change and continuity in her physical appearance and personality. "Facts of Life" ranges from sneaking into her father's consulting room to look for information on sexuality to her "dog's love affair while I was taking him for a walk" (49) to falling in love with words and kissing her horse's neck and calling him "Darling, darling!" (52) when he won a race. For the playfulness of Smile Please to become obvious, one has only to compare this chapter to Bridges on the same subject:

> I passed into the first stages of adolescence entirely incurious as to sex, no more than casually observing the changes which were taking place within me. Running barefoot about the estate, following the stream, swimming in its pools and wading in its shallows, lying

on my rock terrace with all my senses attuned to catch the sight and sounds of Nature I was untouched by any of the soul-searchings, the morbid curiosity, the dreads and distortions, with which the approach of puberty affects so many children. (Bridges 201–2)

Similarly, "The Religious Fit" makes fun of Rhys's youthful desire to transform the unwanted baggage of her racial difference through "good works" among black Dominicans. The play dimension of *Smile Please* is constituted in the adult Rhys's playfully "performing" childhood and making up the rules as she goes along.[28]

The empirical base of these narratives confirms the difficulty of maintaining exclusionist paradigms in respect to identity formation in the Caribbean, even within the narrow confines of a common colonial settler-Creole experience within a specific discursive form. Their narratives suggest that nothing about identity is fixed or monolithic in a multiply-centered diaspora network like the Caribbean, beyond some notion of contiguous cultural connection to the region as an original site of dwelling and return.[29] To use their race or color as the cultural or political sign of inferiority or degeneracy is to devalue their contribution on the basis of race and perpetuate their legacy of skin color as a "visible and natural" object of discrimination (Bhabha, *Location of Culture* 80). In hindsight, their highly localized sense of Caribbean dwelling is an inherently fragile social and cultural achievement. Their legacy takes its place among others in an ever shifting regional ethnoscape of socially and spatially defined networks of community.[30]

Part 4

Autobiography, Elegy, and Gender Identification

Thus far the conventions of self-identification and self-preservation in the autobiographical texts in this study coincide with the conventions of gender identification operative in their different social contexts. Autobiographical constructions of identity may be sympathetic and compassionate toward the opposite sex, as in Mary Prince and Mary Seacole, but a carefully guarded pattern of male or female self-identification is a defining feature of all these narratives. This said, the elegies of Kamau Brathwaite and Jamaica Kincaid both appear to question the exclusiveness of such normative patterns of self-identification by installing the deceased other within the self in a dynamic process of cross-gender identification.

In *The Zea Mexican Diary* and *My Brother*, Brathwaite and Kincaid break with the conventionally drawn gender identifications of antecedent texts. Both Brathwaite and Kincaid question repetitive gender hierarchies and/or binaries as oppressive formulations within the postcolonial body politic. Yet these texts do not overlap, for whereas *The Zea Mexican Diary* questions rigid gender formulations of masculine and feminine as Brathwaite mourns the death of his wife, *My Brother* questions the compulsory heterosexuality that has rendered Kincaid's bisexual brother culturally unintelligible to her otherwise resistant and historically aware consciousness. In *Gender Trouble* Judith Butler observes:

> The rules that govern intelligible identity, i.e., that enable and restrict the intelligible assertion of an "I," rules that are partially structured along matrices of gender hierarchy and compulsory heterosexuality, operate through *repetition*. Indeed, when the subject is said to be constituted, that means simply that the subject is a consequence of certain rule-governed discourses that govern the intelligible invocation of identity. The subject is not *determined* by the rules through which it is generated because signification is *not a founding act, but rather a regulated process of repetition* that both conceals itself and enforces its rules precisely through the production of substantializing effects. (145)

If, as she argues, agency "is to be located within the possibility of a variation on that repetition" (145), the conjunction of elegy and autobiography in the lyric outpouring of these writers' thoughts and feelings in grief and loss appears to create precisely such a possibility in the reconfiguration and redeployment of gendered identity in *The Zea Mexican Diary* and *My Brother*.

Cross-gender identifications are of a very different quality in *The Zea Mexican Diary* and *My Brother*, but what both writers share is a searing personal loss that initiates a revaluation of the terms through which identity has been articulated. The work of mourning fashions new insight into the triangular relationship of self, deceased, and community that in turn invites a reconfiguration of the self and the self's own cultural location.[1] Freud's 1917 essay "Mourning and Melancholia" provides a theoretical framework appropriated by scholars such as Jahan Ramazani and Melissa F. Zeiger in their studies of elegy. In *Beyond Consolation* Zeiger appropriates this model "as a translation into literature of the grieving process following a death, leading to resignation or consolation" (3). In *Poetry of Mourning* Ramazani dilutes Freud's binary distinction between mourning and melancholia, taking the position that "'melancholic mourning' is conceivable as a term for the kind of ambivalent and protracted grief often encountered in the modern elegy" (29). Though not concerned with elegy, Butler's *Gender Trouble* offers intriguing insights on the work of mourning in the context of Freud's "Mourning and Melancholia" and his 1923 *The Ego and the Id,* both in respect to the melancholia of gender and the limits of gender identification.[2] Butler's insights illuminate the complexities of cross-gender identification in ways that are applicable to both *The Zea Mexican Diary* and *My Brother,* because in each case the loss of the loved one is overcome only through specific acts of identification that seek to make the deceased a permanent part of the mourner's identity: "This identification is not simply momentary or occasional, but becomes a new structure of identity; in effect, the other becomes part of the ego through the permanent internalization of the other's attributes" (Butler 58). Butler argues that this process of internalization contributes not only to character formation but to gender formation as well (58). In both *The Zea Mexican Diary* and *My Brother* the signifying practices of gender in the antecedent autobiographical texts are challenged through grief and loss to acts of cross-gender identification that produce uncanny reconfigurations of inherited gender binaries.

For Brathwaite the very process of male mourning challenges the status quo because friends and family construe melancholy as feminine and unmanly. Part of the poet's resolve is to change the culture of death and mourning to make it more accommodating to men who find themselves dispossessed of the feminine in the loss of a wife or partner and also dispossessed of the rituals of mourning, which are culturally available to women but not to men. If the only way that the mourner can survive the loss of his beloved is by internalizing his ties to her as wife and muse, this theoretically entails a gender-altering process of identification and incorporation. It may be that this process of incorporation is a fantasy, not a process, one that is "imagined within a language that can conjure and reify such spaces" (Butler 67). However, fantasy is a moot point within the conventions of elegy and autobiography when established patterns of gender identification are reconfigured through cross-gender identifications that install the object of grief and loss within a reconfigured self.

In the case of the death of Kincaid's brother from AIDS, cross-gender identification and incorporation engage a different set of taboos because of the ambivalence in their sibling relationship, her disapproval of his lifestyle, and her discovery after his death that he was bisexual rather than heterosexual. The internalizing strategy of mourning and melancholia as a point of departure thus engages issues of gender identification and sexual identity in areas that challenge rigidly drawn boundaries of normative heterosexuality, beyond the signifying gender specificity that nearly always characterizes autobiographical narratives of men and women. In *My Brother* the elegiac movement toward apotheosis, the return to the world with fears allayed and faith renewed, is replayed twice: after her brother's death and after she learns of his secret life of closeted homosexual activity.

Cross-gender identification in both texts is played out against the familiar thematic of travel and dwelling, islanders and emigrants, but with some interesting twists in their representation of Caribbean space. In the case of *My Brother* Kincaid is the emigrant to North America who travels back and forth to the island to bring aid to her dying brother and aging mother. Her descriptions of island space are marked by colonial and postcolonial neglect and decay and a reciprocal representation of the prostrate, disfigured body of her dying and deceased brother. For most of the narrative the Antiguan landscape is the body of "my brother," problematizing the representation of both until the very end of the narrative when the inadequacy of her controlling viewpoint becomes apparent to narrator and reader. This reversal of the traditional gendering of landscape as feminine focuses a sense of displacement and a crisis of identity in the errant writer around gender-based issues of cultural dislocation and erasure in an unprecedented way.

In the case of *The Zea Mexican Diary* both Brathwaite and his late wife settled in Jamaica, where they made their home. He is from Barbados and she was from Guyana; her death triggered not only a crisis of identity but also a crisis of identification with the Jamaican landscape as adopted home. By burying Doris's ashes in part and scattering the rest over the Blue Mountains, he in effect fixes Doris in the Jamaican landscape. This use of the landscape restores and makes permanent a positive aspect of his relationship to the Jamaican landscape and his wife. Doris is biologically linked to the natural landscape and deified as earth mother. This feminization of the field of vision proves empowering and restorative to a battered and grieving male ego.

11

Beyond Consolation
Kamau Brathwaite's *The Zea Mexican Diary*

The funeral themes of V. S. Naipaul's *A Way in the World*, and the elegiac components of *The History of Mary Prince, My Green Hills of Jamaica, In the Castle of My Skin, The Pleasures of Exile, Another Life, Child of the Tropics, My Mother's Daughter,* and *Finding the Center* give way in *The Zea Mexican Diary* to full-blown elegy. *The Zea Mexican Diary* memorializes "the perfect poet's wife" (152), records the events leading up to and following her death as the poet experiences them, and launches a critique of social codes and practices that leave him, the male survivor, feeling marginalized and bereft of comfort. In short, Brathwaite introduces issues of gender identity unaddressed in male-authored texts in this study. The traumatic events poeticized in this diary of his wife's death are also about the survival of the male poet subject whose harrowing experience of death and loss is transformed through poetic elegy into a medium for the understanding and transmission of painful truths about self and community; his failures and insecurities are part of the record, as are the failures and insecurities of a community with whom he is in conflict regarding sexual difference and the culture of death.

The elegiac themes of loss, mourning, and melancholia describe a pervasive mood in much of Brathwaite's poetry of the black Atlantic experience, classically embodied in his first trilogy, *The Arrivants,* and variously explored in subsequent trilogies. In fact, the trope of the Middle Passage in Brathwaite's work as a whole lends itself to the work-of-mourning model derived from Freud's "Mourning and Melancholia." Gordon Rohlehr observes that it is possible "to view Brathwaite's presentation of the entire Middle Passage experience as one vast collective night journey made by diasporan Africans" (introduction v).[1] In *The Zea Mexican Diary*, however, the poet's customary panoramic sweep of the black Atlantic and persistent racial melancholia is transformed. The elegiac contours of his diary of death, loss, and displacement are resolutely personal in their fashioning of the poet as a man on the inside of the experience, who struggles toward healing and transcending his wife's death as a condition of his continuance.[2]

On his return to the Caribbean after eight years spent working with the Ministry of Education in Ghana (1955–1962), the activist poet, who sought to embody, in his life and work, the diasporan quest for wholeness, projects an aesthetic sensibility shattered by the circumstances surrounding the death of his beloved wife, Doris Monica, about three months after she was diagnosed as terminally ill with cancer. Brathwaite's cultural project had barely begun when he met and married Doris in 1960 while on long leave in Barbados. She returned to Ghana with him and assumed an active partnership in his life's work. Her dedication to Brathwaite's momentous cultural project remained an unrecorded and unwritten dimension of his life's work until the publication of her exhaustive bibliography, *EKB: His Published Prose and Poetry, 1948–1986*, which came out in the year of her death, and the poet's passionate account of the circumstances surrounding her death in *The Zea Mexican Diary*.

The Zea Mexican Diary makes public a different side of Brathwaite. Black iconic leadership gives way to grief and lamentation in a public examination of hitherto unrevealed aspects of self and community, the author's intimate relationship with his wife, and, by extension, women's role in a male-defined cultural enterprise. At the center of *The Zea Mexican Diary* is the empowering figure of the woman who is also the poet's muse, though not his only muse (78).[3] Yet this is not Doris's story so much as a testament to their passionate and companionate partnership in a shared cultural project that valued his genius over her devotion. It celebrates "the perfect wife of/for the poet" (152). She is represented as intimately bound up with and devoted to the male poet subject of the text: "She made it possible. Created from the very / start & kept it go/ing to the last moments of her very life. The perfect / temperature & space for the poems to be/come" (152). The poet's cultural project is enabled by his wife and threatened by her loss: "But what I fear/fear for is not the fu- / ture me/ but future of the poems" (182). *The Zea Mexican Diary* laments her loss as a threat to the poet's cultural production; it memorializes his "masculine" dependency on and incorporation of her "feminine" attributes in this very public published display of grief.[4] The interdependence of this "loveline life-line" (89), as Brathwaite represents it in *The Zea Mexican Diary*, creates a dynamic space for the poet's exploration and expression of gendered identity as a personal and cultural problematic.

The interdependence of the poet's cultural project and his marriage locates *The Zea Mexican Diary* within the structural paradigm of the Orpheus and Eurydice myth, though not without extensive refiguring of this traditional model.[5] As Eurydice, Doris is immortalized as the poet's wife, now irrevocably lost to him. As Orpheus, the poet is humbled by his grief and loss and his inability to reverse her fate and his. *The Zea Mexican Diary* moves between what Celeste Schenck calls mourning and panegyric: "In the interplay of elegiac and epithalamic strains, the conventions of the one are exchanged for those of the opposite ritual: the procession of the wedding march, for example, finds its complement in the cortege" (11). The elegiac quest is for poetic continuance through the poet's emotionally charged representation of marriage as the celebrated site of artistic emergence and production.[6] In this case the marriage plot turns on Doris's death; her immortality as the poet's wife and muse is ensured in his literary rebirth, ritualized in an act of communion when he places some of her ashes on his tongue and literally ingests some of her remains in what may be read as an attempt to make her a permanent part of his subsequent life: "I put some of the ashes on my / tongue & swallowed her" (199).

This private act of ingestion is mysterious and uncanny in its seeming parody of the Catholic and Anglican rituals of Holy

Communion and in its evocation of cannibalistic practice.[7] In Brathwaite's "Notes" to the recorded version of *Islands*, he links his earlier treatment of this theme in "Eating the Dead" (*The Arrivants* 219–21) to both Vodou's *manger les morts* and Catholicism's Eucharist.[8] Rohlehr explains that the Haitian ritual of *mangé morts* is "a ceremony of remembrance and in-gathering which the Haitian people consider important for the preservation of the psychic wholeness of the tribe. It thus parallels the Catholic eucharist in which Christian ritualists eat the symbolic body (bread) and drink the symbolic blood (wine) of Christ in remembrance of his death and resurrection, and in hope of their attainment of 'everlasting life'" (Rohlehr, *Pathfinder* 258).[9] Beyond issues of organic survival (Rohlehr, *Pathfinder* 222), one might argue that in *The Zea Mexican Diary* this is not an act of negation so much as it is an act self-preservation, an attempt to establish continuity with the deceased and perhaps to ensure her continued participation in his cultural work: "As I experience it, it is the nature of the poet / to base a great deal of his self, poise & creativity, / on his oneness with his wife & the happiness of / shared memories" (146). The token act of ingestion incorporates and sublimates the poet's desire to hold onto his wife's signal virtues—her morality, generosity, courage, and fidelity (22–24)—after her death, but oral ingestion implies transgressive desire and destruction as well as consecration. Thus the poet's transcendent vision of love and self-preservation projects a rather mysterious, contradictory ego ideal in this figure of incorporation that both cancels out and reaffirms gender hierarchies in the name of culture and art.[10]

Using the Orpheus myth to contextualize her analysis of the genre, Melissa Zeiger notes that the myth "also addresses the fear that to grieve at all, but especially to write elegy, is to be unmasculine" (11). This cultural bias that privileges women in rituals of mourning is of course as much Akan as it is British.[11] In *The Zea Mexican Diary* Brathwaite opens up these and other questions about the culture of death as he experiences it in Jamaica. The lyric, meditative, reflective mode of the elegy creates a space for denouncing the way that the "feminine" culture of death disposes of men in grief: "But the widow's Other? *the widower?* In a-we- / culture? Depending on his age/con- dition he's / either useless cock or hot new uneXpected / 'property'/ the newly 'eligible bachelor'" (175). The male poet subject bitterly laments the lack of established avenues for the expression of male grief: "In / either/neither case / NO/BODY bizness wid im grief & / dislocation . im is suppose to cope / ('*real man' na cry* etc etc etc)" (175). In his anger and felt rejection he returns to established gender binaries again and again as a threat to his continuance as a poet: "But it seems to me that we have / so marginalized our males (or have they so / marginalized them- / selves) that we don't even know **how** to / comfort them Xcept perhaps as lovers or / chilldren" (174).

There is a felt struggle in *The Zea Mexican Diary* for "own-ership" of his dying wife and the rituals of death. Unprepared for the struggle and inadequate to the task, the poet stakes his claim to her dying and death in and through his diary. Although his celebration of her devotion to his artistic life, "her life deal-ing with my life" (89), might be read as a celebration of her servi-tude, the struggle between the sexes is modified somewhat as a struggle between culture and anticulture (151), or a contempt for his work as a poet. His poetic power, mocked and derided for its inefficacy in arresting her steady progress toward death, reasserts itself in elegy, in revelations of domestic intimacies, harrowing details of the physical ravages of cancer, in the eroti-cized memory of her body laid out for burial: "[When Sheila stripped her down to sponge her & / xamine her . her naked body stretched there on / the bed was as beautiful & desirable as ever . / I cd have made love to her that Sunday morning" (68). Memories of a courtship, marriage, and companionship inter-change with guilt about his neglect and infidelities and his wife's reassurances of enduring love and devotion: "Said / she'll miss me had enjoyed every minute of our ti- / me together wd do it all over again if she cd" (50–51). Funeral dirge and nuptial song are inextricably mixed in a soulful resistance to the authority of the women who tend to his wife, and they make him more acutely aware of his gender-defined helplessness and dependency when faced with the loss of his wife.

In the gender dynamics of the poet's public display of grief, his wife is represented as muse, guardian, and the stronger of the two in their active partnership in his life's work: "4 yrs younger than her / but the 'weaker sex'. Much weaker" (27).[12] She is uniquely enabling, but the coterie of women who manage her illness and death in the face of his masculine unpreparedness is perceived as threatening in its cultural authority, or ownership, of an experience that he registers as intimate to his male poet psyche. When "V" tells him that his hope for a miraculous recovery is standing in the way of his wife's death, he is defensive and accusatory at the lack of sympathy and understanding of his motivation as "twin and couple" (66). Time and again, *The Zea Mexican Diary* narrates a felt threat to the dependency of the culturally privileged male persona on the enabling feminine in the figure of the beleaguered poet whose existence and function are threatened by the loss of his wife and his subsequent displacement within a community of clearly defined male and female spheres of experience and authority.[13]

The fear of annihilation as an obsessive component of grief and loss, with writing as the only antidote, so central to the writer's motivation in Naipaul's "Prologue to an Autobiography" (in *Finding the Center*) and Lamming's *In the Castle of My Skin,* is resolved here in elegy as consoling apotheosis. In its elegiac focus *The Zea Mexican Diary* constructs a private mechanism for the expression of rage and grief that can find no other outlet and for moving on toward some measure of acceptance and consolation. The process is evaluative, reflective, and revisionary; it is personal and culturally specific. It registers a turning point in the cultural situatedness of the self as male poet subject who finally moves away from grief toward acceptance of the loss of his "perfect poet's wife" and the consolation that accrues from sensing her at-oneness in death with the soaring and majestic beauty of the Blue Mountains of Jamaica. At the end of *The Zea Mexican Diary* she is ensconced as Mountain-Mother, magical and mysterious, whose life was marked by loyalty to her male consort and their joint cultural project.[14]

The dissociative movement in "The Awakening" (213–14) toward acceptance of Doris as disembodied presence in the Blue

Mountains is marked by a qualified acceptance of female authority over the rituals of death. The companionate marriage paradigm
cannot be preserved across the boundaries of life and death, time
and space, without fear of ghostly contagion, or "being exposed
to the danger of catching death from the dead" (Zeiger 45).
Ghostly encounters with Doris after death are menacing and without comfort; as a spirit, she inspires repulsion and fear. In "This
Obeah Business" (159–67) the poet reluctantly takes passing refuge
in the rites of passage of a folk culture that girds itself against the
vengeful, destructive sorties of the restless needy dead with lit can-
dles, sulfur powder, covered mirrors, and other ritual interventions
that are meant to break the bonds between the living and the dead.
In the destabilizing field of Doris's death, the perfect love story,
constructed in the trappings of the companionate marriage of
love, passion, and literary achievement, comes to an end in private-made-public rituals of reversal. He buries some of her ashes
under an African tulip tree on the grounds of their house in Irish
Town in a second funeral service presided over by Mr. Reid, who
is associated with Legba, guardian of the crossroads and pathways,
and Brathwaite secretly puts some of her ashes on his tongue and
swallows her remains in a private-made-public act of communion
in contravention of the public gestures of letting go.[15]

The formal aspects of *The Zea Mexican Diary* are elaborately
and self-consciously drawn. It is elegy and diary, lyric and dramatic. It is ritual lamentation and also petitionary commemora-
tion: "How God has come to punish me not cherishing enough"
(78). It is an autobiography that writes the male poet subject's
experience of his wife's illness and death into the cultural narrative. Frames of reference multiply at every turn, as its title, *The
Zea Mexican Diary,* makes clear with references to ancient Greece,
the Maya of Central America, and a literary form of uncertain historical value except as a way to escape dominant formulations of
identity in the immediacy of the recorded moment. There are
numerous references to African and Caribbean cultural forms and
expressions, from the Adinkra cloth that he uses as a shroud and
the *damarifa due* sung at her funeral service to invocations of God
and gods, obeah practices, and folk customs.[16] In the context of

Ken Boothe's song, which he quotes, it is a love song "that is also an xtremely poignant song of loss and mourning" (5). It is programmed as a funeral service (11), and it is a certificate of death (80). It is a self-portrait fashioned after the straitened condition of the Second Ku'n of the *I Ching,* the Chinese book of divination (*Zea* 12–14). It invokes the nine nights of mourning and the forty days that Jesus wandered in the wilderness, which has its parallel in Akan eighth and fortieth day mourning rituals (Nketia 15). *The Zea Mexican Diary* assimilates all these details in realizing its narrative of grief, loss, and restoration.

In *The Zea Mexican Diary* ritual expressions of grief acquire new aesthetic characteristics as published diary and record of events as they occurred. It is intimate in its attention to details of time and place and people, yet it houses the ultimate expression of cosmic will. It is a rite of passage, a truly communicant ritual in which an anguished continuum of transition occurs. *The Zea Mexican Diary* includes nine extracts from a diary that Brathwaite started when he learned that his wife was terminally ill, nine extracts from letters that he wrote to his sister Mary Morgan in an attempt to reopen lines of communication across the breach created by Doris's suffering and death, a statement that he wrote on the night of her death and that Edward Baugh read at her Thanksgiving service, and a letter written by Ayama, which is interwoven with the author's meditations on the words and the Thanksgiving service that occasioned them. Though the diary and the letters originally were not intended for publication, the completeness and depth of aesthetization in their final form confirm the aesthetic contemplation immanent in any work of art. The text coheres thematically and architecturally in its multifarious parts. In its formal aspects the ritual of grief and lamentation is sculpted on the page with great meticulousness. Lines and fonts are varied to achieve rhythmic effects, to mirror emotional states, and for thematic emphasis. The solitary self-confessional core of the narrative is subsumed periodically in its polyphonic design, in its many voices, and in its intimations of restored community beyond the alienation and marginalization imposed by grief and loss. It is interesting that Brathwaite chooses the circumscribed autobiographical space of the diary as personal communication to restage his changing emotional states around Doris's illness and death. Though it is elegiac in mood and function, in its insistence on names, places, and the sequence of events, *The Zea Mexican Diary* retains the implacable historicity of a memorial carved in stone. It shapes a compelling representation of the tormented end of a life-sustaining relationship that slowly and painfully moves beyond lamentation and recrimination toward acceptance and reconnection. It is a wonderfully concrete, self-reflexive meditation on change and continuance framed by the philosophical directives of the *I Ching*: "If he do repent of former errors, there will be good fortune in his going forward."

The poet calls attention to the unconventional form and style of the narrative, seemingly at every turn: through visual images generated by irregular layout, computer graphics, special font effects, and an irregular, idiosyncratic use of language. The carefully plotted "strangeness" of the text on the page has become a hallmark of Brathwaite's "video" style, but in *The Zea Mexican Diary* it appears utterly invested in the display and emplotment of funereal grief and loss that is both quirky and very personal, and it is ritualized in its formal and very public display of private grief.[17] This calls to mind Thomas Hardy's deployment of strange and awkward diction in *Poems of 1912–13*. Writing about Hardy's remodeling of the genre, Zeiger observes, "To defamiliarize language is, however, to ally oneself with the uncanny, with the irrational, with the feared and the unknown" (46). Rohlehr catalogues many of Brathwaite's special effects: "The practical convention which ideally fills the page with words is undermined by the use of half and quarter pages, or by pages with 16- or 18-point type faces, or with few words or even no words at all. Words are broken randomly; some deliberately misspelt. Brackets, asterisks, abbreviations and various symbols are used sometimes with, sometimes without, clear purpose. Periods appear in places where normally commas would occur" (introduction viii–ix).

In *The Zea Mexican Diary* the "estrangement" of language and form destabilizes generic codes and culturally specific rituals of death and mourning. Psychological crises are reflected with seemingly endless variety on the page. According to Julia Kristeva, the estranging use of language on the page is a sign of melancholia; melancholic mourners do violence to linguistic codes in their rejection of any comfort that might accrue from the very act of writing.[18] In *The Zea Mexican Diary* the poet self-consciously records speechlessness as a kind of disabling affliction: "- like STUPID/ in increasing cleft & shock / & silence - there are no WORDS for this" (91). He tries to describe the quality of his son Michael's grief and the words escape him: "*[still can't find the word for / this - bottomless emotion]*" (92). In "Tano" death is "the dumb speaking god" that afflicts the creative spirit (*Arrivants* 153). The very act of writing *The Zea Mexican Diary* records a war of sorts between factions of the male poet subject self in grief: "But the getting there the 40 days in the wilderness of / waiting for vision - the agonies of wrenching it out rig- / ht - the doubts & temptations of the devil(s) that beset / while all that struggle is in progress - the terror of the / mirror held up by one's own self up to one's broken na- / ture - " (151). The confessional moment dissolves into his continuance as elegist, and a feminine space of grief management is invaded and occupied by the poet as dreamer and mourner turned elegist.

The Zea Mexican Diary asks important questions about the culture of death, about the nature of community, and about Doris's place in it in life and death. The emphasis is on journey rather than arrival, on the intertransmutation of essence, ideal, and materiality into a single immortal form. Doris's death becomes a creative act. Grief becomes a process of creation. *The Zea Mexican Diary* expresses pain and grief and love in a way that is restorative without the customary platitudes. Framing all is the fear of private and public scrutiny, "the terror of the / mirror held up by one's own self up to one's broken na- / ture - " (151). The moral imperative of this new aesthetic privileges the male poet subject's private ritual of grief. The social silencing and isolation of the widower are reversed in the interpenetration of elegy and epithalamium. It marks a poetic victory over the fear of mortality and the threat of annihilation in the face of disabling loss.

12

Death and Sexuality
Jamaica Kincaid's *My Brother*

In *My Brother* cross-gender identification does not revolve around a nuptial bond as in *The Zea Mexican Diary*. Gender dynamics are reconfigured in a sibling relationship devoid of sexuality except as a mark of difference. The elegist is identified in the text as the author, Jamaica Kincaid, a successful writer, happily married with children, and resident in pastoral Vermont. She mourns the death from AIDS of her brother Devon, who succumbs to the "underworld" of Antigua despite her best efforts to rescue him and restore him to life's promise. Her failure triggers an ambivalent grief for her dead brother, a crisis of identification and dissociation that provides insight into the displaced family romance at the heart of *My Brother* and the deep alienation that afflicts Kincaid's on-again, off-again relationship with her Antiguan family and her native land.[1] Writing the circumstances of Devon's death into the cultural narrative with passion and vituperation, the author-narrator not only expresses the depth and violence of her grief and loss but she creates a framework for understanding the circumstances of his life and death as it resonates with hers. In so doing she stages the struggle for literary rebirth that is a hallmark of the orphic quest.[2]

If, as Celeste Schenck argues, elegy and epithalamium continually interpenetrate in the poetics of pastoral ceremony, this interpenetration links discrete parts of Kincaid's life in *My Brother*: her abusive childhood in Antigua and the pastoral romance of her adult life in the United States. The boundaries of elegy and epithalamium are drawn along clearly established binaries: the

243

mourning and melancholia that attend the demonizing of Devon and the site of his perceived self-destructive behavior, Antigua, versus the celebration of her marriage and family and successful writing career in the United States.[3] This double vision of self in its Manichean extremism denies the author-narrator's divided persona much hope of peace and reconciliation through ritual mourning; loss and longing remain unassuaged as funeral dirge interpenetrates and competes with nuptial song. The problematics of mourning here are thematic and structural, generating a back-and-forth motion that appears to work against closure. When Devon dies, the author-narrator-subject attends his funeral in Antigua with her children. Having acquitted her obligations as sibling-mourner, she attempts to achieve closure and thus reestablish the harmonious rhythm of her North American life. When acceptance and accommodation occur, they are linear in customary elegiac fashion; they occur at the end of the narrative when Kincaid links her deceased Antiguan brother Devon to her deceased North American mentor and model reader, her father-in-law, William Shawn, as source and keeper of her recalcitrant creative spirit.

Kincaid's unfulfilled longing for acceptance and reconnection is explained in the act of writing to the dead and for the dead. As an extended conversation with the dead, *My Brother* resonates with forms of ancestor worship in the Caribbean, most notably in Haiti, in which the living speak with the dead: "For the Haitians who serve the spirits there is no 'beyond' in the Christian sense, no redemptive surcease of sorrow, but rather an uncertain realm of obligation, of broken but obstinate communion between the living and the dead" (Dayan 263). In *Powers of Horror* Julia Kristeva explains the dire experience of death, loss, and desire in the symbolic language of abjection (4–5). If, as she argues, artistic experience "is rooted in the abject it utters and by the same token purifies" (17), *My Brother* is also a signifier of the utmost abjection, of death infecting life: "Abject. It is something rejected from which one does not part, from which one does not protect oneself as from an object. Imaginary uncanniness and real threat, it beckons to us and ends up engulfing us" (Kristeva, *Powers* 4).[4] Kincaid's compulsion to write to the dead about things they would not want to hear defines the urgent task, however impossible, of establishing a defensive position against death and annihilation. Writing and life are one and the same impulse; writing keeps death at bay. Thus *My Brother* settles as a symbolic pact in which her dead brother, whom she once rejected as a threat to the sacred values of order and productive life in Vermont, gains a place of privilege at the center of her creative life, where the opposing worlds of Antigua and Vermont meet and collide.

Kincaid's elegiac self-positioning as a writer caught in a felt tension between her black Antiguan brother and her white North American father-in-law is sculpted around the quest for life in the shadow of death: "When I was young, younger than I am now, I started to write about my own life and I came to see that this act saved my life. When I heard about my brother's illness and his dying, I knew, instinctively, that to understand it, or to make an attempt at understanding his dying, and not to die with him, I would write about it" (*Brother* 196). She writes to her deceased father-in-law, Shawn, about Devon; as she explains it, Shawn remains her ideal reader even in death: "I was used to telling him things I knew he didn't like, I couldn't help telling him everything whether he liked it or not. And so I wrote about the dead for the dead, and all along as I was writing I thought, When I am done with this I shall never write for Mr. Shawn again, this will be the end of anything I write for Mr. Shawn; but now I don't suppose that will be so" (*Brother* 197).

She is equally candid about her brother as a focal point of her desire to be a writer: "It was because I had neglected my brother when he was two years old and instead read a book that my mother gathered up all the books I owned and put them on a pile in her stone heap, sprinkling them with kerosene and setting them alight. . . . It would not be strange if I spent the rest of my life trying to bring those books back to my life by writing them again and again until they were perfect, unscathed by fire of any kind" (*Brother* 197–98). The terms of such agonistic mourning are, in Jahan Ramazani's words, "less of solace than of melancholia, less of resolution than of protracted strife" (226), but it is important that her recommitment to writing ensures literary continuance.

Creative agency is sustained in tension with the dead, by writing to the dead about her fear and rage against death.

Writing to keep death at bay is contextualized in *My Brother* by multiple encounters, real and imagined, with death.[5] All these experiences are associated with some threat to her creative imagination and to the integrity of her Antiguan family as guardian of that creativity. The threat begins in earnest with the coincidence of encroaching poverty and the birth of her brother Devon. Encounters with death punctuate the narrative: Red ants attack Devon on the very night of his birth, while "he snuggled in the warmth of his mother's body" (5); not long after Devon's birth a six-year-old girl died "in my mother's arms on the way to the doctor" (4); not long after that, Miss Charlotte, who lived across the street, "died in my mother's arms as my mother tried to give her some comfort from the pain of the heart attack she was having" (5). In another cycle of events, while Kincaid was spending the August holidays with a friend of her mother's in full view of the St. John's city graveyard, she decided "that only people in Antigua died, that people living in other places did not die and as soon as I could, I would move somewhere else, to those places where the people living there did not die" (26–27). She recalls staying in Dominica with her mother's relatives as a safeguard against obeah when she was a child, and she recalls that her pleasure in the moonlit landscape turned to horror as the dreaded figure in Caribbean folklore, the jablesse, possessed her imagination. She sought safety by hiding in bed: "And lying in bed with the sheets over my head, I would become afraid to fall asleep with the sheets over my head, I would become afraid to fall asleep because I might suffocate and die" (38). Other encounters with death include the Dead House, Mr. Straffee's funeral parlor, her mother's decaying house, and the half-dead tree in the botanical gardens.

Her brother's illness and death refocus this pervasive fear of death and annihilation in a long-standing fear of being destroyed by her mother, who burned her books for neglecting to change Devon's diaper when she was left in charge of him. She also feared her mother because she pulled Kincaid out of school prematurely and denied her the chance to pursue her education. Fear of contamination comes from contact with an immoral, scheming, dissembling Devon and by extension from proximity to their mother, whose best efforts at nurturance fail to keep her children safe: "I had sympathy for her then, but still no love, only sympathy, and some revulsion, as if I felt what had just happened to her—her child had died, she would be burying one of her children—was a contagious disease and just to be around her, just to be so near her meant I might catch it, this thing of burying your children when they are still so young, when they have not really lived at all" (*Brother* 173). In a fusion of mother and nature, Kincaid links a menacing maternal authority to her native land. She characterizes Antigua as demoniacal, as the place where "the bitter, cruel mother I now know" possesses her once beautiful, intelligent mother (78). With the aging of her stepfather and the birth of Devon, her Antiguan family began to fall apart. Kincaid represents her mother as a woman who becomes destructive and menacing in her relationships with her children because she was unable to nurture her children's talents and her own. She resembles Kristeva's mother turned into an abject: "Repelling, rejecting; repelling itself, rejecting itself. Ab-jecting" (13). This Antiguan past as displaced family romance haunts Kincaid's idyllic Vermont life as intrusive, disruptive memory and alternative present.

Through Devon the author-narrator reflects on the problematics of a double identity that she shares with her brother through social misplacement and/or displacement. Her rage against his illness and Antigua's social condition acquires some of the characteristics of postwar American family elegy. As Ramazani observes: "More than all other elegiac subgenres, the family elegy best displays the postwar American poet's especially intimate and immediate, impatient and hostile work in the genre" (221).[6] It may be that the ravages of colonial-postcolonial conditions in the Caribbean provide an analogous threat to the psychic and physical well-being of Antiguan survivors of the ordeal, but hers is a comparable rhetoric of denunciation.[7] Her primary targets are her deceased brother, her mother, whom Kincaid fears will outlive her children, and Antigua. For example, she describes Devon as a social misfit who is corrupt and parasitic in his relations with his family and community in Antigua. He is a man so selfish and so dissolute as to have unprotected sex even after he became aware that he had AIDS: "My brother had been having unprotected sex with this woman and he had not told her that he was infected with the HIV virus. He did not tell her, because if he told her he thought she might not want to have sex with him at all" (*Brother* 66). If he is described as innately antilife in his self-destructive behavior, their mother is a sorceress of the Medean variety, who would destroy her own children. Even when she praises their mother's devotion to her sick children, especially her heroic nursing of Devon in his illness and death, Kincaid undercuts praise with exposure of a destructive underside:

> She loves and understands us when we are weak and helpless and need her. . . . Her love for her children when they are children is spectacular, unequaled I am sure in the history of a mother's love. It is when her children are trying to be grown-up people—adults—that her mechanism for loving them falls apart; it is when they are living in a cold apartment in New York, hungry and penniless because they have decided to be a writer, writing to her, seeking sympathy, a word of encouragement, love, that her mechanism for loving falls apart. (*Brother* 16–17)

For all its natural beauty Antigua is represented as a place of death, anachronism, and ineptitude, where broken stoplights remain hanging past usefulness: "It could not be fixed because the parts for it are no longer being made anywhere in the world—and that did not surprise me, because Antigua is a place like that: parts for everything are no longer being made anywhere in the world; in Antigua itself nothing is made" (*Brother* 24).[8] If her brother dies of neglect, it is because he lives in a place where government is corrupt "and did not care whether he or other people like him lived or died" (*Brother* 50).

The displaced family romance is evident in the projected incompatibility of two worlds, two selves. The alienation is represented as multiple; it is familial, cultural, national, and geographic. She attempts to lose her displaced Antiguan self in her successful, happy Vermont self in a place where she is sustained by a loving family and supportive community. She demonizes her Antigua life as destructive of family and community ties. After her mother visits Kincaid in Vermont, the author has a nervous breakdown (*Brother* 28), and she declares that Devon simply would not fit in (*Brother* 105). His illness and death challenge Kincaid's alienation to heroic efforts on his behalf: to rescue him from the ravages of AIDS and to be an agent of positive change in what is left of his life and hers. Her brother's and her mother's need challenges her to recoup her Antiguan self by rescuing them; in the process she resituates herself as the heroic nurse rather than the neglectful babysitter of her Antiguan girlhood and as the writer who restores the burned books of her Antiguan childhood to the status of the lifeline that they are to her and to her Antiguan family. In *My Brother* Kincaid reaches across gaps in time, class, gender, language, and cultural situatedness to heal the emotional and physical wounds that have fed her alienation since Devon was born in 1962 when she was thirteen. In one sense her efforts end in failure: She fails to rescue him, and she fails at reconnection in that he does not recognize her when he names the members of his family before dying, even though she has devoted time, love, and money to his nursing care. "That night as he lay dying and calling the names of his brothers and his mother, he did not call my name, and I was neither glad nor sad about this. For why should he call my name?" (*Brother* 74). His rejection may be hurtful, but it actually appears to facilitate the resumption of her Vermont life. She rejects her mother's words of appreciation: "telling me some God or other would bless me, she did not remember this, she did not remember that if it had been up to her, I would not have been in a position to be blessed by any God, I might in fact be in the same position as my brother right now" (75). Devon's death is conclusive evidence of her mother's limitations and her own.[9]

Despite the recurring cycle of rejection, her troubled relationship with her mother and with Antigua endures in the elegiac rhythms of identification and dissociation that characterize the abjection of this mourner's relationship to the dead, the past, and her native place.[10] Looking for her stepfather's unmarked grave with her mother, she senses the omnipresence of death: "We passed through the door of the Dead House, she and I together, and as we did so, my own complicated and contradictory feelings about the dead came up and lay on the ground before my feet, and each step I took forward they moved forward, too, like a form of shadowing" (*Brother* 121). Given her pervasive fear of death, her mother's offhand graveyard encounter with a lizard—a creature of graveyards and messenger of the dead—adds to the portrait of Mrs. Drew as a "graveyard" figure: "As she shook the lizard off, she said that she hoped it wasn't one of those people, meaning the dead, come to tell her something that would make her want to join them ('Eh-eh, me ah wahrn you, dem people no get me, you know'), and she said this with a laugh" (*Brother* 124).

As displaced family romance, *My Brother* is shrouded in the corpse and phallus imagery of Gede, Vodou's lord of death and destruction, and his female counterpart, Maman Brigitte, who is distinguished, as Mrs. Drew is, by her mound of stones.[11] Mrs. Drew's burning of her daughter's precious books on "her stone heap" (134) associates her with Maman Brigitte as graveyard figure of death and guardian of the dead, but this is only one of numerous references to Mrs. Drew as a devourer and destroyer of her children, who would deny her daughter the lifeline of books and a formal education. The association of Devon with Gede is as an emaciated figure of death and lewdness, since Gede is also lord of eroticism. As phallic deity, writes Maya Deren, life for Gede is "the inevitable and eternal erotic in men" (102). In *My Brother* the erotic, lascivious drive in Devon is anti-intellectual and uncompromisingly destructive, with none of Gede's healing and life-giving dimensions. Devon is represented as preoccupied with his own sexuality as emblematic of male power and unfulfilled fantasies of creative talent. Kincaid is contemptuous: "He had been trying to tell me that there was something unique about him, that he was an unusual person, a powerfully sexual man. Powerfully sexual men sometimes cause people to die right away with a bullet to the head, not first sicken and die slowly from disease" (*Brother* 67). He thought of himself as a good singer and fantasized about a career. He was so convinced that he is good that he tells whoever will listen "that when he sang women who heard him removed their clothes" (*Brother* 68).

Kincaid's hostility to what she perceives as his corrupt and irresponsible sexuality is unrelenting when he pathetically displays his diseased penis to her in a gesture that she finds lewd and revolting (*Brother* 91). She had characterized herself earlier as a prim and proper type, frequently targeted by Gede in ritual possession: "My own life, from a sexual standpoint, can be described as a monument to boring conventionality" (*Brother* 41). Thus Devon is made emblematic of Gede's inevitable and eternal erotic as self-destructive and exploitative: "There he was, diseased and dying, looking as unattractive as a long-dead corpse would look, and he could still try to convince a woman to sleep with him" (*Brother* 43).

In common with Kamau Brathwaite's *The Zea Mexican Diary, My Brother* gives a brutal account of the ravages of disease, except that in the case of Devon, the personality of the deceased, his flamboyant excesses of speech and behavior, create a space for more extended, more explicit accounts of the devastating effect of the disease on the body, which Kincaid describes as a flowering of death, a half-dead tree with no name, the dry rot in the rafters of a house that will collapse on itself. The grimness of her account extends to an enumeration of his body parts in varying stages of decay: "When I first saw him, his entire mouth and tongue, all the way to the back of the inside of his mouth, down his gullet, was paved with a white coat of thrush. He had a small sore near his tonsil, I could see it when he opened his mouth wide, something he did with great effort" (*Brother* 15). The graphic nature of such descriptions of Devon's physical deterioration becomes a measure not of Devon's heroism but of the heroism of those who care for him. Devon's heroic nurses are his mother and sister. There are repeated references to the magnitude of this undertaking on an impoverished, mismanaged island, which is how she describes Antigua.

The other side of this unflinching exposure of the ugliness of Devon's illness and death is the kind of sibling identification with his wasted life that prompts repeated observations about how lucky the author-narrator is to have escaped. The ambivalence in

her feelings for her brother stem in part from a too-certain identification with his inevitable death: "I shall never forget him
because his life is the one I did not have, the life that, for reasons
I hope shall never be too clear to me, I avoided or escaped"
(*Brother* 176); "I would have died at about his age, thirty-three
years, or I would have gone insane" (*Brother* 90). By the same
token, this emphasis begs the question about the stability of her
happy life in Vermont, surrounded by family, friends, and community, where an encroaching animal has eaten some of her prized
evergreens: "And the sight of the evergreens, all eaten up in a ran-
dom way, not as if to satisfy a hunger but to satisfy a sense of
play, suddenly made me sad, suddenly made me wish that this, my
brother dying, had not happened, that I had never become involved
with the people I am from again" (*Brother* 102–3). Zeiger observes
that dividing into categories those who have HIV or AIDS and
those who do not is "a way of always remembering that those who
are not infected have been lucky rather than different in any way
from the infected" (108). Except that this emerges as a political
and poetic principle of gay men's poetry in particular (108), and
the author-narrator's heterosexuality is central to her self-positioning in an autobiographical sense.

This is not traditional poetic elegy; it is a prose narrative written by a woman in grief at the loss of her brother and all she associates with him and has tried to escape since she left Antigua for
the United States at sixteen. She was in search of another life, a
better life, which she has since secured and repeatedly affirms as
a contrasting value as she describes the events leading up to and
following her brother's death. Her brother's being stricken with
AIDS when the narrative begins identifies *My Brother* as one of a
growing body of AIDS elegies, though this one brings together
postcolonial issues of gender and sexual difference, underdevelopment, migration, alienation, neglect, and dependency in a rare
and compelling way.[12] The climax of the narrative is not Devon's
death, which is inevitable, but the author's chance discovery, in a
bookstore in Chicago after his death and burial, that his outra-
geous, destructive sexual conduct with women, before and after
taking the AZT that she procured for him, conceals a secret life

of homosexual relationships. The narrative self-consciously reconstructs the sequence of not knowing and then of knowing, and the
web of deceit, secrecy, guilt, and confusion that it engenders. In
the process another facet of her cultural privilege and alienation
emerges as her heterosexuality. Her guilt and alienation, which find
such a passionate and longed-for outlet in her devotion to her
dying brother, are displaced onto his "secret" homosexual life,
known to strangers but not to her.

The deferral of Devon's homosexual identity to the end of the
narrative raises questions about what this information means to
the narrative as a whole. Is it homophobic? Or is it the reverse, a
refusal to link Devon's self-destructiveness to his homosexuality?
As a context for understanding the author-narrator-subject's
mourning and loss, this information reveals a new and unexplored
relationship between subject and object, sister and brother, Jamaica
Kincaid and Devon Drew. Antiguan taboos against homosexuality, and her own obsessive fixation on the heterosexual family
romance, created a space of cultural intelligibility (Butler 145). The
news of her brother's homosexual relationships has the effect of
reversing her anguished and unforgiving gaze; her presumptive heterosexuality is unmasked as a conditioned misreading of the self's
relationship to community. Erasure of her brother's bisexuality is
countered by her preservation of it in elegy: "He had died without ever understanding or knowing, or being able to let the world
in which he lived know, who he was; that who he really was—not
a single sense of identity but all the complexities of who he was—
he could not express fully: his fear of being laughed at, his fear of
meeting with the scorn of the people he knew best were over-
whelming and he could not live with all of it openly" (*Brother*
162). From this perception comes a more moderate, less contentiousness tone, recognition of judgments too hastily formed, and
a mending of fences: "Perhaps he despaired that the walls sepa-
rating the parts of his life had broken down, and that might have
caused him much anxiety, and such a thing, the anxiety when it
appeared on his face, would have seemed to me, who knew nothing about his internal reality, as another kind of suffering, a suffering I might be able to relieve with medicine I had brought from

the prosperous North; but I did not know then, I only know now" (*Brother* 164). The site of transgression shifts from Devon to the author-narrator. After the fact, her misperception creates a space for sympathetic identification after her rancorous rejection of his wasted life and diseased sexuality: "His homosexuality is one thing, and my becoming a writer is another thing altogether, but this truth is not lost to me: I could not have become a writer while living among the people I knew best" (*Brother* 162).[13]

The subversive possibilities of death and mourning, through a process of identification and incorporation, create a space in this elegy for a thoughtful repositioning of self. In lieu of the rigidly drawn boundaries of opposing worlds in a language of passionate denunciation and rejection, *My Brother* records and allegorizes the circumstances of Kincaid's reengagement with Antigua and her family there in a qualified reversal of her earlier abandonment and flight. Devon, initially an object of unmitigated scorn, is recouped by the end of the narrative in a reversal of moral scrutiny that reveals the sibling-mourner's expressed feelings of superiority to be premised on a failure of perception and to that extent subject to question: "And I remembered this woman, superior and slightly contemptuous of her general surroundings (but I did not fault her for that, I had felt the same way, only more so) and casting blame and making denunciations (and I did not fault her for that, I had futilely gone so far as to write a small book in which I did nothing but cast blame and make denunciations)" (*Brother* 158). Judgments are altered and reproaches represented as self-reproaches through the shifting contours of her denunciatory identification with Devon.

Meaning is elusive in this AIDS elegy because the narrative shifts back and forth, continually interrupting itself with unexplained juxtapositions that are often contrastive and incongruous and generate allegorical frames of their own. Reflecting on her brother's illness, which called her out of her ordered Vermont home and back to her chaotic Antiguan past, Kincaid fashions from her intimate knowledge of his disease and death a trope linking life and death: "On one side, there is life, and the thin shadow of death hovers over it; and on the other, there is death with a small patch of life attached to it" (*Brother* 95–96). On one hand this specifi-cally refers to her brother's affliction and impending death: "This latter is the life of AIDS; this is how I saw my brother as he lay in his bed dying" (*Brother* 95–96). But this is also a conventional representation of Gede, one half of his face whitened to represent the living and the other half blackened to represent the dead (Dun-ham 119). In a personal narrative that is obsessed with death, writ-ten by someone who is clearly acquainted with the signs of ancestor worship and the spiritual practices and rituals of the Caribbean, elegiac design suggests the unifying values of Gede, who straddles "the great divide between the living and the dead," and, as Deren observes, is "not only the lord of both, but the lord of their interaction" (112). Indeed, the unifying values of Gede coincide with those of elegy, whether traditional elegy, family elegy, or AIDS elegy. If Gede embarrasses some with bizarre dis-plays of sexuality and terrifies others with macabre signs of death, Deren observes that "he is also history—the experience from which the living learn—and in this role is as deeply responsible and trust-worthy as he is bizarre in his other aspects" (112). As elegist, Kin-caid is curiously in step with Gede.[14] For one thing, she sees herself as family historian with a memory for events and incidents "that everyone else in my family has forgotten, except me," and, like Gede, on occasion will remind those who would prefer to for-get (*Brother* 6). Through the central event of her brother's death, she projects a Gedean vision of life perpetually shadowed by death: "The dead never die, and I now say this—the dead never die—as if it were new, as if no one had ever noticed this before: but death is like that (I can see); . . . The dead never die, let me just say it again" (*Brother* 121).

A new arrangement of differences generates a different system of meaning and a different speaking subject.[15] In death Devon is no longer a defilement to be excluded; instead he emerges as a puri-fier of the writer's knowledge of suffering and the surrender to death. In an ambiguously staged reversal of value, by the end of the narrative the excluding, rejecting, narrating "I" is in turn rejected in a process of literary rebirth that symbolically links her destiny to her brother's fate. As disembodied spirit, Devon is no longer the preferred son and debased paternal authority; he is sublimated as victim of repressed homosexual passion and an uncomprehending demonic mother. If anything, this reaffirms the threat that Antigua represents to the writer's carefully guarded North American life and represents a deepening of the gulf between the writer and her mother and the writer and her native land. But *My Brother* also propounds a myth of dynamic self-invention in the elegiac process of redefining the dividing lines between self and other, sister and brother.

Conclusion

Although the texts that I have been discussing here vary in composition, all are autobiographical. Most are written by major Caribbean poets, novelists, and dramatists but not all. Some adopt a collective manner of thinking about self-identity, while others seek to establish the contrary; more often than not, group identification and differentiation are part of a complex autobiographical process. The extremely varied, verifiable particularity of these autobiographical texts, whether slave narrative or travel narrative, fiction or poetry, elegy, idyll, memoir, or something else, grounds them in their many mutations in a lived, if sharply differentiated, Caribbean reality. Limiting the primary frame of reference to Anglophone autobiography maximizes the interpenetration of social and historical contexts even further, facilitating connections between the more familiar texts by Prince, Lamming, C. L. R. James, Walcott, Naipaul, and Kincaid and the less well-known writings by the Hart sisters, Claude McKay, Seacole, Bridges, Rhys, Mahase, and Brathwaite, and enabling generalizations about the status of the genre. The selection of texts might easily have been different, but the range of these texts is such that this important literary tradition reflects multidimensionality and difference in Caribbean space in a most distinctive way.

Despite great variation in modes of representation, the consistent expressive need in autobiography is the representation of individual identity and its concomitant burden of difference. Its point of departure is the differentiated self; the functionality of the autobiographical project establishes the boundaries of self-representation. Thus this study of autobiography and autobiographical modes privileges individual identity as a necessary beginning, even when the author attempts to camouflage this dimension in an elaborate architectural design, as in the case of Lamming, C. L. R. James, and Naipaul. Contextual conditions

257

vary enormously from the narratives of the Hart sisters at the turn of the nineteenth century to Kincaid's *My Brother* at the end of the twentieth, from Methodist history to the work of mourning, yet each enables an exploration of a different facet of the genre and its place in Caribbean literary production. While no one work is representative of the range of material in this study, patterns emerge with each successive attempt to resolve individual problems of self-analysis and self-representation within the literary and cultural systems in which they operate.

In respect to the flexibility and range of autobiographical forms in this study, Elizabeth Bruss's observation that "there is no intrinsically autobiographical form" (9) still holds true; the genre is dynamic and freely appropriates forms and techniques of other types of discourse, whether they be church history, slave narrative, travel narrative, narrative of childhood, fiction, lyric poetry, or elegy. Thus autobiography readily takes its place within the symbolic systems that make up the literature and culture more generally. In autobiography differences in the choice of structure and design become a measure of the writer's intention and individual sense of identity and reflect the expressive need of an individual and community at a particular moment in history. The defining element in this study, not surprisingly, is fluidity rather than systematic coherence. The dynamic of self-invention is one of openness and closure, concealment and disclosure, recognition and nonrecognition, as individual autobiographical projects determine.

Generalizations about the distinguishing features of this body of work derive from recurring attitudes and expectations, including a range of cultural distinctions surrounding the autobiographical act that is rooted in the spatial, temporal, and cultural geography of the region. Observably, the literary quest for self-definition consistently takes the individual on a journey in space and/or consciousness beyond the space of the region. In these texts, for example, a distinctly Caribbean material and cultural geography are charted over time in the tension between personal geography and the space of the region. Maps of personal geography consistently extend beyond the space of an island or regional geography to metropolitan centers in Europe, North America,

Central and South America, Africa, and Asia. In fact, concepts of cultural identity and space are subject to multiple configurations, just as autobiographical maps are continually redrawn. Mary Prince travels from Bermuda to the Turks and Caicos, Antigua, and England. Mary Seacole's narrative maps journeys to Colombia and Panama, England, and the Crimea and surrounding areas. Claude McKay emigrates to the United States and traces repeated journeys across the expanse of the United States, as well as journeys to Europe, Russia, and North Africa before returning to the United States. The exceptions are the Hart sisters and Anna Mahase, but they form strong alliances with metropolitan religious organizations, and their psychic space is reconfigured accordingly. And Mahase travels vicariously through her children and follows the progress of relatives in India and Guyana.

Although these texts suggest that regional space does not provide an adequate base for the representation of Caribbean identity, it is also clear that this does not cancel out attachment to place and community. If anything, heightened awareness of the multi-dimensionality and limitations of Caribbean space appear to invite an assertion of lineage inscribed in territory as fundamental to narrative self-definition. Even Seacole's *Wonderful Adventures* and Claude McKay's *A Long Way from Home,* both of which downplay a sense of Jamaican beginnings for functional purposes, are punctuated at key moments with assertions of belonging to their island community.

Within the wide range of textual features that signal the generic function of each text, a distinctly Caribbean cultural geography emerges. In this cartography the map of the Caribbean is an open rather than a closed construct. From the Hart sisters through Walcott, Mahase, and Brathwaite, whatever narrative is called up to provide a frame of reference, the tensions, contradictions, differences, and interpenetrations of heterogeneous community appear. The texts in this study suggest that the cartography of the island, whether as colonial territory or nation, is not sufficient as a staging ground for individual identity, even when that is most keenly desired, as in the case of the Harts, Prince, Walcott, and Mahase. Nonetheless, the rhythm of displacement and dispossession, the trauma of racial and ethnic self-consciousness, and the role of errantry as a site of self-definition and empowerment nurture a consciousness of lineage in territory as a distinctive marker of individual identity that is coexistent with journey in space and/or consciousness beyond regional space. This may account in part for recurring tropes of childhood, departure and return, travel and encounter, and the Caribbean as a site of displaced dwelling in seemingly endless variations.

Yet despite a heightened consciousness of lineage in territory, class, caste, racial, and ethnic distinctions are everywhere in evidence in these representations of Caribbean space. In practice autobiographical discourse tends to erect boundaries around constructions of self and community, even where the intention of the text is a carefully crafted myth of national identity, as in the internally differentiated narratives of Claude McKay, C. L. R. James, Lamming, and Walcott, which are constructed around an African Caribbean dream of liberation. The boundaries of racial and ethnic differentiation erected reflect the contours of colonial history and patterns of colonial settlement in different Caribbean territories. Additionally, the dynamic of cultural localization in autobiography, which seeks to establish a sense of belonging in interpersonal relationships, a neighborhood, and a community, so important to the design of their narratives, is characteristically a dynamic of closure and consolidation. This is most evident in narratives like those of Prince, Bridges, Mahase, and Claude McKay's *My Green Hills*. This is the technical cunning of Rhys's *Smile Please,* which is constructed in vignettes that mitigate against the closure and class consolidation of Bridges's *Child of the Tropics* and Naipaul's rejection of existing territorial boundaries and ethnocentricity in *A Way in the World*.

In respect to issues of gender hierarchy and gender consolidation in these narratives, these reflect familiar distinctions of personality, spatial and temporal context, cultural differences, and available avenues of relation to the world beyond native space. As an intentional structure, autobiographical narrative creates the context for self-representation; theoretically, it provides opportunities for openness and closure that reflect the disposition of the autobiographical subject. There is no discernible continuity of intention that unites the women's narratives in this study, though male privilege is a recurring preoccupation and site of resistant awareness that is not shared by the men's narratives, except in relation to other men. The cross-gender personal narratives of Kincaid and Brathwaite are a remarkable challenge to the gender consolidation that is typical of the other narratives in this study in the way that they structurally recode and reorder normative patterns of gender identification in autobiographical writing. The elegiac structure of *The Zea Mexican Diary* and *My Brother* serves to underscore elegiac undertones in the narratives of Claude McKay, Lamming, Walcott, Naipaul, and Bridges as well, though in these cases the elegiac function is quite different because it registers the pervasive sense of personal loss that accompanies radical social change and clings to predictable formulations of gender identity.

These autobiographical texts offer opportunities for a critical reading of self-representation and strategies of self-preservation in communities with continually changing boundaries of self-definition. Coherence and continuity lie in a recurring pattern of cultural localization that is emblematic of lineage inscribed in regional space and allegiance to community or an idea of community. Taken together, each successive autobiographical act illuminates a historically based element of Caribbean life and culture. They are internally differentiated yet intertextually linked in an ongoing process of interculturation and Creolization, shaped as much by geography as by the sociological and economic contours of a shared colonial history. Their common task is situated and embodied difference. In the autobiographical culture represented here, self is continually reinvented in a contested literary space, and as such it lays the foundations for diverse conceptions of individual and group identity, even in the circumscribed space of the Anglophone Caribbean.

NOTES
BIBLIOGRAPHY
INDEX

Notes

PREFACE

1. Sandra Pouchet Paquet, "West Indian Autobiography," *Black American Literature Forum* (special issue on twentieth-century autobiography) 24, no. 2 (1990): 357–74.

INTRODUCTION

1. As Bruss writes, "We can speculate on what cultural conditions promote an emphasis upon individual identity, but conceptions of individual identity are articulated, extended, and developed through an institution like autobiography" (5).

2. For Raymond Williams in *Keywords* the complexity of community "relates to the difficult interaction between the tendencies originally distinguished in the historical development: on the one hand the sense of direct common concern; on the other hand the materialization of various forms of common organization, which may or may not adequately express this" (66). For Paul James *community* refers to more direct relations of mutuality and commonality (184). In *New Diasporas* Van Hear uses *community* "to suggest a social collectivity with a significant dimension in common" (10); that significant dimension is a migratory background.

3. Foucault's observations clarify the distinction that I am seeking here: "The word archaeology is not supposed to carry any suggestion of anticipation; it simply indicates a possible line of attack for the analysis of verbal performances. . . . By seizing, out of the mass of things said, upon the statement defined as a function of realization of the verbal performance, it distinguishes itself from a search whose field is linguistic competence: while such a description constitutes a generative

model, in order to define the acceptability of statements, archaeology tries to establish rules of formation, in order to define the conditions of their formation, in order to define the conditions of their realization" (*Archaeology* 206–7).

4. This list is far from comprehensive, as the recent books by Henry and Edmondson demonstrate. See Henry's *Caliban's Reason* and Edmondson's *Making Men*.

5. Not everyone welcomes the idea of a growing Caribbean frontier. In "The Emerging West Atlantic System," Patterson sees the development of what he calls the "postnational" environment of Miami, for example, as a threat to the political and economic integrity of the nation-states of the Caribbean (260).

6. Harris makes a distinction between "Caribbean man" as a "civilization-making" animal and as "a derivative tool-making, fence-making animal": "Caribbean man is involved in a civilization-making process (whether he likes it or not) and until this creative authority becomes intimate to his perspectives he will continue to find himself embalmed in his deprivations—embalmed as a derivative tool-making, fence-making animal. As such his dialectic will remain a frozen round of protest" ("History" 29).

7. According to Clifford, "Once the representational challenge is seen to be the portrayal and understanding of local/global historical encounters, co-productions, dominations, and resistances, one needs to focus on hybrid, cosmopolitan experiences as much as on rooted, native ones" (*Routes* 24).

8. Much has been written about the themes of a Caribbean diaspora and intercultural identity. With respect to a distinctly Caribbean literary discourse, I have in mind the works of Paul Gilroy, C. L. R. James, Maryse Condé, Benítez-Rojo, Brathwaite, Davies, Glissant, Stuart Hall, Harris, Laforest, Lamming, and Naipaul, among others.

9. In an unpublished interview conducted by Rick Walker at the University of Hartford on February 22, 1980, Lamming observes that the Caribbean region is a unique kind of laboratory for such a study because the region's inhabitants have lived with many multicultural forces for centuries. In "Western Education and the Caribbean Intellectual" in *Coming, Coming Home,* Lamming adds: "But it is so recent since we assumed responsibility for our own destiny, that the antagonistic weight of the past is felt as an inhibiting menace. And that is the most urgent task and the greatest intellectual challenge: how to control the burden of this history and incorporate it into our collective sense of the future" (25).

10. All recent studies—including those by Sidonie Smith, Andrews, Benstock, Bruss, Olney, Spengemann, and Lejeune, among others—underscore the instability of the genre.

11. For more on the many categories of autobiographical analysis, see Folkenflik's introduction to *The Culture of Autobiography*.

PART 1. GENDER, VOICE, AND SELF-REPRESENTATION

1. The many other examples include Belgrave's *Ti-Marie* (1988), Beryl Gilroy's *Inkle and Yarico* (1996), Nunez-Harrell's *When Rocks Dance* (1986), and Rhys's *Wide Sargasso Sea* (1966).

2. In "Caliban, Ariel, and Unprospero" Brathwaite explores the ambiguity arising from colonialism in the Caribbean and the effects of education on the process, of changing self-image, and of ideology, as well as "the effect of outside influences as a form not only of colonization but also of *modernization*" (43).

3. McClintock reminds us that this is nothing new: "From the outset, people's experiences of desire and rage, memory and power, community and revolt are inflected and mediated by the institutions through which they find their meaning—and which they, in turn, transform" (15).

4. Davies's formulation of "uprising textualities" in respect to black women's writing seems appropriate here: "The 'uprising textualities' . . . capture some of the creative movement upward and outward from constricted and submerged spaces. It signifies resistance, reassertion, renewal and rethinking. . . . It addresses that condition of 'unheardness' to which dominant discourses (patriarchal and imperialistic) relegate a range of voices" (*Black Women* 108–9).

5. As Esteves and Paravisini-Gebert observe, in resisting the double oppression of patriarchal and colonial discourse, Caribbean women's writing "both echoes and subverts" the themes and tropes of patriarchal and colonial institutions that silenced them, "often calling into question accepted notions and well-established 'truths,' revealing aspects of the Caribbean experience not previously gleaned from literary or historical accounts" (xiii).

6. McClintock cautions against the representation of women "as the atavistic and authentic body of national tradition (inert, backward-looking and natural), embodying nationalism's conservative principle of continuity," while men represent the opposite (359). That is not my intention here.

7. Texts like these invite a McClintock style of reading the politics of agency: "I wish to open notions of power and resistance to a more diverse politics of agency, involving the dense web of relations between coercion, negotiation, complicity, refusal, dissembling, mimicry, compromise, affiliation and revolt" (15).

8. "Since the ideology of gender makes a woman's life script a nonstory, a silent space, a gap in patriarchal culture, the ideal woman is self-erasing rather than self-promoting, and her natural story shapes itself not around the public, heroic life, but around the fluid, circumstantial, contingent responsiveness to others that, according to patriarchal ideology, characterizes the life of women but not autobiography. From that point of view, woman has no 'autobiographical self' in the same sense that a man does. From that point of view she has no 'public' story to tell. That situating of the autobiographer in two universes of discourse accounts

for the poetics of women's autobiography and grounds its difference" (S. Smith, *Poetics of Women's Autobiography* 50).

9. Gilmore observes that "much feminist criticism of autobiography has sought thematic, formal, and even broadly epistemological coherence among all women's autobiography, claiming that women represent the self by representing others because that is how women know and experience identity. This 'self' that women represent has frequently been white, heterosexual, and educated; has sought identity in relationships rather than in autonomy; and has been conscripted as a player in the mother-daughter plot" (xiii).

10. Consider, for example, Morrissey's *Slave Women in the New World*, Bush's *Slave Women in Caribbean Society*, and Beckles's *Natural Rebels*, among others.

11. In "Selves in Hiding," Spacks makes the case that even women of accomplishment, in writing of themselves, "use autobiography, paradoxically, partly as a mode of self-denial" (132). In *Autobiographics* Gilmore concludes: "For the most part, feminist critics of autobiography have agreed there is a lived reality that differs for men and women and accounts for much of the difference between men's and women's autobiography. Just how that difference might be represented is still an open question. Indeed, the desirability of difference as an organizing principle for feminist criticism is a newly open question" (x).

12. Gilmore gives this observation even wider application: "I have found that the texts by men which constituted the emerging canon of autobiography are problematical as proof of the principles they have been pressed into service to demonstrate" (xi). McClintock makes a similar observation in *Imperial Leather*: "It is important to note that many of the characteristics of autobiographies that have been defined as female are shared by autobiographies written by people of color, female and male, and by working-class men" (315).

13. "Within this tracking of successful cognitive failure, the most interesting manoeuvre is to examine the production of 'evidence,' the cornerstone of the evidence of historical truth . . . and to anatomize the mechanics of the construction of the self-consolidating Other—the insurgent and the insurgency" (Spivak, *Other Worlds* 199).

14. Exploring the abjection of black women in Olive Schreiner's fiction, Anne McClintock notes a pattern of displacement and denial in their representation. She attributes this to neuroses spawned by the cult of domesticity in the service of colonial patriarchy: "The power of black women is a colonial secret. White domestic life enfolds itself about this secret, as its dreaded, inner shape. Displaced and denied, its pressure is nonetheless felt everywhere, managed by multiple rituals of negation and abasement debasement, suffused with unease. The visible strength of black women presses everywhere on white life so that the energy required to deny it takes the shape of neurosis" (271).

15. In "Nationalism: Irony and Commitment" Eagleton finds an innate logic in this phenomenon: "That negative collective identity, however, is bound over

a period of time to generate a positive particular culture, without which political emancipation is probably impossible. Nobody can live in perpetual deferment of their sense of selfhood, or free themselves from bondage without a strongly affirmative consciousness of who they are" (37).

16. Sidonie Smith maps this territory in *A Poetics of Women's Autobiography*, especially in the chapter entitled "Women's Story and the Engenderings of Self-Representation" (44–59).

CHAPTER 1. TESTING AND TESTIFYING

1. Ferguson's introduction, notes, and appendixes in *The Hart Sisters*, and also her *Colonialism and Gender Relations*, provide a wealth of biographical information and historical detail. An account of the remarkable history of Methodism and the Gilbert family is recorded in Lanaghan's *Antigua and the Antiguans*, vol. 1 (1844), esp. 241–51.

2. According to Lanaghan, in 1793 "the society was found to consist of 6570 members; out of which there were 36 white" (1:246). The figures vary from source to source, but it is clear that the Methodist Church in Antigua was, in effect, an "African" Methodist Church, with direct access to a powerful metropolitan lobby.

3. In 1798 Anne married John Gilbert, cousin of Nathaniel Gilbert, lawyer, planter, speaker of the Antigua House of Assembly in 1764, and a major slaveholder who converted to Methodism and became the island's first self-appointed missionary. In 1805 Elizabeth married Charles Thwaites, a white evangelical educator and committed abolitionist. Ferguson's lengthy introduction to *The Hart Sisters* provides a wealth of biographical information.

4. For example, the Baptist lay preacher Sam Sharpe led the Jamaican revolt of 1831–1832; it involved more than sixty thousand slaves and came to be known as the Baptist War (Rogozinski 184); see also Gordon K. Lewis's *Main Currents in Caribbean Thought* (224–29). The slave rebellion in Antigua in 1831 involved thousands of slaves in arson and widespread unrest; however, the 1735–1736 rebellion involved thousands of Africans and Creoles (Rogozinski 158).

5. In "The Muse of History" Walcott gives us his latter-day Methodist spin on the conversion of slaves to Christianity: "No race is converted against its will. . . . The slave converted himself, he changed weapons, spiritual weapons, and as he adapted his master's religion, he also adapted his language, and it is here that what we can look at as our poetic tradition begins. Now began the new naming of things" (12–13).

6. In *Outside the Fold* Viswanathan makes a strong case for the link between conversion and resistance.

7. In "Nineteenth-Century Black Women's Spiritual Autobiographies," Nellie Y. McKay identifies distinctive features of the genre as it develops, as does Andrews in *To Tell a Free Story* and *Sisters of the Spirit,* and Foster in *Written by Herself.* According to Nellie McKay, the first relatively autonomous black narrative in the United States is a spiritual narrative, namely, *A Brief Account of the Life, Experiences, Travels, and Gospel Labors of George White, an African, Written by Himself and Revised by a Friend (1810).*

8. Writing about African American women's spiritual narratives, Nellie McKay notes: "While they lacked the immediate overt political value of the slave narratives (i.e., they seldom clamored for abolition), they presented readers with a radical revision of prevailing white myths and ideals of black American life" (141).

9. In the note to this excerpt Lanaghan details a long list of the indignities the couple suffered (2:179). Writing about the colored and black middle class in nineteenth-century Trinidad, the historian Bridget Brereton notes: "A person known to have African ancestors could not be accepted into the white upper class, however wealthy or educated he was, however light his complexion, however important the position he occupied" (*Race Relations* 209). However, in *The Development of Creole Society in Jamaica* Brathwaite argues "that the apartheid system was not, perhaps, as rigidly applied at this important personal level as the stereotype of the situation would lead one to expect. There should really have been no marriages of this kind" (189). In *Froudacity* Thomas of Trinidad reports that such marriages were a frequent occurrence in the days of slavery for a variety of reasons, though invariably the parties paid a price socially for their choice (69–70). For a firsthand report on the status of free nonwhites in Trinidad during this period, see Philippe's *Free Mulatto* (1824).

10. The contradictory resistant and assimilative qualities of cricket in the Caribbean are richly explored in C. L. R. James's *Beyond a Boundary,* which may also be described as a self-situating narrative in respect to the intellectual and cultural history of the region and its conspicuous use of an autobiographical frame.

11. These works include Lamming's *The Pleasures of Exile*; C. L. R. James's *Beyond a Boundary*; Brathwaite's *Development of Creole Society, Contradictory Omens,* and "Caliban, Ariel, and Unprospero"; Benítez-Rojo's *The Repeating Island*; Davies's *Black Women, Writing, and Identity*; Glissant's *Poetics of Relation*; and, most recently, Edmondson's *Making Men.*

CHAPTER 2. THE HEARTBEAT OF A WEST INDIAN SLAVE

1. A person could be legally free in England and still be a slave in the West Indies. Writing about the celebrated case of Grace Jones, which was brought

before the High Court of Admiralty in 1827, Shyllon explains: "Temporary residence in England without manumission suspended, but did not extinguish, her status as a slave to which she reverted when she was enticed back to Antigua" (27).

2. In *Colonialism and Gender Relations,* Moira Ferguson identifies Antigua and the Eastern Caribbean as a critical site of British–Caribbean textual and historical contestation that is played out in Jane Austen's *Mansfield Park,* the writings of the Hart sisters, Jean Rhys's *Wide Sargasso Sea,* and Jamaica Kincaid's *Annie John.* Though she has written extensively about *The History of Mary Prince,* the Prince text is not included in this study.

3. For a sympathetic account of the history of the Moravian ministry in Antigua, see Frances Lanaghan's *Antigua and the Antiguans* (185, 248–51).

4. Olney writes: "The theme is the reality of slavery and the necessity of abolishing it; the content is a series of events and descriptions that will make the reader see and feel the realities of slavery; and the form is a chronological, episodic narrative beginning with an assertion of existence and surrounded by various testimonial evidences for that assertion" ("'I Was Born'" 53).

In her introduction to Prince's book Ferguson notes that "the *Reporter's* weekly accounts of such cases usually included details of the legal dispute, authenticating apparatus by eyewitnesses, details of trial testimony, numerous and hideous goings-on and occasional resistance, and some account of abolitionist activity" (25).

5. For more on these issues see Ferguson's *Subject to Others* (281–98).

6. For example, though Joseph Phillips of Antigua wrote a testimonial on Prince's behalf, the letter did not reach England in time to help her or Thomas Pringle in their legal battles. Ferguson explains that Mary Prince's owner brought legal action against Pringle for publishing her *History.* In failing health and short of funds, Pringle was unable to obtain legal evidence in support of her story from the West Indies and was forced to pay damages. Pringle did not have the support of the Anti-Slavery Society in the case of Mary Prince (Ferguson, introduction 39 n44).

7. For more on this subject see Price's *Maroon Societies,* and Benítez-Rojo's *The Repeating Island* (esp. 249–56).

8. I have in mind the distinction that Olney makes: "Autobiography may be understood as a recollective/narrative act in which the writer, from a certain point in his life—the present—, looks back over the events of that life and recounts them in such a way as to show how that past history has led to this present state of being. Exercising memory, in order that he may recollect and narrate, the autobiographer is not a neutral and passive recorder but rather a creative and active shaper" ("'I Was Born'" 47).

9. The issues arising from collaborative autobiography are explored in Lejeune's *On Autobiography* (185–215). In respect to the compromised cultural

practices of the enslaved, see Hartman's *Scenes of Subjection* and Woodward's "History from Slave Sources."

10. Strickland also recorded *The Narrative of Ashton Warner, A Native of St. Vincent's* in Pringle's house. Warner's voice is distinct in style and tone from Prince's. In the same year that *The History of Mary Prince* was published, Strickland published *Enthusiasm and Other Poems* in London. In 1830, shortly after recording Prince's story, Strickland married John Dunbar Moodie and emigrated to Canada with him and their daughter in 1832. She is the author of *Roughing It in the Bush; or, Forest Life in Canada* (1852), and *Flora Lyndsay* (1853). Her sisters, Agnes Strickland and Catherine Paar Traill, were published writers of some reputation in England and Canada.

11. Pringle was a published poet in his own right. He died in 1834. For more information about him see Pringle's *Thomas Pringle, His Life*; *Poetical Works*; and *Thomas Pringle, Narrative*; and Doyle's *Thomas Pringle*. See also Ferguson's introduction (38–40 n44 and 30–31 n15).

12. Sexual activity is subject to conditioned and closeted expression in the text even though the sexual abuse of slaves is a distinctive feature of West Indian life (Ferguson, introduction 25). See also Douglas Hall, *In Miserable Slavery*; Morrissey's *Slave Women*; and Foster's "Adding Color and Contour" and *Witnessing Slavery* (108–9).

13. In respect to issues of authenticity in the autobiography of those who do not write, Lejeune observes: "It is not a metaphysical question to be solved in the absolute; it is an ideological problem, linked to reading contracts, to the possible positions of identification with 'persons,' and to relations of class" (197).

14. Olney applies this descriptive language to Douglass's *Narrative of the Life of a Slave*.

15. According to Lejeune, issues of identity and authorship are everywhere in evidence in autobiographical collaborations: "The question is complicated by the fact that the notion of author refers as much to the idea of *initiative* as to that of *production*, and that the production can itself be shared (equally or in a hierarchical way) among several people" (193).

16. In *Invented Lives* Washington writes: "Narratives by women play an important part in allowing us to hear the voice of slave women; they show women as active agents rather than objects of pity, capable of interpreting their experiences and, like men, able to turn their victimization into triumph" (8).

17. In *Discerning the Subject*, Paul Smith writes: "A person is not simply the actor who follows ideological scripts, but is also an agent who reads them in order to insert him/herself into them—or not" (xxxiv–xxxv). Lamming makes such a positioning central to his conception of the Caribbean writer and the heroine of *Season of Adventure* (Paquet, *Novels* 3–4, 72).

18. Wynter argues that "the African in the New World became a Negro. And the Negro is the world's first uprooted race. He is the only race who is not tied

to a land mass. The African belongs to Africa. The European to Europe. The 'negro' has no such territorial cradle" (review 34). Prince's narrative appears to contradict this; she is specific about her heartland.

19. Prince's use of the trope prefigures its use in such primary texts of modern Caribbean writing as Césaire's *Notebook of a Return*, Lamming's *In the Castle of My Skin*, Brathwaite's *The Arrivants*, and Naipaul's *Finding the Center*, to name but a few.

20. Glissant's definition of a national literature seems tailored to a text like Prince's: "One may speak of a national literature, in the modern sense of the term, only in the instance where a community, faced with a threat to its collective survival, endeavors through the creative use of the spoken and the written word to express the very reason for its existence" (*Caribbean Discourse* 31).

21. Hodge makes this point about women in underdeveloped countries in an interview conducted by Kathleen Balutansky: "The other thing is that the women's movement in the Third World is not only about empowering women, it is very much a liberation process for the whole society" (661).

22. Other slave narratives, like *The Narrative of Ashton Warner* and *Narrative of the Cruel Treatment of James Williams*, make the same point about the de facto equality of men and women in slavery. James Williams gives a gruesome account of pregnant women and nursing mothers alongside him at the treadmill. Warner tells how his pregnant wife is driven to the fields and whipped for being unable to keep up with the others.

23. In "In Respect to Females" Foster finds that slave women's narratives "devote more discussion to familial relationships" in general. She also finds that they "rely less upon litanies of beatings and mutilations of other slaves" (67). The latter is not true of Prince's narrative.

24. Gates's observations about the paradox of representing "the oral within the written, precisely when oral black culture was transforming itself into a written culture" (*Signifying Monkey* 131–32) apply to *The History of Mary Prince* as well.

25. In a footnote to Prince's narrative, Pringle points out the contempt implicit in giving slaves such extravagant names. He does not comment on the contempt for British royalty that is also implicit in such a practice.

26. Stepto distinguishes three phases of slave narrative narration. In the third phase he differentiates the "generic narrative" from the "authenticating narrative": "In the former, authenticating documents and strategies are totally subsumed by the tale; the slave narrative becomes an identifiable generic text, e.g., autobiography, etc." (181–82).

27. The discursive situation is complex. The use of an amanuensis suggests "the unequal relation between colonizer and colonized, oppressor and oppressed," yet the published narrative gives the relationship something of the value of Said's "conversation between equals" (Said, *The World* 48).

28. The issues surrounding Prince's "speakerly text" add yet another dimension to Gates's exemplary analysis of the trope of the talking book in *The Signifying Monkey,* esp. chaps. 4 and 5.

29. Baker stresses the importance of negotiating the economics of slavery as a precondition to freedom in *Blues, Ideology, and Afro-American Literature.* Morrissey reports on the specifics of this practice in *Slave Women in the New World.*

30. Gates's chapter called "The Signifying Monkey and the Language of Signifyin(g)" in *The Signifying Monkey* explores the range of signification as a characteristic feature of black speech and black texts in the United States. What he has to say applies equally well to oral and written figures of signification in the black cultures of the Caribbean.

31. In *Written by Herself* Foster reminds us that the slave's faith in the power of the word came from sources religious and secular, African and European: "Our understanding of the earliest writings by African Americans is considerably enhanced when we consider what Africanists have told us about the primacy of *Nommo* or the Word. . . . Study of the various African literatures and customs, especially the praise songs, the autobiographical writings, and the emphasis on proverbs, masking, and naming, may provide very salient explanations for the prevalence of poetry and political commentary in literature by African American women" (16–17).

32. What Walcott says about the birth of a poetic tradition in "The Muse of History" is pertinent here: "Epic was compressed in the folk legend. The act of imagination was the creative effort of the tribe. Later such legends may be written by individual poets, but their beginnings are oral, familial, the poetry of firelight which illuminates the faces of a tight, primal hierarchy. But even oral literature forces itself toward hieroglyph and alphabet" (13).

33. Abrahams comes to some important conclusions about the importance that black West Indians attached to all forms of speech in *The Man-of-Words in the West Indies*: "The use of talk to proclaim presence of self, to assert oneself vocally in the most anxious and unguarded situations. We are shown the importance of arguing in daily life, as one technique of self-dramatization. And . . . the importance of a highly formal and decorous approach to language in both the intercultural exchanges and intra-group activities" (29).

34. Andrews calls attention to the novelization of slave narratives of the 1850s and 1860s in the concluding chapter of *To Tell a Free Story.*

35. Gates writes that the slave, by definition, "possessed at most a liminal status within the human community. To read and to write was to transgress this nebulous realm of liminality" (*Signifying Monkey* 128). The privileging of orality, in Prince's sophisticated narrative, sets her text at odds with the most influential narratives of the period.

36. Bachelard's observations about a child's reverie and the consciousness of freedom apply here: "To grasp this liberty when it intervenes in a child's reverie

is paradoxical only if one forgets that we still dream of liberty as we dreamed of it when we were children" (*Poetics of Reverie* 101).

37. The narrative does not permit easy generalizations about sexually frustrated and humiliated slave mistresses. Mrs. Williams's kindness is associated with her husband's philandering; the reverse is true of Mrs. I—— and Mrs. Wood. See Gwin's "Green-Eyed Monsters" for a discussion of the psychosexual violence inflicted on slave women by their mistresses.

38. In *The Body in Pain* Scarry describes the throbbing, feeling heart as a metaphor of interiority: "To instead conceive of the body in terms of capacities and needs (not now 'lens' but 'seeing,' not now 'pump' but 'having a beating heart' or, more specifically, 'desiring' or 'fearing') is to move further in toward the interior of felt-experience. To, finally, conceive of the body as 'aliveness' or 'awareness of aliveness' is to reside at last within the felt-experience of sentience" (285).

39. In *The History of the Voice* Brathwaite states the case for "immanence" as the essential feature Caribbean language and culture, "because they come from a historical experience where they had to rely on their very breath rather than paraphernalia like books and museums and machines. They had to depend on immanence, the power within themselves, rather than the technology outside themselves" (19).

CHAPTER 3. THE ENIGMA OF ARRIVAL

1. Mary Seacole is not a medical doctor in British colonial terms. *Doctress* is the term Mary Seacole uses to describe her medical practice. In Jamaica *doctress* was used to describe the black folk healer or nurse who attended sick slaves in the plantation "hot house" or hospital (Cassidy 134; Bush 34, 36). Barbara Bush explains: "Because women in traditional African society had a vital role in healing, particularly in the practical application of herbal remedies . . . they were prominent also in healing in the slave community. . . . women's contribution as healers and nurses outside the plantation hot-house may have exceeded all the health services provided by the white establishment" (155). In her study, Bush establishes an additional link between religion and healing (154–56), but Mary Seacole makes no such claim in *Wonderful Adventures*.

2. With respect to the European culture of travel, Grewal observes that "mobility not only came to signify an unequal relation between the tourist/traveler and the 'native'" but also a new notion of freedom (136–37). Van den Abbeele also links the trope of travel to values embodied in "progress, the quest for knowledge, freedom to move, self-awareness as an Odyssean enterprise, salvation as a destination to be attained by following a prescribed path" (xv).

3. Opposition to colonial protection had no significant support among those who were politically active at the time, even among those who agitated for social and political reforms (Brathwaite, "Caliban" 42–43; Bigelow 46).

4. See Gikandi's *Maps of Englishness* for the contradictory values that Englishness acquires during the colonial period and for an extended study of how this is played out in Seacole's *Wonderful Adventures* (esp. 125–43).

5. Writing about nation, gender, empire, and the culture of travel in colonial India, Grewal makes an important connection between the European discourse of travel and the adoption of comparative structures of value: "Since the forms of European travel above all created the demarcations between 'home' and 'abroad' through comparative perspectives dependent on the binary of Self and Other, the utilization of this binary by Indians was central to creating new forms of the Self" (135).

6. McClintock elaborates on this idea of contagion: "The image of bad blood was drawn from biology but degeneration was less a biological fact than it was a social figure. Central to the idea of degeneration was the idea of *contagion* (the communication of disease, by touching, from body to body), and central to the idea of contagion was the peculiarly Victorian paranoia about boundary order. Panic about blood contiguity, ambiguity and *metissage* expressed intense anxieties about the fallibility of white male and imperial potency. The politics of contagion justified a politics of exclusion and gave social sanction to the middle-class fixation with boundary sanitation, in particular the sanitation of sexual boundaries. Body boundaries were felt to be dangerously permeable and demanding continual purification, so that sexuality, in particular women's sexuality, was cordoned off as the central transmitter of racial and hence cultural contagion" (47).

7. See also Brathwaite's *Contradictory Omens* 17.

8. The Jamaican assembly resisted until the 1865 Morant Bay Rebellion, when Britain imposed a crown colony form of government with an appointed governor. By the end of the nineteenth century, Britain had imposed this form of government in all British colonies except Barbados and the Bahamas (Rogozinski 192–97).

9. Writing about adventurousness and heroism as biographical/autobiographical values, Bakhtin observes: "To strive for glory is to gain consciousness of oneself within the civilized mankind of history (or within a nation); it means to found and build one's own life in the possible consciousness of this civilized mankind" (*Art* 156). The implications of this for the colonized British subject are obvious.

10. In a review of Naipaul's *The Enigma of Arrival*, Walcott makes the point that "there is the real enigma: that the provincial, the colonial, can never civilize himself beyond his province, no matter how deeply he immures himself in the woods of a villa outside Rome or in the leafy lanes of Edwardian England. And that is not pathetic; it is glorious" (31).

11. In a conversation with Robert Stepto, Morrison makes a useful, if conventional, distinction between "the black woman as parent, . . . as a sort of

umbrella figure, culture-bearer," and the fearless, adventurous black woman who is possessed by what she calls "the traveling Ulysses scene" (226–28). Judd makes Seacole's refashioning of the Homeric epic central to her reading of *Wonderful Adventures*: "Through her rewriting of both Homeric epic and the popular hagiography of Florence Nightingale—icons of both British domesticity and imperialism—I argue that Seacole creates a heroic self that cannot be contained by the exigencies of her English audience" (101).

12. It is interesting to compare William Wells Brown's *Three Years in Europe* (1852) and *The American Fugitive in Europe* (1854) with Mary Seacole's pride in her colonial status. Brown and Seacole do not perceive Europe as the source of American slavery and corruption but as the civilizing center of the world.

13. In her reading of *Wonderful Adventures*, Judd privileges the mock heroic and "the jocular style that typifies her autobiography" (108, 109).

14. According to Middleton, a preoccupation with correct female attire was one of the ways that Victorian lady travelers tried to hold on to "a high ideal of womanhood" (8–9).

15. Little is known about Nanny, the legendary Jamaican Windward Maroon, but there is no doubt that she played a crucial role in the success of the Windward Maroons: "Not only was she a tactician and political adviser, but as a spiritual leader she assured communal loyalty and upheld the morale of the maroons" (Bush 70).

16. In "Author and Hero in Aesthetic Activity," Bakhtin describes the heroic constituent in biography/autobiography as "characterized by this organic sense of oneself within the heroicized mankind of history; by the organic sense of being a participant in it, of experiencing one's essential growth within it, of taking root in it and gaining full consciousness and understanding of one's own works and days within it" (*Art* 156).

17. Morrissey also notes that "women's medical role was well established in West Indian slave societies and strongly linked to African practices. It brought slave women prestige and resources. . . . African 'doctors' and healers had superior knowledge of diseases also found in West Africa—yaws, malaria, yellow fever. Women healers and nurses were routinely called on to serve as midwives and attendants to new mothers and to treat reproductive diseases, problems, and maladies that seemed to plague women" (68–69).

18. This is akin to what Morrison describes as the "how I got over—look at me—alone—let me show you how I did it" kind of autobiography, which she contrasts with classic African American autobiography: "My single and solitary life is like the lives of the tribe; it differs in these specific ways, but it is a balanced life because it is both solitary and representative" ("Rootedness" 339–40).

19. It may be that she judged that this would assist the London fund-raising efforts on her behalf to defray financial losses that she incurred when the war ended; one such effort coincided with publication of her book: "On 25 July, 1857 the *Illustrated London News* recommended the book to its readers and in the

same issue announced a Grand Military Festival to be held for Mrs. Seacole's benefit on the four nights of 27–30 July, at the Royal Surrey Gardens" (Alexander and Dewjee 31–32).

20. In exploring the values that "a national-cultural community as a sovereign entity and place set against other places," Said observes that "this idea of place does not cover the nuances, principally of reassurance, fitness, belonging, association, and community, entailed in the phrase at home or in place" (*World* 8).

21. In writing about the travel novel, Bakhtin makes the point that "the author's own real homeland . . . serves as organizing center for the point of view, the scales of comparison, the approaches and evaluations determining how alien cultures are seen and understood (it is not compulsory that the native country be evaluated positively, but it must absolutely provide us with a scale and a background)" (*Dialogic Imagination* 103).

22. "England enters Seacole's childhood imagination—and her adult memories—as a longing, an image without substance, but also as a figure of desire. For this image to be realized, Jamaica must fade into the distance, be reduced to a phantom, so that England can be rewritten as the real place of identity" (Gikandi 128–29).

23. According to Said, culture may be described as "a system of exclusions legislated from above but enacted throughout its polity, by which such things as anarchy, disorder, irrationality, inferiority, bad taste, and immorality can be identified, then deposited outside the culture and kept there by the power of the State and its institutions" (*World* 11).

24. For more on Seacole's use of the trope of the other, see Gikandi 138–39.

PART 2. THE ESTRANGING SEA

1. According to Clifford, "Decentered, lateral connections may be as those formed around a teleology of origin/return. And a shared ongoing history of displacement, suffering, adaptation, or resistance may be as important as the projection of a specific origin" (250).

2. In *Poetics of Relation* Glissant clarifies this point about nomadism: "But is the nomad not overdetermined by the conditions of his existence? Rather than the enjoyment of freedom, is nomadism not a form of obedience to contingencies that are restrictive?" (12).

See Lawrence's *Penelope Voyages,* for a useful study of the Penelope (home)–Circe (foreign) paradigm in relation to phallocentric discourse framed around Hermes as paradigmatic traveler (x).

3. See Paul Gilroy's *The Black Atlantic* for a review of the relative values of ontological as opposed to strategic pan-Africanism (31–35).

4. Brathwaite's epic trilogy, *The Arrivants* (1973), inscribes and affirms a collective African consciousness at the heart of Caribbean community. This was done

earlier by Claude McKay and Césaire, among others, but Brathwaite's mythicized Africa was based on historical knowledge and lived experience.

5. In "Timehri" Brathwaite remarks on the shift in focus from inescapable fragmentation and a sense of rootlessness: "The second phase of West Indian and Caribbean artistic and intellectual life, on which we are now entering, having become conscious of the problem, is seeking to transcend and heal it" (32).

6. In *The Black Atlantic* Paul Gilroy proposes a politics of transfiguration: "This emphasizes the emergence of qualitatively new desires, social relations, and modes of association within the racial community of interpretation and resistance *and* between that group and its erstwhile oppressors. . . . This is not a counter-discourse but a counter that defiantly reconstructs its own critical, intellectual, and moral genealogy in a partially hidden public sphere of it own" (37–38).

7. "Errantry, therefore, does not proceed from renunciation nor from frustration regarding a supposedly deteriorated (deterritorialized) situation of origin; it is not a resolute act of rejection or an uncontrolled impulse of abandonment. Sometimes, by taking up the problems of the Other, it is possible to find oneself . . . prompting the knowledge that identity is no longer completely within the root but also in Relation" (Glissant, *Poetics of Relation* 18).

8. In some respects Glissant's open boat clarifies the method and mission of Lamming's *The Pleasures of Exile*: "Traveling is no longer the locus of power but, rather, a pleasurable, if privileged, time. The ontological obsession with knowledge gives way here to an enjoyment of relation; in its elementary and often caricatural form this is tourism. Those who stay behind thrill to this passion for the world shared by all. Or, indeed, they may suffer the torments of internal exile" (*Poetics of Relation* 19).

9. Caricom (Caribbean Community) is an economic association formed in 1974 by ten Caribbean nations.

10. Molloy fashions an alternative to what she perceives as the tunnel vision of nationalist readings of Spanish American autobiography: "What seems more profitable, instead, is to allow the preoccupation with national identity (undeniably present in Spanish-American self-writing) to reverberate in the text as an ever-renewed scene of crisis necessary to the rhetoric of self-figuration; to see it as a critical space, fraught with anxiety of origins and representation, within which the self stages its presence, and achieves ephemeral unity" (29).

11. In *Routes* Clifford notes the destabilization of time lines in respect to "diaspora": "In diaspora experience, the co-presence of 'here' and 'there' is articulated with an anti-teleological (sometimes messianic) temporality. Linear history is broken, the present is constantly shadowed by a past that is also a desired, but obstructed future: a renewed, painful yearning" (264).

12. A recent study of Claude McKay and Paule Marshall by Hathaway does exactly this. See *Caribbean Waves* (1999). Edmondson also takes up this issue in *Making Men*.

13. In *Black Skin, White Masks* Fanon develops this theme with his own peculiar emphasis: "For the majority of white men the Negro represents the sexual instinct (in its raw state). The Negro is the incarnation of a genital potency beyond all moralities and prohibitions" (159).

14. See Dollimore's *Sexual Dissidence* (1991), including "Fanon: Race and Sexuality" (344–51), for a useful study of transgression and its containment.

15. For example, in *Power/Knowledge* Foucault and Guy Le Gaufey compare the American women's movement with the American homosexual movement:

FOUCAULT: . . . Like women, they [homosexuals] begin to look for new forms of community, co-existence, pleasure. . . .

Yes, but the homosexual liberation movements remain very much caught at the level of demands for the right to their sexuality, the dimension of the sexological. . . . Women on the other hand are able to have much wider economic, political and other kinds of objectives than homosexuals.

LE GAUFEY: Women's sexuality doesn't lead them to depart from the recognized kinship systems, while that of homosexuals places them immediately outside them. (120)

16. LeSeur observes in her study of the bildungsroman: "The West Indian novelists' nostalgia for childhood takes on an extra dimension when we note that they are often displaced from their places of birth in order to pursue a writing career" (150).

17. This pressure mounts through the 1980s, for example, in Parry's "Problems of Current Theories of Colonial Discourse," where she argues: "The labor of producing a counter-discourse displacing imperialism's dominative system of knowledge rests with those engaged in developing a critique from outside its cultural hegemony, and in furthering a contest begun by anti-colonial movements, theorists of colonial discourse will need to pursue the connections between imperialism's material aggression and its epistemic violence, and disclose the relationships between its ideological address to the colonial world and the imperialist culture of the metropolitan world" (55).

18. Gramsci's observations about the link between autobiography and the political or philosophical essay seem to be on point here: "Autobiographies are often an act of pride: one believes one's own life is worth being narrated because it is 'original,' different from others, etc. Autobiography can be conceived 'politically.' One knows that one's life is similar to that of a thousand others, but through 'chance' it has had opportunities that the thousand others in reality could not or did not have. By narrating it, one creates this possibility, suggests the process, indicates the opening. Autobiography therefore replaces the 'political' or 'philosophical essay': it describes in action what otherwise is deduced logically" (132).

19. See Gramsci on the equivocation of nationalism in respect to the punctual expression of the spirit of the group: "The spirit is good to the extent that it adopts a certain *collective* manner of thinking and bad to the extent that it seeks to differentiate itself" (261).

20. See also my earlier study, *The Novels of George Lamming*.

21. Lejeune's observations on the autobiographical space are pertinent here: "We escape accusations of vanity and egocentrism when we seem so aware of the limitations and insufficiencies of our autobiography; and no one notices that, by the same movement, we extend on the contrary the autobiographical pact, in an *indirect* form, to the whole of what we have written" (27).

22. Walcott made these comments as he was chatting informally with my graduate class in Caribbean literature at the University of Pennsylvania, fall 1987.

23. Edmondson's point is well taken: "The inversion of gender characteristics that the English imagined onto black West Indian society circumlocuted the discourse of later West Indian nationalism, such that the nationalist project became inseparable from the epistemological issue of defining West Indian manhood" (8).

CHAPTER 4. "THE TRAVELING ULYSSES SCENE"

1. Claude McKay returned to the United States in 1934. He completed *A Long Way from Home* in the summer and fall of 1936 while working for the Federal Writers Project in New York City (W. Cooper 313).

2. Extracts from the original manuscript were published in *Phylon* as "Boyhood in Jamaica" in 1953. In his introduction to *My Green Hills of Jamaica*, Morris concludes that "Boyhood in Jamaica" was "intrusively edited," with "phrases, sentences, even whole paragraphs which do not appear in the typescript" (v).

3. "Cultural identities are points of identification, the unstable points of identification or suture, which are made, within the discourse of history and culture. Not an essence but a positioning. Hence, there is always a politics of position, which has no absolute guarantee in an unproblematic, transcendental 'law of history'" (S. Hall, "Cultural Identity" 72).

4. Cultural difference within the diaspora has been overlooked in some studies of black autobiography, for example, Butterfield's *Black Autobiography*. Others have observed it with little sympathy, for example, David Levering Lewis's *When Harlem Was in Vogue*.

5. According to Paul Gilroy, a pluralistic position "affirms blackness as an open signifier and seeks to celebrate complex representations of a black particularity that is *internally* divided: by class, sexuality, gender, age and political consciousness" (*Black Atlantic* 123).

6. In this respect Claude McKay has much in common with Harlem Renaissance writers like Langston Hughes and Zora Neale Hurston. In Claude McKay's

work, as in Hurston's fictional and anthropological representations of black urban and rural folk life in the United States, the rhythms of life among the black working class have their own legitimacy and are to be celebrated rather than reconstructed to reflect the values of a black middle class dedicated to "racial uplift." I have in mind Hurston's *Their Eyes Were Watching God, Mules and Men,* and shorter pieces like "Muttsey" and "Story in Harlem Slang." Hughes's "The Negro Artist and the Racial Mountain" is an exemplary statement of these aesthetic values.

7. "Each time the encounter with identity occurs at the point at which something exceeds the frame of the image, it eludes the eye, evacuates the self as site of identity and autonomy and—most important—leaves a resistant trace, a stain of the subject, a sign of resistance" (Bhabha, *Location of Culture* 49).

8. Bachelard argues that the nucleus of childhood is permanent within the human soul, "an immobile but ever living childhood, outside history, hidden from others, disguised in history when it is recounted, but which has real being only in its instants of illumination which is the same as saying in the moments of its poetic existence" (*Poetics of Reverie* 100).

9. This evokes Kincaid's statement to an interviewer: "I'm a West Indian. It's in my blood. But I can't live there" (D4). Though he is domiciled in Barbados, Lamming once expressed similar sentiments: "This may be the dilemma of the West Indian writer abroad: that he hungers for nourishment from a soil which he (as an ordinary citizen) could not at present endure" (*Pleasures* 50). The Caribbean as site of identification to these migrant writers effectively splits the subject.

10. Paul Gilroy, like Bhabha (*Location of Culture* 13), uses the crossroads as a sign of the "new" internationalism: "The crossroads as a special location where unforeseen, magical things can happen might be an appropriate conceptual vehicle for rethinking the dialectical tension between cultural roots and cultural routes between the space constituted through and between places and the space marked by out flows" (*Black Atlantic* 193).

11. Bhabha argues that verticality is "significant for the light it sheds on the *dimension of depth* that provides the language of Identity with its sense of reality—a measure of the 'me,' which emerges from an acknowledgement of my inwardness, the depth of my character, the profundity of my person, to mention only a few of those qualities through which we commonly articulate our self-consciousness" (*Location of Culture* 48).

12. In 1942 Claude McKay estimated that a third of Harlem's black population was of Caribbean origin; this was to be the subject of a new book entitled *The Tropics in New York* (W. Cooper 349–50).

13. In *Black Metropolis* Drake and Clayton describe the contradictoriness of group identification on the basis of race in the contested cultural space that is Harlem: "As Race Leaders, the upper class must identify itself psychologically

with 'the Race,' and the Race includes a lot of people who would never be accepted socially" (563).

14. Gates's analysis of the mask-in-motion as an African and Afro-American cultural phenomenon offers valuable insight into Claude McKay's autobiographical mask: "Once effected, the mask is a vehicle for the primary evocation of a complete hermetic universe, one of force or being, a world autonomous, marked both by a demonstrably interior cohesion and by a complete neutrality to exterior mores or norms. This internal cogency makes it impervious to the accident of place or time" ("Dis and Dat" 89).

15. In *Some Versions of Pastoral* Empson makes the connection between proletarian art and pastoral: "I think good proletarian art is usually covert pastoral" (6). Bone is even more to the point in *Down Home,* when he distinguishes pastoral and antipastoral as definitive discursive modes in the evolution of the black short story through the Harlem Renaissance (109–38).

16. For example, Du Bois's "Criteria of Negro Art" provoked contradictory statements of aesthetic value by writers like Hughes and Hurston.

17. Hathaway provides an interesting account of the contentiousness generated by the miscommunications and misunderstandings that characterized the relationship between West Indians and black Americans in Claude McKay's Harlem (1–28).

18. Writing about Caribbean immigrant communities generally, Stuart Hall observes: "We belong to the marginal, the under-developed, the periphery, the 'Other.' We are at the outer edge, the 'rim,' of the metropolitan world—always 'South' to someone else's *El Norte*" ("Cultural Identity" 73).

19. In describing the play of "difference" within Caribbean identity from the black British point of view, Stuart Hall stresses the importance of the double meaning of *play*: "It suggests, on the one hand, the instability, the permanent unsettlement, the lack of any final resolution. On the other hand, it reminds us that the place where this 'doubleness' is most powerfully to be heard is 'playing' within the varieties of Caribbean music" ("Cultural Identity" 73).

20. Suleiman continues: "Does all playing involve a game? Are all games playful? What's the difference between playing with and playing against? Playing at and playing on? Playing up and playing down, playing to and playing around? And what about 'just playing'? Do all games have players? Does all play have players? Does the game stop if there is no one around to see it—or play it?" (1).

21. Claude McKay's autobiographical "mask" adds another dimension to Gates's assumptions in "Dis and Dat": "In a collective as well as a functional sense, the mask effects the 'spiritual consolidation' of the race, in an especial universe governed only by the laws of cohesive interiority. Mask enmeshes 'the day to day awareness of a people,' surely a fundamental aesthetic value in all of African art" (89).

22. The title of James Weldon Johnson's autobiography, *Along This Way* (1933), also calls attention to the course of his life as an actual spatial course. Zora Neale Hurston does the same thing in *Dust Tracks on a Road* (1942). And

so does Langston Hughes in his autobiographies, *The Big Sea* (1940) and *I Wonder as I Wander* (1956). The latter interestingly reverses coded assumptions of sexual orientation with Claude McKay's "I was gripped by the lust to wander and wonder" (*Long Way* 4).

23. In *Man-of-Words* Abrahams points out that not only is gossip a means of increasing the gossiper's base of esteem through the articulation of interactional channels and friendship networks, in some cultures it is also a narrative form (78–79).

24. In "Rootedness" Morrison makes a clear distinction regarding the aesthetics of black autobiography: "The autobiographical form is classic in Black American or Afro-American literature because it provided an instance in which a writer could be representative, could say, 'My solitary and individual life is like the lives of the tribe; it differs in these specific ways, but it is a balanced life because it is both solitary and representative.' The contemporary autobiography tends to be 'how I got over—look at me—alone—let me show you how I did it'" (339–40).

25. Stuart Hall's notion of Caribbean identities as framed by two interacting axes or vectors, "the vector of similarity and continuity; and the vector of difference and rupture" is fully operative here ("Cultural Identity" 72).

26. In *Roots of Jamaican Culture* Alleyne describes myalism as follows: "Myalism has come to be used to refer to the dominant form of Africa-derived religion that developed among the slaves in Jamaica. It emerged as the first religious organization of Africans in Jamaica; its characteristics are those of the typical West African 'secret cult societies'" (85).

27. Claude McKay writes Max Eastman about a felt "need to settle down": "No place has satisfied me since I left home as much as Morocco. There are many things in the life of the natives, their customs and superstitions, reminiscent of Jamaica" (quoted in W. Cooper 271).

28. Wayne Cooper concludes: "With the creation of *Banana Bottom,* [Claude] McKay's picaresque search for psychic unity and stability, begun in *Home to Harlem,* came full circle to rest again in the lost paradise of his pastoral childhood" (282).

29. According to Bhabha, "to dwell 'in the beyond' is also . . . to be part of a revisionary time, a return to the present to redescribe our cultural contemporaneity; to reinscribe our human historic commonality; *to touch the future on its hither side*" (*Location of Culture* 7).

30. According to Bakhtin, the essence of this kind of historical inversion "is found in the fact that mythological and artistic thinking locates such categories as purpose, ideal, justice, perfection, the harmonious condition of man and society and the like in the *past*" (*Dialogic* 147).

31. The Lewises' class analysis of Claude McKay's Jamaica is sharply critical of his silences about the plight of the landless poor in rural Jamaica. McCleod also documents instances of Claude McKay's misrepresenting Jamaican reality,

from facile conclusions about rape and violence to his account of the 1865 Morant Bay rebellion (252–53).

32. The contrast between the texts is extreme in many respects. For example, the house on the hill in Lamming's fictive village is the white landlord's; in *My Green Hills* it belongs to the McKay family and is the result of the peasant farmer's diligence, intelligence, and courage.

CHAPTER 5. BLURRED GENRES, BLENDED VOICES

1. Coe links the origins of the genre to major social upheavals: "But if this motif is most clearly discernible in recent writings, the fact is that the origins of the Childhood as a genre coincided from the outset with a major period of upheaval, with the French Revolution and the Industrial Revolution" (*Grass* 65). In her recent study of the black bildungsroman, LeSeur makes a similar point, adding that "the West Indian novelist writes a bildungsroman to recall childhood roots and to discover the truth about self and home" (1).

2. Coe writes: "The formal literary structure is complete exactly at the point at which the immature self of childhood is conscious of its transformation into the mature self of the adult who is the narrator of the earlier experiences" (*Grass* 9).

3. Seidel's definition of *exile* is a useful starting point: "Exile is an impetus, a positioning, and a perspective . . . one gets outside a space to look in and see wholly; on the other hand, the space created from outside is, willy-nilly, a projection, subject to the laws generated and inspired by the imagining mind" (87). Also to the point is Lamming's meditation on exile in *The Pleasures of Exile* (24–25).

4. According to Heaney, "We are more and more aware of writing as a place in itself, a destination in art arrived at by way of art. And yet an urge persists to enquire into the inspiration and foundation which place affords in the creative process" (19).

5. In *The Narrative of Liberation* (189–92) Taylor analyzes some of the remarkable parallels between *In the Castle of My Skin* and Fanon's *The Wretched of the Earth*.

6. Cooke links the pattern of spectatorhood in the text to its counterpart, a pattern of concealment (30–31).

7. Stuart Hall's approach to the "problem" of ideology seems particularly appropriate to the encoding/decoding autobiographical project of *In the Castle of My Skin*: "By ideology I mean the mental frameworks—the languages, the concepts, categories, imagery of thought, and systems of representation—which different classes and social groups deploy in order to make sense of, define, figure out and render intelligible the way society works" ("Problem of Ideology" 26).

8. Wright seems to recognize this himself in his introduction to the McGraw Hill edition of *In the Castle of My Skin* in 1954: "I, too, have been long crying

286 / Notes to Pages 117–126

these stern tidings; and, when I catch the echo of yet another voice declaiming in alien accents a description of this same reality, I react with pride and excitement, and I want to urge others to listen to that voice" (vi).

9. Wright is perhaps rhetorically present in the figure of Trumper, whose newly acquired race consciousness as a migrant worker in the United States marks the boundaries of the childhood experience that he shared with G. (*Castle* 298; Taylor 221–22; Ramchand 54–56).

10. For a foundational statement on sexual difference and subaltern subjectivity, see Spivak's "Can the Subaltern Speak?"

11. Kristeva's *Powers of Horror* provides a rich framework for exploring confrontations with the feminine beyond abjection and fright to the ecstatic.

12. In her study of the black bildungsroman LeSeur observes: "The West Indian novel of youth also celebrates life through the use of local color and events. The use of dialect, the names given to characters, and the realism of the depicted scenes enhance the portrayal of the joy and pain of being a child" (3).

13. "Unless it is highly fictionalized, the autobiography of childhood is of necessity largely descriptive. There is, by and large, comparatively little scope for narrative, still less for dialogue, while reflective or analytical passages must be seen strictly as the contribution of the adult" (Coe, *Grass* 117).

14. "Sight says too many things at one time. Being does not see itself. Perhaps it listens to itself," writes Bachelard (*Reverie* 215).

15. This is not dissimilar to Walcott's model in "The Muse of History": "Epic was compressed in the folk legend. The act of the imagination was the creative effort of the tribe. Later such legends may be written by individual poets, but their beginnings are oral, familial, the poetry of firelight which illuminates the faces of a tight, primal hierarchy. But even oral literature forces itself toward hieroglyph and alphabet" (13).

16. Writing about the contribution of folklore to the development of the historical novel in the eighteenth century, Bakhtin observes: "The folksong, the folktale, the heroic and historical legend, and the saga were above all a new and powerful means of humanizing and intensifying one's native space" (*Speech Genres* 52).

17. An important theoretical companion piece to Brathwaite's *History of the Voice* (1984), quoted here, is his earlier essay on nation language, "English in the Caribbean," in Baker's *Reading Black* (1976).

18. Writing on autobiography, Bakhtin concludes that "the boundary between horizon and surrounding world or environment is unstable in biography and has no significance in principle; empathy has maximal significance" (*Art* 166).

19. In her recently published *Making Men*, Belinda Edmondson takes issue with this privileging of a black Caribbean peasantry by writers like Lamming. She observes: "The intellectual's argument that black Caribbean culture constitutes the basis of an indigenous literary tradition is, as I will argue, the basis of

a certain anxiety in West Indian discourse on the question of race and authenticity" (59). I would argue that *In the Castle of My Skin* takes careful measure of this paradox.

20. It may be that the dialogue with self is also a dialogue with Fanon about the death of the colonizer (Taylor 74, 195–96).

21. Writing about *The Education of Henry Adams,* Hayden White observes that "the classic text reveals, indeed actively draws attention to, its own processes of meaning production and makes of these processes its own subject matter, its own 'content'" (211).

22. Because of its deep resonance and complex structure, *In the Castle of My Skin* illuminates the sociocultural processes at work in subsequent Caribbean narratives of childhood and adolescence. "The consummate text of growing up male in the Caribbean" (Cooke 29) provides a useful apperceptive background for investigating texts as different as Naipaul's *Miguel Street* (1959), Anthony's *The Year in San Fernando* (1965), Hodge's *Crick Crack, Monkey* (1970), Erna Brodber's *Jane and Louisa Will Soon Come Home* (1980), and Kincaid's *Annie John* (1985). Cooke's "The Strains of Apocalypse" demonstrates some of the many ways in which Brodber's text repeats and revises key tropes and rhetorical strategies in *In the Castle of My Skin.* The same case can be made for all these texts, even where they explore the different historical reality of growing up female in the Caribbean or place an entirely different value on their Caribbean childhood.

23. I have in mind the castle of the gothic, or black, novel as a space saturated with historical time: "The castle is the place where the lords of the feudal era lived (and consequently also the place of historical figures of the past); the traces of centuries and generations are arranged in it in visible form as various parts of its architecture, in furnishings, weapons, the ancestral portrait gallery, the family archives and in the particular human relationships involving dynastic primacy and the transfer of hereditary rights. And finally legends and traditions animate every corner of the castle and its environs through their constant reminders of past events" (Bakhtin, *Dialogic* 245–46).

CHAPTER 6. AUTOBIOGRAPHICAL FRAMEWORKS AND LINKED DISCOURSES

1. Tiffin identifies *The Pleasures of Exile* as a resistance autobiography, along with Rhys's *Smile Please* and Naipaul's *The Enigma of Arrival*: "In these three resistance autobiographies, then, the unmasking of imperial fictions is important, not just in terms of specific texts, but through the examination of the book as fetish, dream, insignia of authority" (30). Edmondson characterizes this process as a cultural dependency: "The tropistic relationship between nineteenth-century Englishness and twentieth-century West Indianness has structured the meaning

of 'Authorship' and 'nation' in Anglophone Caribbean discourse such that what is now recognized as West Indian oppositional discourse to Britain is still marked by a utilization of a specifically English vision of what constitutes intellectual production" (5).

2. In "Caribbean and African Appropriations of *The Tempest*," Nixon stresses the importance of Lamming's use of collectivity: "Lamming's assertions that his unorthodoxy is collectively grounded is crucial: those who defend a text's universal value can easily discount a solitary dissenting voice as uncultured or quirky, but it is more difficult to ignore entirely a cluster of allied counter judgments, even if the group can still be stigmatized" (558).

3. In some respects the title anticipates the pleasure-bliss principle of Barthes's *The Pleasure of the Text* (1975).

4. In *Exile and the Narrative Imagination* Seidel observes that "the task for the exile, especially the exiled artist, is to transform the figure of rupture back into a figure of connection" (x).

5. In a 1983 interview by Philippe Decraene, the Martiniquan poet and playwright Aimé Césaire takes the position that the wealth and originality of the West Indies are the fruit of synthesis (64).

6. In Wright's "Blueprint for Negro Writing," perspective is a theory about the meaning, structure, and direction of the modern world, a theory that the writer fashions for himself when he has looked and brooded hard and long at the circumstances of his race in relation to subject peoples everywhere: "It is that fixed point in intellectual space where a writer stands to view the struggles, hopes, and sufferings of his people" (400).

7. In "Reading from Elsewhere" Hulme gives Lamming's reading of *The Tempest* in *The Pleasures of Exile* the kind of appreciative critical assessment that it has rarely received. It is usefully read in conjunction with my own introduction to the Ann Arbor edition of *The Pleasures of Exile* (1992).

8. Bakhtin calculates the influence of theomachy and anthromachy on autobiographical self-accounting in *Art and Answerability*: "An element of theomachy and anthromachy is possible in confessional self-accounting, that is, the refusal to accept a possible judgment by God or by man, and as a result tones of resentment, distrust, cynicism, irony, defiance appear" (146).

9. See, for example, Césaire's adaptation of Shakespeare's play, *Une Tempête*; Retamar's *Caliban and Other Essays*; Brathwaite's "Caliban" in *The Arrivants*, and his "Caliban, Ariel, and Unprospero"; Lamming's novel, *Water with Berries*; Wynter's afterword; Joseph's *Caliban in Exile*; Supriya Nair's *Caliban's Curse: George Lamming and the Revisioning of History*, and, more recently Edmondson's *Making Men*. Lamming makes a singular contribution to the discourse around Mannoni's use of *The Tempest* to legitimize his theory of the psychology of colonialism in *Prospero and Caliban: The Psychology of Colonialism* and in the spirited responses to Mannoni's theory in Fanon's *Black Skin, White Masks* and Césaire's *Discourse on Colonialism*.

10. Diawara concludes that *Beyond a Boundary* "shows that West Indian cricket represents the taking-away and the appropriation of the game from Englishness" (41).

11. As Trotsky observes in *Literature and Revolution*: "Artistic creation is always a complicated turning inside out of old forms, under the influence of new stimuli which lie outside of art" (37).

12. The taking of the Amazon from Amerindian people through land titles is a recent example of the preeminence of paper over fact. The legal definition of land claim and possession for purposes of deforestation supplants the moral definition of landownership through hundreds of years of planting nut and fruit trees and harvesting the forest.

13. The collusion of colonization and textual constructions of alterity is the subject of Hulme's *Colonial Encounters* and Cheyfitz's *The Poetics of Imperialism*.

14. In an interview by Ian Munro and Reinhard Sander, Lamming clarified his position: "So although I would make a distinction about functions, I do not make a distinction about responsibilities. I do not think that the responsibility of the professional politician is greater than the responsibility of an artist to his society" (*Kas-Kas* 13).

15. Nonetheless, as Edmondson observes in *Making Men*, in Anglophone Caribbean discourse Lamming bears a special responsibility "for establishing *The Tempest* as the primary text for discourse on the West Indies' relation to Europe and for erecting Caliban as the revolutionary symbol of Caribbean manhood and independence" (111).

16. For more on illocution and autobiography in this context, see Bruss's *Autobiographical Acts* (4–8) and Lejeune's *On Autobiography* (156–58).

17. See Lejeune for more on the limitations of the biographical model (235).

18. As Bruss observes in respect to the idiosyncrasies of perspective in autobiography: "The order, the meaning or rhythm of the composition, becomes clear only when we look for the person and the personality which holds it all together, whether by means of publicly ascertainable religious convictions or by a private, implicit set of values and associations" (164).

19. As Bruss concludes: "Indeed, with so much of life and identity beyond our personal control, we perhaps cling all the more fiercely to an institution which offers us at least one remaining arc of symbolic power over our destiny as individuals. For despite attacks upon the notion of individuality, it is still at the center of the way we organize and imagine life in our society and in our literature" (163–64).

20. Sensitive to the pressures of shaping a literary tradition in midcentury, Walcott observes: "It may be, then, that the first impulse of West Indian writing is not towards fiction, because that is another device that conceals our identity, another mask" (notebooks entry dd. 2.65). According to Baugh, Walcott began writing what was to be the first version of *Another Life* in April 1965: "By early November he had filled a quarto-size exercise book of 76 pages in closely written

longhand and had started on a second such book. Up to that time the work was proceeding as a prose memoir, and was to that extent conventional; but in January 1966 it begins to break into verse, after an entry in which Walcott reflects on the difference between verse and prose. . . . Through various subsequent drafts, Walcott reworked the whole thing as a poem" (*Derek Walcott* 4).

What I am referring to as notebooks refers to the first of these drafts. Pagination and dates in the original are erratic and difficult to follow.

CHAPTER 7. POETIC AUTOBIOGRAPHY

1. On the first page of one of his notebooks (Sun, July 10, 1966), Walcott quotes Boris Pasternak on self and community: "And life itself is only an instant, / Only the dissolving / Of ourselves in all others / As though in gift to them."

2. Writing about Wordsworth's *The Prelude* in particular and "philosophical" autobiography generally, Spengemann observes: "The conditions—the need to locate the fixed personal center that lends pattern and value to unstable reality, and the necessity of approaching that center through one's own moving experiences—stipulate autobiography as the prime intrument of Romantic knowledge, and movement as its method" (77).

3. Gunn explains: "As the reader of his or her life, the autobiographer inhabits the hermeneutic universe where all understanding takes place. The autobiographer serves, by this habitation, as the paradigmatic reader; and the autobiographical text, embodying this reading, becomes, in turn, a model of possibilities and problems of all interpretive activity" (22).

4. "Et c'est l'heure, o Poête, de décliner ton nom, ta naissance, at ta race" [And the time is come, O Poet, to declare your name, your birth, and your race] (St. John Perse, quoted by Walcott in notebooks, Oct. 11, 1965).

5. A classic American precedent in the forging of an aesthetic personality based on self and collective culture is Whitman's *Leaves of Grass*: "This was a feeling or ambition to articulate and faithfully express in literary or poetic form, and uncompromisingly, my own physical, emotional, moral, intellectual, and aesthetic Personality, in the midst of, and tallying, the momentous spirit and facts of its immediate days, and of current America—and to exploit that Personality, identified with place and date, in a far more candid and comprehensive sense than any hitherto poem or book" (*Complete Poetry* 444). Even more specific to the evolution of Caribbean literary discourse is the affinity with Césaire's poet-hero in *Notebook of a Return to the Native Land*. Terada observes that "Walcott considers himself the type of the American poet, and . . . that the American poet is for him the type of the poet" (7).

6. This is Perse's national poetic ideal: "What a prodigious destiny for a poet, creator of his language, to be at the same time the unifier of a national tongue long before the political unity that it promises. Through him, speech restored to

a living community becomes the life lived by an entire people in search of unity" (Perse 21). This unity, Walcott acknowledged, may be possible only in art: "I see no possibility of the country becoming unified and having its own strengths except in art," he told Hirsch in 1979 (284).

7. Discourse in the essays and *Another Life* is characteristically male centered; thus "Caribbean man" seems the appropriate designation.

8. Walcott conceives of his poetic sensibility as a bridge between different ancestries, Europe and the Third World of Africa and Asia ("Muse" 20). He is not alone in this. In a 1983 interview for *Callaloo*, Césaire told Philippe Decraene: "The Amerindian, even the Indian component, the African foundation and three centuries of life in common with France, all that makes up an indivisible whole. How do you slough that off, I mean one or another of these elements, without impoverishing reality, without sterilizing it?" (64). Wilson Harris uses the term *gateway complex* to describe the metamorphosis of the poetic imagination after the shock of the Atlantic crossing and the interpenetration of different cultures that followed ("History" 12).

9. To the contrary, Terada finds Walcott's use of the American Adam mythology duplicitous: "Each of Adam's words is indeed a beginning; but these are beginnings over, not primal beginnings" (151).

10. In *Discourse on Colonialism* Césaire makes the same point: "I said to myself: it's true that superficially we are French, we bear the marks of French customs; we have been branded by Cartesian philosophy, by French rhetoric; but if we break with all that, if we plumb the depths, then what we will find is fundamentally black" (68).

11. As Harris, one of the great architects of Caribbean literary culture, explains: "Caribbean man is involved in a civilization-making process (whether he likes it or not) and until this creative authority becomes intimate to his perspectives he will continue to find himself embalmed in his deprivations—embalmed as a derivative tool-making, fence-making animal. As such his dialectic will remain a frozen round of protest" ("History" 29).

12. In *Derek Walcott's Poetry* Terada explores a wide range of issues around the dichotomy of mimicry and originality on an individual scale, a cultural scale, and as expressive of the relations between representation and the object world and between culture and nature in Walcott's poetry. Note especially her introductory chapter, "American Mimicry" (1–12).

13. In "History, Fable and Myth," Harris identifies such cultural phenomena as part of an original "West Indian architecture of consciousness" (21).

14. Césaire told Decraene in the 1983 *Callaloo* interview: "That dualism, that ambiguity if you will, is the very basis of the West Indian soul. It is the ambiguity one has to accept and make one's own" (66–67).

15. In *Memoirs* Neruda writes: "With feelings, beings, books, events, and battles, I am omnivorous" (264). In *Song of Myself* Whitman writes: "I know perfectly well my own egotism, / Know my omnivorous lines and must not write

any less, / And would fetch you whoever you are flush with myself" (60). In a 1989 interview for *Callaloo* Césaire explained to Charles H. Rowell: "I am a man who loves—I won't say culture—cultures, all cultures" (55). Walcott seemed to prefer the more violent image: "You know that you just ravage and cannibalize everything as a young poet; you have a very voracious appetite for literature," he told Hirsch in 1979 (282).

16. Harris's emphasis on the primacy of the subjective imagination in Caribbean societies is illuminating here: "In the first place the limbo imagination of the West Indies possesses no formal or collective sanction as in the old Tribal World. Therefore the gateway complex between cultures implies a new catholic unpredictable threshold which places far greater emphasis on the integrity of the individual imagination" ("History" 16).

17. In his conversation with Drecraene, Césaire made a careful distinction between assimilating French culture and being assimilated. Like Walcott, Césaire resists the alienation of the culturally assimilated by rooting himself culturally in the Caribbean rather than Europe (1983 interview 64).

18. In effect, Walcott repeats a central tenet of Lamming's *The Pleasures of Exile* in respect to the centrality of the folk in Caribbean literature and culture and revises another in respect to Lamming's emphasis on politically determined cultural formula.

19. Here I am referring to the creative aspect of Ogun, a Yoruba and Afro-Caribbean god.

20. An authoritative interpretive text on *Another Life* is Baugh's *Derek Walcott*. Baugh richly explores the autobiographical detail underlying the poem in relation to the overarching themes of memory, history, art, and life.

21. "Only those who need it know how parasitic is the literary principle, how a single, borrowed phrase can germinate a book" (Walcott, notebooks, May 5.65).

22. In "Ballad of the Two Grandfathers" Guillen conjures his prototypical grandfathers, black and white, from the shadows of his mind and brings them together (67).

23. Walcott adds a new dimension to Césaire's substitution of acceptance and love for hatred and anger in his notebook (73, 77).

24. In *Notebook of a Return to the Native Land* Césaire's celebrated "Eia for those who have never invented anything" also ends in a celebration of the poet-hero as "a man of germination" (70–71).

25. An essential feature of Trinidad's Carnival is the invention and discarding of costumes on an annual basis. Where the costumes are retained and reused, the performance is characteristically satirical, obscene, or grotesquely humorous. Walcott comments on this phenomenon at some length in "Caribbean" (9–10).

26. In the Farrar, Straus and Giroux edition of Walcott's Nobel lecture, the pages are unnumbered. A shortened version of the Nobel lecture appears in *The Routledge Reader in Caribbean Literature*, edited by Donnell and Welch; this quote appears on page 506.

PART 3. BIRTHRIGHTS AND LEGACIES

1. In respect to the West Indian artist, Brathwaite writes: "The poverty, this shortage of material on which the spirit is sustained, becomes a famine in the soul of the West Indian artist. He comes to recognize the grave limitations of his social existence, and seeks a solution in moving away" (*Roots* 9).

2. Brathwaite elaborates on the spiritual dimension of this angst: "The dichotomy expresses itself in the West Indian through a certain psychic tension, an excitability, a definite feeling of having no past, of not really belonging (which some people prefer to call 'adaptability'); and finds relief in laughter and (more seriously) in movement—dance, cricket, carnival, emigration" (*Roots* 30).

3. As I pointed out in the introduction, Brathwaite eventually concludes that conceptualizing the "multilingual multi-ethnic many ancestored" Caribbean is limited inevitably "by the scholar's aboriginal concept and perception of wholes" ("Caribbean Man" 1).

4. The pages of the text are not numbered; I deduced these page numbers from the arrangement of the text.

5. In *Modernity at Large* Appadurai argues the point: "Local knowledge is substantially about producing reliably local subjects as well as about producing reliably local neighborhoods within which such subjects can be recognized and organized. In this sense, local knowledge is what it is not principally by contrast with other knowledges . . . but by virtue of its local teleology and ethos" (181).

6. Statistically, Mahase's achievements are extraordinary: "Up to 1946 only 30% of Indian women in Trinidad were literate (against 50% for men) and amongst those over 45 only 10.6% were literate. In the census of 1931, only 4% of Indian women were listed as having professions, 72 as teachers (there were 368 male Indian teachers); about 13% were classified as self-employed shop-keepers, peasant farmers and other proprietors, but over 83% of all women in paid employment were domestic servants, general laborers or, the biggest group, agricultural laborers" (Poynting 235).

7. Brereton clarifies the caste/class distinction in postemancipation Trinidad: "It was a caste line which separated the white upper class from all other groups. A person known to have African ancestors could not be accepted into the white upper class, however wealthy or educated he was, however light his complexion, however important the position he occupied. . . . Strictly speaking, the only truly caste-like group in late nineteenth-century Trinidad (excluding the Asian population) was the white elite. It depended on a complex ideology, which involved racial fears and hostilities, an obsession with 'purity of blood,' and an exaggerated deference to birth, breeding, and family connections" (*Race Relations* 209).

8. Brathwaite writes: "These are, historically, the colonizers, the plantation owners. In the Caribbean they started as a settler group but became exploiters of land and (imported) labour with the introduction of sugar (early in the 17th

century in the case of the English and French islands; in the mid-19th century in Cuba)" (*Contradictory Omens* 33–34).

9. As O'Callaghan observes: "The trouble is, we are dealing with a disparate group of writers and to specify racial or political, or indeed class, criteria for 'belonging' to West Indian literature, inevitably leads to more and more pre- scriptive injunctions about who is 'in' and who is 'out'" (21).

10. As Butler observes in respect to contemporary discourse of identity: "The language of appropriation, instrumentality, and distanciation germane to the epistemological mode also belongs to a strategy of domination that pits the 'I' against an 'Other' and, once that separation is effected, creates an artificial set of questions about the knowability and recoverability of that Other" (144). Bruss makes a similar observation: "It may be that the conditions of the autobio- graphical act actually exacerbate idiosyncratic perspectives" (163).

CHAPTER 8. FRAGMENTS OF EPIC MEMORY

1. "Prologue to an Autobiography" originally appeared in *Vanity Fair,* April 1983, pp. 51–59, 138–56; the text is dated July–October 1982. "The Crocodiles of Yamoussoukro" originally appeared in the *New Yorker,* May 14, 1984, pp. 52–119; the text is dated November 1982–July 1983.

2. The problematic of autobiography on the global level of *publication,* argues Lejeune, is grounded alternatively in "the implicit or explicit contract proposed by the *author* to the *reader,* a contract which determines the mode of reading of the text and engenders the effects which, attributed to the text, seem to us to define it as autobiography" (29).

3. "Necessarily, then, in these symbolic acts of self-creation, 'the creator,' as T. S. Eliot put it, 'is everywhere present, and everywhere hidden'" (Spengemann 168).

4. "To deploy migrancy as an interpretive figure is not at all to repress the crucial situatedness of cultures, or to suggest that colonial encounter can be reread only as an abstraction so slender as to be effete. Instead, it implies that the sto- ries of colonialism—in which heterogeneous cultures are yoked by violence—offer nuances of trauma that cannot neatly be partitioned between colonizer and col- onized" (Suleri 5).

5. As in Wordsworth's *The Prelude,* which, according to Spengemann, "was intended to be a means to something beyond itself—a prelude to something else. Instead, it became a prelude to itself" (91).

6. In the context of Naipaul's *An Area of Darkness* and *The Middle Passage,* Suleri observes that "the genre of the travelogue launches a writer into the lan- guage of ignorance rather than that of experience" (157).

7. *A Way in the World* was first published in the United Kingdom as *A Sequence* and then in the United States as *A Novel.*

8. Clifford's reconfiguration of "Traveling Cultures," "Spatial History," and "Diasporas" in *Routes* seems designed with the colonial and postcolonial Caribbean in mind; rootedness as the basis of identity configuration has not proved to be a sustainable concept, no matter how it is configured.

9. For more on the concept of "ex-centric natives," see Clifford's *Routes* (25).

10. Benítez-Rojo and Glissant are both defensive about the idea of Caribbean insularity as a positive rather than a negative value, for example: "Ordinarily, insularity is treated as a form of isolation, a neurotic reaction to place. However, in the Caribbean each island embodies openness. . . . A Caribbean imagination liberates us from being smothered" (Glissant, *Caribbean Discourse* 139); "The Antilleans' insularity does not impel them toward isolation, but on the contrary, toward travel, toward exploration, toward the search for fluvial and marine routes" (Benítez-Rojo 25).

11. "I hang on to 'travel' as a term of cultural comparison precisely because of its historical taintedness, its associations with gendered, racial bodies, class privilege, specific means of conveyance, beaten paths, agents, frontiers, documents, and the like" (Clifford, *Routes* 39). These are very much the associations that Naipaul enacts in his reinvention of place and identity.

12. One powerful North American model for the protean traveling trickster is, of course, Melville's *The Confidence Man: His Masquerade* (1857), but there are others closer to home in the African Caribbean figures of Brer Anansi, Elegba, and Eshu.

13. "Once traveling is foregrounded as cultural practice then dwelling, too, needs to be reconceived—no longer simply the ground from which traveling departs, and to which it returns" (Clifford, *Routes* 44).

14. Benítez-Rojo reminds us that "there are few things as exhibitionistic as a text. It should be remembered that what a performer writes . . . is not a text, but something previous and qualitatively different: a pre-text. . . . The text is born when it is read by the Other: the reader. From this moment on text and reader connect with each other like a machine of reciprocal seductions" (23).

15. "The notion of the Apocalypse is not important within the culture of the Caribbean. . . . These are ideological propositions articulated in Europe which the Caribbean shares only in declamatory terms, or, better, in terms of a first reading" (Benítez-Rojo 10).

CHAPTER 9. MATERNAL BONDS

1. "Partly as a result of the indentureship, partly because of the Indians' culture and religions, a whole collection of unfavourable stereotypes was built up during the nineteenth century, which did much to form the attitudes of the host society towards the immigrants and their descendants. . . . From the Euro-Christian perspective of the dominant groups, Indians were generally judged to be an immoral

people. John Morton, the pioneer Canadian missionary, thought they were morally unprincipled and degraded; husbands and wives were unfaithful, the women were 'quite as wicked as the men, and more ignorant and prejudiced'" (Brereton, *Race Relations* 186).

2. From the Trinidad newspaper *New Era,* October 26, 1885, quoted in Brereton's *Race Relations* (188).

3. For more on John Morton, see Morton's *John Morton of Trinidad.*

4. Between 1838 and 1917 the British brought 145,000 Indians to Trinidad as indentured laborers; they worked in the sugar industry, which had previously relied on slave labor (Knight 143).

5. For more on spatial practices see de Certeau's *The Practice of Everyday Life* and Clifford's application of his concept in *Routes* (52–91): "For de Certeau, 'space' is never ontologically given. It is discursively mapped and corporeally practiced" (Clifford 54).

6. Clifford makes this point in *Routes*: "This *use* criterion opens a space for a history and sociology of meanings" (55).

7. In *Coming, Coming Home* Lamming invites us to reconceptualize the nation-states of the Caribbean as a "nation that is not defined by specific territorial boundaries, and whose peoples, scattered across a variety of latitudes within and beyond the archipelago, show loyalty to the 'nation state' laws of their particular location without any severance of cultural contiguity to their original worlds of childhood" (32).

CHAPTER 10. COLONIST AND CREOLE

1. In *The Poetics of Relation* Glissant makes this observation about myths of filiation: "These myths express communities, each one innocently transparent for self and threateningly opaque for the other. . . . They suggest that the self's opacity for the other is insurmountable, and, consequently, no matter how opaque the other is for oneself (no myth ever provides for the legitimacy of the other), it will always be a question of reducing this other to the transparency experienced by oneself" (49).

2. Eric Williams writes: "By a curious irony Kingsley, when asked to speak as a historian, spoke as an inferior novelist, and when writing as a novelist [in] a travel book, wrote as a superior historian" (105). For the full text see Eric Williams's *British Historians* (101–5).

3. Bridges is the author of two novels, *Questing Heart* (1934) and *Red Fruit [Creole Enchantment]* (1936), and several studies of famous crimes: *Saint—with Red Hands?* (1954), *How Charles Bravo Died* (1956), *Two Studies in Crime* (1959), and *Poison and Adelaide Bartlett* (1962).

4. Pratt's observations about the ideological bias of the ethnographic portrait of manners and customs in "Scratches on the Face of the Country," are readily

applied to a "settler" narrative like *Child of the Tropics* (139–40). Harris also outlines these issues in relation to the consolidation of dominant social and cultural values in colonial literary culture in *Tradition, the Writer and Society* (45–49).

5. This is in keeping with Coe's observations about childhood as a literary genre: It "is transformational or dynamic: in every case, the basic materials out of which the Childhood is compounded (the experiential archetypes) are combined in new and original patterns" (*When the Grass Was Taller* 272).

6. The strategy is not dissimilar to that used by Claude McKay in his utopian *My Green Hills of Jamaica.*

7. In *When the Grass Was Taller* Coe divides exotic material in childhood narratives into three categories, "the didactic, the interpretive, and the schizophrenic" (225–28).

8. For more on fence building as a descriptor, see Harris's "History" (29).

9. The constraints of Bridges's intimacy with nature become more apparent when juxtaposed with Selvon's *Those Who Eat the Cascadura* (1972) and *Turn Again Tiger* (1958), for example, where the cocoa estate and the sugar estate are detailed from the laborer's point of view.

10. McClintock reminds us that in Victorian England "the elaborate and expensive costumery worn by women became the visible icons of male prosperity and class status"; it was one of the material divisions of women by labor and class (98).

11. By 1902 Indians comprised 33 percent of the island's population and were the principal laborers on Bridges's father's estate in Santa Cruz (Brereton, *Race Relations* 177).

12. Brereton reports that in the nineteenth century Indians largely kept to themselves in communities of their own making after indenture; however, in the towns they were subject to physical and verbal abuse: "Casual abuse and ill-usage of Indian porters and domestics were commonplace; policemen would prosecute them for trivial misdeeds; provocation of defenceless Indians was a kind of game for lower-class urban blacks" (*Race Relations* 189).

13. Of course, others stereotyped the Indians as morally degraded and deceitful. The stereotype could run in either direction (Brereton, *Race Relations* 186).

14. "The difference of the object of discrimination is at once visible and natural—colour as the cultural/political *sign* of inferiority or degeneracy, skin as its natural '*identity*'" (Bhabha, *Location of Culture* 80).

15. Brereton observes: "There were indeed intimate relationships between upper-class whites and lower-class blacks—black mistresses, black domestics—but they were relationships in which social equality was carefully preserved" (*Race Relations* 210).

16. McClintock's observations about the limits of colonial feminism are applicable here: "For Schreiner [Olive], as for most colonials, African women serve principally as boundary markers. Their labor function is to perform boundary work. They stand at thresholds, windows and walls, opening and shutting doors. . . .

They scrub verandahs, clean windows, wash clothes, welcome newcomers and generally mediate the traffic between colonials and between Africans and colonials, marking by their presence and maintaining through their labor the newly invented borders between private and public, family and market, race and race" (268).

17. McClintock notes the pervasiveness of such fears: "In the last decades of the nineteenth century, the urban crowd became a fetish for ruling-class fears of social unrest and underclass militancy. . . . The degenerate crowd occupied a dangerous threshold zone on the border between factory and family, labor and domesticity, where the public world of propertied power and the private world of familial decorum met their conceptual limit" (118–19).

18. This incident reads like a replay of Fanon's "Look a Negro" episode in *Black Skin, White Masks* (111–15).

19. "The taking up of any one position, within a specific discursive form, in a particular historical juncture, is thus always problematic—the site of both fixity and fantasy. It provides a 'colonial' identity that is played out—like all fantasies of originality and origination—in the face and space of the disruption and threat from the heterogeneity of other subject positions" (Bhabha, *Location of Culture* 77).

20. In "Text, Testimony and Gender" Brereton, a social historian, goes to the heart of the matter: "These female-authored texts do not provide a consistently gendered testimony, nor do they always bring a clearly feminine perspective to bear on the Caribbean societies with which they deal. The authors' ethnicity and class, the values and limitations of the societies and eras to which they belonged, make this inevitable" (90).

21. See Athill's foreword, "Jean Rhys and Her Autobiography" (3–9). I am referring to Long's *History of Jamaica*; Trollope's *The West Indies and the Spanish Main*; Kingsley's *At Last*; and Froude's *The English in the West Indies* (1888).

22. Athill explains: "It amounts to being some, and only some, of what she wanted to say in the form of first drafts, or notes towards first drafts. . . . She did not get far enough with this second part of the book, dealing with her life after her arrival in England at the age of sixteen, to put the record straight in the ways she intended" (6).

23. Of course, the departure that marks the end of a childhood is not exclusive to these narratives; in fact, it is useful to compare the language of departure with other autobiographical narratives in this study, including Lamming's *The Pleasures of Exile* and *In the Castle of My Skin*, and Claude McKay's *My Green Hills of Jamaica*. It also appears in the novel of childhood, for example, in Kincaid's *Annie John*.

24. Gregg notes: "The self that Jean Rhys writes/invents can be read as a site where narratives of empire; ideologies of race and gender, memory, and imagi-

nation; and theories of reading and writing are all structured interdependently and sometimes contradictorily" (53).

25. Gregg situates Rhys's representation of the mulatto in the discourses of the white plantocracy of the region: "The major themes are racial contamination and economic threat. These are often figured as the loose sexual behavior of white men, which is a function of the innate promiscuity of black women, and the general animality of the black Other" (109).

26. Writing about Englishness and the culture of travel, Gikandi observes: "The black woman is a particularly revealing site for such desires and anxieties: her body is the standard conceptualization of the strangeness of the other, the doubleness of its attraction and revulsion; as the most radical figure of alterity, the black woman is the space in which theories of blackness are constituted and reformulated" (111).

27. "Thus, childhood images, images which a child could make, images which a poet tells us a child has made are, for us, manifestations of a permanent childhood. . . . They tell of the continuity of the great childhood reveries with the reveries of the poet" (Bachelard, *Poetics of Reverie* 100).

28. This calls to mind the jazz improvisation model that Benítez-Rojo uses in *The Repeating Island* and Brathwaite uses in "Jazz and the West Indian Novel" (in *Roots*); for example, "And so the Caribbean text is excessive, dense, uncanny, asymmetrical, entropic, hermetic, all this because, in the fashion of a zoo or bestiary, it opens its doors to great orders of reading: one of a secondary type, epistemological, profane, diurnal, and linked to the West—the world outside—where the text uncoils itself and quivers like a fantastic beast to be the object of knowledge and desire, another the principal order, teleological, ritual, nocturnal, and referring to the Caribbean itself, where the text unfolds its bisexual sphinxlike monstrosity toward the void of its impossible origin, and dreams, that it incorporates this, or is incorporated by it" (Benítez-Rojo 23). "Jazz is one of those forms where creation and performance are simultaneous. The jazz man composes as he plays. What he plays—based on some basic chord structure or agreed on theme—is peculiar to himself and to each performance. Each performance is different in some way because of its improvisational character, and each successful improvisation is a true creation and is an expression not only of the individual artist or artists, but of the group of which the artists are apart" (Brathwaite, *Roots* 57).

29. As Clifford observes, "the term 'diaspora' is a signifier not simply of transnationality and movement but of political struggles to define the local, as distinctive community, in historical contexts of displacement" (*Routes* 252).

30. Appadurai uses *Ethnoscape* "to get away from the idea that group identities necessarily imply that cultures need to be seen as spatially bounded, historically unselfconscious, or ethnically homogenous forms" (183).

PART 4. AUTOBIOGRAPHY, ELEGY, AND GENDER IDENTIFICATION

1. According to Sacks, "Each elegy is to be regarded, therefore, as a *work*, both in the commonly accepted meaning of a product and in the more dynamic sense of the working through of an impulse or experience—the sense that underlies Freud's phrase 'the work of mourning'" (1).

2. Bringing Freud's "Mourning and Melancholy" to bear on Tennyson's *In Memoriam*, Shaw makes this distinction: "But melancholy differs from mere grief or melancholy in one important way: the loss its victims suffer is a loss inside themselves" (61).

CHAPTER 11. BEYOND CONSOLATION

1. This point is more fully developed in Rohlehr's *Pathfinder* (238–73).

2. Rohlehr observes that in Brathwaite's "pre-1986 work the protagonist remains a symbolic and collective voice, even when closely associated with the poet's personal quest or ordeal," whereas in *The Zea Mexican Diary*, "Brathwaite, removing masks, openly assumes the role of subject, the straitened man of the *I Ching*" (introduction vi).

3. "A muse is typically personified as a female force external to and radically different from the poet, capable of drawing poetry out of the poet and into the world. The muse is therefore distinct from, although often associated with, a beloved woman who is imagined as having an actual presence for the poet" (Zeiger 45).

4. Rohlehr notes that with the "unmasking" of *The Zea Mexican Diary* and *Trench Town Rock*, Brathwaite's writing as whole "becomes at once more personal and more public" (introduction vi).

5. For a rich and complex study of Orpheus and Eurydice as a structural paradigm for elegiac production, see Zeiger's *Beyond Consolation*.

6. "Central to the Orphic story and to traditional elegy has been a highly charged representation of marriage—'the nuptial moment' which, as Schenck has shown, functions as a climactic moment in a ritual drama of initiation into (masculine) literary production" (Zeiger 109).

7. In "Self-Consuming Fictions" Matibag observes that cannibalism "displays the uncanny quality of binary oppositions: it is a sign both of animalistic nature and cultural practice; of affection and aggression, of transgression and consecration" (3).

8. This Haitian ritual is a ceremony held after the funeral rites of the dead have been performed and on anniversaries of the death. See Deren's *Divine Horsemen* (28–29).

9. Rohlehr explains one African origin of the ritual: "The Akan ritual of

'Eating the Dead' or 'Drinking the Gods' was associated with the taking of oaths involving the affirmation of loyalty to the chiefs and people of the Asantehene" (*Pathfinder* 258).

10. In *Divine Hunger* Sanday explains that cannibal practice can either affirm or negate "the relationships that join or separate the subject vis-a-vis the other. Thus, parts of the body may be consumed to imbibe the characteristics of the fertile force of the other; or, consumption may break down and destroy characteristics of the other in the self" (36).

11. See Nketia's *Funeral Dirges of the Akan People,* for more on women's role in the work of mourning (8, 101).

12. Zeiger frames these issues around Orpheus as Ur-elegist in her reading of Matthew Arnold's "Thrysis": "If the poem laments a failure of Orphean power and masculine poetic identity, the discovery of that 'lack' facilitates an appropriation of the 'feminine' and a simultaneous erasure of women. The gender politics of this self-consciously 'weak' Orphean scenario are not necessarily more hospitable to women than are those of the 'strong' ones" (11).

13. "As we have seen, female figures abound in the major, canonical English elegies, occupying constantly shifting roles as enabling or threatening adjuncts to the poetic process. Although the proliferation and multiple functioning of female figures in the traditional English elegy may serve to consolidate male literary authority, the sheer excess of these figures tends to betray an insecurity at the heart of that authority" (Zeiger 11).

14. Deren explains that "the flesh of the original human personality withers away." There is left "only the distilled, depersonalized" essence of the principles with which the deceased is identified. The person becomes a principle, and the principle is eventually transfigured into a archetypal figure of devotion who in turn exacts dedication (28–29).

15. Writing about *The Arrivants,* Rohlehr explains that Brathwaite invokes Legba as a symbol of Caribbean Man's potential for cultural wholeness, psychic wholeness, and historical continuity, a reconciliation of opposites that is Brathwaite's ultimate goal as a poet (*Pathfinder* 245–46).

16. The *damarifa due,* a traditional Akan funeral lament, is a recurring theme in Brathwaite's poetry, for example, "Tano" in *Masks* (*Arrivants* 151–55).

17. "In *DreamStories* and much of the post-1986 work, the video style exploits several fonts and type sizes rendered on the page in a variety of imaginative ways. Conventional modes of representation of the text are constantly under attack, the aim being to unsettle the reader's expectations by an unfixing or unhinging of word and image" (Rohlehr, introduction viii). See also Bobb's *Beating a Restless Drum* (135–38).

18. "Speech delivery is slow, silences are long and frequent, rhythms slacken, intonations become monotonous, and the very syntactic structures . . . are often characterized by nonrecoverable elisions" (Kristeva, *Black Sun* 34).

CHAPTER 12. DEATH AND SEXUALITY

1. Ramazani identifies the displaced family romance as a distinguishing feature of postwar American elegy: "It is in their parental elegies that Lowell, Plath, Sexton, Ginsberg, Rich, and Berryman most forcefully revise the displaced family romance at the heart of the elegy, denouncing, mocking, ravaging, and exposing their parents in stunning poetic acts of confrontation" (221–22).

2. Schenck writes: "The orphic task, as understood by the poets, is the search for literary rebirth by means of an initiatory descent. The subsequent recovery (and continuance) of voice is a guarantee of literary immortality" (2).

3. "To make connections between sensual celebration and mourning is a way to reconstruct the epithalamium-elegy nexus of poetic tradition in a non-sacrificial mode, and this becomes one of the most consistent endeavors of AIDS elegies" (Zeiger 124).

4. "There looms, within abjection, one of those violent, dark revolts of being, directed against a threat that seems to emanate from an exorbitant outside or inside, ejected beyond the scope of the possible, the tolerable, the thinkable. It ties there, quite close, but it cannot be assimilated. It beseeches, worries, and fascinates desire, which, nevertheless, does not let itself be seduced. Apprehensive, desire turns aside; sickened, it rejects. . . . Like an inescapable boomerang, a vortex of summons and repulsion places the one haunted by it literally beside himself" (Kristeva, *Powers of Horror* 1).

5. Schenck identifies such encounters as part of the structure of elegy: "Built into the structure of elegy is a confrontation with death, a homeopathic administration of fear, and ultimate transcendence of the crisis" (7).

6. "Defying social taboos on public mourning and on female anger, they used the parental elegy to vent continuing rage, to reinspect childhood worries, and to scrutinize paternal power in its absence" (Ramazani 22).

7. "In the family elegy, American poets duel fiercely with the dead, refusing to temper their belligerence and sometimes deliberately inflaming it" (Ramazani 221).

8. Parallels with Naipaul's *The Middle Passage* are inescapable here, especially the chapter on his native island, Trinidad.

9. "If dung signifies the other side of the border, the place where I am not and which permits me to be, the corpse, the most sickening of wastes, is a border that has encroached upon everything. It is no longer I who expel, 'I' is expelled" (Kristeva, *Powers of Horror* 3–4).

10. "While these curses, condemnations, and exorcisms may help to free the living from the dead, they may also help paradoxically, to make the dead more emotionally accessible to the living" (Ramazani 221).

11. Deren notes that the graves that are under the special protection of Maman Brigitte are marked by a mound of stones (193).

12. Zeiger's study includes a chapter entitled "Beyond Mourning and Melancholia: AIDS Elegies" (107–34).

13. In Butler's appropriation of Freud, when "an ambivalent relationship is severed through loss, that ambivalence becomes internalized as a self-critical or self-debasing disposition in which the role of the other is now occupied and directed by the ego itself" (58).

14. "Gede is probably the most complex character in Haitian folklore, for he reveals more than thirty personae, each of which is associated with a different function. As Petro Baron Sanmdi, whose fearless wife is Maman Brijit, the guardian of the past, he is the preserver of the community's religious heritage, and the protector of the history of the human race" (Desmangles 116). Also worth noting is Hurston's account of Gede's orchestration of a lesbian's suicide in *Tell My Horse* (222).

15. See Kristeva's *Powers of Horror* (112).

Bibliography

Abrahams, Roger D. *The Man-of-Words in the West Indies.* Baltimore, Md.: Johns Hopkins University Press, 1983.

Alexander, Jacqui. Review of *The History of Mary Prince. Women's Studies International Forum* 13, nos. 1–2 (1990): 159.

Alexander, Ziggi, and Audrey Dewjee. Editors' introduction to *Wonderful Adventures of Mrs. Seacole in Many Lands* by Mary Seacole, 9–45. Bristol, U.K.: Falling Wall Press, 1984.

Alleyne, Mervyn. *Roots of Jamaican Culture.* London: Pluto, 1988.

Anderson, Benedict. *Imagined Communities: Reflections on the Origins and Spread of Nationalism.* London: Verso, 1983.

Andrews, William L. "The Changing Moral Discourse of Nineteenth-Century African-American Women's Autobiography: Harriet Jacobs and Elizabeth Keckley." In *Decolonizing the Subject: The Politics of Gender in Women's Autobiography,* edited by Sidonie Smith and Julia Watson, 225–41. Minneapolis: University of Minnesota Press, 1992.

Andrews, William L. *Sisters of the Spirit: Three Black Women's Autobiographies of the Nineteenth Century.* Bloomington: Indiana University Press, 1986.

Andrews, William L. *To Tell a Free Story: The First Century of Afro-American Autobiography, 1760–1865.* Urbana: University of Illinois Press, 1986.

Anthony, Michael. *The Year in San Fernando.* 1965. Reprint, London: Heinemann, 1970.

Appadurai, Arjun. *Modernity at Large: Cultural Dimensions of Globalization.* Minneapolis: University of Minnesota Press, 1996.

Appiah, Kwame Anthony. *In My Father's House: Africa in the Philosophy of Culture.* New York: Oxford University Press, 1992.

Asa-Asa, Louis. "Narrative of Louis Asa-Asa, a Captured African." In Mary Prince, *The History of Mary Prince, a West Indian Slave, Related by Herself,* 121–24. 1831. Reprint, London: Pandora, 1987.

Athill, Diana. Foreword to Jean Rhys, *Smile Please: An Unfinished Autobiography*. Berkeley, Calif.: Creative Arts Book Co., 1979.

Bachelard, Gaston. *The Poetics of Reverie*, translated by Daniel Russell. Boston: Beacon, 1971.

Bachelard, Gaston. *The Poetics of Space*, translated by Maria Jolas. Boston: Beacon, 1969.

Baker, Houston A., Jr. *Blues, Ideology, and Afro-American Literature: A Vernacular Theory*. Chicago: University of Chicago Press, 1980.

Bakhtin, Mikhail M. *Art and Answerability*, edited by Michael Holquist and Vadim Liapunov and translated by Vadim Liapunov and Kenneth Brostrom. Austin: University of Texas Press, 1990.

Bakhtin, M[ikhail]. M. *The Dialogic Imagination: Four Essays*, translated by Caryl Emerson and Michael Holquist. Austin: University of Texas Press, 1981.

Bakhtin, Mikhail M. "Discourse Typology in Prose." In *Readings in Russian Poetics: Formalist and Structuralist Views*, edited by Ladislav Matejka and Krystyna Pomorska, 176–96. Cambridge, Mass.: MIT Press, 1971.

Bakhtin, M[ikhail]. M. *Speech Genres and Other Late Essays*, translated by Vern W. McGee. Austin: University of Texas Press, 1986.

Barthes, Roland. *The Pleasure of the Text*, translated by R. Miller. New York: Hill and Wang, 1975.

Baugh, Edward. "Cuckoo and Culture: *In the Castle of My Skin*." *Ariel* 8, no. 3 (July 1977): 23–33.

Baugh, Edward. *Derek Walcott: Memory as Vision: Another Life*. London: Longman, 1978.

Baugh, Edward. "Travel as Self-Invention." Paper presented at the 14th Annual Conference on West Indian Literature, Antigua State College, Antigua, March 9–11, 1995.

Beckles, Hilary. *Natural Rebels: A Social History of Enslaved Black Women in Barbados*. New Brunswick, N.J.: Rutgers University Press, 1989.

Beckles, Hilary. "Sex and Gender in the Historiography of Caribbean Slavery." In *Engendering History: Caribbean Women in Historical Perspective*, edited by Verene Shepherd, Bridget Brereton, and Barbara Bailey, 125–40. London: James Currey, 1995.

Belgrave, Valerie. *Ti Marie*. Oxford, U.K.: Heinemann, 1988.

Benítez-Rojo, Antonio. *The Repeating Island: The Caribbean and the Post-modern Perspective*, translated by James E. Maraniss. Durham, N.C.: Duke University Press, 1992.

Benstock, Shari, ed. *The Private Self: Theory and Practice of Women's Auto-biographical Writings*. Chapel Hill: University of North Carolina Press, 1988.

Bhabha, Homi. "Interrogating Identity." *ICA Documents* 6 (1989): 5–11.

Bhabha, Homi. *The Location of Culture*. London: Routledge, 1994.

Bigelow, John. *Jamaica in 1850. Or the Effects of Sixteen Years of Freedom on a Slave Colony*. 1851. Reprint, Westport, Conn.: Negro University Press, 1970.

Blunt, Alison, and Gillian Rose, eds. *Writing Women and Space: Colonial and Postcolonial Geographies*. New York: Guilford, 1994.

Bobb, June D. *Beating a Restless Drum: The Poetics of Kamau Brathwaite and Derek Walcott*. Trenton, N.J.: Africa World Press, 1998.

Bone, Robert. *Down Home*. New York: Columbia University Press, 1988.

Boose, Lynda E. "'The Getting of a Lawful Race': Racial Discourse in Early Modern England and the Unrepresentable Black Woman." In *Women, "Race," and Writing in the Early Period*, edited by Margo Hendricks and Patricia Parker, 35–54. London: Routledge, 1994.

Brathwaite, Edward [Kamau]. *The Arrivants: A New World Trilogy*. London: Oxford University Press, 1973.

Brathwaite, Edward Kamau. "Caliban, Ariel, and Unprospero in the Conflict of Creolization: A Study of the Slave Revolt in Jamaica in 1831–32." In *Comparative Perspectives on Slavery in New World Plantation Societies*, edited by Vera Rubin and Arthur Tuden, 41–62. New York: New York Academy of Sciences, 1977.

Brathwaite, Edward Kamau. "Caribbean Man in Space and Time." *Savacou* 11/12 (September 1975): 1–11, 106–8.

Brathwaite, Edward Kamau. *Contradictory Omens: Cultural Diversity and Integration in the Caribbean*. Mona, Jamaica: Savacou, 1978.

Brathwaite, Edward [Kamau]. *The Development of Creole Society in Jamaica, 1770–1820*. Oxford, U.K.: Clarendon, 1974.

Brathwaite, [Edward] Kamau. *DreamStories*. Essex, U.K.: Longman Group, 1994.

Brathwaite, Edward Kamau. "English in the Caribbean." In *Reading Black: Essays in the Criticism of African, Caribbean and Black American Literature*, edited by Houston A. Baker, Jr., 15–53. Ithaca, N.Y.: African Studies and Research Center, Cornell University, 1976.

Brathwaite, Edward Kamau. *The History of the Voice: The Development of Nation Language in Anglophone Poetry*. London: New Beacon, 1984.

Brathwaite, Edward [Kamau]. "Notes to *Islands*." ARGO 33 rpm. LP Record, PLP 1184/5. London, 1973.

Brathwaite, [Edward] Kamau. *Roots*. Ann Arbor: University of Michigan Press, 1993.

Brathwaite, Edward [Kamau]. "Sir Galahad and the Islands." *Bim* 7, no. 25 (1957): 8–16.

Brathwaite, Edward [Kamau]. "Timehri." In *Is Massa Day Dead? Black Moods in the Caribbean*, edited by Orde Coombs, 30–44. New York: Anchor, 1974.

Brathwaite, [Edward] Kamau. *The Zea Mexican Diary, 7 Sept 1926–7 Sept 1986*. Madison: University of Wisconsin Press, 1993.

Brereton, Bridget. *Race Relations in Colonial Trinidad 1970–1900*. Cambridge: Cambridge University Press, 1979.

Brereton, Bridget. "Text, Testimony and Gender: An Examination of Some Texts by Women on the English-Speaking Caribbean, from the 1770s to the 1920s." In *Engendering History: Caribbean Women in Historical Perspective,* edited by Verene Shepherd, Bridget Brereton, and Barbara Bailey, 63–93. Kingston, Jamaica: Ian Randle, 1995.

Bridges, Yseult. *Child of the Tropics: Victorian Memoirs,* edited by Nicholas Guppy. 1980. Reprint, Trinidad: Aquarela Galleries, 1988.

Bruss, Elizabeth. *Autobiographical Acts: The Changing Situation of a Literary Genre.* Baltimore, Md.: Johns Hopkins University Press, 1974.

Bush, Barbara. *Slave Women in Caribbean Society, 1650–1838.* Bloomington: Indiana University Press, 1990.

Butler, Judith. *Gender Trouble: Feminism and the Subversion of Identity.* New York: Routledge, 1990.

Butterfield, Stephen. *Black Autobiography.* Amherst: University of Massachusetts Press, 1974.

Carby, Hazel. *Reconstructing Womanhood: The Emergence of the Afro-American Woman Novelist.* New York: Oxford University Press, 1987.

Cartey, Wilfred. *Whispers from the Caribbean: I Going Away, I Going Home.* Los Angeles: Center for Afro-American Studies, University of California, Los Angeles, 1991.

Cassidy, Frederic C. *Jamaica Talk: Three Hundred Years of the English Language in Jamaica.* Basingstoke: Macmillan Education Ltd., 1971.

Césaire, Aimé. *Discourse on Colonialism,* translated by Joan Pinkham. 1955. Reprint, New York: Monthly Review Press, 1972.

Césaire, Aimé. Interview by Philippe Decraene. *Callaloo* 6, no. 1 (1983): 63–70.

Césaire, Aimé. Interview by Charles H. Rowell. *Callaloo* 12, no. 1 (1989): 47–67.

Césaire, Aimé. *Notebook of a Return to the Native Land.* In *The Collected Poetry,* translated by Clayton Eshleman and Annette Smith, 32–85. 1947. Reprint, Berkeley: University of California Press, 1983.

Césaire, Aimé. *Une Tempête; d'après "La Tempête" de Shakespeare. Adaptation pour un théâtre de nègre.* Paris: Éditions du Seuil, 1969.

Chamberlain, May. "Gender and Memory: Oral History and Women's History." In *Engendering History: Caribbean Women in Historical Perspective,* edited by Verene Shepherd, Bridget Brereton, and Barbara Bailey, 94–110. London: James Currey, 1995.

Chaudhuri, Nupur, and Margaret Stroebel, eds. *Western Women and Imperialism: Complicity and Resistance.* Bloomington: Indiana University Press, 1992.

Chauncey, George. *Gay New York: Gender, Urban Culture, and the Making of the Gay Male World, 1890–1940.* New York: Basic, 1994.

Cheyfitz, Eric. *The Poetics of Imperialism: Translation and Colonization from The Tempest to Tarzan.* New York: Oxford University Press, 1991.

Clifford, James. *Routes: Travel and Translation in the Late Twentieth Century.* Cambridge, Mass.: Harvard University Press, 1997.

Coe, Richard N. *Reminiscences of Childhood: An Approach to a Comparative Mythology.* Leeds, U.K.: Leeds Philosophical and Literary Society, 1984.

Coe, Richard N. *When the Grass Was Taller: Autobiography and the Experience of Childhood.* New Haven, Conn.: Yale University Press, 1984.

Collier, Eugenia W. "The Four-Way Dilemma of Claude McKay." *College Language Association Journal* 15 (1972): 345–53.

Condé, Maryse. *I, Tituba: Black Witch of Salem,* translated by Richard Philcox. Charlottesville: University Press of Virginia, 1992.

Cooke, Michael G. "The Strains of Apocalypse: Lamming's *Castle* and Brodber's *Jane and Louisa.*" *Journal of West Indian Literature* 4, no. 1 (January 1990): 28–40.

Cooper, Helen M., Adrienne Auslander Munich, and Susan Merrill Squier. *Arms and the Woman: War, Gender, and Literary Representation.* Chapel Hill: University of North Carolina Press, 1989.

Cooper, Philip. *The Autobiographical Myth of Robert Lowell.* Chapel Hill: University of North Carolina Press, 1970.

Cooper, Wayne F. *Claude McKay: Rebel Sojourner in the Harlem Renaissance.* New York: Schocken, 1987.

Craig, Christine. "*Wonderful Adventures of Mrs. Seacole in Many Lands*: Autobiography as Literary Genre and a Window to Character." *Caribbean Quarterly* 30, no. 2 (1984): 33–47.

Cruse, Harold. *The Crisis of the Negro Intellectual.* New York: Morrow, 1967.

Dash, J. Michael. *The Other America: Caribbean Literature in a New World Context.* Charlottesville: University Press of Virginia, 1998.

Davies, Carole Boyce. *Black Women, Writing, and Identity: Migrations of the Subject.* London: Routledge, 1994.

Davies, Carole Boyce. "Collaboration and the Ordering Imperative in Life Story Production." In *Decolonizing the Subject: The Politics of Gender in Women's Autobiography,* edited by Sidonie Smith and Julia Watson, 3–19. Minneapolis: University of Minnesota Press, 1992.

Davies, Carole Boyce, and Elaine Savory Fido, eds. *Out of the Kumbla: Caribbean Women and Literature.* Trenton, N.J.: Africa World Press, 1990.

Dayan, Joan. *Haiti, History, and the Gods.* Berkeley: University of California Press, 1995.

de Certeau, Michel. *The Practice of Everyday Life.* Berkeley: University of California Press, 1984.

Deren, Maya. *Divine Horsemen: The Voodoo Gods of Haiti.* New York: Dell, 1972.

Desmangles, Leslie G. *The Faces of the Gods: Vodou and Roman Catholicism in Haiti.* Chapel Hill: University of North Carolina Press, 1992.

Diawara, Manthia. "Black British Cinema: Spectatorship and Identity Formation in Territories." *Public Culture* 3, no. 1 (fall 1990): 33–48.

Dollimore, Jonathan. *Sexual Dissidence: Augustine to Wilde, Freud to Foucault.* Oxford: Clarendon, 1991.

Donnell, Alison, and Sarah Lawson Welch, eds. *The Routledge Reader in Caribbean Literature.* New York: Routledge, 1996.

Doyle, John R., Jr. *Thomas Pringle.* New York: Twayne, 1972.

Drake, St. Clair, and Horace Clayton. *Black Metropolis.* New York: Harcourt Brace, 1945.

Du Bois, W. E. B. "Criteria of Negro Art." *Crisis* 32 (1926): 290–97.

Du Bois, W. E. B. *The Souls of Black Folk.* 1903. In *Three Negro Classics.* New York: Avon, 1995.

Dunham, Katherine. *Island Possessed.* 1969. Reprint, Chicago: University of Chicago Press, 1994.

Eagleton, Terry. "Nationalism: Irony and Commitment." In *Nationalism, Colonialism and Literature,* edited by Terry Eagleton, Frederic Jameson, and Edward Said, 69–75. Minneapolis: University of Minnesota Press, 1990.

Eagleton, Terry, Frederic Jameson, and Edward Said. *Nationalism, Colonialism and Literature.* Minneapolis: University of Minnesota Press, 1990.

Echevarria, Roberto Gonzales. *The Voice of the Masters: Writing and Authority in Modern Latin American Literature.* Austin: University of Texas Press, 1988.

Edmondson, Belinda. *Making Men: Gender, Literary Authority and Women's Writing in Caribbean Narrative.* Durham, N.C.: Duke University Press, 1999.

Empson, William. *Some Versions of Pastoral.* 1935. Reprint, Norfolk, Conn.: New Directions, 1960.

Equiano, Olaudah. *The Interesting Narrative of the Life of Olaudah Equiano, or Gustavas Vassa, the African. Written by Himself.* London, 1789.

Esteves, Carmen C., and Lizabeth Paravisini-Gebert, eds. *Green Cane and Juicy Flotsam: Short Stories by Caribbean Women.* New Brunswick, N.J.: Rutgers University Press, 1991.

Fanon, Frantz. *Black Skin, White Masks,* translated by Charles Lam Markmann. 1952. Reprint, London: Pluto, 1986.

Fanon, Frantz. *The Wretched of the Earth.* 1961. Reprint, Harmondsworth, U.K.: Penguin, 1967.

Ferguson, Moira. *Colonialism and Gender Relations from Mary Wollstonecraft to Jamaica Kincaid: East Caribbean Connections.* New York: Columbia University Press, 1993.

Ferguson, Moira. *Subject to Others: British Women Writers and Colonial Slavery, 1670–1834.* New York: Routledge, 1992.

Ferguson, Moira, ed. *The Hart Sisters: Early African Caribbean Writers, Evangelicals and Radicals.* Lincoln: University of Nebraska Press, 1993.

Ferguson, Moira, ed. Introduction to *The History of Mary Prince, a West Indian Slave, Related by Herself* by Mary Prince. London: Pandora, 1987.

Folkenflik, Robert. *The Culture of Autobiography: Constructions of Self-Representation.* Stanford, Calif.: Stanford University Press, 1993.

Foster, Frances Smith. "Adding Color and Contour to Early American Self-Portraitures: Autobiographical Writings of Afro-American Women." In *Conjuring: Black Women, Fiction, and Literary Tradition,* edited by Marjorie Pryse and Hortense J. Spillers, 25–38. Bloomington: Indiana University Press, 1985.

Foster, Frances Smith. "'In Respect to Females . . .': Differences in the Portrayals of Women by Male and Female Narrators." *Black American Literature Forum* 15, no. 2 (1981): 60–69.

Foster, Frances Smith. *Witnessing Slavery: The Development of Ante-Bellum Slave Narratives.* Westport, Conn.: Greenwood, 1979.

Foster, Frances Smith. *Written by Herself: Literary Production by African American Women, 1746–1892.* Bloomington: Indiana University Press, 1993.

Foucault, Michel. *The Archaeology of Knowledge and the Discourse on Language,* translated by A. M. Sheridan Smith. New York: Pantheon, 1972.

Foucault, Michel. *Power/Knowledge: Selected Interviews and Other Writings, 1972–1977,* edited by Colin Gordon and translated by Colin Gordon, Leo Marshall, John Mepham, and Kate Soper. New York: Pantheon, 1980.

Freud, Sigmund. "Mourning and Melancholia." In *The Standard Edition of the Complete Psychological Works of Sigmund Freud,* edited by James Strachey, 14:243–58. London: Hogarth, 1953.

Froude, J. *The English in the West Indies; or, The Bow of Ulysses.* New York: C. Scribner's Sons, 1888.

Garber, Eric. "A Spectacle in Color: The Lesbian and Gay Subculture of Jazz Age Harlem." In *Hidden from History: Reclaiming the Gay and Lesbian Past,* edited by Martin Duberman, Martha Vicinus, and George Chauncey, 318–33. New York: New American Library, 1989.

Gates, Henry Louis, Jr. "Dis and Dat: Dialect and Descent." In *Afro-American Literature,* edited by Dexter Fisher and Robert Stepto, 88–119. New York: Modern Language Association, 1978.

Gates, Henry Louis, Jr. *The Signifying Monkey: A Theory of African-American Literary Criticism.* New York: Oxford University Press, 1988.

Gates, Henry Louis, Jr., ed. *"Race," Writing, and Difference.* Chicago: University of Chicago Press, 1986.

Gikandi, Simon. *Maps of Englishness: Writing Identity in the Culture of Colonialism.* New York: Columbia University Press, 1996.

Gilmore, Leigh. *Autobiographics: A Feminist Theory of Women's Self-Representation.* Ithaca, N.Y.: Cornell University Press, 1994.

Gilroy, Beryl. *Inkle and Yarico.* Leeds, U.K.: Peepal Tree Press, 1996.

Gilroy, Paul. *The Black Atlantic: Modernity and Double Consciousness.* Cambridge, Mass.: Harvard University Press, 1993.

Glissant, Edouard. *Caribbean Discourse: Selected Essays (Le Discours Antillais),* translated by J. Michael Dash. Charlottesville: University Press of Virginia, 1989.

Glissant, Edouard. "Literature and the Nation in Martinique." *Caliban* 4, no. 1 (1981): 3–7.

Glissant, Edouard. *The Poetics of Relation,* translated by Betsy Wing. 1990. Reprint, Ann Arbor: University of Michigan Press, 1997.

Goodison, Lorna. *Selected Poems.* Ann Arbor: University of Michigan Press, 1992.

Gramsci, Antonio. *Selections from Cultural Writings,* edited by David Forgacs and Geoffrey Nowell-Smith and translated by William Boelhower. Cambridge, Mass.: Harvard University Press, 1985.

Gregg, Veronica Marie. *Jean Rhys's Historical Imagination: Reading and Writing the Creole.* Chapel Hill: University of North Carolina Press, 1995.

Grewal, Inderpal. *Home and Harem: Nation, Gender, Empire, and the Cultures of Travel.* Durham, N.C.: Duke University Press, 1996.

Guillen, Nicolas. *Man-Making Words,* translated by Robert Marquez and David Arthur McMurray. Amherst: University of Massachusetts Press, 1972.

Gunn, Janet Varner. *Autobiography: Towards a Poetics of Experience.* Philadelphia: University of Pennsylvania Press, 1982.

Gwin, Minrose C. "Green-Eyed Monsters of the Slavocracy: Jealous Mistress in Two Slave Narratives." In *Conjuring: Black Women, Fiction, and Literary Tradition,* edited by Marjorie Pryse and Hortense J. Spillers, 39–52. Bloomington: Indiana University Press, 1985.

Hall, Douglas. *In Miserable Slavery: Thomas Thistlewood in Jamaica, 1750–1886.* London: Macmillan, 1989.

Hall, Stuart. "Cultural Identity and Cinematic Representation." *Framework* 36 (1989): 68–81.

Hall, Stuart. "The Problem of Ideology: Marxism without Guarantees." In *Stuart Hall: Critical Dialogues in Cultural Studies,* edited by David Morley and Kuan-Hsing Chen, 25–46. London: Routledge, 1996.

Harris, Wilson. "History, Fable and Myth in the Caribbean and the Guianas." *Caribbean Quarterly* 16, no. 2 (1970): 1–32.

Harris, Wilson. *The Palace of the Peacock.* London: Faber, 1960.

Harris, Wilson. *Tradition, the Writer and Society.* London: New Beacon, 1967.

Harris, Wilson. *The Womb of Space: The Cross-Cultural Imagination.* New York: Greenwood, 1983.

Hartman, Saidiya V. *Scenes of Subjection: Terror, Slavery, and Self-Making in Nineteenth-Century America.* New York: Oxford University Press, 1997.

Hathaway, Heather. *Caribbean Waves: Relocating Claude McKay and Paule Marshall.* Bloomington: Indiana University Press, 1999.

Heaney, Seamus. *The Place of Writing.* Atlanta: Scholars, 1989.

Henry, Paget. *Caliban's Reason: Introducing Afro-Caribbean Philosophy.* New York: Routledge, 2000.

Hodge, Merle. *Crick Crack, Monkey.* 1970. Reprint, London: Heinemann, 1981.

Hodge, Merle. Interview by Kathleen M. Balutansky. *Callaloo* 12, no. 4 (1989): 651–62.

Hodge, Merle. "The Shadow of the Whip." In *Is Massa Day Dead?*, edited by Orde Coombs, 111–42. New York: Anchor, 1974.

Hughes, Langston. "The Negro Artist and the Racial Mountain." In *Voices from the Harlem Renaissance*, edited by Nathan Irvin Huggins, 305–9. New York: Oxford University Press, 1976.

Hulme, Peter. *Colonial Encounters: Europe and the Native Caribbean, 1492–1797*. London: Methuen, 1986.

Hulme, Peter. "Reading from Elsewhere: George Lamming and the Paradox of Exile." In *'The Tempest' and Its Travels*, edited by Peter Hulme and William H. Sherman, 220–35. London: Reaktion, 2000.

Hurston, Zora Neale. "Muttsey" and "Story in Harlem Slang." In *Spunk: Selected Short Stories of Zora Neale Hurston*, 19–37 and 82–90. Berkeley, Calif.: Turtle Island Foundation, 1985.

Hurston, Zora Neale. *Tell My Horse: Voodoo and Life in Haiti and Jamaica*. 1938. Reprint, New York: Harper & Row, 1990.

James, C. L. R. *Beyond a Boundary*. 1963. Reprint, Durham, N.C.: Duke University Press, 1993.

James, C. L. R. *The Black Jacobins: Toussaint L'Ouverture and the San Domingo Revolution*. 1938. Reprint, New York: Vintage, 1963.

James, Paul. *Nation Formation: Towards a Theory of Abstract Community*. London: Sage, 1996.

Joseph, Margaret. *Caliban in Exile*. New York: Greenwood, 1992.

Joyce, James. *A Portrait of the Artist as a Young Man*. 1916. Reprint, New York: Viking, 1963.

Judd, Catherine. *Bedside Seductions: Nursing and the Victorian Imagination, 1830–1880*. New York: St. Martin's, 1998.

Kanhai, Rosanne. *Matikor: The Politics of Identity for Indo-Caribbean Women*. Trinidad: University of the West Indies, 1999.

Kincaid, Jamaica. *Annie John*. New York: Farrar, Straus and Giroux, 1985.

Kincaid, Jamaica. Interview by Jacqueline Trescott. *Washington Post*, April 10, 1985, p. D1.

Kincaid, Jamaica. *My Brother*. New York: Farrar, Straus and Giroux, 1997.

Kingsley, Charles. *At Last: A Christmas in the West Indies*. London, 1869.

Knight, Franklin W. *The Caribbean: The Genesis of a Fragmented Nationalism*. New York: Oxford University Press, 1978.

Kristeva, Julia. *Black Sun: Depression and Melancholia*, translated by Leon S. Roudiez. New York: Columbia University Press, 1989.

Kristeva, Julia. *Powers of Horror: An Essay in Abjection*, translated by Leon S. Roudiez. New York: Columbia University Press, 1982.

Laforest, Marie-Helene. *Diasporic Encounters: Remapping the Caribbean*. Naples: Liguori Editore, 2000.

Lamming, George. *Coming, Coming Home: Conversations II*. St. Martin: House of Nehesi, 1995.

Lamming, George. Interview by George E. Kent. *Black World* 22, no. 5 (1973): 4–14, 88–97.

Lamming, George. Interview by Rick Walker. University of Hartford, Hartford, Conn., February 22, 1980. Tape in author's possession.

Lamming, George. *In the Castle of My Skin.* 1953. Reprint, Ann Arbor: University of Michigan Press, 1991. This edition includes the introduction that Lamming wrote for the 1983 Schocken edition.

Lamming, George. Introduction to *The Pleasures of Exile.* London: Allison and Busby, 1984.

Lamming, George. *Natives of My Person.* London: Longman Caribbean, 1972.

Lamming, George. *The Pleasures of Exile.* 1960. Reprint, Ann Arbor: University of Michigan Press, 1992.

Lamming, George. *Season of Adventure.* 1960. Reprint, London: Allison and Busby, 1979.

Lamming, George. *Water with Berries.* London: Longman Caribbean, 1971.

Lamming, George. "The West Indian People." *New World Quarterly* 2, no. 2 (1966): 63–74.

Lanaghan, Frances. *Antigua and the Antiguans: A Full Account of the Colony and its Inhabitants from the Time of the Caribs to the Present Day, Interspersed with Anecdotes and Legends.* 2 vols. Published anonymously, 1844. Reprint, London: Spottiswoode, Ballantyne, 1967.

Lawrence, Karen R. *Penelope Voyages: Women and Travel in the British Literary Tradition.* Ithaca, N.Y.: Cornell University Press, 1994.

Laye, Camara. *The Dark Child,* translated by James Kifkup and Ernest Jones. New York: Farrar, Strauss and Giroux, 1975.

Lejeune, Philippe. *On Autobiography,* translated by Katherine Leary. Minneapolis: University of Minnesota Press, 1989.

LeSeur, Geta. *Ten Is the Age of Darkness: The Black Bildungsroman.* Columbia: University of Missouri Press, 1995.

Lewis, David Levering. *When Harlem Was in Vogue.* New York: Alfred E. Knopf, 1981.

Lewis, Gordon K. *Main Currents in Caribbean Thought: The Historical Evolution of Caribbean Society in Its Ideological Aspects.* Baltimore, Md.: Johns Hopkins University Press, 1983.

Lewis, Rupert, and Maureen Warner Lewis. "Claude McKay's Jamaica." *Caribbean Quarterly* 23, nos. 2–3 (1977): 38–53.

Long, Edward. *History of Jamaica.* 3 vols. London, 1774.

Lorde, Audre. *Zami: A New Spelling of My Name.* New York: Crossing, 1982.

Mahase, Anna, Sr. *My Mother's Daughter: The Autobiography of Anna Mahase Snr., 1899–1978.* Trinidad: Royards, 1992.

Mannoni, O. *Prospero and Caliban: The Psychology of Colonization,* translated by Pamela Powesland. 1950. Reprint, Ann Arbor: University of Michigan Press, 1990.

Mason, Mary. "The Other Voice: Autobiographies of Women Writers." In *Autobiography: Essays Theoretical and Critical,* edited by James Olney, 207–35. Princeton, N.J.: Princeton University Press, 1980.

Matibag, Eugenio D. "Self-Consuming Fictions: The Dialectics of Cannibalism in Modern Caribbean Narratives." *Postmodern Culture* 1, no. 3 (May 1991): 1–19.

McCleod, A. L. "Memory and the Edenic Myth: Claude McKay's *Green Hills of Jamaica.*" *World Literature Written in English* 18 (1979): 245–54.

McClintock, Anne. *Imperial Leather: Race, Gender and Sexuality in the Colonial Context.* New York: Routledge, 1995.

McKay, Claude. *Home to Harlem.* 1928. Reprint, Boston: Northeastern University Press, 1987.

McKay, Claude. *A Long Way from Home.* 1937. Reprint, New York: Harcourt, Brace and World, 1970.

McKay, Claude. *My Green Hills of Jamaica.* Kingston: Heinemann Educational Books, 1979.

McKay, Nellie. "Nineteenth-Century Black Women's Spiritual Autobiographies: Religious Faith and Self-Empowerment." In *Interpreting Women's Lives: Feminist Theory and Personal Narratives,* edited by Personal Narratives Group, 139–54. Bloomington: Indian University Press, 1989.

Middleton, Dorothy. *Victorian Lady Travellers.* Chicago: Academy Chicago Press, 1965.

Mohammed, Patricia. "Midnight's Children and the Legacy of Nationalism." *Callaloo* 20, no. 4 (1997): 737–52.

Molloy, Sylvia. "The Unquiet Self: Spanish American Autobiography and the Question of National Identity." In *Comparative American Identities: Race, Sex, and Nationality in the Modern Text,* 26–39. New York: Routledge, 1991.

Morgan, Paula. "East/West Indian/Woman/Other: At the Cross-Roads of Gender and Ethnicity." *Macomère* 3 (2000): 107–22.

Morris, Mervyn. Introduction to *My Green Hills of Jamaica* by Claude McKay. Kingston: Heinemann, 1979.

Morrison, Toni. Interview by Robert B. Stepto. In *Chant of Saints: A Gathering of Afro-American Literature, Art, and Scholarship,* edited by Michael S. Harper and Robert B. Stepto, 213–29. Urbana: University of Illinois Press, 1979.

Morrison, Toni. "Rootedness: The Ancestor as Foundation." In *Black Women Writers,* edited by Mari Evans, 339–45. New York: Anchor, 1984.

Morrissey, Marietta. *Slave Women in the New World: Gender Stratification in the Caribbean.* Lawrence: University of Kansas Press, 1989.

Morton, S. E. *John Morton of Trinidad, Pioneer Missionary of the Presbyterian Church in Canada to the East Indians in the British West Indies: Journals, Letters and Papers.* Toronto: Westminster, 1916.

Munro, Ian, and Reinhard Sander, eds. *Kas-Kas: Interviews with Three Caribbean Writers in Texas: George Lamming, C. L. R. James, Wilson Harris,* 5–21.

Austin: African and Afro-American Research Institute, University of Texas at Austin, 1972.

Naipaul, V. S. *The Enigma of Arrival*. New York: Alfred E. Knopf, 1987.

Naipaul, V. S. *Finding the Center: Two Narratives*. 1984. Reprint, New York: Vintage, 1986.

Naipaul, V. S. *A House for Mr. Biswas*. 1961. Reprint, New York: Vintage, 1984.

Naipaul, V. S. *In a Free State*. London: Deutsch, 1971.

Naipaul, V. S. Interview by Derek Walcott. In *Conversations with V. S. Naipaul*, edited by Feroza Jussawalla, 5–9. Jackson: University Press of Mississippi, 1997.

Naipaul, V. S. *The Loss of El Dorado: A History*. 1969. Reprint, Harmondsworth, U.K.: Penguin, 1973.

Naipaul, V. S. *The Middle Passage: Impressions of Five Societies—British, French, and Dutch—in the West Indies and South America*. 1962. Reprint, Harmondsworth, U.K.: Penguin, 1975.

Naipaul, V. S. *Miguel Street*. 1959. Reprint, London: Heinemann, 1974.

Naipaul, V. S. *A Way in the World: A Novel*. New York: Vintage, 1995. Originally published as *A Way in the World: A Sequence*. London: Heinemann, 1994.

Neruda, Pablo. *Memoirs,* translated by Hardie St. Martin. New York: Farrar, 1977.

Nichols, Grace. *I Is a Long Memoried Woman*. London: Karnak House, 1983.

Nixon, Rob. "Caribbean and African Appropriations of *The Tempest*." *Critical Inquiry* 13 (spring 1987): 557–78.

Nketia, J. H. *Funeral Dirges of the Akan People*. 1955. Reprint, New York: Negro Universities Press, 1969.

Nunez-Harrell, Elizabeth. *When Rocks Dance*. New York: Putnam, 1996.

O'Callaghan, Evelyn. *Woman Version: Theoretical Approaches to West Indian Fiction by Women*. London: Macmillan, 1993.

Olney, James. *Autobiography: Essays Theoretical and Critical*. Princeton, N.J.: Princeton University Press, 1980.

Olney, James. "'I Was Born': Slave Narratives, Their Status as Autobiography and as Literature." *Callaloo* 7, no. 1 (1984): 46–73.

Paquet, Sandra Pouchet. "The Enigma of Arrival: *Wonderful Adventures of Mrs. Seacole in Many Lands*." *African American Review* 26, no. 4 (1992): 651–63.

Paquet, Sandra Pouchet. Foreword to *The Pleasures of Exile* by George Lamming. Ann Arbor: University of Michigan Press, 1992.

Paquet, Sandra Pouchet. "The Heartbeat of a West Indian Slave: *The History of Mary Prince*." *African American Review* 26, no. 1 (1992): 131–46.

Paquet, Sandra Pouchet. *The Novels of George Lamming*. London: Heinemann, 1982.

Paquet, Sandra Pouchet. "West Indian Autobiography." *Black American Literature Forum* (Special Issue on Twentieth-Century Autobiography) 24, no. 2 (1990): 357–74.

Parry, Benita. "Problems of Current Theories of Colonial Discourse." *Oxford Literary Review* 9, nos. 1–2 (1987): 27–57.

Patterson, Orlando. "The Emerging West Atlantic System: Migration, Culture and Underdevelopment in the United States and the Circum-Caribbean Region." In *Population in an Interacting World,* edited by William Alonso, 227–60. Cambridge, Mass.: Harvard University Press, 1987.

Patterson, Orlando. *Slavery and Social Death: A Comparative Study.* Cambridge, Mass.: Harvard University Press, 1982.

Persaud, Lakshmi. *Butterflies in the Wind.* Leeds, U.K.: Peepal Tree Press, 1990.

Perse, St. John. *Two Addresses.* New York: Pantheon, 1966.

Philippe, J. B. *Free Mulatto: Being, an Address . . . Relative to the Claims Which the Coloured Population of Trinidad Have to the Same Civil and Political Privileges with Their White Fellow Subjects. By a Free Mulatto of the Island.* 1824. Reprint, Trinidad: Paria Publishing, 1987.

Poynting, Jeremy. "East Indian Women in the Caribbean: Experience and Voice." In *India in the Caribbean,* edited by David Dabydee and Brinsley Samaroo, 231–63. London: Hansib, 1987.

Pratt, Mary Louise. *Imperial Eyes: Travel Writing and Transculturation.* London: Routledge, 1992.

Pratt, Mary Louise. "Scratches on the Face of the Country; or, What Mr. Barrow Saw in the Land of the Bushmen." In *"Race," Writing, and Difference,* edited by Henry Louis Gates, Jr., 138–62. Chicago: University of Chicago Press, 1986.

Price, Richard. *Maroon Societies: Rebel Slave Communities in the Americas.* 1973. Reprint, Baltimore, Md.: Johns Hopkins University Press, 1979.

Prince, Mary. *The History of Mary Prince, a West Indian Slave, Related by Herself.* 1831. Reprint, Ann Arbor: University of Michigan Press, 1993. This edition, like most others, includes the "Supplement" by Pringle, the postscript to the second edition, and the appendix to the third edition.

Pringle, Thomas. *The Poetical Works of Thomas Pringle, With a Sketch of his Life by Leigh Ritchie.* London: Edward Moxon, 1838.

Pringle, Thomas. Preface to *The History of Mary Prince, a West Indian Slave, Related by Herself* by Mary Prince. Ann Arbor: University of Michigan Press, 1993.

Pringle, Thomas. *Thomas Pringle, His Life, Times, and Poems.* Cape Town, South Africa: J. C. Juta, 1912.

Pringle, Thomas. *Thomas Pringle, Narrative of a Residence in South Africa, a New Edition, to Which Is Prefixed a Biographical Sketch of the Author by Josiah Conder.* London: Edward Moxon, 1840.

Ramazani, Jahan. *Poetry of Mourning: The Modern Elegy from Hardy to Heaney.* Chicago: University of Chicago Press, 1994.

Ramchand, Kenneth. *The West Indian Novel and Its Background.* London: Faber & Faber, 1970.

Retamar, Roberto Fernández. *Caliban and Other Essays,* translated by Edward Baker. Minneapolis: University of Minnesota Press, 1989.

Rhys, Jean. *Smile Please: An Unfinished Autobiography*. Berkeley, Calif.: Creative Arts, 1979.

Rhys, Jean. *Wide Sargasso Sea*. 1966. Reprint, New York: Popular Library, 1975.

Robinson, Amy. "Authority and the Public Display of Identity: *Wonderful Adventures of Mrs. Seacole in Many Lands*." *Feminist Studies* 20, no. 3 (fall 1994): 537–57.

Rogozinski, Jan. *A Brief History of the Caribbean: From the Arawak and the Carib to the Present*. New York: Meridian, 1994.

Rohlehr, Gordon. Introduction to *DreamStories* by Kamau Brathwaite. Essex, U.K.: Longman Group, 1994.

Rohlehr, Gordon. *Pathfinder: Black Awakening in* The Arrivants *of Edward Kamau Brathwaite*. Trinidad: author, 1981.

Rubin, Vera, and Marisa Zavalloni. *We Wish to Be Looked Upon: A Study of the Aspirations of Youth in a Developing Society*. New York: Teachers College Press, 1969.

Ruhe, Edward L. "Pastoral Paradigms and Displacements, with Some Proposals." In *Survivals of Pastoral*, edited by Richard F. Hardin, 103–50. Lawrence: University of Kansas Press, 1979.

Sacks, Peter M. *The English Elegy: Studies in the Genre from Spenser to Yeats*. Baltimore, Md.: Johns Hopkins University Press, 1985.

Said, Edward W. "Identity, Authority and Freedom: The Potentate and the Traveler." *Transition* 54 (1991): 4–18.

Said, Edward W. *The World, the Text, and the Critic*. Cambridge, Mass.: Harvard University Press, 1983.

Said, Edward W. "Yeats and Decolonization." In *Nationalism, Colonialism and Literature*, edited by Terry Eagleton, Frederic Jameson, and Edward W. Said, 69–95. Minneapolis: University of Minnesota Press, 1990.

Sanday, Peggy Reeves. *Divine Hunger: Cannibalism as a Cultural System*. Cambridge: Cambridge University Press, 1986.

Scarry, Elaine. *The Body in Pain*. New York: Oxford University Press, 1985.

Schenck, Celeste. *Mourning and Panegyric: The Poetics of Pastoral Ceremony*. University Park: Pennsylvania State University Press, 1988.

Schwartz, Roberto. *Misplaced Ideas*. London: Verso. 1992.

Seacole, Mary. *Wonderful Adventures of Mrs. Seacole in Many Lands*. 1857. Reprint, New York: Oxford University Press, 1988.

Seidel, Michael. *Exile and the Narrative Imagination*. New Haven, Conn.: Yale University Press, 1986.

Selvon, Samuel. *Those Who Eat the Cascadura*. London: Davis Pynter, 1972.

Selvon, Samuel. *Turn Again Tiger*. 1958. Reprint, London: Heinemann, 1979.

Senior, Olive. "The Panama Railway." *Jamaica Journal* 44 (1980): 67–77.

Shaw, W. David. *Elegy and Paradox: Testing the Conventions*. Baltimore, Md.: Johns Hopkins University Press, 1994.

Shyllon, F. O. *Black People in Britain, 1555–1833*. London: Oxford University Press, 1977.

Smith, Ian. "Critics in the Dark." Paper delivered at the Sixteenth Annual West Indian Literature Conference, University of Miami, Coral Gables, April 1–4, 1997; subsequently published in *Journal of West Indian Literature* 8, no. 2 (April 1999): 2–9.

Smith, Paul. *Discerning the Subject*. Minneapolis: University of Minnesota Press, 1986.

Smith, Sidonie. *A Poetics of Women's Autobiography: Marginality and the Fictions of Self-Representation*. Bloomington: Indiana University Press, 1980.

Smith, Sidonie. "Self, Subject, and Resistance: Marginalities and Twentieth-Century Autobiographical Practice." *Tulsa Studies in Women's Literature* 9, no. 1 (1990): 11–24.

Smith, Sidonie. *Subjectivity, Identity, and the Body: Women's Autobiographical Practices in the Twentieth Century*. Bloomington: Indiana University Press, 1993.

Spacks, Patricia Meyer. "Selves in Hiding." In *Women's Autobiography: Essays in Criticism*, edited by Estelle C. Jelinek, 112–32. Bloomington: Indiana University Press, 1980.

Spengemann, William C. *The Forms of Autobiography: Episodes in the History of a Literary Genre*. New Haven, Conn.: Yale University Press, 1980.

Spivak, Gayatri Chakravorty. "Can the Subaltern Speak?" In *Marxism and the Interpretation of Culture*, edited by Cary Nelson and Lawrence Grossberg, 271–313. Urbana: University of Illinois Press, 1988.

Spivak, Gayatri Chakravorty. *In Other Worlds: Essays in Cultural Politics*. New York: Routledge, 1988.

Stepto, Robert B. "Narration, Authentication, and Authorial Control in Frederick Douglass' *Narrative of 1845*." In *Afro-American Literature: The Reconstruction of Instruction*, edited by Dexter Fisher and Robert B. Stepto, 178–91. New York: Modern Language Association, 1979.

Suleiman, Susan Rubin. *Subversive Intent: Gender, Politics, and the Avant-Garde*. Cambridge, Mass.: Harvard University Press, 1990.

Suleri, Sara. *The Rhetoric of English India*. Chicago: University of Chicago Press, 1992.

Taylor, Patrick. *The Narrative of Liberation*. Ithaca, N.Y.: Cornell University Press, 1989.

Terada, Rei. *Derek Walcott's Poetry: American Mimicry*. Boston: Northeastern University Press, 1992.

Thomas, J. J. *Froudacity: West Indian Fables by James Anthony Froude*. 1889. Reprint, London: New Beacon, 1969.

Tiffin, Helen. "Rites of Resistance: Counter-Discourse and West Indian Autobiography." *Journal of West Indian Literature* 3, no. 1 (January 1989): 28–46.

Trollope, Anthony. *The West Indies and the Spanish Main.* 1859. Reprint, Gloucester: Alan Sutton, 1985.

Trotsky, Leon. *Literature and Revolution.* In *Trotsky on Literature and Art,* edited by Paul N. Siegel. New York: Pathfinder, 1970.

Van den Abbeele, Georges. *Travel as Metaphor: From Montaigne to Rousseau.* Minneapolis: University of Minnesota Press, 1996.

Van Hear, Nicholas. *New Diasporas: The Mass Exodus, Dispersal and Regrouping of Migrant Communities.* Seattle: University of Washington Press, 1998.

Visel, Robin. "A Half-Colonization: The Problem of the White Colonial Woman Writer." *Kunapippi* 10, no. 3 (1988): 39–45.

Viswanathan, Gauri. *Outside the Fold: Conversion, Modernity, and Belief.* Princeton, N.J.: Princeton University Press, 1998.

Wachtel, Nathan. *The Vision of the Vanquished: The Spanish Exploration of Peru through Indian Eyes.* 1971. Reprint, New York: Harper & Row, 1977.

Walcott, Derek. *Another Life.* 1973. Reprint, Washington, D.C.: Three Continents Press, 1982.

Walcott, Derek. *The Antilles: Fragments of Epic Memory.* New York: Farrar, Straus and Giroux, 1992.

Walcott, Derek. "The Caribbean: Culture or Mimicry?" *Journal of Interamerican Studies and World Affairs* 16, no. 1 (February 1974): 3–14.

Walcott, Derek. *Epitaph of the Young: A Poem in XII Cantos.* Bridgetown, Barbados: Advocate Co., 1949.

Walcott, Derek. "The Garden Path: V. S. Naipaul." In *What the Twilight Says: Essays,* 121–33. New York: Farrar, Straus and Giroux, 1998.

Walcott, Derek. Interview by Edward Hirsch. *Contemporary Literature* 20 (1979): 280–92.

Walcott, Derek. Interview by Edward Hirsch. *Paris Review* 101 (1986): 197–230.

Walcott, Derek. Interview by Robert Hamner. *World Literature Written in English* 16 (1977): 409–20.

Walcott, Derek. "Leaving School." *London Magazine* 5, no. 6 (1965): 4–14.

Walcott, Derek. "Meanings." *Savacou* 2 (1970): 45–51.

Walcott, Derek. "The Muse of History." In *Is Massa Day Dead?,* edited by Orde Coombs, 1–27. New York: Anchor, 1974.

Walcott, Derek. "Necessity of Negritude" (1964). In *Critical Perspectives on Derek Walcott,* edited by Robert D. Hamner, 20–23. Washington, D.C.: Three Continents Press, 1993.

Walcott, Derek. Notebooks, 1965–1967. Holograph for *Another Life,* prose and poetry. Mona, Jamaica: Library of the University of the West Indies.

Walcott, Derek. "What the Twilight Says: An Overture." In *Dream on Monkey Mountain and Other Plays,* 3–40. New York: Farrar, 1970.

Warner, Ashton. *The Narrative of Ashton Warner, a Native of St. Vincent's.* Related to Susanna Strickland. London, 1831.

Washington, Mary Helen. *Invented Lives.* New York: Anchor, 1988.

White, George. *A Brief Account of the Life, Experiences, Travels, and Gospel Labors of George White, an African.* New York: John C. Totten, 1810.

White, Hayden. *The Content of the Form: Narrative Discourse and Historical Representation.* Baltimore, Md.: Johns Hopkins University Press, 1987.

Whitman, Walt. *Complete Poetry and Selected Prose,* edited by James E. Miller, Jr. Cambridge, Mass.: Riverside, 1959.

Williams, Eric. *British Historians and the West Indies.* Trinidad: P. N. M. Publishing, 1964.

Williams, Eric. *Capitalism and Slavery.* 1944. Reprint, London: Andre Deutsch, 1964.

Williams, James. *Narrative of the Cruel Treatment of James Williams, a Negro Apprentice in Jamaica from 1st August, 1834 till the Purchase of His Freedom in 1837, by Joseph Sturge Esq., of Birmingham, by Whom He Was Brought to England.* Glasgow, 1837.

Williams, Raymond. *Keywords: A Vocabulary of Culture and Society.* New York: Oxford University Press, 1976.

Woodward, C. Vann. "History from Slave Sources." In *The Slave's Narrative,* edited by Charles T. Davis and Henry Louis Gates, Jr., 48–59. New York: Oxford University Press, 1985.

Wright, Richard. "Blueprint for Negro Writing." In *Voices from the Harlem Renaissance,* edited by Nathan I. Huggins, 394–402. New York: Oxford University Press, 1976.

Wright, Richard. Introduction to *In the Castle of My Skin* by George Lamming. New York: McGraw Hill, 1954.

Wynter, Sylvia. Afterword to *Out of the Kumbla,* edited by Carole Boyce Davies and Elaine Savory Fido. Trenton, N.J.: Africa World Press, 1990.

Wynter, Sylvia. Review of *Lady Nugent's Journal. Jamaica Journal,* December 1967, pp. 23–34.

Zeiger, Melissa F. *Beyond Consolation: Death, Sexuality, and the Changing Shapes of Elegy.* Ithaca, N.Y.: Cornell University Press, 1997.

Zimra, Clarisse. "Righting the Calabash: Writing History in the Female Francophone Narrative." In *Out of the Kumbla,* edited by Carole Boyce Davies and Elaine Savory Fido, 143–59. Trenton, N.J.: Africa World Press, 1990.

Index

abjection, 244, 247, 249, 302n4
Abrahams, Roger D., 90, 274n33, 284n23
accommodation, 13, 20, 56, 244
acculturation, 21, 23
Adam mythology, 291n9
Africa/Africans: in Brathwaite's works, 75, 76, 145, 176, 180–81, 234, 239, 278–79n4; in Bridges' works, 219, 220; colonialism in, 83; and complexity of Caribbean culture and society, 5; and cultural base of Caribbean, 177; and departure and return paradigm, 74; and diaspora themes in Caribbean, 6; eating the dead in, 300–301n8; European rejection of culture of, 23; healing in, 275n1, 277n17; influence on Caribbean of, 178; in James' works, 85, 158; in Lamming's works, 75, 76, 125, 133, 137, 138, 144, 145; and Lorde, 82; in McKay's works, 75, 91–92, 94, 278–79n4; and Mahase, 179, 212; and maps of personal geography, 259; masks in, 283n14; and models of historical analysis, 7; mythicized, 278–79n4; in Naipaul's works, 185, 190–91, 193, 205; as New World Negroes, 272–73n18; and Prince's narrative, 36; religion in, 284n26; and Seacole's narrative, 48; and silencing, 12; in Walcott's works, 159, 160, 161, 163, 167, 171
African Americans, 80, 82, 93, 274n31
Afrocentrism, 75, 86

AIDS, 230, 243, 248, 249, 252, 254, 255, 302n3
Akan people, 40, 236, 240, 300–301n8, 301n16
Alcee, Andreuille, 154, 166, 170–71
Alexander, Jacqui, 32
Alexander, Ziggi, 61, 67
alienation: Appiah's views about, 180; in Brathwaite's works, 240; Césaire's views about, 292n17; of Creoles, 176; and evolution of anti-colonialist discourse, 83; in Kincaid's works, 243, 248–49, 252, 253; in Lamming's works, 76, 84, 111–12, 115, 116, 135, 137, 138, 176; in McKay's works, 90, 105; in Mahase's narrative, 213; in Naipaul's works, 189, 191; O'Callaghan's views about, 181; and Rhys' works, 222. See also marginalization
Alleyne, Mervyn, 284n26
Allfrey, Phyllis Shand, 73
America/Americans: as audience for McKay's works, 96; colonialism in, 58; as expatriates, 75; and Hart sisters' narratives, 14; in Kincaid's works, 230, 243, 244, 245, 247, 252, 256; in Lamming's works, 76, 79–80, 126, 129, 133, 137, 138, 145; and McKay, 75, 79, 80, 83, 87, 88–89, 90, 91, 92, 93, 94, 95, 96, 98, 99, 100, 101, 102, 103–4, 105, 107, 109, 214, 259, 281n1; in Mahase's narrative, 206, 212; and models of historical analysis, 7; in

Bridges' works, 216, 217, 218–19, 220; as civilizing presence, 55–56, 64, 69, 120; consumers of intellectual and cultural history of, 134–35; and cultural dependency, 23, 140, 287–88n1; cultural supremacy of, 54–55, 56; death and funerals in, 236; and English as absentee owners, 106; gender characteristics imagined onto black West Indian society by, 281n23; and grounding of Caribbean subjectivities, 7; in Hart sisters' narratives, 23; in James' works, 141, 148, 149, 151, 152; in Lamming's works, 54–55, 76, 79–80, 111–12, 113, 114, 120, 122, 126, 129, 133, 136, 137, 140, 143, 144, 148; as location of authentic British subject, 54; in McKay's works, 93, 94, 100; in Mahase's narrative, 207, 212; in Naipaul's works, 185, 186, 189, 200, 202; in Prince's narrative, 28, 29, 31, 32, 34, 36, 37, 38–39, 42, 49, 259, 271n6; privilege of intellectuals of, 135; racism in, 56–58, 100; in Rhys' works, 214, 221, 224; as safety and security, 58; and Seacole, 15, 51, 53, 55–59, 61, 62, 63, 64, 65, 66, 68, 69, 79, 96, 100, 259, 278n22; sexism in, 56–57; and slavery, 14, 28, 30, 31, 38, 270–71n1; as source of culture, 148; supremacy of, 148; and travel, 299n26; Victorian era in, 41, 59, 60, 85, 215, 216, 277n14, 297n10; vision of intellectual production in, 287–88n1; in Walcott's works, 162, 167, 170. See also colonialism; imperialism
English Harbour (Antigua), 24, 25
equality, 17, 23, 273n22, 273n27, 297n15
Equiano, Olaudah (Gustavas Vassa the African), 34, 142
erasure/silencing: in Brathwaite's works, 242; and Caliban paradigm, 11–12; of East Indians, 178; and homoeroticism, 81; and identity, 17; in Kincaid's works, 230; in Mahase's narrative, 213; in Naipaul's works, 178, 189–90, 191, 208; and quest for female ancestors, 11–13; self-, 16, 18, 267–68n8; of women, 11–12, 16–17, 73, 146, 267–68n8, 301n12

errantry, 55, 75, 76, 78, 81, 184, 185, 189–90, 214, 230, 260, 279n7
Esteves, Carmen C., 269n5
ethnicity: Brereton's views about, 298n20; in Bridges' works, 177, 181, 214; and colonialism, 260; and commonalities among autobiographies, 260; and consciousness, 9; and diaspora themes, 6; and identity, 176; in ay's works, 101; in Mahase's narrative, 177, 205–6, 208, 209, 210; in Naipaul's works, 177, 178, 187, 190, 195, 197, 199, 205, 260; in Rhys' works, 177, 181
ethnoscape, 299n30
Europe/European: African intellectuals' use of canon from, 141; authority of traditions in, 159; in Brathwaite's works, 181; Caribbean mythology differentiated from, 143; and complexity of Caribbean culture and society, 5; cultural superiority and civilizing mission of, 142, 277n12; and diaspora themes, 6; and Hart sisters' narratives, 14; in Lamming's works, 138, 142; in McKay's works, 75, 80, 87, 88, 94, 95, 259; in Mahase's narrative, 206; and maps of personal geography, 259; and models of historical analysis, 7; in Naipaul's works, 191, 193, 205; in Pratt's works, 192; in Prince's narrative, 34, 36; rejection of African and Caribbean culture in, 23; in Seacole's narrative, 61, 63, 277n12; as source of slavery, 277n12; Tempest as primary text for discourse on West Indies' relation to, 289n15; in Walcott's works, 158, 159, 160, 161, 163, 165, 166, 168, 169, 170, 171; women's suffrage in, 14. See also specific nation
Eurydice myth, 235
exile: Bhabha's views about, 97; in Brathwaite's works, 76; and colonialism, 132; definitions of, 285n3; distancing perspective of, 32; and errantry, 55, 78; in Glissant's works, 214; and identity, 55; and imagination, 146; internal, 279n8; in James' works, 85; in Kincaid works, 146; in Naipaul's works, 196; paradox of, 135; and presencing, 97; in Prince's narrative, 146; and progress and social development, 79; task of, 288n4. See

exile (*continued*)
  also James, C. L. R.; Lamming, George;
  McKay, Claude; Walcott, Derek
expatriate, the writer as, 135, 144–45,
  190–91, 192

family: in Brathwaite's works, 229; in
  Bridges' works, 218, 221; and childhood, 180; and colonial feminism,
  297–98n16; and fear of black crowds,
  298n17; and gender, 18; in James'
  works, 149–50, 153; in Kincaid's
  works, 243, 244, 247, 249, 250, 252,
  254, 255; in Lamming's works, 115,
  123, 131; in McKay's works, 88, 89,
  90, 104, 105, 106, 109; in Mahase's
  narrative, 2–9, 207, 208, 210–11; in
  Naipaul's works, 178, 186, 187, 188;
  and pastoral paradigms, 105; in Prince's
  narrative, 45, 46, 48, 49, 273n23; in
  Rhys' works, 215, 221–22; in Seacole's
  narrative, 53; self as creation of, 109;
  and slave narratives by women,
  273n23; in Walcott's works, 163, 171
family romance: as displaced, 302n1
Fanon, Frantz, 78, 81, 83, 88, 89, 140,
  180, 280n13, 285n5, 287n20, 288n9,
  298n18
father/Pa: in Bridges' works, 218, 219,
  220; in Lamming's works, 115, 117,
  118, 123, 124, 125–26, 127, 132–33; in
  McKay's works, 107; in Mahase's
  narrative, 208, 210; in Naipaul's works,
  183, 184, 186, 187, 188–89, 191, 192,
  207; in Rhys' works, 221, 224
Federal Writers Project; McKay's work
  for, 281n1
feminism, 59, 213, 215, 268n9, 268n11,
  297–98n16
Ferguson, Moira, 13, 21–22, 23, 24, 25,
  27, 29, 30, 269n1, 269n3, 271n2,
  271n4, 271n6
Fido, Elaine Savory, 11, 146
folklore, 155, 286n16, 303n14
Foster, Frances Smith, 27, 273n23,
  274n31
Foucault, Michel, 82, 265–66n3,
  280n15framework, autobiographical: in
  Bridges' works, 216; in James' works,
  84, 148–49, 152, 153; in Lamming's
  works, 130, 134, 136–37, 138, 146,
  148,

153; in Naipaul's works, 184–85, 193;
  in Rhys' works, 216; in Walcott's
  works, 173
France/French, 5, 59, 70, 75, 78, 94, 98,
  100, 102, 127, 216, 291n10, 292n17
freedom: and childhood, 274–75n36; and
  gender, 146; and homosexuality,
  280n15; in James' works, 141, 260; in
  Lamming's works, 138, 139, 140, 143,
  146, 260; in McKay's works, 93, 102,
  109, 260; in Mahase's narrative, 213;
  reverie as, 216; in Rhys' works, 223; in
  Seacole's narrative, 52; and travel,
  275n2; in Walcott's works, 172, 260; in
  Wynter's works, 146. *See also* Prince,
  Mary
Freud, Sigmund, 228, 229, 234, 300n1,
  300n2, 303n13
Froude, J., 221

Garber, Eric, 92
garden: Jamaica as exotic, 108, 159-60
Garvey, Marcus, 103
Gates, Henry Louis, Jr., 36, 37, 99, 142,
  273n24, 274n28, 274n30, 274n35,
  283n14, 283n21
gateway complex, 291n8, 292n16
gender: and absence of woman writers'
  text, 11–13; and autobiographies by
  male Caribbean writers, 17–18; and
  blackness as open signifier, 281n5; in
  Brathwaite's works, 227–28, 229, 230,
  231, 233, 234, 235, 236–38, 261;
  Brereton's views about, 298n20; in
  Bridges' works, 177, 179, 215, 220;
  and centrality and complexity of autobiographic modes, 4; and childhood,
  287n22; and colonialism, 16, 17, 18,
  19, 86, 117–18, 268n14, 269n5; and
  commonalities among autobiographies,
  260–61; and consciousness, 9, 228;
  cross-, 9, 227, 228, 229, 230, 243, 261;
  and death, 230; and departure and
  return paradigm, 74; and elegy, 261,
  301n13; and equality, 17; and
  erasure/silencing of women, 16, 146;
  and freedom, 146; and grounding of
  Caribbean subjectivities, 7; in Hart
  sisters' narrative, 19, 20; Hodge's views
  about, 16–17; and identity, 4, 227,
  268–69n15; and ideology, 15–16; and
  internalization, 229; in James' works,

Wisconsin Studies in Autobiography

William L. Andrews
General Editor

Robert F. Sayre
The Examined Self: Benjamin Franklin, Henry Adams, Henry James

Daniel B. Shea
Spiritual Autobiography in Early America

Lois Mark Stalvey
The Education of a WASP

Margaret Sams
Forbidden Family: A Wartime Memoir of the Philippines, 1941–1945
Edited, with an introduction, by Lynn Z. Bloom

Charlotte Perkins Gilman
The Living of Charlotte Perkins Gilman: An Autobiography
Introduction by Ann J. Lane

Mark Twain
*Mark Twain's Own Autobiography: The Chapters from the North
American Review*
Edited, with an introduction, by Michael Kiskik

Journeys in New Worlds: Early American Women's Narratives
Edited by William L. Andrews

American Autobiography: Retrospect and Prospect
Edited by Paul John Eakin

Caroline Seabury
The Diary of Caroline Seabury, 1854–1863
Edited, with an introduction, by Suzanne L. Bunkers

Marian Anderson
My Lord, What a Morning
Introduction by Nellie Y. McKay

American Women's Autobiography: Fea(s)ts of Memory
Edited, with an introduction, by Margo Culley

Frank Marshall Davis
Livin' the Blues: Memoirs of a Black Journalist and Poet
Edited, with an introduction, by John Edgar Tidwell

Joanne Jacobson
Authority and Alliance in the Letters of Henry Adams

Cornelia Peake McDonald
A Woman's Civil War: A Diary with Reminiscences of the War, from March 1862
Edited, with an introduction, by Minrose C. Gwin

Kamau Brathwaite
The Zea Mexican Diary: 7 Sept. 1926–7 Sept. 1986
Foreword by Sandra Pouchet Paquet

Genaro M. Padilla
My History, Not Yours: The Formation of Mexican American Autobiography

Frances Smith Foster
Witnessing Slavery: The Development of Ante-bellum Slave Narratives

Native American Autobiography: An Anthology
Edited, with an introduction, by Arnold Krupat

Henry Bibb
The Life and Adventures of Henry Bibb: An American Slave
With a new introduction by Charles J. Heglar

Suzanne L. Bunkers
Diaries of Girls and Women: A Midwestern American Sampler

Jim Lane
The Autobiographical Documentary in America

Sandra Pouchet Paquet
Caribbean Autobiography: Cultural Identity and Self-Representation